THE COLLEGE
OF
EARTH AND MINERAL
SCIENCES
AT
PENN STATE

THE COLLEGE
OF
EARTH AND MINERAL
SCIENCES
AT
PENN STATE

E. Willard Miller

The Pennsylvania State University Press
University Park, Pennsylvania

Library of Congress Cataloging-in-Publication Data

Miller, E. Willard (Eugene Willard), 1915–
    The College of Earth and Mineral Sciences at Penn State /
  E. Willard Miller.

       p.   cm.
    Includes bibliographical references and index.
    ISBN 0-271-00796-6
    1. Pennsylvania State University. College of Earth and
  Mineral Sciences—History.   I. Title.
QE47.P43P45   1992
550'.71'1748—dc20   91–41068
                                              CIP

It is the policy of The Pennsylvania State University Press to use
acid-free paper for the first printing of all clothbound books.
Publications on uncoated stock satisfy the minimum requirements of
American National Standard for Information Sciences—Permanence of
Paper for Printed Library Materials, ANSI Z39.48–1984.

Frontispiece: Steidle Building, view of portico.

*This book is dedicated to the
more than 12,000 graduates of the College.*

Contents

Foreword
by John A. Dutton, Dean

The concept that history is a guidepost to the future seems relevant in searching for the origins of eminence of a person, a nation, or perhaps a college or university. In examining the life of a distinguished person, we look for antecedents of attitudes, for those experiences that determined the mind-set necessary for superior achievement or performance. In searching for the origins of eminence of a college or university, we similarly try to identify the assumptions, shared beliefs, opportunities, and perhaps the tensions that shaped its development and made it unusual.

A college is a collection of people. A distinguished college is not only a collection of distinguished people, it is also a collection of people who consciously or unconsciously share a vision of excellence and who instill confidence in each other. The exhilaration of a prestigious college is transmitted over the years from one generation to the next, from faculty to students, from alumni to faculty. The expectations endure. The task of the historian is thus both simple and severe: determine what the shared vision and the expectations actually are, and then ascertain how they were created and how they are maintained.

The College of Earth and Mineral Sciences will celebrate its centennial in this decade. We have evolved from our beginnings as a poor relation among the Penn State schools to our present position as a jewel in the Penn State crown. We are still one of the smallest colleges at Penn State, but our expectations and achievements are among the highest at the University. We have grown from an initial focus on mining engineering to global involvement in the sciences of the Earth and its atmosphere, to examination of human interactions with the planet, and to leadership in the science, engineering, and economics of fuels and materials. The EMS family—faculty, students, staff, and alumni—are an exhilarated group indeed.

A single individual stands out in the history of the College of Earth and Mineral Sciences for his paramount influence on its development: Dean Edward Steidle, who in 1931 re-created the college in its modern image as the School of Mineral Industries. By force of intellect and personality, Dean Steidle made a respectable but quite ordinary school of the Pennsylvania State College both self-conscious and self-confident. His remarkable ability to motivate a sense of pride in both faculty and students stimulated development of the school's distinctive vision. Once in motion, the transformation was self-perpetuating and subsequent leaders advanced their own initiatives, strengthening but not altering the essence of the basic assumptions.

For disentangling the web of events, ideas, and people that make the history of our college, we were indeed fortunate to enlist the talent of E. Willard Miller, a prolific author and distinguished geographer who brought to the task his prodigious industry and deep understanding of the goals of the College. As founding head of the Department of Geography, as Associate Dean for Resident Instruction, and now in busy "retirement," Dr. Miller has been intimately involved in the life and development of the College since 1945. From the outset, he recognized that the true story of the College lay in its people and their focus on excellence and achievement. His historical account of how a collection of disparate individuals shared and perpetuated an academic vision suggests the source of our contemporary success and exuberance. For those who follow, it is a guidepost toward the traditions and the triumphs of this extraordinary college.

Preface

The College of Earth and Mineral Sciences at The Pennsylvania State University has had a long and distinguished history. From its origin in 1859, when earth science courses were offered in the agricultural program, to the establishment of the School of Mines in 1890 with its single major in mining engineering, to the creation of a College of Mineral Industries by Dean Edward Steidle in the 1930s, and to the present with the development of a comprehensive College of Earth and Mineral Sciences dedicated to the study of the total Earth, the College has been at the cutting edge in advancing knowledge.

One major tradition in the College has been the recognition that the success of the teaching and research programs rests squarely on the abilities of the faculty, and an established goal has been to secure the best-qualified faculty possible. At times this has meant a worldwide search for certain positions. Because the faculty is always attempting to extend the boundaries of knowledge, whether it be in basic or applied research, graduates of the College acquire the most up-to-date knowledge on how to attack problems in dynamically changing fields. In this context, teaching and research are entwined in a single endeavor; they are not separate entities.

This volume has two basic goals: to reveal the evolution of a uniquely structured college in the American university system and to highlight the work of individual faculty members in each discipline of the College. To accomplish this, many sources of information were consulted. The *Mineral Industries* bulletin and later the *Earth and Mineral Sciences* bulletin provided a long-running record of College activities, with particular emphasis on the years between 1930 and the 1960s. Quotations from those sources are by permission of the College of Earth and Mineral Sciences. Quotations that have no source given are from personal interviews with, letters to the author, or personal papers in the Penn State Room at the Pattee Library. The Penn State Room also provided much additional information and many photographs on many aspects of the history of the College. Photographs were also obtained from College and departmental collections. Many faculty were generous with their time and provided information about present and past developments, and I myself, a part of the College since 1945, have relied heavily on personal recollections. Special thanks are given to the faculty who read and commented on the manuscript in its many stages of development. I, however, take complete responsibility for its accuracy.

—E. Willard Miller

The College of Earth and Mineral Sciences
Sources of Success

The College has succeeded owing to:

A stress on excellence

The extraordinary freedom granted faculty to pursue promising research and teaching initiatives

Recognition that the best instruction is provided by people engaged in actively contributing to development of important knowledge

Sustained commitment to its academic and research programs without undue influence by current fads

Openness to new ideas

Willingness to accept diverse viewpoints on critical issues

These sources of success will be the most important guideposts for the future.

—Richard L. Gordon
Professor of Mineral Economics

Deike Building.

PART ONE | THE EVOLUTION OF THE COLLEGE

Deike Building, facing Burrowes Road.

Chapter 1 | The Beginning

S tudy of the Earth has been a fundamental part of the curriculum of the University since its beginning as the Farmers' High School. In the early years, students were trained exclusively in the practical aspects of agriculture. A meeting of the Trustees on July 13, 1854, provided the foundation for the initial program: "It is a fact universally known, that the literary institutions of the country, as at present constituted, educate young men to a state of total unfitness not only for the pursuit of a farmer but as a companion for his parents, brothers and sisters, with whom he is expected to spend a life. He is thus driven from them—from his father's estate—and into a profession for which he has perhaps little capacity, where he is subject to all the temptations of an idle life; whereas the farm school proposes to impart an education which is appropriate to a farm, which educates his body to act as well as his mind to the science of farming, and which will have the feature of making the institution so nearly self-sustaining as to bring education, in part of expense, within the reach of every man who claims to make his son an educated farmer."

The Farmers' High School was established on April 13, 1854, when Pennsylvania Governor William Bigler signed the Act of Incorporation. The act stated: "The teachers are to be capable of imparting a knowledge of the English language, grammar, geography, history, mathematics and such other branches of the natural and applied sciences, as would conduce to the proper education of a farmer." Actual instruction began in 1859 when Evan Pugh, a thirty-one-year-old native of Chester County with a Ph.D. in agricultural chemistry from Germany's University of Göttingen, became president.

EARLY EARTH SCIENCE INSTRUCTION

According to the school's first catalog in 1859, a single program led to a degree of bachelor of scientific agriculture (Steidle, 1939). The importance of the earth sciences was recognized in the agricultural program. A geography and elementary astronomy course was required in the first year, and physical geography, meteorology, geology, and paleontology were required in the second year of study. Four courses were described as follows in the catalog:

Geography and Elementary Astronomy
  With use of the globe.
Physical Geography and Meteorology
  Embracing the general principles and their special application to agriculture, involving questions of the influence of temperature, rainfall and the general outline of the earth upon the productive power of the soil for deficient vegetable substances.
Geology and Paleontology
  Embracing the general principle of these sciences, and the special development in regard to the origins of soils and substances capable of fertilizing the latter. Also the special geology of Pennsylvania, with excursions in the neighborhood.
Mineralogy and Crystallography
  Embracing the description of minerals, their classification and means of determining them.

The catalog does not identify the faculty members who taught these courses, but we do know that President Evan Pugh had the title "Professor of Chemistry, Scientific and Practical Agriculture and Mineralogy," and it is possible he taught the course in mineralogy because his microscope and other research and instructional equipment have been preserved in the College of Earth and Mineral Sciences Museum.

The Old Mining Building, circa 1920.

The geological sciences were recognized as important in the study of agriculture. In 1860, by act of the state legislature, the State Mineralogical and Geological Collection was transferred from Harrisburg to the institution. The 1861 catalog states: "A collection of nearly 6,800 specimens of rocks, limestone, fossils, ores, are collected from all parts of the state together with a large collection from Europe. The neighborhood is one of the finest in the world for the study of numerous subdivisions of the Paleozoic rocks . . . all of which the student will have an opportunity of obtaining good specimens on geological excursions."

The first graduation ceremonies were held in December 1861, when eleven students received bachelor's degrees. They had completed the normal four-year course of study in three years because they were admitted in 1859 with advanced standing, having transferred to the Farmers' High School from other colleges. The eleven students who graduated collectively produced six theses to meet graduation requirements. Two students were assigned to each thesis topic, "concentrating upon a single dissertation." Of the six theses, three were entitled: "On the Limestone of Nittany Valley" (by J. W. Eckman and C. A. Smith); "On the Iron Ores of Nittany Valley" (by J. D. Isett and J. N. Banks); and "On the Slags of Iron Furnaces and the Residual Products Obtained in Converting Pig into Bar Irons" (by L. C. Troutman and C. E. Troutman). The theses titles indicated that two of the three research projects were in the geological sciences and that the third was on high-temperature reactions among minerals; hence, six of the eleven students graduating did their research on projects in the geological and metallurgical sciences.

In 1862 U.S. Representative Justin S. Morrill's land-grant bill (introduced in 1857) was passed by the U.S. Congress. The Land-Grant Act, also known as the first (1862) Morrill Act, was signed by Abraham Lincoln and created the land-grant colleges. As a result, the name of the Farmers' High School was changed to the Agricultural College of Pennsylvania. The purpose of the Land Grant Act was: "The endowment, support, and maintenance of at least one college where the leading object shall be, without excluding other scientific and classical studies, and including military tactics, to teach such branches of learning as are related to agriculture and the mechanic arts in such manner as the legislature of the state may respectively prescribe in order to promote the liberal and practical education of the industrial classes in the several pursuits and professions of life."

THE EDUCATIONAL GOALS OF A LAND-GRANT INSTITUTION

The basic aims of the classical school in emphasizing such courses as Greek and Latin deeply disturbed President Pugh, and he wrote a lengthy pamphlet in support of the importance given to agriculture and the mechanical arts at Pennsylvania's only land-grant school (Jones, 1955). In order to develop the mechanical arts program, President Pugh proposed in 1864 to add two faculty members in the mineral industries: a professor of agricultural chemistry and geology, and a professor of metallurgy, mining, and mineralogy. He proposed also that equipment should be provided for instruction in several mineral industries fields. Unfortunately, President Pugh was not able to get the necessary funds for the equipment, and his dream for expanding the offerings of the college ended when he contracted typhoid fever in the spring of 1864 and died on April 29.

In 1866 a committee of three faculty members was appointed to study revision of the agricultural curriculum because, according to the committee, "the entire educational policy of the

The mining engineering class of 1903, gaining practical experience at the Mosgrove Mine of the Mosgrove Coal Works, a subsidiary of the Pittsburgh Plate Glass Company. The mine was located about five miles north of Kittanning. Left to right, seated on the ground, are Horatio C. Ray '04 and Paul G. Elder '04, and left to right, standing or seated on the car, are George H. Deike '03, Bruce McCamant '04, William H. Robinson '04, Jere E. Zullinger '05, Arthur C. Clay '05, William K. McDowell '04, and Harold C. George '04.

institution has failed and cannot but fail to satisfy the expectation of the enlightened friends of education." The committee instead proposed four four-year courses of instruction: general science and agriculture; literature; mechanical and civil engineering; and mining and metallurgy. The influence of the late President Pugh was clearly evident in these proposals, but the committee's recommendations were not implemented because of lack of funds. Mineral industries education could have had a much earlier start had it not been for the impoverished condition of the college.

For most of the years during the 1870s and 1880s, physical geography and the geological sciences were required areas of study in the agricultural and scientific programs. Courses were usually taught by individuals who were trained in biology or the physical sciences. The first instructor who held the title "Professor of Zoology, Biology, and Geology" was Henry James Clark, who taught at the college in the late 1860s. From 1871 to at least 1881, William A. Buckhout was professor of botany, geology, and zoology; in 1871–72 Albert H. Tuttle was professor of geology and physiology; and from 1882 to 1884 A. L. Ewing was professor of geology and zoology. These professors taught a number of courses in the geological sciences.

Fieldwork was considered important in the study of geology. In 1881–82 the college catalog stated: "Geology is one of the important studies of the senior year. Sufficient time is given to enable students to understand clearly the general principles of the science, and so far as possible, illustrations and specimens are drawn from the vicinity. To special students the neighboring valleys and mountains afford rare opportunities for the study of botany, zoology and geology. The great synclinal and anticlinal Paleozoic waves east of the Alleghenies are here shown in every position and angle of inclination, while good outcrops are to be seen of nearly all the subdivisions of the Paleozoic rocks, from the lowest to the coal measures."

ESTABLISHMENT OF A MINING ENGINEERING CURRICULUM

With the coming of President George W. Atherton in 1882, the educational goals of the college were enlarged (Neilly, 1980). The industrial economy of the state was expanding rapidly with the growth of the coal-mining industries. In the 1880s bituminous coal production in Pennsylvania grew from 16,514,000 tons in 1880 to 79,318,000 tons in 1890, and the labor force increased from 33,290 to 108,735. In the same period, anthracite production rose from 27,974,000 tons to 44,986,000, and the number of miners grew from 73,300 to 120,000. Trained miners were desperately needed by the rapidly growing industry. Coal-mining was a "pick and shovel" industry that lagged behind the rapid growth of technology in other engineering fields.

Reaffirming the goals of the institution to conform to those of the 1862 Morrill Act, President Atherton moved to strengthen the mechanical arts. For the first time, training in the mining industry was as important as training in other engineering fields. Thus, on October 4, 1890, the Executive Committee of the Board of Trustees established the procedure for creating a Department of Mining Engineering. The minutes of the committee state: "On motion, four thousand dollars ($4,000) was appropriated for the immediate establishment of mining engineering and the President of the College was authorized to make all necessary preliminary inquiries and arrangements for the beginning of such work and to report to the committee as early as practical."

To implement the program, the Pennsylvania state legislature in 1891 funded a building for the mechanical arts, including mining engineering, and in 1893 the state appropriated an additional $16,000 to develop the mining engineering program. On June 15, 1893, the minutes of the Executive Committee of the Board of Trustees state: "In order to place the Department of Mining Engineering upon a suitable footing, the Chairman and Secretary of the Committee were authorized to employ as head of the Department a Professor of such rank as to give it at once a commanding position. For that purpose they were authorized to pay a salary of $2,500. With a house or allowance for the same, with an understanding that the amount might be raised to $3,000 if special circumstances might justify it."

Magnus C. Ihlseng, from the Colorado School of Mines, was appointed the first head and professor of mining engineering and geology. He was assisted by Harry H. Stoek, assistant professor of mining engineering and metallurgy; Franklin E. Tuttle, assistant professor of chemistry and mineralogy; and Thomas C. Hopkins, instructor in geology. The 1893–94 catalog states:

Administration
School of Mines and
Metallurgy, 1890–1928

Department of Mining Engineering

Magnus C. Ihlseng   1893–1896

School of Mines

Magnus C. Ihlseng   1896–1899

Department of Mining Engineering

M. E. Wadsworth   1901–1906

School of Mines and Metallurgy

M. E. Wadsworth   1906–1908
Walter R. Crane   1908–1910

School of Mines

Walter R. Crane   1910–1918
Elwood S. Moore   1918–1922

School of Mines and Metallurgy

Elmer A. Holbrook   1922–1927
David F. McFarland   1927–1928

"This course aims to fit students for practical work in mining, geology and metallurgy by combining practice with theory. The course coordinates with the other engineering courses, but gives an option in mining or metallurgy. [The metallurgy option was not developed at the time.] These options are rendered necessary by the extent of the field of mining engineering, which embraces the three specialties, geology, metallurgy, and mining. The divergence between these is not great, but is sufficient to enable the student to specialize according to his preference for mechanical or chemical lines. A third option in geology may be offered hereafter."

Nine students enrolled in mining, including one graduate student, the first year and twenty-two the second year. Henry P. Dowler of Clearfield, who initially enrolled in civil engineering but transferred to mining in 1893, was the first graduate in mining engineering in 1894. Charles W. Hardt of DuBois, who enrolled as a mining student in 1893, received his degree in 1897 and was the first graduate to complete the entire curriculum.

A review of the early activities of the department indicates that there was concern for serving the needs of the mining industry. In January 1894 a bimonthly publication, *The Mining Bulletin,* was first published, with the avowed purpose of keeping "in sympathetic relations with the industrial interests of the Commonwealth." The second issue (March 1894) called attention to the recently established tuition-free short courses in mining: a two-year program designed to give a basic knowledge of the principles of mining, and a twelve-week course arranged to accommodate miners and others, which was listed as beginning on January 2, 1895. The third issue of *The Mining Bulletin* (June 1894) publicized what is probably the first extension service in the mining industry in the United States. It proposed that department members give free lectures to "mine employees at their customary place of assembly upon matters of interest to them in their occupations."

THE SCHOOL OF MINES IS CREATED

The rapid growth of students in the mining engineering program indicated the growing need for an increase in the program. As a consequence, the faculty was increased to five in 1896, and the department was upgraded and given the name "School of Mines," with Dr. Ihlseng named dean.

Magnus C. Ihlseng

Magnus C. Ihlseng was born on May 2, 1855, in Christiania, Norway (now Oslo). He received his C.E., E.M., and Ph.D. degrees from Columbia University. Dr. Ihlseng was instructor of physics at Columbia from 1875 to 1881 and professor of engineering at the Colorado School of Mines from 1881 to 1893. He came to Penn State in 1893, where from 1893 to 1896 he was professor of mining engineering and geology, and from 1896 to 1899 he was dean of the School of Mines. Because of lack of funds the School of Mines was discontinued in 1899 and Dr. Ihlseng stayed on one more year as professor of mining engineering and geology. On leaving Penn State in 1900, Dr. Ihlseng taught at Brooklyn Polytechnic Institute for six years. In 1906 he became president of Blairsville College, and he continued at that post for the next fifteen years. Dr. Ihlseng's chief areas of research were the velocity of sound through solids, the coefficient of elasticity of metals, and an antidote for white damp. He was active in the affairs of the American Institute of Mining, Metallurgical, and Petroleum Engineering.

The Obelisk, Armory on left, Old Main on right.

The Penn State Obelisk

The Penn State Obelisk, a polylith made up of Pennsylvania stones located immediately east of Willard Building, is the oldest monument on the campus. Its construction was completed in 1896 by Magnus C. Ihlseng, the first Penn State professor of mining engineering and geology. In 1894 William Clinton B. Alexander, a freshman in the mining program, was employed by Dr. Ihlseng to secure the stones for the monument. Fifty-five years later, in 1949, Mr. Alexander wrote: "Letters explaining the proposition and soliciting specimen building stones were sent to Pennsylvania operators and others interested. As some inducement, prospects were given the privilege of cutting their names on the face of the stones donated."

The idea of the polylith was well received in the state. To further the project during the summer of 1894, Mr. Alexander took an extended bicycle trip in Pennsylvania, visiting many of the quarries that provided specimens. Some 281 stones from 139 locations were collected. Thomas C. Hopkins, assistant professor of economic geology, assembled the stones in the obelisk in their natural geologic order, starting at the base with the older igneous rocks. As reflected in the minutes of the Executive Committee of the school, the site for the polylith was selected "In accordance with President Atherton's suggestion, on the right hand corner of the intersection of the main avenue and the crossing in front of the Armory, going toward the Inn, 20 feet from each intersection."

The Obelisk has been not only an object of natural curiosity but also a monument of important scientific value. It has made it possible for students of geology to study the stones of Pennsylvania, and, from a practical viewpoint, it is now possible— after nearly a century of the stones' standing in the open—for students to evaluate the relative ability of each stone to withstand weathering and erosion.

Despite the need for the program, however, a legislative cut in the 1899 appropriations necessitated a retrenchment. On August 29, 1899, the Executive Committee of the Board of Trustees stated: "In view of the fact that it has been necessary to dispense with the services of one-half of the teaching force in the School of Mining, it was voted that the title 'School of Mining' be for the present, discontinued and that Professor Ihlseng rank as head of the Department of Mining Engineering in the School of Engineering."

In September 1899 Dr. Ihlseng described the department's difficulties in *The Mining Bulletin:* It was necessary "at least for two years," he wrote, "to stop printing the Bulletin, give up the system of free lectures in the mining regions, and defer plans for additional field work." Financial difficulties finally led Dr. Ihlseng and other faculty members to resign. In the 1900–1901 catalog, no faculty members in mining were listed.

Because mining was becoming such a dominant industry in the state, it was recognized that the training of mining engineers was necessary, and at the July 20, 1901, meeting of the Executive Committee of the Board of Trustees, President Atherton announced the appointment of Marshman E. Wadsworth. On September 3, 1901, Dr. Wadsworth recommended to the Executive Committee "that the Department be known for the present as the Department of Mines and

Marshman E. Wadsworth

Marshman E. Wadsworth was born in Livermore Falls, Maine, on May 6, 1847. He was a graduate of Bowdoin College and received a Ph.D. from Harvard University in 1869. He was an instructor at Harvard from 1874 to 1885; professor of mineralogy and geology at Colby College from 1885 to 1887; president of Michigan College of Mines from 1887 to 1899; state geologist of Michigan from 1888 to 1893; and geologist and mining expert for the Keweenawan Association from 1898 to 1903. In 1901 he came to the Pennsylvania State College as professor of mines and geology and head of the mining engineering program. From 1906 to 1908 he headed the School of Mines and Metallurgy. From 1908 to 1912 he was a faculty member at the University of Pittsburgh. He was a pioneer in microscopic petrology and taught the first course in that subject in the United States. He was a fellow of the AAAS, the Geological Society of London, and the Geological Society of America. He was the author of *Geology of the Iron and Copper Districts of Lake Superior* (1880), *Lithological Studies* (1884), *Crystallography* (1909), and some two hundred other books and papers.

Mining; that the title of the head professor be that of Mines and Geology, and that the title of Mr. Shed be Assistant Professor of Mining and Metallurgy."

In 1901 the department had twenty-one students, the average for the 1890s. Although the department was poorly equipped and was considered a "poor relation" in the School of Engineering, new courses were developed to serve the needs of the students. In 1906 the department was once again reorganized to become the School of Mines and Metallurgy, with Dr. Wadsworth as dean. By this time the new school ranked fifth among the nation's mining schools, and first in Pennsylvania.

From its origin, the School was housed in the least desirable building on the campus, initially in an old frame building formerly used for mechanical arts instruction. This building was moved to a site now occupied by the power plant at the corner of College Avenue and Burrowes Road. With a gift of $5,000 from Andrew Carnegie, which defrayed part of the expenses, the building was increased to a length of 270 feet. In 1907 the legislature appropriated an additional $20,000 to

Walter R. Crane

Walter R. Crane was born in Grafton, Massachusetts, on February 5, 1870. He received A.B. and A.M. degrees from the University of Kansas in 1895 and 1896 and a Ph.D. from Columbia University in 1901. He was director of manual training in the city schools of Janesville, Wisconsin, from 1898 to 1899; assistant geologist of the Geological Survey of Kansas from 1893 to 1905; and assistant professor of mining at the University of Kansas from 1900 to 1905. From 1905 to 1908 he was a faculty member at the Columbia University School of Mines. In 1908 he became professor of mining and dean of the School of Mines of the Pennsylvania State College, a position he held until 1918. In 1918 he left Penn State to take a position at the U.S. Bureau of Mines. In 1920 he was chief of the War Minerals Relief Commission of the U.S. Department of the Interior. In 1921 he became superintendent of the Southern Mining Experiment Station of the U.S. Bureau of Mines in Birmingham, Alabama. He was the author of *A Treatise on Gold and Silver* (1908), *Index of Mining Engineering Literature* (1909), and *Ore Mining Methods* (1910). He wrote numerous reports, papers, and monographs on mining and similar subjects.

build a new wing. In time this structure came to be known as the Old Mining Building, and it remained the home of the School until the Mineral Industries Building (now Edward Steidle Building) was completed in 1930.

DEVELOPMENT OF A MINERAL INDUSTRIES PROGRAM

In 1908 Dr. Wadsworth resigned and was replaced by Walter R. Crane, who served as dean for ten years. In spite of financial difficulties and frequent lack of support from the administration, Dean Crane continued the development of the School. He restructured it, and in 1910 the name was changed back to "School of Mines" to conform with other schools throughout the nation.

It was recognized that there was a need to develop the training of students in other areas of work besides mining. The study of the geology of minerals was advancing, as the easily discoverable mineral deposits had been found. There was both a need to discover new deposits and a need to understand the earth's structure in order to develop sound mining principles. The mining geology major was added to the program in 1910.

The availability of bituminous coal provided the basis for development of the modern iron and steel industry in Pennsylvania. In 1900 the value of Pennsylvania iron and steel production was 54 percent of the nation's total. The number of workers in iron and steel rose from about 10,000 in 1860 to 110,000 in 1900 and 186,000 in 1920. In 1919 the iron and steel industry of Pennsylvania consumed 20,935,000 tons of iron ore, 1,468,000 tons of scrap, and 13,335,000 tons of coke, to produce 12,014,000 tons of pig iron and 12,011,000 tons of steel. As the industry became

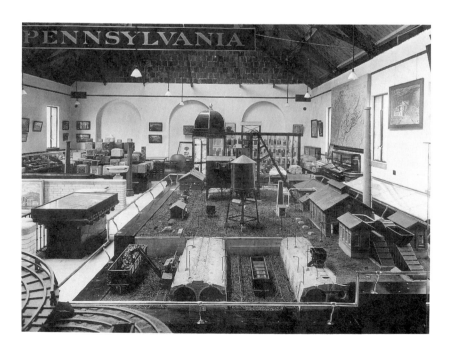

The Mining Museum, circa 1917, on top floor of the Old Mining Building.

technologically more advanced, personnel with technical training were required. Penn State responded to that need by establishing a bachelor's degree in metallurgical engineering. In 1913 the first ceramic course was offered, and in 1917 a course in physical and commercial geography was added.

The faculty varied in size from nine to twelve members during the Crane era. Between twenty and thirty bachelor's degrees were granted each year. For example, at the June 11, 1913, commencement, sixteen degrees were awarded in mining engineering, nine in metallurgical engineering, and one in mining geology. The first advanced degree in mining engineering was awarded on June 14, 1905, to David Lloyd Eynon, who was a 1901 B.S. graduate. Eynon's thesis was entitled "The Flow of Iron and Steel: A Discussion of the Flow of Iron and Steel in Rolling Mill Processes," part 2, "The Design of a 12-inch Merhant Train." The graduate program developed slowly, with one or two advanced degrees awarded annually.

Although extension courses had been discontinued because of financial problems, the need for these courses was recognized and the program was reactivated. The development of the programs was aided by the Pennsylvania YMCA and the Central Pennsylvania Coal Producers Association.

During Dean Crane's administration there were some attempts to improve the facilities of the School. In the summer of 1911 a 100-foot tunnel was constructed adjacent to the School for the purpose of carrying on mine-rescue instruction and conducting ventilation experiments. The School became one of the national leaders in these endeavors.

In 1915 the first wing of a new building to house the School was built with a state appropriation of $50,000. (This building was ultimately named "Textile Chemistry" and was later demolished to provide space for "Home Economics, South.") However, the location was deemed unsuitable for future development of the School of Mines and so the structure served only to house the mining museum on the top floor.

Elwood S. Moore

Elwood S. Moore was born in Heathcote, Ontario, on August 3, 1878. He received B.A. and M.A. degrees from the University of Toronto in 1904 and 1908 and his Ph.D. in geology from the University of Chicago in 1909. He came to Penn State in 1909 to teach geology and mineralogy. In 1917 he was appointed acting dean, and in 1920 he became dean, serving until 1922. He was a member of the Pennsylvania Topographic and Geologic Survey from 1911 to 1922. On leaving Penn State, he returned to Canada, where he pursued a career in the geological sciences.

In 1918 Dean Crane resigned and Elwood S. Moore, professor of geology, was named acting dean, becoming dean in 1920. Dr. Moore continued the struggle to secure adequate funds to develop the School's programs. He increased the faculty from twelve to eighteen members, and in 1921 he created the Department of Mining with four members, the Department of Metallurgy with four members, the Department of Geology with five members, and the Department of Mineralogy with three members.

An experiment station was established in 1919, and the initial impetus to develop a research program began, although handicapped by lack of funds. Some research was carried out by the faculty, who presented their findings either at professional society meetings or in original School bulletins. Harold J. Sloman, assistant professor of coal-mining, published the first bulletin, "An Investigation of the Properties of Smithing Coals," on March 1, 1922. Bulletin No. 2, published in October 1926 by Arthur P. Honess, associate professor of mineralogy, and Charles K. Graeber, instructor in geology, presented Honess's and Graeber's results on "Petrography of the Mica Peridotite Dike at Dixonville, Pennsylvania." Although several other bulletins were published in the 1920s, lack of funds prevented development of an organized research program. Not until 1929 did the Baldwin-Wilson Act provide a small funded research program in the School.

Elmer A. Holbrook

Elmer A. Holbrook was born in Litchburg, Massachusetts, on June 23, 1880. He received a B.S. degree from the Massachusetts Institute of Technology in 1904 and an E.M. degree from the University of Illinois in 1915. From 1905 to 1911 he did mining engineering work in the eastern United States, Canada, and Mexico. From 1911 to 1913 he was professor of mining and metallurgy at the Nova Scotia Technical College at Halifax. In 1913 he went to the University of Illinois as an assistant professor and in 1915 was made professor. In 1917 he took a position with the U.S. Bureau of Mines as engineer in charge of the Central West Division, and in 1920 he became assistant director of the Bureau of Mines. In 1922 he came to Penn State as dean of the School of Mines and Metallurgy, a position he held until 1927. In 1928 he went to the University of Pittsburgh. He wrote more than forty-five professional papers on coal-mining engineering. He was active in the Coal Mining Institute of America and the American Institute of Mining, Metallurgical, and Petroleum Engineers.

A mineralogy class, meeting in the Old Mining Building in the 1920s, identifying rock specimens.

A mining extension division was also established in 1919 with funds provided by the Smith-Hughes Act of 1917. This work was organized in cooperation with the state Department of Public Instruction. Resident summer classes to prepare miners for the Pennsylvania Department of Mines competitive examination, similar to the "12-week courses" of 1897, were initiated in 1919 but discontinued in 1920.

THE SCHOOL OF MINES AND METALLURGY

When Dean Moore resigned in 1922, Elmer A. Holbrook was appointed dean of the School of Mines. One of his first acts was to have the school renamed the School of Mines and Metallurgy, a name that was in use until 1929. In 1924 a fourth major, in ceramic engineering, was begun. Although enrollment in the School totaled only 126 in 1926, it was the largest enrollment east of the Mississippi and the second largest in the United States. During this period, the metallurgy program expanded and equaled the mining program in enrollment. Dean Holbrook resigned in 1927 and David F. McFarland, head of the Department of Metallurgy, served as acting dean until 1928, when Edward Steidle was elected dean.

From 1893 to 1929 the School was directed by five deans, all of whom reportedly left because the programs were underfunded, poorly housed, and underequipped. In spite of great adversity, however, the School persisted and the faculty built the fundamental programs in the mineral industries. Many of the students who graduated from these programs became leaders in their fields.

The School of Mines and Metallurgy, 1928

Dean

David F. McFarland (acting)

Budget

Instruction	$59,840
Research (postage)	50
Extension	3,200

Programs and Administrations

Mining Engineering	William R. Chedsey
Metallurgical Engineering	David F. McFarland
Ceramic Engineering	Joseph B. Shaw
Geology	Chesleigh A. Bonine

Students

Undergraduate	144
General Service Course	300

The Steidle (Mineral Industries) Building under construction and completed.

Chapter 2 | The Creation of a School of Mineral Industries

In 1928 Pennsylvania was the leading mineral-producing state in the nation. One of the pillars of the Pennsylvania economy was its mineral wealth. Penn State President Ralph D. Hetzel recognized that the School of Mines and Metallurgy had to be strengthened and that to accomplish this, strong leadership was required at the dean's level. Penn State could no longer ignore the rightful place of mineral industries education in its programs. As Dean Elburt F. Osborn stated in 1953 at the retirement of Dean Steidle:

Instruction [in 1928] was being given in few areas, but graduate work, research, and extension were virtually nonexistent. From the emphasis given this work in the College, one would have judged that we were living in an agrarian economy, and that little was needed in the way of instruction and research in the sciences, technology and engineering of minerals—this despite the fact that we were running out of our lush mineral deposits and were losing our competitive advantage in the mineral fields. One would have judged that service to the Commonwealth in these fields was largely unnecessary.

What was needed was a "spark plug," an organizer, a man of vision, and that's what the College got in Edward Steidle. He developed the idea for a program and an organization to carry it out, and then he made the idea a fact by his ceaseless and ingenious efforts. (Mineral Industries 22 [1953], 3)

Dean Edward Steidle with the Steidle (Mineral Industries) Building in the background, about 1950.

SELECTION OF A DEAN

In the 1920s Edward Steidle's work at the Carnegie Institute of Technology had earned him the reputation of a major academic leader in the mining industries. When a new dean was sought for the School of Mining and Metallurgy in 1928, a number of members of the Pennsylvania State College Board of Trustees knew of his work and recommended him to President Hetzel. Steidle also received support from a number of influential men in industry and in the U.S. Bureau of Mines. (The selection of Dean Steidle is well documented in Louis J. Venuto's *Creation of a College* [1965].)

President Hetzel received a letter from A. S. Wilson, general manager of the Cosgrove-Meehan Coal Company of Johnstown, Pennsylvania, and an alumnus of the Pennsylvania State College, recommending Steidle for the deanship. Wilson wrote: "In going over the names of former students whom I knew and who would probably be interested, Captain Edward Steidle, head of the Department of Mining at Carnegie Tech, seems first on my list. He has the necessary business instincts, energy and common sense as well as experience and contact within the industry to do justice to this position" (Venuto, 1965, p. 24).

A. C. Fieldner of the U.S. Bureau of Mines wrote a similar letter to President Hetzel: "I can realize that one of the most important duties of this position is to establish contacts with industry and develop further financial support, which is badly needed by most of our universities. For this particular phase of work, I know of no one better qualified than Professor Edward Steidle. . . . I have been in close contact with Professor Steidle while I was Superintendent of the Pittsburgh Experiment Station. I can say without reserve that he is one of the most energetic men that I have ever seen in the position of developing the industrial support for a university department. He has been very successful at Carnegie Tech. Professor Steidle is a man whose qualities of a modern salesman are well developed" (Venuto, 1965, pp. 24–25). J. T. Ryan, Sr., of the Pittsburgh Mine Safety Appliance Company gave his impressions about the abilities of Steidle to Raymond H. Smith, comptroller of the Pennsylvania State College: "I have been associated with Steidle more or less ever since he came out of college and know intimately of his work, both with the Bureau of Mines and at Carnegie Tech. I have for several years, been a member of the Mining Advisory Board of Carnegie Tech, of which Steidle is Secretary and active head—in fact, he organized it, and this organization has given wonderful assistance to Carnegie Tech in bringing the school in close contact with the mining industry in Western Pennsylvania. The important thing, as I see it, in bringing in an outside man to head the Mining Department of State, is to get a man who not only has the ability but who will be diplomatic and receive the full and hearty cooperation of the various department heads. I am positive, judging from my contact with Steidle, that he can do this and that if he is appointed to the deanship he will very soon have the department welded into a happy cooperative family" (Venuto, 1965, p. 25).

President Hetzel offered Steidle the deanship on May 25, 1928, indicating the past limitations on the School and his hope for development in the future. He wrote: "We are exceedingly anxious to bring the School into a position where it will function to the maximum as a constructive and helpful factor in the improvement of the whole mining situation and in the up-building of the ceramic and metallurgical industries. We have not had much money for research but we believe that there is great opportunity ahead for us for general expansion of our services both in research and in extension teaching. We feel that several interests immediately concerned with the work of our School are going to look in increasing measure to the College for trained men and also for leadership in research" (quoted in Venuto, 1965, pp. 25–26).

Location of the Steidle (Mineral Industries) Building. Armory on the right, Carnegie and Sparks Buildings in the center, 1929.

Steidle accepted the appointment and revealed his aspirations in his letter to President Hetzel: "Mining, metallurgy, ceramics and oil and gas production have entered a new era requiring more technical applications. Education will always play an important part in these movements and your School of Mines must serve the industries in the state in a large and efficient manner. When this service is recognized, the support of the industries, financial and otherwise, will be forthcoming" (quoted in Venuto, 1965, p. 26).

THE LAND-GRANT TRADITION

Dean Steidle developed the School of Mineral Industries in the land-grant tradition: each program was to provide both knowledge for solving the problems of the day and a sound foundation for the future. He strongly believed that educated individuals should be capable of utilizing all their natural talents. This philosophy was particularly important in American society, where the people had control over their own political system. Only an educated individual could make the decisions necessary for the healthy functioning of the democratic system.

EDUCATIONAL PHILOSOPHY

Early in his career at Penn State, Dean Steidle made known his educational philosophy. In a paper presented at the February 1933 meeting of the American Institute of Mining Engineers he said, "Mineral industries as presented in American colleges covers two fields for studies: cultural and professional, both of which must be considered." Furthermore, he said, "As a part of institutions

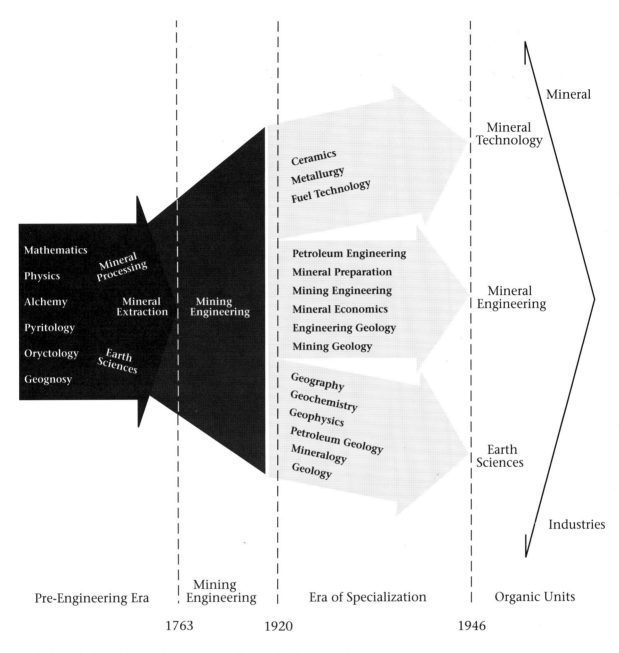

Evolution of mineral industries education, first unified by Agricola in 1556.

dependent upon public support, mineral industry schools must produce graduates who are, primarily, better citizens, and secondly, they must produce trained technicians. Ideal graduates should view technical advances in light of social effects, and social requirements as technical problems." Then he pointed out, "This requires a nice balance between liberal arts and professional subjects. We can present professional curricula in detail, but we can only indicate the path liberal arts teaching should follow."

Further, Dean Steidle also recognized the importance of the accomplishments of the individual in the educational process. In his book *Mineral Industries Education* (1950) he wrote: "The instrument of progress is the human brain. Under the urge of spiritual drive, the brain acts as a focal point to utilize the forces of nature and put them to work for the benefit of mankind. Besides intelligence, which is an innate quality, the tasks of the human brain are knowledge, experience, training, initiative and skill. Given sufficient intelligence, the human brain can make an amazing amount of progress, provided it is supplied with an adequate spiritual and moral urge and a good technical background. It is the role of education to supply such a background."

In order to achieve the desired educational results, Dean Steidle believed there must be a well-rounded curriculum with strict standards over an adequate period of time, and training that would enable individuals to solve the problems they encountered. If students in this curriculum did not receive such training, they would be mere technicians capable only of mechanical operations requiring no thought-processes. Dean Steidle compared the development of a student to the conditions governing the growth of a crystal in this way:

1. Proper concentration and physico-chemical fields and phases	1. Adequate curricula and courses
2. Proper intensity of crystallization (temperature and pressure)	2. Rigid standards
3. Proper balance between various physico-chemical processes going on in the solution and symmetrically directed flow of nutrient solution toward crystal faces	3. Teamwork between different divisions and curricula, cooperation between subjects; observance of prerequisites
4. Adequate length of time for crystallization	4. Sufficient length of education (four years basic curriculum and at least one year of graduate work under traditional standards)

INITIAL DEVELOPMENTS

Dean Steidle made four early decisions that established the pattern the development of the School would take. His first fundamental decision after accepting the deanship was to change the name, on September 20, 1929, to the School of Mineral Industries. This change symbolized a philosophy that the School would provide an all-inclusive educational program for the mineral industries of the state and nation. It also reflected the philosophy of the federal land-grant legislation in the first and second Morrill Acts (1862 and 1890).

Dean Steidle's second endeavor was the improvement of the physical plant. The School was housed in an antiquated structure, and at the dean's insistence the Pennsylvania state legislature appropriated $500,000 for a new Mineral Industries Building (now Steidle Building), which was occupied in 1930. In 1938 the central wing, which had been omitted from the original building, was added at a cost of $250,000. For the first time in the history of the School there was a satisfactory academic building, and perhaps even more important, space was now available for the development of new programs.

In 1931 Dean Steidle established the basic administrative structure with the appointment of Alfred W. Gauger as director of the Mineral Industries Experiment Station, modeled after the Agricultural Experiment Station, and the first professor of fuel science, and the appointment of Harry B. Northrup as director of Mineral Industries Extension. With these appointments, the School began exercising its responsibilities of serving the demands of all of the mineral industries. Most important, research and extension were now full partners with the instructional program.

The year 1931 also witnessed the first expansion of the programs of the School to provide development of a total mineral industries program. A major in petroleum and natural gas engineering was established in the Department of Geology. George H. Fancher was appointed to head the development of the petroleum and natural gas program. Raymond E. Murphy, the first professional geographer at Penn State, was appointed assistant professor of economic geography to begin the development of the geography program.

The Mineral Sciences Building with Steidle Building in the background, about 1955.

THE STRUCTURE OF THE SCHOOL

In the 1930s Dean Steidle initiated the policy that the School of Mineral Industries must provide resident instruction, research, and extension training and that there be no differentiation as to the value of each function. All were educational services that had to be well coordinated for effective application to a progressive mineral industries program. To illustrate the unity of these functions, Dean Steidle wrote: "It will be remembered that weavers use a loom to unite many diverse strands into a useful and attractive cloth, a product far better than the warp and the woof alone. Using all the subject-matter fields in a mineral college accomplishes a like effect."

Dean Steidle provided guidelines and a framework for effective programs in resident instruction, research, and extension training. He believed that the character of an institution, the varying demands made on it, its geographical location, its own internal organization, the types of research programs, and the development of extension services were all important factors in curriculum-making.

RESIDENT INSTRUCTION

During Dean Steidle's era the undergraduate program was viewed as the core of the School. The philosophy behind this contained a set of inviolable principles: a mineral industries education must give undergraduates a broad and general background that was compatible with the times and with future work demands, and good citizenship was a prerequisite for sound technical training. It was the personal conviction of Dean Steidle "that there should be no sectionalized curricula for the first two years of college work." He continued: "These years should be confined to a general, truly liberal education. The decision to enter the technical or nontechnical field could be made with some degree of reason at the end of two years. Properly qualified students should then spend three additional years in any one of the several mineral industries curricula leading to undergraduate degrees. All of this does not seem possible under present academic customs and egoisms. Secondary schools would have to raise their standards under the plan, but the day may come when the now lowly Bachelor will be able to hold its head as a product of true accomplishment and bask in the educational sun" (Steidle, 1950a, p. 201).

In carrying out the philosophy of resident education, a common freshman and sophomore year in all programs was established. This provided not only a sound base for all programs but also an opportunity for students to transfer within the School with no loss of credits. During these two years, training in mathematics, chemistry, physics, English, drawing, geology, and mineralogy were required and there were no electives. In the junior and senior years the programs embraced required fundamental subjects common to all divisions, required professional subjects for departmental curricula, and selected lists of humanistic, labor relations, and technical electives.

In the development of these programs the value of English was recognized. Dean Steidle wrote that English had to have multiple objectives: "(1) To develop in the student the ability to use reference material with facility so that he learns to keep abreast of current developments, technical and humanistic; (2) to provide extensive practice in the writing of reports and papers of all kinds which are criticized in detail on the basis of both grammar and content; (3) to give experience in the preparation, organization, and oral presentation of reports and papers; and (4) to give practice in participation in formal sessions as speaker, chairman, or contributor to floor

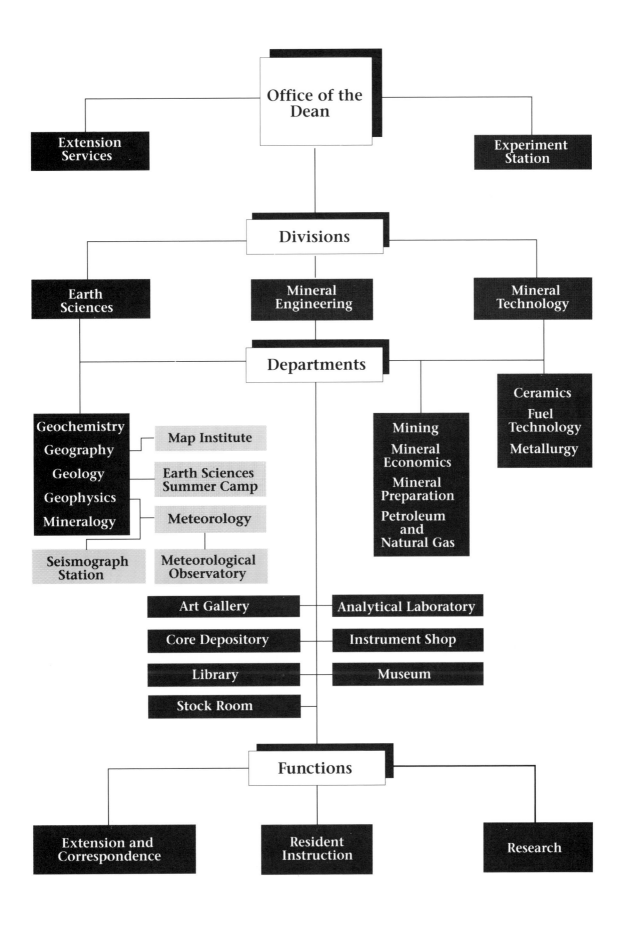

discussion. Compiling a technical report is not too difficult when the facts are available. On the other hand, philosophical expression worth reading for its own sake is a laborious contrivance that can be accomplished only in rare moments of meditation. Excellence is something that counts; ability and facility to express an idea are almost as important as the idea itself" (Steidle, 1950a, p. 204).

English was considered a responsibility of every faculty member in the School of Mineral Industries. It was not left to formal courses. Instruction revolved around the enthusiasm of the student, because topics that were important in a technical, humanistic, and often controversial way were assigned or approved for study. In response, the students exerted themselves in a manner not likely to be found in English classes where the instructor does not have a technical background.

In essence, Dean Steidle postulated, "Formal education is society's endeavor to put old heads on young shoulders, to implant the experience of centuries in the youthful generation. Seen in this light, it is evident that isolated facts have little place in formal education; that presentation of any subject without correlating it to other material, and to life itself, fails its purpose. Liberal arts men must reintegrate their material, weave individual subjects together so as to develop a perspective for students. They must present the past so that it becomes vital today; they must link cause to effect through the ages; delineate the ends for which man struggled, the ideals which motivated him, the results he obtained, and show how all this affects the present" (Steidle, 1950a, p. 204).

RESEARCH AND THE EXPERIMENT STATION

Research in the School of Mineral Industries was tied directly to the experiment station. Dean Steidle believed that "organized research which emphasizes the practical application of new theories has been one of the greatest agencies in advancing the broad base of science" and that it "should be sustained on a continuing basis and should be devoted primarily to substantially increasing the reservoir of fundamental knowledge."

Dean Steidle felt that there was both worthwhile research and worthless research, and that the word "research" could be used far too loosely. In order to restore the value of research, the Mineral Industries Experiment Station was organized to exemplify the research spirit of the School. "Its objectives were to increase knowledge and to establish fundamental principles that had a wide practical application; to promote the most effective utilization of the products and production capacity of the mineral industries of the Commonwealth by seeking new products, new users and more efficient processes; to conserve natural resources; to train men for research work" (Steidle, 1950a, p. 204).

In recognition that teamwork is needed in research, all members of the School's faculty who were engaged in research were automatically members of the experiment station. This provided the foundation for teamwork, which was considered essential where several specialists and much expensive equipment were needed. A basic policy adhered to was that in scholastic research no one preempts a field for his own exclusive use. As Dean Steidle stated, "The net result of one man's work may be zero, whereas the non-fertilization resulting from the contributions of two men may produce partial or complete results on a given problem" (Steidle, 1950a, p. 204). A policy of the School was to encourage in the mineral industries long-range programs treating the discovery, extraction, treatment, or processing of minerals that had particular value for the state of Pennsylvania.

Graduate study was also recognized as an integral part of the research program. It was implemented in two ways: first, through scholarships, fellowships, and graduate assistantships, which provided the means for students to get advanced training while at the same time developing a greater comprehension of their chosen profession; and second, through research assistantships, which permitted young graduates to work under a senior professor.

Dean Steidle felt that little thought had been given to the social significance of college research and that graduate study must be encouraged for the welfare of the nation. Therefore, the graduate program must produce a continuous flow of scholars and teachers. As Dean Steidle said, "We must explore the frontiers of science because the geographical frontiers have vanished. Most important the stature of research must be raised." In his remarks Dean Steidle put forth a challenge: research, to be worthwhile, must not be trivial. To clarify his position and encourage improvements in quality, he said: "Today anything passes for research. Label a simple inquiry 'research' and it acquires a mystic dignity. We must distinguish between investigation and research. Re-search into the postulates, theories, laws pertaining to the subject, careful scrutiny into the initial framework of the field of knowledge—such, in sum, represents the realm of research. All else is investigation. Einstein and classical physics, Lobachevsky and Euclidean geometry, Pasteur and medicine—all are representatives of research of the highest and purest order, a thorough re-searching of the foundations in the respective fields of learning" (Steidle, 1950a, pp. 209–10).

EXTENSION TRAINING

The third major function of the School of Mineral Industries was extension training. The basic purpose of these programs was, in essence, continuing education, to provide training courses that would help workers to secure industrial advancement and to provide employees with greater competence in their jobs. The major part of the program consisted of establishing training classes in communities where there were a sufficient number of industrial workers to support a class, or

Mrs. Edward Steidle serving punch in the Mineral Industries Museum, early 1940s.

in locations that were central to areas from which students could be drawn. Correspondence instruction provided training for those who could not attend classes. The goal was to reach as many as possible of the 600,000 workers employed in the mineral industries of Pennsylvania.

Extension classes developed along three distinct lines. The most common was on-the-job vocational training provided to workers who would be promoted to positions on a supervisory or equivalent technical level. The second type was designed for workers who were already on a supervisory level but who needed to improve their supervisory abilities in the technical phases of their work. The third type of class provided specialized training for the technicians.

Classes of the first type, for workers not yet at the supervisory grade, were organized largely under public school supervision and control, and state and federal funds were used to reimburse local school districts for instruction expenses. This program was free to students, except for costs for textbooks and incidental expenses. The work was approved by the State Department of Public Instruction and carried out with the cooperation of local school officials. Only local instructors, qualified by training and experience, were used.

In the second type of instruction, for training of workers at the supervisory level, programs were designed according to the particular needs of the company served. Each group was limited to twelve to fifteen supervisors from a company and was under the guidance of a trained conference leader provided by the School. The technical training of these supervisory personnel contributed greatly to the modernization of the mineral industries in the state.

The special training programs were developed solely on request by a group. These programs were provided at various levels from less-than-college-credit to college credit and occasionally were offered at the graduate level. Local instructors were employed, and classes operated on a fee basis. Although these programs were few in number, they provided a progressive service that could not be obtained anywhere else in the state.

Correspondence instruction consisted of both college-credit and less-than-college-credit courses. The college-credit courses were developed and administered by the resident instruction faculty. The less-than-college-level courses were developed by extension personnel from material used in extension classes. The texts and other materials used in extension work and correspondence classes were developed by the extension staff.

UNIFICATION OF THE MINERAL INDUSTRIES EDUCATION

Dean Steidle was quite concerned about the low standing and reputation of mineral industries education in the eyes of American colleges and universities. He wrote: "Few branches of mineral industries education have a very high standing in the engineering and scientific world, occupying a stepchild position as they do. Some are considered a nuisance by college administrators and therefore are relegated to basement or attic space in old buildings on campus. Values are based on enrollment rather than the unique services to be rendered by graduates" (Steidle, 1950a, p. 148). In many instances this low status of mineral industries education was due to dispersal of the fields in different colleges where the dean's interest was primarily in other fields.

Dean Steidle believed that the mineral industry programs had to be centralized in a single school for the study of the total physical resources of the Earth: land, water, and air. Thus, a

Grade-school students visit the Mineral Industries Museum, early 1950s.

unified program that would permit students in the various branches to organize an interdisciplinary awareness of related fields could be developed. If this did not occur, the dean believed, "there can be no unity: department is against department on a divide and conquer basis, and the work is ineffective and uneconomical . . . and every bit of friction costs money."

From the moment of his appointment as dean, Dean Steidle planned for a unification of the disciplines oriented to the study of the Earth's resources. He molded a unified program from disciplines that had been rejected by or not been established in any other schools. The School of Engineering had traditionally exhibited little or no interest in developing mining, metallurgy, or ceramics. Geology was associated with mining at Penn State and did not have a traditional development in the School of Science. The programs of petroleum and natural gas engineering, geography, meteorology, and mineral economics originated in the School of Mineral Industries.

Dean Steidle's reforms were firmly implemented by January 1944, when the Board of Trustees of the Pennsylvania State College approved his new organization. In the November 1944 issue of *Mineral Industries* Dean Steidle wrote:

> The new plan provides greater opportunity for unity, policy, purpose, and more integration of programs. The conventional departments have been replaced by three new departments, Earth Sciences, Mineral Engineering, and Mineral Technology. Heads of the departments will coordinate twelve divisions of work, geology, mineralogy, geophysics, meteorology, geography, mineral economics, mining, mineral preparation, petroleum and natural gas, fuel technology, metallurgy and ceramics. Chiefs of the divisions are key men and will give close attention to student personnel and guidance. In addition, Mineral Industries Extension Services and the Mineral Industries Experiment Station each will be served by a director.

Under the new plan all fences whatsoever are eliminated, and the total resources of the School will be made available for each of the three functions of resident instruction, extension and correspondence instruction, and research. The School faces the greatest opportunities and greatest obligations of all times, and the new organization is in accordance with the spirit of the organic Land-Grant Act [the 1890 Morrill Act].

The mineral industries are dependent functions of independent variables—the rates of mineral discovery. The three general classifications of mineral industries education are established on a basis of the needs for tomorrow's mineral world.

The earth sciences are concerned with those divisions of *natural sciences* which relate specifically to the earth-land, air and water. The term earth science is a direct translation of "geo-logy." Geology, mineralogy, geophysics, meteorology and geography are included under Earth Sciences.

Mineral engineering is concerned with extracting minerals from the earth and preparing them for use. In other words, it is the means by which mineral matter, including mineral fuels, is made available to man, with due regard to conservation. Mineral economics, mining, mineral preparation, and petroleum and natural gas production and transportation are grouped under this classification. These involve design, construction and operation, together with the application of the earth sciences.

Mineral technology is the science and systematic knowledge of primary methods of processing and treating mineral matters and directing its industrial utilization. It is concerned with those industrial arts and sciences which involve the transformation of mineral fuels into energy and the conversion of minerals of all classes into raw materials of industry or finished articles of commerce. Modern fuel technology, metallurgy, and ceramics are classified as Mineral Technology. These involve advanced phases of chemistry and physics, as well as basic engineering.

In the 1945 and 1946 issues of *Mineral Industries* the chairmen of the newly established divisions provided information on the new organization (Gensamer, 1946). Maxwell Gensamer, the first chairman of the Department of Mineral Technology, recognized certain curricular advantages resulting from the new organization. He wrote: "From the point of view of teaching . . . there is much more uniformity in objectives and methods among the three divisions of the department—fuel technology, metallurgy and ceramics—than in the School as a whole. While it is possible to have a common freshman year for the whole school, differences develop by the sophomore year that make it advisable to differentiate these departments from the departments of the other two divisions at this level. But within the division there is no need for specialization in the sophomore year. . . . This high degree of uniformity in the curriculum is possible because the emphasis placed on the basic courses is about the same in each department and different from the emphasis placed on the courses in the other divisions."

Dr. Gensamer also believed that a strength of the research program in the Department of Mineral Technology was that the faculty in the three departments were permitted to cooperate on joint research projects.

The chairman of the Department of Earth Sciences, Herbert Insley, also believed that the new organization would make it possible to unify fields: "This closer coordination will bring a greater appreciation in research of the fruitfulness of cooperation among the departments in the collection of data, the common use of facilities, and the interchange of information. The broadening of viewpoint is as essential to teaching as it is to research. In graduate instruction the value of cooperation is self-evident, for if this exists among faculty members, the graduate student will almost automatically turn to others as well as his own supervision for information" (Insley, 1945).

David R. Mitchell, chairman of the Department of Mineral Engineering, noted that separate, isolated departments produced a climate conducive to duplication and waste (Mitchell, 1945). He believed the new organization would enhance the overall academic programs of the School: "There has been a tendency during the past 25 years as special professional work developed in certain schools, to establish a department, and let it function as an independent unit even though closely related to other departments in the school. Under such procedures inefficiencies and duplications of effort tend to grow. For instance, where there are separate departments in mining engineering, petroleum engineering, mining geology and mineral economics, four separate courses may be given in Mineral Property Examination and Valuation, covering the same fundamental material. . . . To prevent this condition from developing, and to promote efficiency by providing a close relationship for professional fields of activity dealing with the engineering phase of the mineral extraction industries, these divisions of instruction were brought together into a single department of Mineral Engineering."

ADMINISTRATIVE STRUCTURE

The administrative structure established in 1945 was based on a hierarchical system. The dean was the chief administrative officer, and directly responsible to him was the Executive Committee, composed of the dean, the directors of the extension service and the experiment station, and the heads of the three departments. Within the departments were twelve programs administered by division chiefs.

The dean was responsible for the overall program but concentrated on undergraduate resident instruction, a primary function. The directors coordinated extension training and graduate training and research. The department heads conferred regularly with the division chiefs and integrated the subject-matter fields. The chiefs of the divisions formed the cutting edge of the overall program.

Within this structure Daisy Rowe (1919–53) played a unique role. At the time of her death in 1953, she had spent thirty-four years in the School, a term that spanned the graduation of three-fourths of the College's alumni. She was known not only for the counsel she provided for undergraduate students, but also for the information and counsel she offered administrators. Her opinion was highly respected. The value of Daisy Rowe's service and extra hours of work during the development of the College of Mineral Industries can hardly be estimated. In the absence of the dean she was the source of information on the college. Dean Steidle considered her an executive secretary, private secretary, and office manager. As a memorial, alumni and friends provided funds for a bronze plaque, now located in Steidle Building.

The development of departments and divisions strengthened the organization of the School. In selecting personnel for these positions, the traditional policy of advancement from within was strongly adhered to. Personnel from outside were brought in only when the School faculty did not have someone with the special qualifications for the position. Of particular importance was the hiring policy provided by the executive officer of each unit. The standard policy was that every executive officer employ the finest talent available. At times a professor with greater professional and financial status than the executive officer could be hired, for, as Dean Steidle said, "He who surpasses me the furthest, loves me the most."

This organization evolved over many years. Dean Steidle recognized that the organization was an evolutionary process:

> Reorganization without purpose is more dangerous than no organization at all. It often takes much longer to plan a project than it does to build it; similarly, much longer to prepare a program than it does to put it into action. The success of the reorganization rests heavily on chairmen and heads of departments.
>
> The attitude of the faculty must be positive. Leadership on the part of responsive officers renders it positive. Once leadership is withdrawn, the attitude inevitably becomes negative. If an officer slackens or fails, someone must be ready to assume leadership or the School will disintegrate as a functional body. The net result is a weak spot that must be plugged with an interested able man. Methods, too, can be improved again and again as human ingenuity and a fresh viewpoint are brought to bear upon them. Open minds are not in themselves sufficient. Initiatives must be taken in originating projects if results are to be accomplished. (Steidle, 1950a, p. 175)

The School of Mineral Industries, 1953

Edward Steidle, Dean
Alfred W. Gauger, Director of the Experiment Station
Donald C. Jones, Director of Extension

College Organization

Earth Sciences	Elburt F. Osborn
Division of Geography	E. Willard Miller
Division of Geology	Frank M. Swartz
Division of Geophysics and Geochemistry	Benjamin F. Howell, Jr.
Division of Meteorology	Hans Neuberger
Division of Mineralogy	Paul D. Krynine
Mineral Engineering	David R. Mitchell
Division of Mineral Economics	John D. Ridge
Division of Mineral Preparation	H. Beecher Charmbury
Division of Mining	Arnold W. Asman
Division of Petroleum and Natural Gas	John C. Calhoun
Mineral Technology	Woldemar Weyl
Division of Ceramics	Edward C. Henry
Division of Fuel Technology	Calvert C. Wright
Division of Metallurgy	Jay W. Fredrickson

Students

Undergraduate	500
Graduate	170

ENROLLMENT TRENDS

In 1929, when Edward Steidle became dean, the resident student body in the departments was 197. Enrollment dropped to a low of 180 in 1933. Following this dip, in spite of the continued economic depression, enrollment increased to 400 in 1940. After World War II the undergraduate enrollment remained stable. In 1954 undergraduate enrollment totaled 444 at the State College campus, and 21 at the Commonwealth Campuses. Major growth had occurred, however, in graduate enrollment, and by 1954 the School had 193 graduate students.

Because Dean Steidle believed that the undergraduate student body was the core of the program, he assumed responsibility for the growth of the undergraduate programs. Only after the undergraduate programs were structured was emphasis placed on the development of graduate enrollment. As the programs of the School grew, it became evident that many of the departments—but particularly the geological sciences, geography, and meteorology—had knowledge that needed to be imparted to the entire student body at Penn State. The demand for service courses grew. In 1930 the enrollment in service courses was about 900; by 1940 enrollment had doubled to about 1,800, and it again doubled by 1953. As enrollment increased, the number of graduates also increased. In the early 1950s between 129 and 143 students received bachelor of science degrees each year. The growth in graduate degrees was even more striking, going from twenty-four in 1947 to forty-two in 1953, and for the Ph.D. degree from one degree in 1947 to fourteen in 1952.

MINERAL INDUSTRIES CONFERENCES

A major goal of Dean Steidle was to make the School of Mineral Industries the center of mineral training and research in the state. To accomplish this he encouraged the mineral industry societies to meet at the School. In 1930 the initial conference at the School was devoted to the problems of petroleum and natural gas. Interest in these conferences grew each year, and by 1933 each conference had an attendance of more than 100. These early conferences were so successful that the School began to develop plans to sponsor conferences in all fields of activity in which it offered programs.

The conferences provided a tangible link to the mineral industries in the states. At all the conferences papers providing information on developments in specific industries were presented. Most important, the conferences gave leaders of mineral industries an opportunity to assemble at the only School of Mineral Industries in the state. Through these conferences, the industry leaders came to realize the value of the School.

EDUCATIONAL FACILITIES

In order to provide a quality education, Dean Steidle recognized the need for an adequate physical plant for faculty and students and for other facilities, including a ready-reference library, a museum and art gallery, and a publication to inform the public about the activities of the School.

He also wrote: "Likewise, there should be proper arrangement of offices, classrooms, and laboratories in order to provide the quiet and solitude so necessary for mental pioneering" (Steidle, 1950a, p. 223).

GROWTH OF THE PHYSICAL PLANT

It became evident that a single building was not adequate to house the expanding activities of the School. In July 1938 Dean Steidle sent a detailed report to President Hetzel explaining the need for more laboratory space. This thirty-two-page report traced the economic position of the mineral industries in Pennsylvania, summarized the work of the School, and detailed urgently needed research. The space allocations of the overcrowded Mineral Industries Building were detailed, as was a precise plan for use of the proposed building. Although funds were not available in 1938 and the construction of new buildings did not occur during the World War II period, the groundwork had been laid for the Mineral Sciences Building.

The Mineral Sciences Building was authorized under Governor James H. Duff's postwar building program, and cornerstone exercises were held on March 25, 1949. The facility was to be used for instruction in geophysics, geochemistry, geography, mineral economics, steel-making, coal-processing, and mineral beneficiation and would also provide offices for the Mineral Industries Experiment Station and the Mineral Industries Extension Services. On December 6, 1950, the proposal to add a wing to the new Mineral Sciences Building was approved.

The securing of funds for the Mineral Sciences Building immediately after World War II is attributable to Dean Steidle's continued insistence that space was inadequate. In 1946, in an unpublished paper to the central administration, he wrote: "The new laboratory building will not meet our present needs in any sense. It singly will not relieve the over-crowded, inefficient situation existing throughout our School whether resident instruction, extension instruction, or research. No space is available in the present building for the exclusive use of our Departments of Geophysics and Geochemistry, Geography, and Mineral Economics. There are no specific laboratories available for research in any of the twelve major departments of work of the School excepting petroleum, natural gas and coal. The space allocated to Extension Services in the present building is wholly inadequate—office space, demonstration space, or storage. The problem of accommodating our work is so acute that we were compelled to give up our Historical Museum to Army and Navy graduate study and research, in spite of the fact that we believe Museum projects are a definite part of our education service to Pennsylvania."

Dean Steidle connected the new Mineral Sciences Building to the Mineral Industries Building. This made physical access between the two buildings easy, but it also symbolized the interrelationship and interdependence among the various disciplines. Two other buildings were constructed too. A Combustion Laboratory was built adjacent to and interconnected with a small heating plant servicing one of the dormitory developments. The equipment available permitted study of a wide variety of operating conditions on units with burning ranges from 20 to 1,000 pounds an hour, including twin 6-by-6-foot stokers firing twin 178 horsepower boilers metered and instrumented so that comparative performance could be observed and recorded.

The Mineral Industries Summer Camp constructed by the Farm Security Administration in 1937 was located in Stone Valley, about thirteen miles south of State College. The main building consisted of an attractive, rustic hall combined with a dining hall and living rooms and offices. A total of thirty-six students and staff could be housed in twelve cabins furnished with steel cots, dressers, and electric lights. The camp had its own well and reservoir and modern sewage disposal plants. It was used not only as a geology field camp but also as a recreational facility for faculty and staff.

THE MINERAL INDUSTRIES LIBRARY

The foundations for a School library were laid in the 1890s. Periodicals were subscribed to and kept bound, and the departments managed to collect a few books. With these as a nucleus, the modern college library was created in 1930 and M. Lucille Jackson was appointed the first librarian. She was a graduate of the Pennsylvania College for Women (Chatham College) and received her master's degree in chemistry from Penn State in 1930.

In March 1932 the purpose and need for a library were stated in *Mineral Industries:* "As a vital part of the School, its purpose is to build and maintain a collection of books pertinent to the various phases of the mineral industries such that undergraduates may be encouraged to broaden their academic interests and also that research may be provided with a satisfactory tool. As research grows, one of the most important sources is the library, and preparation must be made for its demands. The library in a school such as this is as necessary as classrooms and laboratories, since the work done there must often be preceded by investigations of the literature. Thus, there is a definite need for a book collection of a specific scientific nature and to this end are library activities being directed."

Dean Steidle recognized that the library was of fundamental importance to the development of the School: "The libraries may be considered as storehouses of scientific and technologic knowledge. But storehouses are, so to speak, locked, and a student must be taught to use the keys to them. The student must learn how to avail himself of the funds of information at his disposal and to use it efficiently. The keys are a card catalog. The catalog, however, is in reality only introductory. The student must familiarize himself with still other keys, such as indexes, abstracts, and bibliographies of special fields, which open to him vistas of what has been published, even though his own library may not have it all on its shelves." He then quoted Lord Beaconsfield, "The more extensive a man's knowledge of what has been done, the greater will be his power of knowing what to do," and continued: "Research usually implies a laboratory with flasks, retorts and delicate apparatus, all skillfully manipulated by a scientist. The technical library, the universal

---

Librarians

Mineral Industries Library

M. Lucille Jackson	1930–1941
E. Paul Jones	1941–1942
Liberata Emmerich	1942–1965

Earth and Mineral Sciences Library

Emilie T. McWilliams	1966–1989
Linda R. Musser	1990–

tool, must nowadays be included in the picture. Library research will prevent two serious mistakes often made by scientists: duplication of studies already made and failure to employ established methods and procedures" (Steidle, 1950a, pp. 235–36).

The Mineral Industries Library was located on the third floor of the Mineral Industries Building. The main room, under a circular dome, made an architecturally interesting arrangement with walls and ceiling in white plaster. A skylight provided an indirect lighting system. On either side of the main room were two smaller rooms, each with wall space for about 5,000 volumes.

By the early 1950s the working collection had grown to more than 15,000 books, but journals, in foreign languages and in English, constituted the greatest part of the collection. More than 300 leading periodicals, plus transactions, proceedings, annuals, and monographs relating to the mineral industries, were received. Geological reports, bulletins, investigations, and circulars of the technical departments of state and federal governments, as well as those of foreign governments, were also obtained, as were publications of the professional societies and institutions, domestic and foreign, that applied to the mineral industries. The value of journals and special publications was recognized. Dean Steidle wrote: "Books are necessary, even though their research value is of secondary importance to that of journals. The value of sets of periodicals increases with the years, while that of books decreases. Authors frequently publish their findings in the former as soon as they arrive at safe conclusions, long before they are put into book form for the convenient use of students."

During the early years of the library a small rare book collection was begun. Included were Agricola's *De Ortu & Causis Subterraneorum* (1546), *De Re Metallica* (1556, as well as the Hoover translation of 1912), and the German edition of the *Berckwerck Buch* (1580). Other early mineral industry books included Pettus's *Fleta Minor: The Laws of Art and Nature, in Knowing, Judging, Assaying, Fining, Refining, and Inlarging the Bodies of Confin'd Metals* (1683), Schonberg's *Ausführliche Berg-Information* (1693), Delius's *Anleitung zu der Bergbaukunst* (1773), de Saussure's *Essais sur l'Hygrométrie* (1783), Maclure's *Observations on the Geology of the United States of America* (1817), Berzelius's *Nouveau Système de Minéralogie* (1819), Davy's *On the Safety Lamp for Preventing Explosions in Mines* (1825), Brongniart's *Traité des Arts Ceramiques* (1854), and Wright's *Oil Regions of Pennsylvania* (1865).

Lucille Jackson served as librarian from 1930 to 1941, when she was replaced by E. Paul Jones, a graduate of Temple University with a degree in chemistry and a library science degree from the Drexel Institute Library School. As a scientist and a librarian, he continued the tradition of having a librarian trained in the sciences as well as in library work. He was succeeded by Liberata Emmerich, who held the position from 1942 to 1965. From 1966 to 1989 the librarian was Emilie T. McWilliams. The present librarian is Linda R. Musser. By 1966 the library had outgrown the space in the Mineral Industries Building (Steidle Building) and was moved to a more spacious area in Deike Building.

The Earth and Mineral Sciences Library now has more than 80,000 volumes and more than 1,800 serials and periodical titles. In addition to books and periodicals, the library has much to offer students and faculty. Among its holdings are Earth Resource Technology Satellite (ERTS) photographs covering the continental United States and Alaska; more than thirty abstracting and indexing tools, including *Chemical Abstracts*, the *Bibliography and Index of Geology*, the *Engineering Index, Fuel Abstracts, Metal Abstracts*, and *Meteorological and Geophysical Abstracts;* 14,000 maps and a variety of atlases; foreign-language technical dictionaries; encyclopedias; company directories; biographical listings; and all the theses prepared by earth and mineral sciences students.

There is seating for 150 in the library's spacious, well-lighted reading room, a popular place for studying or using the library facilities. Copies of the current *Daily Collegian* and the *New York Times* are always available. The library has four to five full-time library staff available, plus part-time students help to provide service.

THE MINERAL INDUSTRIES ART GALLERY

One of Dean Steidle's primary objectives was to provide "educational forces" to help make the people of Pennsylvania more "mineral conscious." The establishment of the Mineral Industries Art Gallery was one way of attaining this objective. In order to accomplish this goal, the dean began to acquire oil paintings of the mineral industries.

In the 1930s the dean's office and conference room served as an art gallery. At the art gallery's first public exhibition, held in the State Museum in Harrisburg from March 9 to April 10, 1935, Gertrude B. Fuller, then assistant director in charge of the State Museum, said, "These are not dreary pictures of depressing scenes; they are vivid with scenic beauty, life, action, color and drama. Here are greystone towers against the loveliest hills in spring coloring; here are night skies and curving water lighted by the fiery glow of iron blast furnaces; men of strength and skill interested in pouring molten glass for a great lens for the service of science."

In the late 1930s the General State Authority approved the construction of the central wing of the Mineral Industries Building. The first floor of this wing included the Mineral Industries Art Gallery, which was conceived, designed, and constructed as a permanent institution. On April 11, 1942, when the gallery was formally opened, three hundred guests were present, including College administrators and members of the College Senate, the Board of Trustees, and the State College Ministerium. The 165 canvases and most of the minerals housed in the art gallery were donated by artists, alumni, and friends of the School.

The Mineral Industries Art Gallery is the only gallery in the world devoted solely to mineral industries scenes. The collection has won international recognition and has been the subject of articles in several publications. Paintings from the collection have been used to illustrate articles in many technical and industrial journals. In 1986 some of the paintings were reproduced in *Pennsylvania: Keystone to Progress*, written by E. Willard Miller. At the dedication of the art gallery, J. Burne Helme, a professor in the Division of Fine Arts, stated: "The nucleus of the collection was the representation of the Black Diamond Colliery near Scranton, one of the oldest collieries in the anthracite region painted by John W. Raight and already belonging to the College as a gift of the artist. Eighty-six artists are now represented. Each activity in the mineral industries field of Pennsylvania is covered. It is most appropriate that a collection of pictures about the mineral

Museum and Art Gallery Curators	
Clair W. Robinson	1934–1948
Howard Lucas	1948–1951
Arthur Jaffe	1952–1953
David E. Snell	1953–1991

The art gallery of the College, 1946. Dean Edward Steidle, left, and John E. Gaus view an 1846 oil painting showing the rolling of steel ingots in the Richard Foundry, Philadelphia. The painting, purchased for the Mineral Industries Art Gallery, was painted by George Caleb Bingham.

industries should have been housed at The Pennsylvania State College. The predominant part these industries play in the economic life of the Commonwealth of Pennsylvania is of profound significance for the development of such a collection. Here is the Mineral Industries Art Gallery, colorful fruit of a germinating idea, fraught with impact for our growth and understanding. May it be a symbol of future rich acquisitions by the College in the realm of art."

All the paintings in the collection are originals. One shows the last beehive coke ovens to operate continuously in Pennsylvania. A painting made in Johnstown depicts one of the first by-product coke plants installed in this country. Another painting shows the now dismantled Schollenberg rolling mill on the Monongahela River near Pittsburgh. The painting of Lucy Furnace, one of the oldest iron blast furnaces on the Allegheny River near Pittsburgh, provides a view of the traditional iron industry of Pennsylvania.

As part of the opening program of the art gallery, Theodore Roethke of the Department of English Composition wrote a dedicatory poem:

> Here on the cushioned wall
> In richly-gelded frame,
> Furnaces bulge and flare
> Against a Pittsburgh night,
> Diminish, cinder-charred;
> Hard pressed anthracite
> Moves from a narrow vein
> As fine-strong muscles heave;
> Magyar, Welshmen, Lett,
> Cunning technicians tame
> Metals richer than grain;
> Glassworkers coddle and coal
> A telescopic lens
> To prove a star immense

And more than beautiful
For whoever labors with ore,
Coal, clay, oil-bearing sand,
Probers of rock and air,
Live not by work alone;
Rig, tackle, pit-beast, man,
Above or under earth,
Brings more than mineral forth
More than the secret of stone.

And Dean Steidle summed it all up when he wrote at the dedication ceremony: "The Art Gallery at the Pennsylvania State College's School of Mineral Industries truly represents the mineral arts; as it shows both the art created by man as well as art created by nature."

THE *MINERAL INDUSTRIES* BULLETIN

The first issue of the *Mineral Industries* bulletin, October 31, 1931, stated: "Since its inception as the old School of Mines and more recently as the School of Mines and Metallurgy, this division of the Pennsylvania State College has been the least known throughout the state and nation, of any of the schools on the campus. Its sole method of publicity was through the medium of its graduates, and because these were few, the School did not receive the attention merited." As a response to a revitalization of the School in the early 1930s, there had been a revived interest in its activities. Because former graduates knew little of the major changes of the School, a publication

Bulletin Editors

Mineral Industries Bulletin

John T. Ryan, Jr.	1931–1932
Harry B. Northrup	1932–1947
Donald C. Jones	1947–1953
Frederick R. Axelson	1953–1956
Roy G. Ehman	1956–1957
Jeanne L. Slobod	1957–1961
Roy G. Ehman	1961–1964
Mary Neilly	1964–1965
Pamela L. Slingluff	1966

Earth and Mineral Sciences Bulletin

Pamela L. Slingluff	1967–1972
Mary Neilly	1973–1985
Judith Kiusalaas	1985–

to bring them up-to-date was needed. There was perhaps even a greater need for a publication to inform the general public of activities of the School. The first issue reported: "It is our intention to continue this organ monthly throughout most of the year and for many years to come for your benefits and that of our many friends and associates in the mineral industries."

The title of the *Mineral Industries* bulletin was changed to *Earth and Mineral Sciences* with the change in the name of the College. At the same time, the professional content of the Bulletin was increased to reflect the expanding research activities of the College. Mary S. Neilly was editor of the Bulletin from the 1960s to the mid-1980s. The Bulletin is presently under the editorship of Judith Kiusalaas. It has been published for more than sixty years and continues to inform students, alumni, and friends about the professional activities of the College.

THE DEAN'S PHILOSOPHY

Dean Steidle expressed many of his ideas and educational philosophy in editorials in the *Mineral Industries* bulletin.

"THE ROOTS OF HUMAN PROGRESS"

The following excerpts from some 1948 and 1949 editorials summarize his views on "the roots of human progress."

> Most men in their quest for comfort and security have paid little attention to the higher value of mind and spirit. The inclination has always been to measure progress in terms of material developments which are at best of a fugitive nature. The neglect of mental and spiritual aspects has an important bearing on present world turmoil.
>
> Man is born on Mother Earth without knowledge or skills. Soon he finds physical needs for food, clothing, shelter, exercise and relaxation. His personal needs are self-expression, new experiences, and amusements, while his social needs have been classified as work, status, security, friendship, companionship, and love. He finds himself infinitesimal in comparison to the whole. And when he feels smart and made, he is actually dumb and broke.
>
> I advance the idea that we must make a new approach to arouse the interest of the general student in the bases for the progress of mankind. We must return to fundamentals, discarding for this purpose the highly departmentalized and specialized type of course, and turn to two closely integrated courses that will highlight man's basic needs, problems and resources. I would like to call the course "Roots of Human Progress," Parts I and II. Part I would include subject matter designated "Man and Nature" and "Man and Man"; Part II [would include] subject matter designated "Man and Land" and "Man and Conservation."

Dean Steidle's Executive Committee in 1951. From left, A. W. Gauger, director of the Mineral Industries Experiment Station; David R. Mitchell, head of the Department of Mineral Engineering; Daisy Rowe, dean's secretary; Edward Steidle, dean; E. F. Osborn, head of the Department of Earth Sciences; Woldemar Weyl, head of the Department of Mineral Technology; and Donald C. Jones, director of Mineral Industries Extension.

Thinking man has been concerned with his place and purpose in the universe since the time of the earliest Egyptian and Chinese philosophies. Ancient creeds, as well as modern religions and philosophies of life, are concerned with the same problem. While such considerations and concepts have been valuable, theoretical philosophizing and dogmatic concepts are inadequate for a satisfactory solution of world problems of today. The concepts of man and life and their ultimate purpose should be looked for in the relations of intelligent man to man and their relationship to the physical world.

Progress must be of a balanced nature, and mankind's goal is manysided perfection. Life should be a process of individual perfection and creation, and is as much of mind and spirit as of matter.

Man becomes more self-reliant as he extends his scientific and technological discoveries and learns how to shape natural condition to his own desires.

The purpose of the School of Mineral Industries is not only to train potential human resources in the use of scientific and technological devices, or in the ability to create bigger and better machines and devices, or in the capacity to solve Nature's secrets and discover Nature's laws and the way to control them, but to produce a better and more decent citizen for a great democracy, a man who will be able to use his training and brains with proper self-control and humility in order to improve the fate of all mankind.

Research and more research, teamwork and more teamwork, in all fields of endeavors, are needed to create the man of the future; not the fatalistic man ready to accept whatever nation generously or niggardly gives him, but the man who can control nature and his own fate.

CONSERVATION

In 1949 and 1950 Dean Steidle wrote a series of editorials in *Mineral Industries* entitled "A Philosophy of Conservation." The wise use of minerals was one of his major themes, as the following excerpts show:

Standards of living depend upon two factors: human resources—intelligence, imagination, initiative, know-how, work; and natural resources—plants, animals and minerals, including water, air, soil, heat and light from the sun, and all other such resources that are useful to man. Human relationships have not kept pace with scientific achievement; as a result

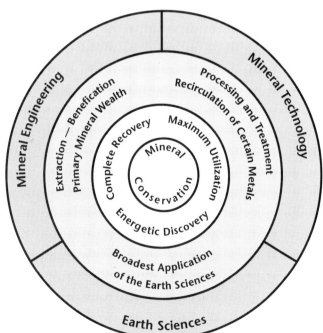

Conception of the development and conservation of irreplaceable minerals.

man, in desperation, wittingly, premeditatively sacrifices freedom for security. Many natural resources, through overproduction, mismanagement, and greed, have definitely moved over into the exhausted and exhaustible category. There must be a philosophy for conservation now in order to reach the ultimate goal of human improvement.

The theory of Malthus that the food supply is increasing in an arithmetic ratio while the population increases in a geometric ratio has required a new value in the modern industrial age. For a time this theory seemed disproved by the tremendous advances of chemical and mechanized agriculture, but now statistics show that the yield of the cultivable land of the world will soon be insufficient to sustain the ever-increasing world population. A parallel drawn in the industrial field shows that the per capita consumption of raw mineral materials is increasing while the supplies are decreasing. Malthus' ominous prediction now applies not only to agriculture, but ever more to mining.

No one can deny the serious impact of the situation. No one can contest the implications of the facts that are at man's disposal. Nevertheless, though the need for conservation is undeniable, the majority of people continue to content themselves with paying new lip service to the ideal. When will man realize that there is very little time left to establish world peace, and that he must take definite and practical steps now to put his heart in conservation?

The greatest single obstacle in the path of constructive action in making conservation a reality is the inherent discord in the hearts of men. A perfect society doubtless is many millennia removed from the present generation, but it must be admitted that progress toward a conservative use of our natural heritage with an altruistic concept of the greatest good for the greatest number for the greatest time can be attained only by a society in which discord is reduced to a minimum compatible with the limitations of human nature.

Conservation of the soil, one of the most valuable natural mineral resources, is definitely needed. However, the program must not stop with the prevention of soil erosion. It must take definite steps toward restoring vitality to soil that is growing increasingly sterile. Education of the farmer in practical and understandable terms can do it.

Man sees the surface of the earth as a blank wall. It need not be so blank if the signs are read correctly. Progress in the mineral arts and sciences, like progress in most affairs, depends on that peculiar quality, so rarely developed in humanity, imagination. Imagination must be put to work to convert the images to the reality of fact. With the aid of modern science this can be done.

THE NEED FOR MINERAL INDUSTRIES COLLEGES

In 1951 Dean Steidle proposed a series of editorials in *Mineral Industries* entitled "Wanted: Mineral Industries Colleges." The following are excerpts from this series on the importance of mineral industries education:

The United States owes much of its industrial greatness to the work of pioneers in the mineral industries. The task of the pioneer was to locate and develop in a rude way the mineral resources of the nation. Today, mineral industries leaders are still in great demand, but for a different purpose—to direct intelligent utilization of the limited, waning, submarginal mineral resources. Today the need is for trained earth scientists, mineral engineers, and mineral technologists rather than the unskilled prospectors of earlier days.

Everyone who can read and think should consider the needs of higher education of tomorrow—its scope, its aims, its values. Along with improved technical education, there must be improved moral education. Man is not born human, he becomes so, and those responsible for the transformation are the teachers and parents.

Mineral industries education must be considered on the broadest possible terms. Thinking must extend beyond the campus to the public, to governmental agencies, whose influence is expanding, and to the industries themselves. Accept the challenge to meet the growing needs for coordinated action which must represent all the various units concerned with mineral industries education. Establish a broad classification of mineral industries education on a basis of earth sciences, mineral engineering and mineral technology.

THE NEED FOR A NATIONAL MINERALS POLICY

A pervasive theme of Dean Steidle was the wise use of the nation's mineral resources and the need for a national minerals policy. In 1952 he wrote:

> The United States has evolved a mineral economy during the past fifty years. That is, the fundamental base of agriculture and industry has become adjusted to and dependent upon the steady flow of mineral products in constantly increasing tonnages, . . . the problems of supply are acute, and the country is not self-sufficient.
>   Mineral supply has become a matter of national concern as a guarantee of national existence. To what extent atomic energy may be applied to the peaceful parameter of industry is yet to be established. . . . Mineral industries people must think of more than minerals and rocks. Now they must ask penetrating questions in order to find fundamental answers to mineral problems. (Steidle, 1952)

Dean Steidle viewed conservation as the "prudent and intelligent use of all types of resources," not "the parsimonious and misguided avarice of the miser." He continued: "There is a fundamental need for a national mineral policy." A sound policy would be developed in two stages as follows:

Phase One:
1. A survey of the world's mineral resources
2. A survey of the world's mineral demands, including an estimate of future demands
    a. Change of the mineral position of creditor mineral nations to debtor mineral nations
    b. Migration of mineral exploration in the world and its effect on the stability of national and international economies

    c. Effects on the economy of a region or nation in the development of a new mineral or in the new application of a known mineral

    d. Distribution of mineral resources as a factor in industrial locations

    e. Area studies of problem mineral regions, such as the declining Bradford Oil Field of Pennsylvania

3. An evaluation of national and international demands for minerals in relation to existing resources and the economic and political structure under which they are developed

    a. Effects of wars on the rate of depletion of the world's mineral resources

    b. Effects of a growing world population on demands for mineral resources

    c. Conservation as a factor in mineral resources exploitation

    d. Effects of programs of nationalization of natural resources on mineral exploration and exploitation

    e. Analysis of needs for technical education in foreign lands

4. Establishment of a United States Department of Mineral Industries with a Secretary of Cabinet rank

5. The development of state, national, and international mineral policies

Phase Two:

1. Implementation of the proposed mineral policy. The goal of the individual studies occurring in phase two in which the recommended mineral policies are applied on a state, national, and international basis to create a sound mineral economy in the world. (Steidle, 1952, pp. 197–98)

The School of Mineral Industries faculty in 1954.

A MODEL OF EXCELLENCE

Dean Steidle based his development of the School of Mineral Industries on the philosophy that the Pennsylvania State College had a responsibility to provide resources to advance the welfare of the nation's people. He often said that the richest deposits of minerals had been exhausted and that future supplies would come only from the lower-grade deposits. Combined with this viewpoint was the need for conservation, so that all minerals would be utilized for the benefit of the greatest number.

Edgar C. Weichel, left, member of the executive committee, PSU Board of Trustees, accepts the portrait of Dean Steidle in 1953 from George H. Deike, Sr., '03, vice president of the PSU Board of Trustees, acting on behalf of the faculty and alumni of the School of Mineral Industries, which had authorized the painting by Malcolm S. Parcell.

In order to achieve these objectives, a unified program that integrated each part into a single endeavor was needed. When Dean Steidle began to build this unified program in 1929, the core consisted of mining engineering, metallurgy, ceramics, and geology. In the next fifteen years, he added petroleum and natural gas engineering, fuel technology, mineral economics, geography, and meteorology. These programs were organized in 1945 under the three Departments of Mineral Engineering, Materials Technology, and Earth Sciences. Time has proven this structure to be academically sound.

While the structure of the School of Mineral Industries was fundamental in providing the basic organization, it did not create an atmosphere of excellence. This could be done only by a dedicated faculty. Dean Steidle recognized that the quality of the faculty would determine the true worth of the School. His goal was therefore to obtain the best qualified persons in each academic area. No area was of lesser importance, for one weak link in the system would weaken the entire program. Faculty members with the highest qualifications were sought in Europe as well as in the United States, and many faculty were recruited from industry.

As the academic structure and faculty evolved, Dean Steidle recognized that teaching and research needed to be integrated: a research program was needed to exploit the leaner mineral resources, and if the research was to be utilized it had to be disseminated as part of the instructional program, either as resident instruction or through continuing education. The research was thus primarily applied research, although there were a few notable exceptions. Dean Steidle believed that all members of the faculty, including administrators, should teach, and the dean himself taught an introductory course to all freshmen. This tradition is still being maintained.

The cornerstones of Dean Steidle's model of excellence were structure, faculty, and academic achievement. This grouping provided goals that were the foundation of a unique academic experience, and a newly created esprit de corps provided an incentive for work of the highest quality.

Lieutenant Governor Singel and Dean Dutton at the dedication of the Coal-Water Fuel Demonstration Facility.

C. Drew Stahl and President Bryce Jordon at the dedication of the C. Drew Stahl Enhanced Petroleum Recovery Laboratory.

President Joab Thomas, left, and Mimi Coppersmith Fredman, president of the Board of Trustees, far right, with Dr. and Mrs. E. Willard Miller, center, at the ceremony making the Millers honorary alumni of the University.

Chapter 3 | The Modern College of Earth and Mineral Sciences

The College of Earth and Mineral Sciences has evolved dramatically in the last forty years. The focus on research and graduate education that began in the 1950s and 1960s became an established characteristic of the College, bringing with it expanding horizons, new opportunities, and increasing national and international recognition for faculty contributions to the disciplines.

Involvement in the international scientific community became routine for virtually all faculty members. Meanwhile, the environmental movement, beginning in the 1960s, and the energy crisis of the 1970s brought stimulating challenges and emphasized the College's special capacity for interdisciplinary cooperation in major projects. The concurrent revolution in materials led to creation of the Department of Materials Science and Engineering, the addition of a program in polymer science, and major changes in emphasis in both teaching and research.

Even more dramatic was the impact of the technological revolution, which transformed every aspect of the College's operation and demanded huge capital expenditures for computers and sophisticated instrumentation, as well as new laboratory facilities in every department. A steady increase in personnel and facilities necessitated new construction and numerous alterations to the physical space occupied by the College.

Throughout these times of drastic and exciting change, the individual and group achievements of the faculty and the distinguished careers of its alumni gave the College a solid reputation as a leader in its disciplines and as an effective center for research and higher education.

Under the leadership of each dean, basic research was a fundamental objective. Within this framework, the training of students at both the undergraduate and the graduate level remains a primary goal, so that students are at the cutting edge of their field.

It is now recognized that many of the most difficult scientific and engineering problems will not be solved from the perspective of a single discipline. Interdisciplinary endeavors have become increasingly important. These develop in many ways. The simplest way is for two or more professors to form an informed group in which their collective expertise is focused on a particular problem. Presently, because of the importance of investigating interdisciplinary problems, more formal structures have evolved in such groups as the Earth System Science Center and the Center for Advanced Materials.

In these structures several faculty groups exist as long as needed to investigate a problem. These groups are dynamic with complete flexibility as a situation warrants. The freedom to select critical problems and then assemble a team that focuses their collective expertise is the essence of modern research and ultimately provides the foundation for the state-of-the-art teaching.

The six deans of the College from 1928 to 1985. Left to right, Charles L. Hosler, Richard Jahns, O. Frank Tuttle, Edward Steidle, Elburt F. Osborn, and David R. Mitchell.

COLLEGE ADMINISTRATION

Between 1953 and 1992 six deans provided leadership and direction in the development of the College. Of these, Charles L. Hosler, Jr., was dean for twenty years, from 1965 to 1985. Elburt F. Osborn had the next longest term of office, serving the College for six years from 1953 to 1959. Since 1985 John A. Dutton has been dean. In the period from 1959 to 1965 three deans served the College for short periods: O. Frank Tuttle from 1959 to 1960, David R. Mitchell from 1960 to 1962, and Richard H. Jahns from 1962 to 1965.

ELBURT F. OSBORN

Elburt F. Osborn came to Penn State as head of the Department of Earth Sciences in 1946. He became dean of the College in 1953, continuing until he became vice president for research in the administration of Eric A. Walker.

When Dr. Osborn became dean, he recognized the major endeavors of Dean Edward Steidle: "Development of the highly unusual and successful College of Mineral Industries was primarily the work of Dean Steidle in his twenty-five years as dean. He established the skeleton and brought in several top people. His driving idea was that the study of mineral resources at a land-grant college should be organized and supported as the study of agricultural resources has been since the Hatch Act of 1887 and succeeding federal legislation that established an agricultural experiment station and extension service at a university in each state. Penn State was the land-grant college of Pennsylvania. When I came to Penn State in 1946, Dean Steidle had succeeded in establishing the three-part structure—instruction, experiment station, and extension—as in an agricultural college. The whole field of mineral resources was covered—earth sciences, mineral technology, and mineral engineering. During the 1930s, for geology instruction, he received support from the federal agencies to construct summer camp facilities for the geology summer field course in Stone Valley. In addition, it was his idea to establish the Mineral Constitution Laboratories to provide essential support for laboratory research. Here were collected the extensive high-technology pieces of analytical equipment for the use of all. This central analytical facility made it possible to obtain funds for such instruments as x-ray diffraction units, an electron microscope, emission spectrographs, and mass spectrometers, as well as chemical analysis labs. Full-time technicians were hired to care for the instruments and instruct in their use. This was a unique feature in any university at that time."

Concepts of the Positions of Department Head and Dean

Dr. Osborn believed that the most important function of a department head and dean was to get good people for the faculty and staff and then be able to keep them. Furthermore, he states, "For me . . . just as important was to develop a strong personal research program with graduate students, continuing my previous career as a researcher in academic and industrial science and engineering. This I did by spending half my time on research and the teaching of graduate students and half on academic administration in a very long week. In addition, there was a need to obtain strong financial support for my research from industry and government sources."

Elburt F. Osborn, Dean, College of Mineral Industries, 1953–59. Dean Osborn accepting the Regional Technical Meeting Award of the American Iron and Steel Institute from Max D. Howell, executive vice president of the American Iron and Steel Institute.

The Importance of Professional Contacts

Dr. Osborn reports: "A very important part of my efforts as they helped to build our program was an active participation in scientific societies and strong contacts with federal government agencies and the National Academy of Engineering. Students, colleagues, and I delivered numerous papers at meetings, and I served as president of four of the societies—the American Ceramic Society, the Mineralogical Society of America, the Geochemical Society, and the Society of Economic Geologists. In the federal government I was active on many committees and panels, especially the National Science Foundation, the National Bureau of Standards, the National Research Council, the National Academy of Engineering, the Department of the Interior, the Department of Commerce, and the Congressional Office of Technology Assessment."

Establishing a Research Foundation

Although he was not aware of it at the time, Dr. Osborn's training for his appointment as dean began during his college days. He earned his degree, including a Ph.D. at the California Institute of Technology, in geology and also had training in chemistry and thermodynamics—"Simply because I liked it, not because you thought you could get a job back in those days." In 1937, at the conclusion of his college career, he worked in northern Quebec as a geologist for a mining company.

In 1938 he took a position at the Geophysical Laboratory at the Carnegie Institution of Washington. The Carnegie Institution had been established by a grant from Andrew Carnegie in 1903, and its Geophysical Laboratory was established in 1907. Over the years it became world renowned for its phase equilibrium research. Dr. Osborn reflects: "So here was a laboratory which would do basic research that was not a government laboratory or an industry laboratory. The intent was to do basic research that would give us some fundamental facts and some theories on the origin of igneous rocks."

Dr. Osborn remained with the Geophysical Laboratory until 1945. As he reminisced about this long research experience he said: "This was a greater opportunity in retrospect than I realized at the time, because here I had a chance to work with those people in a field that was mature but still with the chance to expand, working with the top scientists in the world." During the World War II years, he worked on many military problems, such as internal ballistics and temperature control in gun barrels, broadening his background in metallurgy and electrochemistry.

In December 1945 an opportunity to work on optical glasses opened up at the Eastman Kodak Company, which had developed some glasses with unusual optical properties in order to produce better lenses for cameras to reduce defraction effects. The work entailed basic research with fluoride systems rather than oxide systems, but still in fundamental phase equilibriums.

Dr. Osborn was at Eastman Kodak only a few months when he received a letter from Dean Steidle asking him to become chairman of the Department of Earth Sciences. He accepted the opportunity and brought with him a research contract from Eastman Kodak. Eastman Kodak had never had a contract with a university before, but they provided the equipment and the funds for Dr. Osborn to continue his work at Penn State. He arrived with funds for two graduate assistants and thousands of dollars of platinum for experimentation in glass and ceramic technology. Among his early graduate students were Della Martin Roy, Rustum Roy, and Arnulf Muan.

Between 1946 and 1950, contacts continued to be made with industry. Bethlehem Steel provided funds for a research project in the field of refractories and slags and related chemical aspects, Harbison Walker provided funds for refractory studies, and the American Iron & Steel Institute supported a large research contract. In 1950 Dean Osborn secured the first grant made by the U.S. Office of Naval Research, awarded to Penn State for study in the field of igneous petrology.

Administration
Earth Sciences

Department of Earth Sciences

Herbert Insley	1945–1947
Elburt F. Osborn	1947–1953

Division of Earth Sciences

O. Frank Tuttle	1953–1959
Richard H. Jahns	1959–1964

Cooperative Research

These endeavors established a pattern of cooperative research across departmental boundaries, which was the hallmark of Dr. Osborn's tenure as department head and dean. Dean Osborn observed: "This approach was possible because of Dean Steidle's remarkable organizational structure, which put all the fields that ought to cooperate in the general mineral area together in such a way that they could. And there's no question that cooperation in research is essential in these fields." Dean Osborn continued, "If we had been at a school, like, for example, Ohio State University, which had a strong ceramics department but no connection whatsoever with a geological science program, we couldn't have had cooperation such as we had here with, for example, Dr. Weyl, an outstanding glass scientist, and I working very closely together—my research being in the geological sciences and his being in ceramics. Throughout our College we're able to go very easily across boundaries, using very often the same research equipment, having students from different departments taking courses in each of the fields. For example, in my graduate course I had just about as many students from ceramics as I had in the geological sciences. There developed a feeling among some of us in the College that it was very important to be cooperative. Because of these interdepartmental endeavors, I did not have any particular departmental allegiances when I became dean. As a result, we were able to develop a very fine interdepartmental research program."

O. FRANK TUTTLE

O. Frank Tuttle, born in Olean, New York, on June 25, 1916, spent his youth in McKean County, Pennsylvania. He first enrolled at Penn State at the Bradford center, and after transferring to State College he completed his bachelor of science degree in 1939 and his master of science degree in geology in 1940. His Ph.D. in petrology was conferred in 1948 by the Massachusetts Institute of Technology, where he served as a teaching fellow.

While at the Geophysical Laboratory of the Carnegie Institute of Washington from 1947 to 1953, Dr. Tuttle and Dr. N. L. Bowen made a major advancement in experimental petrology by developing a technique for the systematic study of phase equilibria in igneous mineral systems with temperatures up to 1,000° C simultaneously with hydrostatic pressures of many thousands of pounds per square inch, duplicating conditions in the earth's crust.

In 1952 Dr. Tuttle received the signal honor of being the first recipient of the Mineralogical Society of America's Award. This was established by the Society to honor a scientist thirty-five years of age or under who had made an outstanding contribution to mineralogy and petrology. Dr. Tuttle was selected as the initial recipient on the basis of the excellence of his 1952 paper, "Variable Inversion Temperature of Quartz as a Geologic Thermometer," in which he demonstrated that the inversion temperature of quartz was variable within more than a degree, depending on its origin. This study provided a new basis for analysis.

Dr. Tuttle joined the Penn State faculty in 1953 as professor of geochemistry and chairman of the Division of Earth Sciences. As part of his research work, he made field studies on various areas not only in the United States but also in Scotland, Norway, Finland, and southern France. He was the author or co-author of many scientific papers, among the most outstanding of which was a paper published in 1958 by the Geological Society of America with Dr. Tuttle as senior author and Dr. Bowen as collaborator: "Origin of Granite in the Light of Experimental Studies in the System $NaAlSi_3O_8$-$KAlSi_3O_8$-SiO_2-H_2O." This was a major scientific contribution.

O. Frank Tuttle, Dean, College of
Mineral Industries, 1959–60.

In 1959 Dr. Tuttle became dean of the College of Mineral Industries, but within a few months his health deteriorated as a result of Parkinson's disease, and he resigned from the deanship on October 31, 1960.

When informed of the impending retirement of the dean, the mineral industries faculty at its fall meeting on October 13, 1960, adopted the following resolution:

> The faculty of the College of Mineral Industries wish to record their gratitude to Dean O. F. Tuttle for his period of service as Dean. They greatly regret the circumstances which led to his early relinquishing of these responsibilities, but are very pleased to note that he will continue his research and activities on the faculty. Dean Tuttle stood squarely in the fine tradition of Deans of the Mineral Industries College that not only inherited one of the best organizations of its kind, but started those necessary changes to keep M.I. in the position of leadership it now occupies.

Dean Tuttle remained a professor of geochemistry in the College until 1965, at which time he moved to Stanford University as professor of geology (geochemistry). In 1967 he was forced to take a medical leave of absence, and in 1970 he resigned from Stanford University. He died on December 13, 1983.

DAVID R. MITCHELL

David R. Mitchell was born at Bells Landing, Pennsylvania, on June 12, 1898, and during World War I from 1917 to 1918 served in the Aviation Section of the Signal Corps of the U.S. Army. He earned a bachelor of science degree in mining engineering from Penn State in 1924, a master of science degree in 1926, and the professional degree of engineer of mining from the University of Illinois in 1930. He also completed a considerable amount of graduate work in mineral industries subjects and physical chemistry while working toward a doctorate. Professor Mitchell had practical mining experience in both coal and clay mines and held both fire boss and mine foreman certificates for the bituminous region of Pennsylvania. After graduating from Penn State, he worked for Bethlehem Mines Corporation and Lincoln Gas Coal Company.

Appointed as an instructor in mining engineering at the University of Illinois in 1929, Mitchell rose through the ranks to become professor of mining and metallurgical engineering in 1938. During this period he did much research and consulting work on the design and operation of coal and clay mines and preparation plants, as well as on the utilization of fuels, including carbonization. During 1934–35 he was adviser to the Illinois Emergency Relief Commission.

In 1938 he came to Penn State as chairman of the Division of Mineral Engineering. In the period from 1938 to 1960 he assumed the role of acting head of each department in his division, served as acting director of the Mineral Industries Experiment Station in 1952, and from February 1, 1958, to July 31, 1958, was acting dean of the College. He also wrote nearly one hundred professional articles during this period, and his book, *Coal Preparation,* was recognized as the

David R. Mitchell, Dean, College of Earth and Mineral Sciences, 1960–62.

primary volume in the field. With the untimely resignation of Dean Tuttle, Professor Mitchell became dean of the College in 1960, serving for two years. After leaving the deanship in 1962, he continued as professor of mining engineering until his retirement in 1964.

Besides serving Penn State for nearly three decades, he served his profession in a number of special ways. In 1942 he published an article on the qualifications and selection of young men for the coal industry, in which, to aid Penn State in training miners and advising employers, he discussed the kinds of psychological tests, experience records, personal interviews, and physical examinations that should be part of the selection process for young men seeking to enter the coal industry. In 1959 Professor Mitchell was asked to be technical adviser to a legislative committee probing the Knox Coal Company flood disaster, which took the lives of twelve men. He acted as a consultant for the design and operation of many large coal preparation plants, and when he retired in 1964 he was appointed chairman of Pennsylvania Governor Scranton's Committee on Mine Safety.

RICHARD H. JAHNS

Born in Los Angeles, California, on March 10, 1915, Richard H. Jahns attended high school in Seattle, Washington, and then entered the California Institute of Technology. With majors in chemistry and geology, he graduated with honors in 1935. In 1937 he received an M.S. in geology at Northwestern University and then returned to Cal Tech for two more years of graduate work. His Ph.D. from the California Institute of Technology was awarded in 1943.

Dr. Jahns joined the U.S. Geological Survey as a junior geologist in 1937 and worked full-time for this organization from 1939 to 1946, after which he continued part-time. He rose through the ranks from assistant geologist (1940–42), to associate geologist (1942–44), to geologist (1944–48), and to senior geologist (1948–60). In 1946 he joined the faculty of the California Institute of Technology as assistant professor of geology, becoming associate professor in 1947 and professor of geology from 1949 to 1960. His rise from assistant professor to professor in three years at Cal Tech must have been a record at an institution not noted for rapid or easy promotions.

His early professional work was aimed at problems of structure, stratigraphy, and vertebrate paleontology in complex tertiary basins of southern California and at problems of igneous petrology in South Park, Colorado. From 1937 to 1942 his work for the U.S. Geological Survey was done in New York and the New England states, chiefly in igneous and metamorphic petrology, structural geology, flood sedimentation, glacial geology, engineering geology, and the geology and technology of graphite, refractories, construction materials, and dimension stone. Between 1942 and 1960 his work shifted to control-metamorphic deposits of beryllium and tungsten in New Mexico, Colorado, Arizona, California, Virginia, North and South Carolina, Georgia, and Alabama. He was also concerned with petrology and glacial geology in New England, regional geology in southern California, the mechanics of landsliding, and the geology of metalliferous deposits in many areas. When asked to characterize his geological work, he stated: "I am a general geologist, with special interests in igneous petrology and a conviction that many of geology's ultimate truths will be recognized most effectively through a combination of observational, experimental, and theoretical approaches. The smoother the combination among earth scientists, the more truth obtained."

Dr. Jahns's first official contact with Penn State came in 1958 when he was a visiting professor. Two years later he came to the College of Mineral Industries to head the Division of Earth

Richard H. Jahns, dean of the College of Earth and Mineral Sciences, 1962–65, in the geochemistry laboratory at Penn State and doing field work.

Sciences, and in 1962 he became dean of the College. Although as dean his administrative duties increased tremendously, he tried to leave his basic lifestyle intact, maintaining major commitments to teaching, to graduate students, and to an active research program while remaining available to faculty and staff.

Although he was active in many aspects of his career while a dean at Penn State, Dr. Jahns's people-oriented side assumed a dominant role. Lauren Wright, professor of geology, wrote in his memorial: "As an administrator he was guided by a conviction that groups function most effectively when permitted, within broad limits, to make their own decisions. He was quite firm, however, in enforcing matters of fundamental policy. He used to say, half seriously and half in jest, that on some matters some of his associates were so consistently wrong that he relied upon their judgment to help him make the correct decisions."

His assistant dean for resident instruction, E. Willard Miller, remarks: "Dr. Jahns had a remarkable ability to foster harmonious working relationships. He was completely supportive of his colleagues, and he spent endless hours with his graduate students. He was a master teller of funny stories, for he loved to make people laugh, but probably more important, he believed that people could work together better if they recognized that humor provided a common bond."

In 1965 Wallace Sterling, then president of Stanford University, persuaded Dr. Jahns to return to the familiar landscapes and geology of the West Coast, and Jahns accepted an offer to become dean of the earth sciences at Stanford. He served in that capacity for fourteen years and then returned to teaching for more than four years. On the evening of December 31, 1983, while preparing to spend New Year's Eve with friends, he was felled by a fatal heart attack.

CHARLES L. HOSLER, JR.

Charles Hosler has spent his entire professional career at Penn State, from the time he entered the University as a student in 1942. In the Department of Meteorology he advanced from instructor to professor and was head of the department from 1961 to 1965. In 1965 he became dean of the College, a position he held until 1985, when he became dean of the Graduate School and vice president for research. In 1987 he became senior vice president for research and in 1990 acting executive vice president and provost of the University. He retired on December 30, 1991.

Charles L. Hosler, Jr., Dean, College of Mineral Industries and College of Earth and Mineral Sciences, 1965–85.

The Philosophy of Dean Hosler's Administration

Although Dean Hosler had been at Penn State many years before he became dean, he knew little about the functions of the dean's office. In his own words:

> As a professor and head of the Department of Meteorology, I didn't have much of an idea of what a dean did. Once a week at the meeting of the Executive Council, we heard the announcements of what was going on in the University. When I walked into the office on my first day on the job, I found that the former dean had taken the entire staff except for one secretary, so I started from scratch to learn what a dean did and what had to happen— and in retrospect that wasn't a bad way to begin. But I soon assessed the College and said, "Look, this is a pretty good college, but it has the potential to become a lot better and it was my job to do that." It was thus my overall goal to make a good College of Mineral Industries into the best College of Earth and Mineral Sciences in the world. To do this as a dean, I was a facilitator and an enabler. I didn't really run anything, but I could certainly

help ensure that we hired only the best faculty and kept only the best and most productive faculty. It was also necessary to get the highest-quality undergraduate and graduate students. In all these endeavors the faculty was the key element. You had to give the faculty free rein, and so my philosophy was to allow a highly independent faculty—which gives you trouble sometimes because people don't want to pull in the same direction. But nevertheless, I think the faculty came to realize that I was there to help them do what it was they did best. As a response, they created a very, very productive College.

In order to achieve these goals the unwritten strategy I followed was:

1. To build on our research strengths to make a good faculty better. This included hiring faculty who had research potential, counseling out those who were not productive, supporting the productive people, and providing incentives for excellent teaching and research, such as the establishment of the Wilson Teaching Award.

2. To improve the esprit de corps. A Wilson Awards dinner was initiated for faculty and students, and an annual appreciation luncheon for the staff and clerical personnel. Posters touting the accomplishments of the College and its graduates were published.

An open-door policy was followed in the dean's office. This provided an intimate knowledge as to what the faculty were doing. No appointment was ever refused or delayed, and any faculty member or student could walk in if someone wasn't already in the office. The faculty got used to this, and I believe it contributed in large amount to a high esprit de corps and personal loyalty to the College and dean.

A self-evaluation form was initiated which each faculty member submitted each year. Reading these forms enabled the dean to have a good knowledge about the expertise and concerns of every faculty member. Annual raise letters included comments on their specific accomplishments. This was a great deal of work but contributed strongly to the faculty feeling that they were appreciated.

3. To improve salaries. The salary plan was changed from forty-eight to thirty-six weeks.

4. To build the College budget. All funds were shifted to salaries in the zero budget. Other expenses were then covered by unused salaries or salaries released by research funds. This meant that each year the inflationary adjustments in salary, which were very large between 1965 and 1984, were applied to the entire budget and compounded over twenty years. Since there were very small increases in other expense budgets—or none at all—the other colleges in the University fell behind inflation in proportion to how much money they kept in budgets for other purposes than salaries, whereas EMS kept pace. There wasn't another dean at Penn State who used this procedure. The only people in the administration who understood this procedure were the budget officer and the controller.

In 1965 there were no discretionary funds in the College. With the help of faculty who relinquished payment for continuing education work and had consulting fees paid to the University, a miscellaneous fund was created in the Dean's Office. When this amounted to $100,000, I negotiated with the University treasurer to receive interest on the fund. Thus we have our own endowment that has been built to over one million dollars.

There had never been an organized fund-raising effort in the College. In 1966 Mrs. Anne Wilson visited me to discuss her husband's estate. In a bequest he gave a considerable part of his estate that was to revert to the College on the death of Mrs. Wilson. She indicated she didn't need the money and we discussed how it might be used. I convinced her that, rather than be specific about its use for loans, salaries, etc., it should be set up simply "for the benefit of the faculty." This fund provides income for teaching awards, the awards banquet, and miscellaneous expenses beyond the ability of the general budget to cover.

In 1977 we began an organized campaign to secure funds. By 1985 we were at the level of $3 million a year in contributions to the College. Funds invested in accounts amounted to about $7 million, the income of which comes to the College.

5. To make our courses and curricula more attractive. To increase student credit hours in a way that would not endanger the budget, emphasis was placed on the development of general education courses in the geological sciences, geography, and meteorology and to a lesser extent in material sciences. Excellent professors were selected to teach these courses, so they became very popular. Because student credit hours increased, other departments, also seeking to increase student credit hours, wanted to remove many of the courses from satisfying general education graduation requirements.

A number of the engineering majors had increased graduation requirements to the maximum of 144 credits. These majors were competing with programs that required as few as 124 credits. At the same time, the mineral engineering program was accepting the students with a lower number of credits as graduate students.

There were two new programs developed in the College. The degree in polymer science located in the Materials Science and Engineering Department provided instruction and research in a rapidly growing materials area not emphasized at Penn State. The earth sciences program was developed to provide a broad interdisciplinary degree in the fields of the geological sciences, geography, and meteorology.

Location of the Walker Building

When Dean Hosler assumed the deanship in 1965 he immediately initiated the process of securing a new building that ultimately became the Walker Building. He wrote a long justification for the building based on environmental concerns and the expansion of programs in the College during the environmental era. The University administrative planning group accepted the proposal and placed it on the Capital Budget request, but at a relatively low priority.

With persistence from Dean Hosler and help from Dr. Osborn, who was vice president for research at the time, the building was moved to the top-priority list. The next step was approval by the Pennsylvania State Assembly and governor. This hurdle was achieved, but Pennsylvania Governor Milton Shapp decided that there would be no more major buildings constructed at University Park and canceled the building. As a result the justification and procedures had to begin anew in the early 1970s, at which time the building was justified on the basis of needed energy research. After long delays the funds for the building were approved.

But the exact location for the new building had not been determined. Dean Hosler wanted the building located on Atherton Street, on the site of old maintenance buildings. President Eric Walker opposed this location because he wanted the building on the north side of the campus near the parking lots for the stadium. But that site would have separated the departments in the College and would have provided a classroom building that was far from other classroom buildings. A stalemate resulted, and the site of the building was not determined until President Walker left office.

Soon after John Oswald became president, Dean Hosler took him to the roof of Deike Building to show him the dilapidated buildings he wanted to replace with the new building. The dean also indicated how the College's instruction and research program would be handicapped if the building were far removed from existing College buildings. He also pointed out that the existing structures on Atherton Street were an eyesore. Standing on the roof of Deike Building, President Oswald made the decision that the new building would be built at the Atherton site, and the six-

The Eric Walker Building, about 1975.

story building was constructed and dedicated as the Eric A. Walker Building. It had taken fourteen years of justifying and rejustifying in the face of strong opposition before the Walker Building was completed.

The Preservation of Mining and Petroleum and Natural Gas Engineering

In the 1960s, enrollment in programs in mining and petroleum and natural gas engineering fell dramatically not only at Penn State but also in other eastern universities. In Pennsylvania all programs were discontinued except at Penn State. The central administration of the University frequently expressed concern that these programs were not viable and that there would be no future need for them.

Dean Hosler relates the following incident on a visit of President Oswald to the College: "When John Oswald became president at Penn State his initial visit to my office was focused on the discussion of mining and petroleum and natural-gas engineering programs. He had been advised by others that these programs should be abandoned. At the same time, Governor Shapp and members of the legislature were questioning why Penn State was wasting money on coal research (the governor abolished the Coal Research Board in 1972). In my defense of these fields of study and research, I indicated that it was inevitable that these fields would be highly valued and essential in the future, and I refused to consider eliminating them. The subsequent Arab oil embargo made my point for me, and President Oswald had many occasions to boast that only Penn State had the foresight to preserve the programs."

A New Name: The College of Earth and Mineral Sciences

Originally the College was dominated by programs in the mineral industries—mining, petroleum, metallurgy, and ceramics, but as the College developed, new programs—such as the geological sciences, meteorology, and geography—came to play a more important role. As a result, Dean

Hosler states, "In order to give the name a little more visibility and relevance, we had quite a bit of discussion, but in the long run there wasn't a very strong consensus for anything. At the same time there wasn't a tremendous amount of objection to the name "Earth and Mineral Sciences," which, I believe, was pretty much my own choice. After many years now, it has withstood the test of time. The College is unique in that it has everything from liberal arts to engineering. With that kind of mix, I don't think there is any name that everyone would agree on. But I think we did about the best we could."

Departmental Structure

In 1965, when Dean Hosler assumed office, there were twelve departments in the College. He soon recognized that "the territorial prerogatives of these twelve departments were divided up in so many pieces that none could really be effective. People couldn't expand or contract on any side." In order to solve this problem, six departments were created. A Department of Geosciences brought together geochemists, geophysicists, paleontologists, mineralogists, and geologists. In the field of mineral engineering the fields of mining, mineral processing, and petroleum and natural gas engineering were combined into a single department, and in the materials science the fields of metallurgy, ceramics, fuel science, and polymers formed a unit. The bringing together of programs that had similar objectives recognized that many of the modern-day complex problems can be approached only through interdisciplinary approaches.

Laboratories and Equipment

A college with science and engineering programs has a fundamental need for well-equipped laboratories, but also a continual need to keep the laboratories modern. Although equipment funds from the state were modest, Dean Hosler remarks, "because of the high level of sponsored research in the College we fared pretty well on equipment. This was due to the aggressiveness of the faculty in getting outside funds, and, with the availability of matching funds, the College is one of the best equipped in the nation."

The Tuesday Tea

The Students' Tuesday Tea was important in bringing a sense that the College was a human and likeable place to study and work. This weekly event was held in the dean's office. If students were in nearby laboratories or in the library, they interrupted their work for a few minutes to have refreshments and, more important, to have friendly discussions. The students made new friends, and the faculty got to know the students, hearing sometimes about their pleasures and sometimes about their problems. It was a time that students could talk with the dean, the associate deans, and the faculty about anything on their minds. These teas have become traditions in the College.

The Interest House

In the late 1960s a large number of interest houses were formed on the campus. Many of these reflected the radical period of the time and disappeared very quickly, but the Earth and Mineral Sciences Interest House located in Irvin Hall was developed by students who had similar academic interests and has survived the test of time. A major function of this interest house is to bring students with similar interests together. This provides a fine learning environment, for there are

Tuesday afternoon tea in the dean's office, about 1985.

usually a number of students who are taking the same course and they thus can not only discuss the course content but also study as a group for examinations. There is a large lounge where students can relax, play cards, watch television, or talk. The students have their own organization to plan events during the year, such as fieldtrips, special dinners, and sports events. A member of the College faculty acts as adviser to the group. The students of the interest house develop a camaraderie that persists long after graduation.

Spring Student Science Fair

Every other year for two days in late spring, the students have an open house for the public—known as EMEX—for which they develop demonstrations to illustrate the activities in their programs. While these are fun days, development of the students' exhibits not only takes a great deal of ingenuity but also provides a showcase for the great breadth of programs found in the College. Thousands of people come to view the marvels of a scientific and engineering carnival.

Dean Hosler Reflects

In reflecting on a twenty-year career as dean of the College of Earth and Mineral Sciences, Dean Hosler comments:

> The highlights were positive and accumulative. In other words, I felt we made progress during every one of my twenty years as dean in terms of the strength of the College, and I am proud of what the faculty has accomplished. There were several specific highlights that provided personal satisfaction. The completion of the Walker Building, the last major building, completed in the 1970s with state funds, was a major accomplishment.
>
> The other major accomplishment was when I convinced the University—and it wasn't easy—to change the faculty in the College from a twelve-month salary plan to a nine-month salary plan, that is, from forty-eight to thirty-six weeks at the same salary. This represented a considerable raise for everybody in the College and made it possible for faculty to go out and seek grants to supplement their salaries by one-third each year. Most of the other colleges of the University have now switched to the academic year plan.

The College of Earth and Mineral Sciences, 1973

Charles L. Hosler, Jr., Dean
E. Willard Miller, Associate Dean for Resident Instruction
Maurice E. Bell, Associate Dean for Research; Director of the Experiment Station
Robert Stefanko, Assistant Dean for Continuing Education
H. Beecher Charmbury, Assistant Dean for Planning and Development

College Organization

Earth Sciences	E. Willard Miller, In Charge
Geography	Wilbur Zelinsky, Head
Geosciences	Arnulf Muan, Head
Geochemistry, Mineralogy, Petrology	Arthur L. Boettcher, In Charge
Geology	Robert F. Schmalz, In Charge
Geophysics	Shelton S. Alexander, In Charge
Materials Science	Philip L. Walker, Jr., Head
Ceramic Science	Guy E. Rindone, In Charge
Metallurgy	William R. Bitler, In Charge
Polymer Science	Philip L. Walker, Jr., In Charge
Meteorology	Alfred K. Blackadar, Head
Mineral Economics	John D. Ridge, Head
Mineral Engineering	Thomas V. Falkie, Head
Mining Engineering	Thomas V. Falkie, In Charge
Petroleum and Natural Gas Engineering	C. Drew Stahl, In Charge

Students

Undergraduate	800
Graduate	400

The other thing that has given me great satisfaction was my role in getting some of the young faculty to come to Penn State. Although the recruitment is shared with the rest of the faculty, the department heads, and the associate deans, the key to a great university is to be able to recruit dynamic young people and keep them.

JOHN A. DUTTON

John A. Dutton did his college work at the University of Wisconsin, receiving his Ph.D. in 1962. He began his career at Penn State in 1965 and had been head of the Department of Meteorology for five years when he became dean of the College of Earth and Mineral Sciences in 1986. From 1971 to 1972 he was visiting scientist at the Riso Research Establishment in Roskilde, Denmark, and from 1978 to 1979 he was visiting professor at the Technical University of Denmark. He has served on many meteorological and science policy organizations, including the University Corporation for Atmospheric Research, the Board of Atmospheric Sciences and Climate of the National Research Council, the Space Studies Board, and the Space and Earth Science Advisory Committee of NASA. He is also a fellow of the American Meteorological Society. Dean Dutton has written many articles in professional journals on theoretical aspects of atmospheric science and more recently on policy issues. He is author of *The Ceaseless Wind: An Introduction to the Theory of Atmospheric Motion* (1976), cited as an outstanding academic book by the American Library Association, and, with Hans A. Panofsky, *Atmospheric Turbulence: Models and Methods for Engineering Applications* (1985).

Philosophy of Dean Dutton's Administration

A major function of the dean is to act as a facilitator, providing an environment in which students and faculty can be as creative and effective as possible. Dean Dutton states: "I've sometimes described my job as being a cheerleader who encourages people to do things they are good at. I do think that there is an added dimension to the job of leadership in a scientific organization of looking toward the future and being well attuned to significant trends so you can aid faculty in structuring programs that take advantage of future opportunities. This virtually demands involvement at national scientific policy levels. Academic leadership is different from that found in

John A. Dutton, Dean, College of Earth and Mineral Sciences, 1985– .

government, business, and industry, which have tended to be hierarchical. A university faculty does not operate on a system of orders down the chain of command. Rather, things are accomplished by force of logic and imaginative persuasion."

The Relationship of the College to the Central Administration

If excellence is to be sustained, there must be a cooperative relationship between the College and the central administration. According to Dean Dutton, "A major objective is to identify key areas for growth or attention, then present budget proposals based on this policy to the central budget committee. Once a budget is established, the dean may use the funds at his discretion, and it is his responsibility to see that they are used effectively. In other words, he can buy equipment if this is most essential, or he can hire faculty at the academic posts of greatest value to the identified policy. With this budget policy, I think things have worked out pretty well."

The College of Earth and Mineral Sciences, 1991

John A. Dutton, Dean
Everett P. Tiffany, Assistant to the Dean
John J. Cahir, Associate Dean for Resident Instruction
Peter T. Luckie, Associate Dean for Research
Robert L. Frantz, Associate Dean for Continuing Education and Industry Programs

College Organization

Earth Sciences	Charles P. Thornton, Program Chair
Geography	Rodney A. Erickson, Head
Geosciences	Michael A. Arthur, Head
Geosciences	Albert L. Guber, Associate Head
Materials Science and Engineering	Richard E. Tressler, Head
Ceramic Science and Engineering	Karl E. Spear, Program Chair
Fuel Science	Harold H. Schobert, Program Chair
Metals Science and Engineering	Donald A. Koss, Program Chair
Polymer Science	James P. Runt, Program Chair
Meteorology	William M. Frank, Head
Mineral Economics	Adam Z. Rose, Head
Mineral Engineering	Raja V. Ramani, Head
Mineral Processing	Richard Hogg, Section Chair
Mining Engineering	Stanley C. Suboleski, Section Chair
Petroleum and Natural Gas Engineering	Turgay Ertekin, Section Chair

Students

Undergraduate	900
Graduate	525

A major advance introduced by Penn State President Bryce Jordan (1984–1990) was the formal strategic planning procedure that links budget allocations to programs. Because the College has been able to prepare long-range plans for such major initiatives as the Earth System Science Center, these fledgling units have gained immediate credibility and widespread recognition.

Research Goals

Dean Dutton reaffirms the College's commitment to both fundamental and applied research:

> The first responsibility and the foundation for all future success is basic research that examines fundamental questions closely related to the intellectual progress of the disciplines. But, beyond this, we have a societal responsibility to address major issues of our times that are related to the work we do in the College. Our disciplines have never been more relevant than they are today. We have important contributions to make in defining, understanding, and helping to ameliorate global environmental change, in finding responsible answers to the global energy problems our society attempts to ignore, and in assisting the development of new technologies based on the imaginative use of new high-performance materials that will be important to the future social and economic well-being of our nation. Our response to these issues will determine a major dimension of the College's future success, and we are actively involved in pursuing research opportunities arising in each of these areas.
>
> These types of complex societal problems involve knowledge from several disciplines and can be dealt with effectively only by groups of researchers, each applying his or her own expertise. To focus these interdisciplinary efforts, we have created a number of research centers over the past five years, drawing on the College's established tradition and rich experience in cooperative research. We have had considerable success.
>
> The Center for Advanced Materials has attracted widespread interest and funding in the highly competitive area of high-performance high-temperature materials. The Earth System Science Center, one of the earliest university centers for the study of global change, has already gained an international reputation for its innovative work in studying complex interactions in the water cycle and other biogeochemical cycles and in modeling stages in natural global change. Our two energy centers, the Center for Energy and Fuels Research and the Center for Energy and Mineral Policy Research, have many constructive ideas and interesting work under way in the environmentally responsible utilization of fuels and examining current economic and structural changes in coal and steel industries, but initially both these centers suffer from the general lack of funding available for energy research at the moment. We will have to wait and see what future changes in world attitudes toward energy issues will bring.

The College's research programs face other changes. Dean Dutton states:

> In common with other scientific institutions, we face a challenge posed by the very success of modern technology. The proliferation of data and information unleashed by advanced computing and remote-sensing systems has created a range of new opportunities, and the innovative management and intelligent use of information has become a critical activity for academic institutions as well as governments and corporations.

Consequently, in 1990, we established EMSnet, a College-wide communications network, to link us together and provide improved connections with national and international networks. We strive constantly to keep our instrumentation up-to-date and to be attuned to the latest developments. In the Department of Geography, for example, we have a group working in data systems and management involved in advances in geographical information systems, and the Deasy GeoGraphics Laboratory is directing work in scientific visualization techniques.

Curriculum Developments

Dean Dutton has placed strong emphasis on the undergraduate programs. He says:

The lower enrollment that accompanied the economic downturn in mining, metals, and petroleum industries in the mid-1980s gave us an opportunity to examine all the programs, to work on curriculum content and structure, and to set new performance standards. We are now confident that the education we are able to offer young people is unsurpassed both in value and in quality. EMS has all the advantages of being a small college within the context of a major research university. We are able to offer students unparalleled individual attention and in most cases the increasingly rare advantage of small classes, and at the same time, the vast array of opportunities and facilities of a large institution are at the door ready to be explored.

In reviewing our programs we kept in mind the relentless change and ever-increasing complexity our graduates will undoubtedly face in their careers. They will need the ability and motivation to succeed in learning throughout their lives; they'll need the skills and confidence to address complex scientific and technological issues and to attack problems that have no unique solution; they'll need superior skills in the analysis and organization of complex ideas and in the effective communication of difficult concepts; and they must have a strong sense of scientific integrity and personal values in order to thrive in a globally interdependent environment and appreciate the disparate and often conflicting interests of diverse constituencies.

Thus we have increased the rigor of our curriculums, yet at the same time we have reduced the overall number of required credit hours to allow greater flexibility and provide more opportunities for in-depth study and specialization. We have added new writing and presentation requirements in numerous courses and provided a professional writing tutor to assist both faculty and students college-wide. Work with advanced computers and modern instrumentation has been integrated more fully into the curriculum. We have added or redefined undergraduate thesis requirements for the senior year to bring almost all our students the experience of learning through research.

But far beyond "requirements," we are vigorously encouraging a spirit of excitement and adventure in our undergraduate programs, promoting in-depth study of open-ended issues and fostering multidisciplinary initiatives throughout the college, and encouraging students to consider academic "minors" in such areas as marine sciences, materials economics, environmental protection, and hydrosciences. Faculty are being asked to reexamine their courses with a view to engaging students even further in the learning process. Student and faculty response to our renewed focus on undergraduate programs has been overwhelming.

The College and General Education

In 1987 the University established new guidelines for general education courses, and the College expanded and revised its offerings. Dean Dutton stresses that understanding energy issues and global environmental problems, and comprehending the basis of our high-technology society, has educational value for all students. "We depend ultimately on an informed society. If we can get students to look at this world a little more knowingly, to appreciate what some of the challenges are, to recognize their roles as stewards of the Earth, we will have been socially effective."

Earth and Mineral Sciences and the Commonwealth Campuses

It is now recognized that the University Park Campus is an integral part of the Commonwealth Campus system. Most students enter the Penn State system through a Commonwealth Campus. Because Earth and Mineral Sciences is a major transfer College, it must rely on students that transfer from other majors. Consequently, the College must be able to admit students from the Commonwealth Campuses.

To solve this problem, there are plans to create small earth and mineral science centers at several campuses in strategic locations, where a group of faculty knowledgeable about their disciplines would be available to students, who would be encouraged to seek them out. Thus, rather than spreading faculty across the total campus system, it may make sense to concentrate them in terms of earth and mineral science (EMS) majors.

The Earth and Mineral Sciences Library in Deike Building, early 1970s.

Providing EMS coursework in general education is more difficult. There has been some success in the use of satellites and television in providing courses on some campuses, but the faculty at the larger campuses needs to be increased. This remains an important issue that must be resolved in the near future.

The Space Problem

Space is a traditional problem in a college with expanding research programs. Dean Dutton notes: "One of the department heads refers to it as the space wars, and space wars it is. An essential difficulty is that in the past the College acquired one major new building each decade—the Mineral Sciences Building was built in the 1950s, Deike Building in the 1960s, and Walker Building in the 1970s. We didn't build anything in the 1980s, and we're suffering because of it." He continues, "We have grown in numbers of students and particularly graduate students, and we've been increasing in the complexity of the research requiring more equipment. We have a severe space problem. To compound this problem, such new endeavors as the Center for Advanced Materials and the Earth System Science Center require additional space as programs develop."

Although space will continue to be a problem, the College has received a small amount of funds to improve the coal research facility for coal-utilization research. In the longer run, as the College of Engineering builds new buildings the College will acquire Electrical Engineering East and West.

ACADEMIC FUNCTIONS

The academic functions—instruction, research, and continuing education—are administered by associate deans in the College. These positions have evolved over time. Resident instruction began with the origin of Penn State; continuing education and the earliest research dates from the 1890s. Dean Steidle recognized the importance of these functions by establishing positions to direct the continuing education and research of the School of Mineral Industries.

RESIDENT INSTRUCTION

Dean Steidle assumed responsibility for developing the instructional program. In 1954 Dean Osborn created the position of assistant dean of resident instruction, and John D. Ridge held this position until 1964. In that year E. Willard Miller became the assistant dean for resident instruction. In 1972 the position was raised to associate dean, a position Dr. Miller held until his retirement in 1980. Since then, John J. Cahir has been associate dean for resident instruction.

The associate deans for resident instruction are responsible for implementing the instructional program of the College. Dean Miller says: "I considered my primary responsibility was to mold and articulate the educational programs of the College. This involved the development of new courses and programs and their guidance through University procedures. A second major responsibility was to make the courses and programs visible in the University system in order for students to be

Administration
EMS Resident Instruction

Assistant Dean

John D. Ridge	1954–1964
E. Willard Miller	1964–1972

Associate Dean

E. Willard Miller	1972–1980
John J. Cahir	1980–

aware of the educational opportunities within the College. Many hours were spent with University faculty members providing information on the course content of the earth, mineral, and materials science and engineering courses. A third responsibility was to create an environment of excellence in teaching. The research and teaching programs are intimately intertwined. Only through research can teaching remain at the cutting edge of each discipline." This basic philosophy of the office of associate dean has changed little over the years. In Dean Cahir's words: "Emphasis on skills in the fundamentals—mathematics, physics, chemistry, and communications—along with great care taken to ensure breadth and an involvement in the humanities and social sciences, has been a constant. There has been a growing emphasis on undergraduate research, on computing, and on the importance of lifelong learning. However, for a College whose goals are heavily practical and applied, fundamentals remain in the ascendancy."

Because most high school students are not aware of the disciplines in the College, or, worse, are misinformed about the opportunities within the discipline, a large percentage of the College's student body are transfers from other majors at the University. A primary responsibility of Garry L. Burkle is to inform students about the College's programs and career opportunities. In 1990 an undergraduate center directed by Garry Burkle, where students can obtain such information, was opened.

Enrollment in the College of Earth and Mineral Sciences reflects employment demands, so there are periods of very high enrollment in the undergraduate programs, and at other times enrollment decreases. In modern times, undergraduate enrollment reached a peak of more than 2,200 students in the early 1980s but declined to about 1,000 in 1990. When this occurs, a rigorous recruitment program is required to inform students about the career opportunities the many programs in the College offer.

Since the first program was established in 1890, there have been more than 12,000 graduates from the College, of which just over 1,000 are women. Meteorology leads with the largest number of graduates, totaling over 1,700, followed by petroleum and natural gas engineering, metals science and engineering, and mining engineering, all with more than 1,100 graduates. Geography, with over 800 graduates, has the largest number of women graduates, more than 160.

The graduates are widely distributed geographically, with the state of Pennsylvania having the largest number: about 4,500. Graduates are located in every county of the state and in every state

A part of the student body of the School of Mineral Industries in 1954, on the steps of Steidle Building.

in the United States (see Figures 4 and 5). In addition, more than 400 graduates are found in seventy-two foreign countries; Canada has the largest number, with 80 graduates, followed by Venezuela, Japan, Australia, United Kingdom, and India (Figure 6). The College typically has a higher proportion of out-of-state students than any other college in the University, and the graduate student body has a wide U.S. and world distribution (Figures 7 and 8). Every major in the College attracts foreign students, who come from the most advanced industrial nations to the least industrialized countries of the Third World. (Figures 4–9 appeared in the Spring 1987 issue of the *Earth and Mineral Sciences* bulletin, published by the College.) Graduate instruction is an integral part of the instructional program of the College. As the research program has expanded, graduate enrollment has risen steadily from about 140 students in the early 1950s to 330 in the mid-1960s to more than 500 in the early 1980s (Figure 9). Most of the graduate students are supported by teaching or research graduate assistantships. As in the undergraduate enrollment, the number of women has increased greatly and now totals about 25 percent of the student body. In the 1980s the number of Ph.D.'s granted annually rose from about 40 to 65, and the number of M.S. degrees rose from about 85 to more than 100.

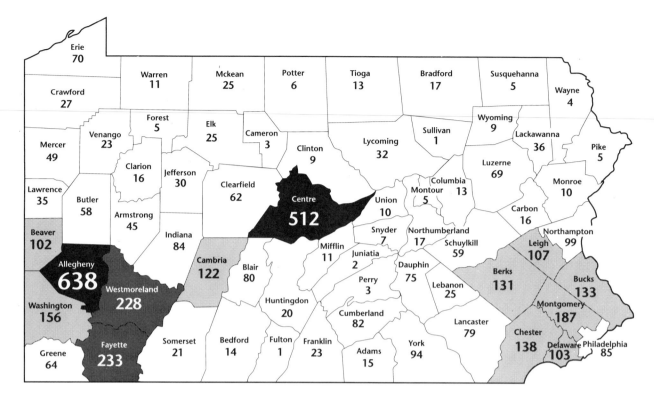

Distribution of alumni in Pennsylvania, 1986.

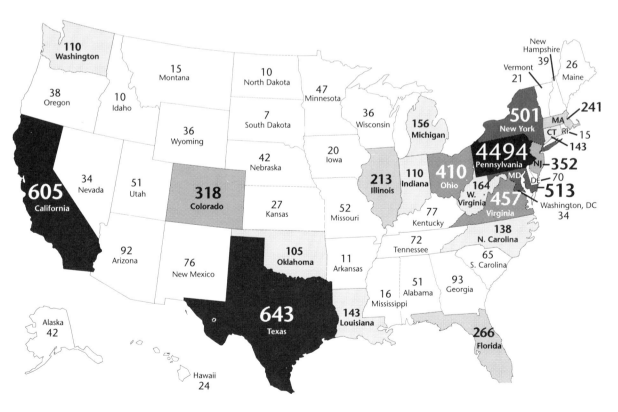

Distribution of alumni by states, 1986.

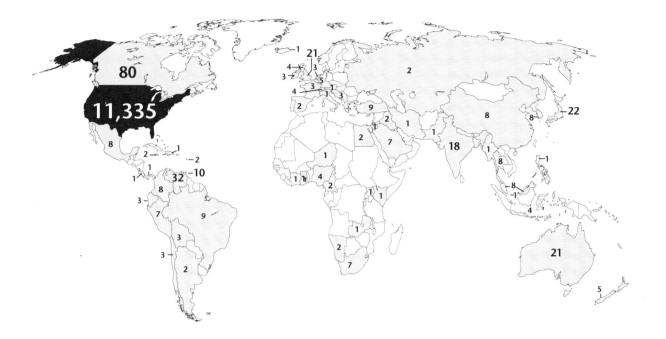

Distribution of alumni by country, 1986.

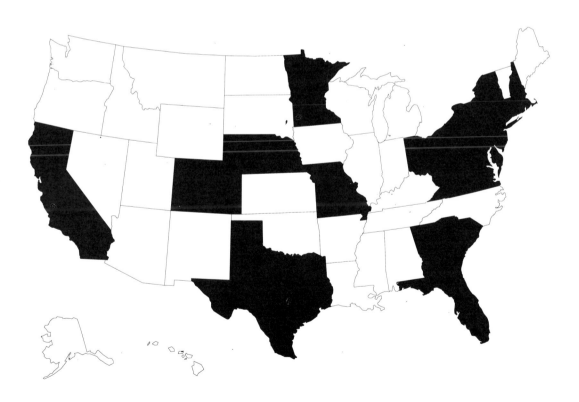

Distribution of graduate students by states, 1986.

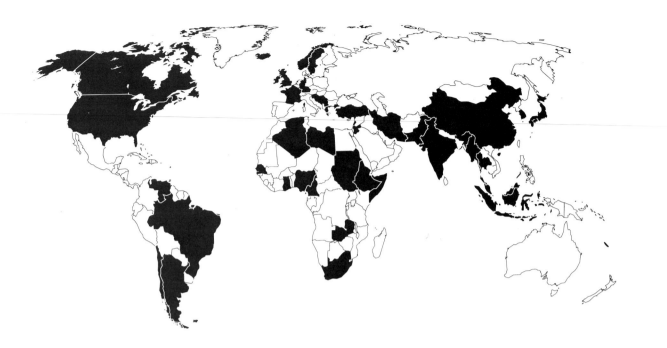

Distribution of graduate students by country, 1986.

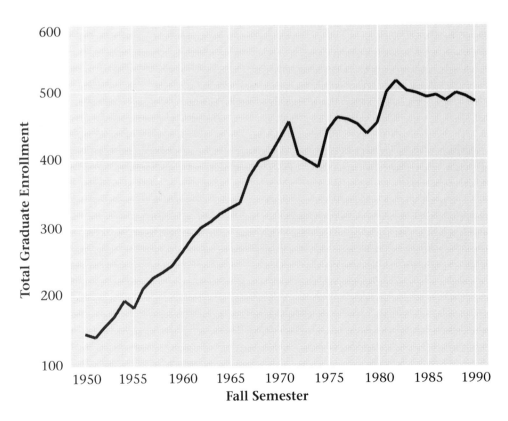

Graduate student enrollment, 1950–1990.

Besides the overall trends in enrollment, there are three special trends in undergraduate enrollment. The first is the increasing number of Earth and Mineral Sciences students that are beginning their college career on one of the Commonwealth Campuses. In the late 1980s some 20 to 25 percent of the EMS student body was located on a Commonwealth Campus. In order to advise these students and provide courses, a strong effort is being made to have EMS faculty at the Commonwealth Campuses. The first permanent position was at the Behrend Campus when Eva Tucker introduced the teaching of the geological sciences in the early 1960s. The second position was at the Ogontz Campus, where Peter C. Bazakas taught courses in geography and the geological sciences. In the late 1960s and early 1970s, Garry L. Burkle was appointed at the Altoona Campus, August H. Simonsen at the McKeesport Campus, John A. Ciciarelli at the Beaver Campus, John A. Vargas at the DuBois Campus, and John R. Ousey at the Delaware County Campus. In 1980 Brian B. Tormey replaced Burkle at the Altoona Campus when Burkle came to the University Park Campus in the associate dean's office.

The most recent appointments were made in 1989 when George K. Tseo was appointed at the Hazelton Campus, James E. Alcock at the Ogontz Campus, and Jon M. Nese at the Beaver Campus. From time to time there have been temporary appointments of individuals at a number of the campuses who were qualified to teach a particular course. The television network has also been used to teach meteorology and the geological sciences at other campuses.

August H. Simonsen received the Excellence in Teaching Award in 1972, the 1980 Outstanding Teaching Award from McKeesport Campus, the AMOCO Foundation Teaching Award in 1982, and in 1990 the Matthew J. Wilson Outstanding Teaching Award.

There has also been a major trend in the growing number of women in the College. As late as 1970, women students made up fewer than 5 percent of the student body. By the late 1980s this number had increased from 20 percent to 25 percent. Although all majors have attracted women, the largest numbers are in the earth sciences.

There has also been a serious effort in the College to increase the proportion of minority groups—Afro-Americans, Native Americans, and Hispanics. The College began to actively recruit minority students in the late 1960s. Faculty members visited high schools in the large cities, particularly Philadelphia, to inform minority students about the opportunities for careers in the College. In spite of limited success, these efforts have continued. In order to enhance the efforts, an Office of Minority and International Programs has been established in the College, headed by John D. Lee. A number of projects have been initiated. Of these, the summer programs of the Perry Academy and the Westinghouse High School in Pittsburgh, in which minority high school students are brought to the main campus for several weeks, have been most encouraging. In this way high school students receive a taste of college life. There are high expectations that these programs will attract some fine students.

General Education

The College has traditionally developed courses of interest to the entire University student body. These courses, in the fields of the geosciences, geography, meteorology, and materials science, provide an understanding of the natural world and cover a wide range of material. For example, the Energy and Fuels in Society course stresses energy utilization and technological developments as well as trends in human use of energy; the geoscience course "Planet Earth" emphasizes earth processes, materials, and the evolution of the earth; and the meteorology course "Wealth and Society" treats the effects of weather and climate on society and its activities. Geography, in

Donald F. Stock, Alumni Fellow, talks with William Williamson in the College museum, 1985.

describing, analyzing, and explaining patterns of physical and human behavior, is simultaneously an environmental and social-behavioral science.

Each semester thousands of students from every major on the campus elect courses in the College of Earth and Mineral Sciences to satisfy graduation requirements. These courses give students a view of Earth processes that provides them with an enlarged perspective and enriches their lives permanently. The natural landscape has greater meaning to them than before.

Participation in Interdisciplinary Programs

In the University structure a number of teaching and research programs that are intercollege in character have developed. The faculty for these programs are associated with a particular college, and earth and mineral sciences faculty have been active participants. In the Materials Research Laboratory at least seventeen faculty from such EMS programs as mining engineering, geosciences, ceramic science and engineering, fuel science, metals science, and engineering and polymer science are members of the laboratory. Rustum Roy, professor of geochemistry, established the Materials Research Laboratory and was its director until 1988.

A number of the faculty are members of interdisciplinary teaching programs. The Science, Technology, and Society Program is directed by Dr. Roy and has faculty from fuel science, materials science, and geography. The Marine Science Program conducts an undergraduate laboratory program each spring semester at Chincoteague Island in Virginia. The present chair of the program is Eric J. Barron, associate professor of geoscience. For many years Albert Guber was director of the program. Five geoscience faculty members are associated with the program. C. Gregory Knight is a member of the Advisory Committee to the Black Studies Program.

RESEARCH

The modern development of research began with the appointment of Alfred W. Gauger as the first director of the Mineral Industries Research in 1931, a position he held until his retirement in 1954. Dr. Gauger, son of a geologist at Johns Hopkins University, was recognized as one of the nation's outstanding scientists in fuel technology. His Priestley Lectures on coal technology remain classic contributions in their field. Dr. Gauger saw Pennsylvania as a state with a remarkable endowment of both minerals and agriculture. His 1943 article entitled "Mineral Industries Research: An Endowment Policy for Pennsylvania" (Gauger, 1943) called for researchers and industrialists to use the minerals and agriculture of Pennsylvania wisely, always looking to the future in this work and combating the depletion of Pennsylvania's natural resources. He was constantly looking for ways to use resources in the most complete fashion.

In order to encourage faculty research, Dr. Gauger developed four types of research publications issued by the Experiment Station. The "bulletins" presented accounts of original research; between 1932 and 1974, the year of final publication, eighty-eight bulletins were published. The "technical publications," 197 of which were issued between 1932 and 1953, were reprints from professional journals. The "circulars," eighty-six of which were issued, contained reviews of research in progress, reports of scientific information presented at technical meetings, and other matters of interest. There were also special publications about projects being developed in the School of Mineral Industries.

Administration
Research

Director of Mineral Industries Research

Alfred W. Gauger   1931–1945

Director of Mineral Industries Experiment Station

Alfred W. Gauger   1945–1954

Assistant Dean for Research and Director of the Mineral Industries Experiment Station

John A. Hipple   1954–1956
Maurice E. Bell   1956–1967

Assistant Dean for Research and Director of the Earth and Mineral Sciences Experiment Station

Maurice E. Bell   1967–1972

Associate Dean for Research and Director of the Earth and Mineral Sciences Experiment Station

Maurice E. Bell   1972–1976
Arnulf Muan   1976–1986
Peter T. Luckie   1986–

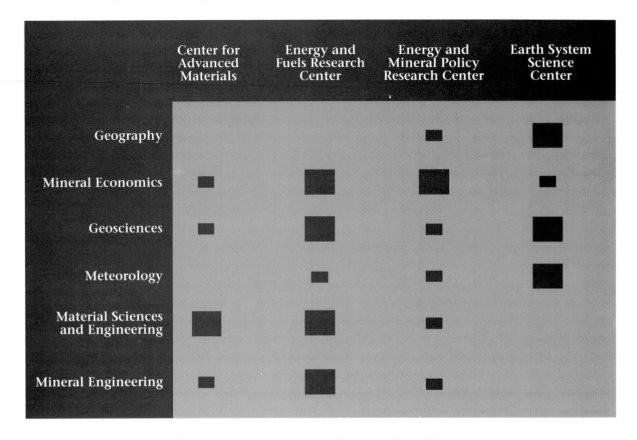

	Center for Advanced Materials	Energy and Fuels Research Center	Energy and Mineral Policy Research Center	Earth System Science Center
Geography			■	■
Mineral Economics	■	■	■	■
Geosciences	■	■	■	■
Meteorology		■	■	■
Material Sciences and Engineering	■	■	■	
Mineral Engineering	■	■	■	

Matrix of Earth and Mineral Sciences initiatives in the research centers of the College.

In the 1930s a mineral industries machine shop was established. It was responsible for the upkeep of equipment and the construction of special new equipment used in instructional research. The staff of the shop are highly trained and experienced mechanics. There was also a storeroom for storing and dispensing supplies and necessary equipment. These activities were coordinated by a supervisor of technical services, a position presently held by Charles E. Houser.

In 1954 John Hipple held the position of director of the Mineral Industries Experiment Station for two years until the appointment of Maurice E. Bell in 1956 as assistant dean for research and director of the Mineral Industries Experiment Station. In 1972 Dr. Bell became associate dean and director of the Earth and Mineral Sciences Experiment Station, a position he held until his retirement in 1976.

Of his responsibilities, Dean Bell writes: "I wanted to create an administrative atmosphere conducive to the conduct of valid research by the faculty and graduate students and not disturbed by unsolved administrative problems. Second, I wanted to administer the research program in the College in such a manner that it resembled the experience the students might encounter after graduation and would thus serve as a valuable learning experience. For example, certain funds in the Experiment Station could have been used for direct subsidy of the research services, such as the shop, the Mineral Constitution Laboratories, or services in the University Computation Center. Instead, I chose to make these funds available to graduate students or faculty members for their use in paying the established rates for the services required in actually doing the research on the basis of proposals to the Experiment Station, with endorsements from those in the auxiliary enterprises who would actually do the work. Many students, who initially were diffident about asking for money, learned that requesting money to support research was the *modus operandi* of the modern research establishment."

Because the associate deans have been active in research, a number of new programs have originated in the research office (Figure 10). As Dean Arnulf Muan relates on the establishment of the Mining and Mineral Resources Institute: "I wrote the proposal for the establishment of the program, and at the urging of Dean Hosler I assumed the directorship on a part-time basis. This was in line with the general philosophy of the time when continued funding from governmental sources in Washington was uncertain. A new organization was not created until it was on a sound financial basis. After I had been directing the program for two years, it became evident that funding was going to be available on a continuing basis. At that time a separate program was created with a permanent director."

In the development of the responsibilities of the associate dean, at both the research and the instructional level, the view that associate deans should remain professors in their respective disciplines has persisted. Dean Muan states: "It has been the pattern of the College that the persons holding the positions of dean and associate deans—and in most cases department heads—continue as active researchers and teachers. This has set us apart from other colleges, and

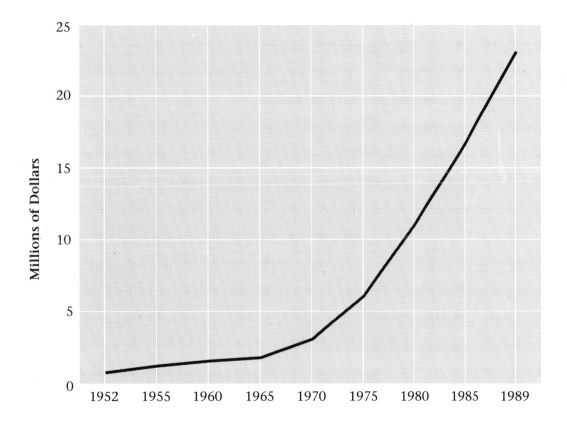

Research funds, 1952–1989.

I think it has contributed to the strength of this College." It has also made it possible for the associate deans to understand the research problems of the individual faculty members.

There has been remarkable continuity of policies in the responsibilities of the associate dean for research. Dean Peter Luckie states: "This office, as it evolved, and as I hope to have it continue to evolve, is a service group that takes its philosophy from former Dean Hosler, who always stated that the function of an administrator was to keep the paper off the back of the faculty. We're a service group trying to make it as simple as possible for faculty to get their proposals to potential funding agencies with a minimum of difficulty."

As the research programs of the College have grown, the research funds have increased (Figure 11). In 1955–56 the total research budget was $818,140, of which federal sources provided $315,451, industrial sources provided $296,610, and the state provided $206,079. In the period from 1955 to 1970 the research funds of the College increased moderately each year, reaching a total of $3,147,563. In the 1970s the research funds escalated to a total of $11,194,085 in 1980–81. This trend continued in the 1980s with funds rising to $20,847,354 in 1990–91. The federal research budget in the College supported 168 projects, the state budget supported 50 projects, and the industrial research budget supported 218 projects. The grants ranged from $100 to $1,203,000. The average federal grant was $62,463, and the average industrial grant was $22,935.

It is difficult to provide a measure of the value of research. Pure research may appear to have no applied value at the moment, but without it the foundation for applied research does not exist. Many attempts have been made to evaluate research. The increase in dollar expenditures gives some indication of the importance of the research performed, for the funds are granted by industry and government only after a long and thorough peer evaluation of the importance of the project. The number of invited papers presented at national and international meetings also provides a recognition of the value of a faculty member's work. Possibly most important is the number of referred articles and chapters in books written by a faculty member. When this criterion is used, there is strong evidence that faculty in the College have increased their productivity for many years. In 1960 the 66 faculty members produced 134 refereed articles, an average annual rate of 2.0 papers per faculty member; in 1970 some 121 faculty produced 288 articles, or 2.3 articles per faculty member; and in 1987–88 there were 416 articles produced by 145 faculty, or 2.8 articles per faculty member.

CONTINUING EDUCATION

A program of continuing education began in the 1890s in the newly created School of Mines. Although the program was accepted by the workers in the mineral industries, lack of funds limited the activities of the faculty. Until the arrival of Dean Steidle in 1929, extension programs had been developed primarily in the field of mining engineering.

The Division of Mineral Industries Extension

When Edward Steidle came to Penn State, he recognized the need for an expanded continuing education program to train workers in the mineral industries. These industries were becoming increasingly complex, and specialized skills were needed. The establishment of the Extension Division provided the structure through which mineral industries information and the results of

Administration
Continuing Education

Director

Harry B. Northrup	1931–1947
Donald C. Jones	1947–1964

Assistant Dean

John J. Schanz	1964–1967
E. Willard Miller	1967–1969
Robert Stefanko	1969–1972

Associate Dean

Robert Stefanko	1972–1980

Director

James D. Bennett	1981–1984

Associate Dean

Robert L. Frantz	1984–

new technology could be disseminated throughout Pennsylvania. Dean Steidle stated: "The Extension Division aims to give every mineral industries worker a broad view and a more comprehensive understanding of the entire field in which he is engaged, so that he will fully recognize his place in the industrial operating plan."

The initial division director was Harry B. Northrup, who served from 1931 to 1947. Professor Northrup came to the extension job with an understanding of the working problems of the mine. After graduating from Ohio State University in 1911 with a mining degree, he came to Penn State as an associate in the Metallurgy Department and just prior to World War I became head of that department. After the war he worked in the iron mines of Michigan and the coal mines of Ohio and Pennsylvania until his return to the School of Mineral Industries.

To initiate the program, the director was charged with the responsibility of developing a program of training for the mineral industries workers of Pennsylvania. To secure assistance from the industry, an advisory board was appointed to provide input on the types of courses to be offered, to review course outlines and content, and to act as a contact with industry in advancing extension proposals. To implement the new extension programs, an agreement was signed between the state Departments of Public Instruction, Mines, Labor, and Industry and the Pennsylvania State College.

While the coal-mining extension program spearheaded the development of extension training, demand soon arose for similar types of programs in other mineral industries. In the 1930s, programs were developed for ceramic technology, petroleum, metallurgy, and natural gas engineering, and in 1942 a program for fuel technology was created. A course could be started anywhere in the state upon petition of a sufficient number of workers, all of whom had to be residents of the same local school district. Because the course of instruction required three years to complete, the extension supervisor recommended that no program be started in a locality with an enrollment lower than twenty-five. The workers had to be more than eighteen years of age and employed in the industry for which the training curriculum was prepared. Workers who completed the program were given a diploma.

A distinctive feature of the extension program was the preparation of books exclusively for these courses. As Donald C. Jones, director of Earth and Mineral Sciences Continuing Education, states: "In the place of developing mimeographed material and passing it out in some flimsy form, the class materials were developed in book form. There was one text for each year of study. The books were printed by a number of publishers, but eventually we settled on Gray Printing Company of DuBois because they would save type for us and reproduce additional copies at minimal cost. At the height of the program there was a budgeted item of $50,000 for printing books." These books were used for extension courses in twenty-eight states and a number of foreign countries.

By the 1930s, when extension instruction was introduced, technological advancements in the mineral industries required highly skilled workers. As a consequence, the programs were remarkably successful. In 1931 there were 1,750 students enrolled in the programs, of which 1,100 completed the course and received certification. By 1935 the number of students had risen to 3,800, some 1,800 of which ultimately completed the course. The student body grew to a total of 4,334 in 1940–41 (Table 1). Between 1931 and 1944, students in the regular extension courses

Table 1.   Extension Classes, 1940–1941

Curriculum	Centers	Classes	Counties	Teachers	Enrollment
Ceramics	7	8	7	8	152
Metallurgy	18	50	14	50	1,173
Coal mining	60	77	16	61	1,788
Mine modernization	4	9	3	9	500
Petroleum and natural gas	8	31	8	31	721
Total	106	188	49	166	4,334

SOURCE: *Mineral Industries* 10 (May 1941), 3.

totaled 38,888. In addition, during World War II, some 7,138 students were instructed in a special defense and war training program. The grand total of students was 45,726. During this period, classes were offered in 287 districts and in 50 of the 67 counties.

By the 1940s, the extension program of the School of Mineral Industries was recognized as the prototype for on-the-job training not only in the United States but also throughout the world. The program was successful because there was a demand and because standards were maintained at the highest possible level. In addition, extension classes were a fundamental part of the entire program of the School.

Administrative Reorganization

As the demand for extension courses declined in the 1950s and 1960s, the objectives of the program changed. There was no longer a need for faculty to supervise the extension courses in the field. A different type of continuing education was evolving: shorter courses and more specialized programs were now needed to serve the mineral industries.

As a response to the changing demands for continuing education, a new administrative structure was developed. The Continuing Education Division was abolished in 1964 and the continuing education instructors were placed in the appropriate departments. Robert B. Hewes and Joseph W. Hunt went to the mining program, John L. Fisher and Michael Zulkoski to metallurgy, and Richard W. Harding transferred to the petroleum and natural gas program. When Donald C. Jones, who became director of extension in 1947, retired in 1964, the administration of continuing education was placed under John J. Schanz, assistant dean for continuing education, who served until 1967, when E. Willard Miller became assistant dean serving until 1969. Robert Stefanko served as assistant dean and later as associate dean until 1980. From 1981 to 1984 continuing education was directed by James D. Bennett. In 1984 Robert Frantz became associate dean for continuing education and industrial programs.

Mining Engineering Continuing Education

The continuing education of the College is presently concentrated in mining engineering. A complete discussion of programs is presented in Chapter 10.

Correspondence Instruction

Correspondence instruction initially began in 1932. In order to serve as large a population as possible, both college-credit and non-college-credit courses were developed. By 1940, lessons had been prepared for a large number of the mineral industry fields. Of the college-credit courses offered, six were in the field of geography, six in geology, three in geophysics, and one in mineralogy. Non-college-credit courses included three in coal-mining, three in petroleum and natural gas engineering, ten in ceramic technology, three in metallurgy, and three in petroleum refining. For many years the non-credit college courses were highly successful. However, as the continuing education work in those areas declined in the 1950s, the demand for correspondence work also decreased, and correspondence work in these areas was gradually phased out.

However, correspondence work in meteorology developed during World War II, and for many years hundreds of students enrolled in a group of meteorology courses. Correspondence instruction in meteorology continues in the department at the present time. By contrast, correspondence instruction declined in the other disciplines and has been discontinued.

THE FACULTY ORGANIZATION

The University Faculty Senate has delegated a number of functions to the colleges. In order to accomplish these functions the Earth and Mineral Sciences faculty has prepared an Organization

Dean Hosler talking to a delegation of Chinese scientists, early 1980s.

Statement, the preamble of which states: "The primary responsibility for the academic program, its quality and growth, rests with the faculty." The Faculty Organization is defined "as the structure which will enable the faculty to realize its maximum potential in contributing to the functions of the College and supporting its administration." Such an organization provides avenues for the faculty to serve as a group discharging the aims and objectives of the College, and for submittal of proposed actions through appropriate channels to the University Faculty Senate and to the University administration. The organization also provides a faculty forum for flow of ideas and information in promoting faculty unity and morale. The Faculty Organization is divided into four parts: the faculty, faculty meetings, committees of the College, and the Executive Committee.

THE FACULTY

The faculty of the College of Earth and Mineral Sciences consists of all members who hold academic rank either in teaching or in research. Student members of the Faculty Organization are graduate and undergraduate members of faculty committees plus student officers of the student council. The dean or faculty may extend the membership to other members of the staff who would not otherwise qualify.

The faculty have such major responsibilities as establishing admission standards for the College, developing the instructional program within the objectives of the College, and initiating programs of study to meet the changing needs of society. In addition, they participate in governing the units within the College, including making recommendations to the dean for promotion and tenure and for appointment of new faculty members, department heads, and section chairs. In selecting a new dean, a special meeting of the faculty develops a list of nominees, which is forwarded to the President's Search Committee.

The faculty affects and helps to develop policies and procedures in the College through such College-wide committees as the Faculty Steering Committee, the EMS College Planning Committee, and the Research Committee.

COMMITTEES OF THE COLLEGE

All EMS faculty are eligible to hold committee membership. In addition, nonfaculty staff may serve on certain select committees. Faculty appointments are made by the dean on recommendation of the EMS Committee on Committees. Depending on responsibilities, some committees report to the dean (the Executive Council, the Plenary, the Committee on Committees, and the Library), others report to the associate dean for research (Research, Safety, Shop, and Stockroom), and some report directly to the faculty (Faculty Steering, Scholarships and Awards, and Affirmative Action).

THE EXECUTIVE COUNCIL

The Executive Council, originally established by Dean Edward Steidle, is the policy-making body of the College. The dean of the College presides over the council, which consists of the associate deans, the department heads, and the chairs of the Faculty Steering Committee. The Executive

George Deike, Jr., beside a portrait of his father, George Deike, Sr., about 1975.

Council has always had open discussion on any topic pertinent to the function of the College. Rarely is a motion made and a vote taken. The discussion continues until a consensus is reached. On the operation of the council, Dean Hosler remarks: "Since I left the College in 1985 I have come to appreciate even more the integrity and ability of the Executive Council members to maintain the confidentiality of critical matters discussed by the council. The council provided the opportunity to work directly with the problems of the departments, and if we disagreed we always worked things out, reaching a reasonable compromise. I was always very positive in the leadership I had in the departments and with the associate deans of the College. The fine and candid exchanges at council meetings created a collaborative effort essential to the operation of a good organization. If the discussions are not free and candid, people bottle things up so that tensions increase and eventually there is an explosion."

FACULTY MEETINGS

A minimum of two faculty meetings are held each calendar year, with provision for special meetings when necessary. The faculty meeting agendas are proposed through the Faculty Steering Committee. The dean is chair and presides over the meetings. The 80 to 90 percent attendance at faculty meetings demonstrates that the faculty consider the meetings important. The meetings not only serve to keep faculty informed about happenings within the College, but also provide a place where faculty members can discuss important issues of the day. Particularly important is the dean's report on development within the College at faculty meetings.

THE EMS FACULTY'S ROLE IN THE UNIVERSITY

ADMINISTRATIVE POSITIONS

The faculty of the College of Earth and Mineral Sciences have long been active in University affairs. A number of the faculty have left the College to assume positions in the central administration. In the 1950s Elburt F. Osborn, dean of the College of Mineral Industries, became vice president for research in President Eric Walker's administration, and in the 1960s Thomas Bates became assistant dean of the Graduate School and vice president for planning in the Walker administration. In 1985 Charles Hosler, dean of the College, was appointed by President Bryce Jordan to the position of vice president for research and dean of the Graduate School. In 1989 C. Gregory Knight, the head of the Department of Geography, was appointed vice provost and dean for undergraduate education.

Many EMS faculty members have served as officers of the University Senate and have chaired Senate committees. Robert F. Schmalz served as vice chairman of the Senate, C. Gregory Knight served as vice chairman and as chairman, and Peter Deines served as vice chairman in 1989–90 and as chairman of the Senate in 1990–91. E. Willard Miller and Dr. Deines served as chairmen of the University Curriculum Committee for a number of years.

GIFTS AND ENDOWMENTS

Gifts of money and equipment from individuals, companies, and government agencies are important to the instructional and research programs of the College. As early as the 1930s the School of Mineral Industries received gifts, usually equipment, from various industries and government agencies. Most of the paintings in the museum, and many of the mineral displays, were gifts from individuals and industries. At that time there was no program of planned giving by Penn State. The individual faculty members contacted industry and government agencies to let them know certain equipment was needed. This personal approach was effective in acquiring equipment for many of the School's programs.

The first concerted fund-raising effort by the College began in 1980–81. In this initial year, gifts totaled $1,240,405, and in the following year the gifts were 19 percent higher, totaling $1,479,888. Particularly significant has been the growing response of the alumni to the College's fund-raising. Between 1980–81 and 1981–82 the number of alumni participating increased by almost 51 percent to a total of 1,173. At the time Dean Hosler wrote: "Our expressed hope was that we would see the alumni participation figure pass 10 percent in 1981–82, and we did—more than 13 percent of our graduates sent contributions." Gifts from business and corporations were up almost 20 percent in 1981–82, with 439 giving a total of $1,125,017. Included in this total was more than $38,000 from companies that matched alumni gifts. Private gifts have continued to rise to a total of $2,552,005 in 1991 (Table 2).

Table 2.   Gifts and Endowments

1978	$ 450,865
1979	537,436
1980	816,904
1981	1,240,405
1982	1,479,887
1983	1,760,589
1984	3,096,542
1985	2,047,963
1986	2,481,790
1987	2,323,863
1988	2,466,900
1989	2,193,870
1990	2,409,802
1991	2,552,005

Many of the gifts are in the form of endowments. Between 1981 and 1991 the endowment fund principal increased from $2,775,455 to $12,264,014. The endowment funds are particularly important for the establishment of chairs, professorships, fellowships, scholarships, awards, student loans, and the purchase of equipment. They are also essential to attract the best students and faculty.

The Obelisk Society

Members of the Society, 1991

Dixie V. Bayer	Thomas M. and Eleanor Krebs
Howard O. and Jean S. Beaver, Jr.	Adolph J. Lena
Victor G. Beghini	Harold P. and Betty J. Meabon
William and Dee Bellano	E. Willard and Ruby S. Miller
Luther T. and Martha A. Bissey	Henry E. Reif, Jr.
James H. Brannigan	William H. and Jeanne Renton
Samuel H. Byers	Norman J. Rubash
Fletcher L. Byrom	Frank and Lucy Rusinko
Helen H. Chelius	Gladys D. Snyder
Anne Deike	Donald F. Stock
George R. and Janet E. Desko	Donald B. and Mary E. Tait
Donald L. and Ellen M. Eberly	Miriam Taylor
Thomas V. and Jean Falkie	George H. Todd
Lawrence D. Gent	George E. Trimble
Carl P. and Mary Ann Giardini	Dennis A. Trout
Howard L. Hartman	Philip L. Walker, Jr.
Milton E. Holmberg	Cecilia E. Weidhaas
Richard O. Hommel	Ernest S. and Julia F. Weidhaas
J. Robert Jones	John P. Weir
Donald E. Kline	Thomas H. and Kathleen C. Wentzler
Charles E. Knopf, Jr.	Quentin E. and Louise Wood

Members in Memoriam

Gus A. Beard	H. Herbert and Mary Hughes
George H. Deike, Jr.	Harvey P. Kocher
William H. Gosnell	Van H. and Helen R. Leichliter
Edward C. Hammond, Jr.	J. Murray Mitchell
William A. Haven	Livingston P. Teas
John P. Herrick	Anne C. Wilson
James S. Hudnall	Matthew J. Wilson, Jr.

THE OBELISK SOCIETY

The Obelisk Society of the College of Earth and Mineral Sciences was formed in 1981 to give special honor and recognition to individuals who make extraordinary contributions to the College. Membership in the Obelisk Society is open to all alumni and friends of the College.

As a memento of membership, each member or member couple receives a framed print of the watercolor "The Obelisk in Winter." Nancy Strailey, a State College, Pennsylvania, artist, was commissioned to paint the picture, which shows the stone column for which the Society was named, with Old Main in the background. In 1991 there were seventy-four members of the Society.

ENDOWED POSITIONS

A number of endowed professorships and faculty and graduate student fellowships have been established in the College.

Centennial Professorship

The Centennial Professorship in Mining Engineering was the first endowed professorship in the College. In 1990 Stanley Suboleski was the first appointment to the professorship. Its purpose is to supplement departmental support for an outstanding faculty member by providing the resources to further the faculty member's contribution to teaching, research, and public service. The principal of the fund, $250,000, has been provided by gifts from alumni and friends of the College. The funds are used to supplement the holder's salary, provide for research, education, travel expenses, graduate assistant salaries, and support the holder's program.

Faculty Fellowships

Three endowed faculty fellowships are now in the College. The Quentin E. and Louise L. Wood and the Victor and Anna Mae Beghini faculty fellowships are in petroleum and natural gas engineering, and the MICASU University endowed Fellowship is in mineral economics. Each of these fellowships has a principal fund of $100,000. The funds for the Wood and Beghini fellowships were contributed by the donors, and the MICASU Fellowship was provided by an anonymous donor. The fellowships provide an outstanding faculty member with supplementary funds so that he or she can make further contributions in teaching, research, and public service. The funds can be used for research, education, travel, and other expenses, or for graduate assistant salaries.

Faculty Fellowships

Quentin E. and Louise L. Wood	Petroleum and Natural Gas
Victor G. and Anna Mae Beghini	Petroleum and Natural Gas
MICASU	Mineral Economics

Graduate Student Fellowships

The most capable graduate students are attracted to universities that have endowed graduate fellowships. The College of Earth and Mineral Sciences had three endowed graduate fellowships in 1990. The Anne C. Wilson Graduate Fellowship, established in 1988 by transferring $100,000 to a separate endowment from the Matthew J. Wilson, Jr., Loan Fund, is open to all graduate programs in the College. The purpose of this fellowship is to recognize and support outstanding graduate students enrolled or planning to enroll in the College. Preference is given to students who receive honorable mention in the NSF Fellowship or NSF Minority Fellowship Competition.

The Carl and Mary Ann Giardini and the Joseph and Anne Rubash fellowships have been established to recognize and support outstanding graduate students enrolled or planning to enroll in Petroleum and Natural Gas Engineering. An initial fund has been provided for each of these fellowships, and interested persons or organizations may make additional contributions. Full-time graduate students exhibiting academic excellence and financial need are considered for these fellowships.

Graduate Student Fellowships

Anne C. Wilson Graduate Fellowship	College
Carl P. and Mary Ann Giardini	Petroleum and Natural Gas
Joseph and Anne Rubash Fellowship	Petroleum and Natural Gas

THE RESEARCH ENDOWMENT FUND

The George H. Deike, Jr., Research Endowment Fund has been established to assist and enhance the research programs of the various disciplines in the College, with preference to be given to mining engineering and special attention paid to innovative and independent research not likely to be funded elsewhere. The initial endowment totaled $675,000. Expenditures from this fund are used for research work of faculty and graduate students, equipment purchases, library assistance, graduate fellowships, and travel and fieldwork expenses.

STUDENT SCHOLARSHIPS, AWARDS, AND MEMORIAL FUNDS

It has long been a tradition in the College to provide financial aid to as many worthy students as possible. Beginning in the 1930s the first scholarships were provided by mining, metallurgical, and ceramic companies. The College now has a number of endowed student fellowships and scholarships that have been established by gifts from alumni and friends of the College and from companies and corporations.

Undergraduate Scholarships

College Scholarships

John and Elizabeth Teas Scholarship Fund
Edwin L. Drake Memorial Scholarship Fund
Matthew J. Wilson Honor Scholarship
Dean's Freshman Scholarship Fund
Michael and Dorothy Deutsch Scholarship
Frances H. Byers Scholarship Fund
Edward C. Hammond, Jr., Memorial Scholarship
John G. Miller Memorial Scholarship

Discipline Scholarships

Robert Stefanko Memorial Scholarship Fund —
    Mining Engineering
Hartman Honor Scholarship — Mining Engineering
Mossy Foundation Scholarship
Bruce Miller Scholarship
E. J. Schulze Scholarship Fund
Hommel Scholarship
C. Philip Cook, Jr., Memorial Scholarship
Samuel Zerfoss Memorial Scholarship
TRW Foundation Scholarship
Hans Panofsky Scholarship
Carpenter Technology Corp. Metallurgical Scholarship
Charles E. Knopf Memorial Scholarship

The undergraduate scholarship program now provides the largest student support at Penn State. Gifts and endowed funds given over the years enabled the College to present $224,805 in scholarships to 274 students in 1991. The largest single source of general scholarship funds in the College is the John and Elizabeth Holmes Teas Scholarship Fund. Between twenty-five and thirty students are granted Teas scholarships each year. Some of the scholarships are available to all students, others are designated for a particular program. Besides scholarships, there are a number of other funds that aid students. Some memorial funds have been created to honor former faculty members. For example, the Charles B. Manula Memorial Fund assists mining engineering students who have demonstrated potential in the application of computers to problems in mining.

The College also presents a student award in recognition of academic achievement and special services to the College. The Ellen Steidle Achievement Award, established by Dean Edward Steidle in memory of his wife, was the initial award. It is presented to a student who has performed outstanding service to the College or community. Other awards have been established to honor faculty members or friends of the College.

Memorial Funds

Paul D. Krynine Memorial Fund	Geosciences
J. Bruce Inswiler Memorial Fund	Geosciences
David R. Mitchell Memorial Engineering Assistance Fund	Mineral Engineering
Charles B. Manula Memorial Fund	Mining Engineering

Awards

Dean Edward Steidle Memorial Scholar Award	College
Ellen Steidle Achievement Award	College
George W. Brindley Award	Crystal Chemistry
Robert W. Lindsay Award	Metallurgy
Arthur P. Honess Memorial Award	Geosciences
Jerome N. Behrmann Award	Meteorology
E. Willard Miller Award	Geography
William Grundy Haven Memorial Award	College
Benjamin F. Howell, Jr., Award	Geophysics
C. C. Wright Award	Fuel Science
Hans Neuberger Award	Meteorology
George H. K. Schenck Award	Mineral Economics
DuPont Polymer Science Award	Polymer Science

WILSON TEACHING AND RESEARCH AWARDS

The annual teaching and research awards are made possible by the Matthew J., Jr., and Anne C. Wilson Trust Fund. The income from this fund is used to benefit the EMS faculty. In 1969 the faculty teaching award was established, and in 1989 a research award was added. The students nominate faculty members for the awards, and the dean of the College makes the final decision. Since 1969 forty-three faculty have been honored, each receiving a plaque and a monetary award (Table 3). The awards are presented at the Annual Awards Banquet, which is the major social event of the year for the faculty and also is made possible by the Wilson Trust Fund. Student awards are presented at the banquet as well. The Fund is an outstanding example of how beneficial to the College bequests can be in providing support for activities for which there is no other funding.

Table 3.   Matthew J. and Anne C. Wilson Awards

Outstanding Teaching Awards

1991	Earl K. Graham	Geosciences
1991	Peter A. Thrower	Materials Science
1990	August H. Simonsen	Environmental Sciences
1990	J. Michael Fritsch	Meteorology
1990	Abraham S. Grader	Petroleum and Natural Gas Engineering
1989	Peirce F. Lewis	Geography
1989	Roger J. Cuffey	Geosciences
1988	Harold H. Schobert	Fuel Science
1988	Kevin P. Furlong	Geosciences
1987	Hampton N. Shirer	Meteorology
1987	Raja V. Ramani	Mineral Engineering
1986	Richard R. Parizek	Geosciences
1986	Peter T. Luckie	Mineral Processing
1985	Paul R. Howell	Metals Science and Engineering
1985	Christopher J. Bise	Mining Engineering
1984	George Simkovich	Metals Science and Engineering
1984	Carlo G. Pantano	Ceramic Science and Engineering
1983	Robert Scholten	Geosciences
1983	Michael M. Coleman	Polymer Science
1982	Turgay Ertekin	Petroleum and Natural Gas Engineering
1982	Craig F. Bohren	Meteorology
1981	Frederick L. Wernstedt	Geography
1981	C. Drew Stahl	Petroleum and Natural Gas Engineering
1980	Lloyd A. Morley	Mining Engineering
1980	Richard Hogg	Mineral Processing
1979	John E. Tilton	Mineral Economics
1979	John H. Hoke	Metals Science and Engineering
1978	Ian R. Harrison	Polymer Science
1978	Earle Ryba	Metals Science and Engineering
1977	Frank F. Aplan	Mineral Processing
1977	Peter M. Lavin	Geosciences
1976	Alistair B. Fraser	Meteorology
1976	Emilie T. McWilliams	EMS Library
1975	William O. Williamson	Ceramic Science and Engineering
1975	Roger M. Downs	Geography
1974	William B. White	Geosciences
1974	Paul D. Simkins	Geography
1973	Anthony V. Williams	Geography
1973	Richard C. Bradt	Ceramic Science and Engineering
1972	Charles P. Thornton	Geosciences
1972	Robert E. Newnham	Solid State Science
1971	H. Reginald Hardy	Mining Engineering
1971	John J. Cahir	Meteorology
1970	Eugene G. Williams	Geosciences
1970	S. M. Farouq-Ali	Petroleum and Natural Gas Engineering
1970	David P. Gold	Geosciences
1969	Robert F. Schmalz	Geosciences
1969	George C. Brindley	Ceramic Science and Engineering

Table 3.   Matthew J. and Anne C. Wilson Awards, *continued*

	Outstanding Research Awards	
1991	Michael M. Coleman	Polymer Science
1991	Paul C. Painter	Polymer Science
1990	Barry Voight	Geosciences
1989	Peter J. Webster	Meteorology
1989	Howard W. Pickering	Metals Science and Engineering

THE WILSON STUDENT LOAN FUND

It is not likely that Matthew J. Wilson, Jr., a 1918 graduate in mining engineering, realized the importance of the bequest in his will for the establishment of a fund in the College to make low-interest loans available to Earth and Mineral Sciences undergraduates and graduate students. This loan fund has made it possible for hundreds of students to complete their college education. Since the establishment of the Matthew J. Wilson, Jr., Trust Fund in 1967, in accordance with his wishes, more than $2,952,000 has been loaned by the College to students. In the 1988–89 academic year alone, more than $295,000 was provided for student loans. In 1989 the endowment fund principal totaled $1,746, 670.

Associate Dean E. Willard Miller with award-winning students of the College, late 1970s.

ALUMNI CONSTITUENT SOCIETY

In 1989 more than 1,200 alumni of the College of Earth and Mineral Sciences petitioned the University for the establishment of an Alumni Society. The petition was accepted, and the initial membership was 4,891—comprising the graduates of the College who were already members of the Penn State Alumni Association. There is a potential membership of 12,000, the entire EMS alumni body.

The goals of the EMS Alumni Constituent Society are simply to encourage alumni to get to know one another and help one another, to support the goals of the College, and to help the College by supporting the student recruiting effort, providing internship opportunities for EMS students, and helping new graduates get established within the professions. It is the desire of the Society to expand the professional contacts among the presumably well-established network of alumni. Beyond the specialist groups, however, the Society recognizes a need to establish stronger connections across the disciplines, to broaden everyone's horizon so that EMS meteorologists know some EMS ceramic scientists, mineral engineers visit geophysicists, and geographers learn more what fuel scientists do.

To accomplish this goal, a regional structure is being developed in areas where a significant number of EMS graduates are located. The initial board of directors comes from many parts of the United States that have set up regional groups. On the board of directors are George R. Desko (Western Pennsylvania region), mining engineering, chairman of the board and president of the Canterbury Coal Company of Avonmore, Pennsylvania; Gail Gockley Frassetta (Mid-Atlantic region), mineral economics, associate utilities specialist with the Virginia State Corporation Commission in the Division of Energy Regulations; G. David Golder (Gulf Coast region), petroleum and natural gas engineering, Marathon Oil Company's production manager for the United States; W. John Hussey (Washington, D.C., and alumni overseas), meteorology, director of the Office of Systems Development for the National Environmental Satellite Data and Information Service of the National Oceanic and Atmospheric Administration; Richard H. Merkel (Denver region), geosciences, senior geophysicist for Marathon Oil; Eric J. Minford (Eastern Pennsylvania region), ceramic science and engineering, senior research ceramist with Air Products and Chemicals Inc. in Allentown, Pennsylvania; John C. Redmond (New England region), geosciences, GTE corporate vice president for research and engineering and president of GTE Laboratories, Waltham, Massachusetts; Frank Rusinko, Jr. (Midwest region), fuel science, president of Intech, EPM, Hinsdale, Illinois; and Richard E. Zeller (Florida region), geography, a planner with the Florida Department of Highway Safety and Motor Vehicles, Tallahassee, Florida.

ALUMNI HONORS

The University honors its alumni with two types of awards: the Distinguished Alumnus Award and the Alumni Fellow Award.

DISTINGUISHED ALUMNI

The Distinguished Alumnus Award was proposed by Penn State President Milton S. Eisenhower and approved by the Board of Trustees in January 1951. The principal purpose of this award, as stated on the medallion, is to recognize and salute achievement of outstanding alumni "whose personal and profession achievements, and community service exemplify the objectives of the Pennsylvania State College." In 1952, the first year alumni were honored in the College, three of the five recipients were from Mineral Industries. In that year incumbent trustee George H. Deike '03 became the first Trustee to receive the award; the other recipients were John V. Forbes and Lewis E. Young. By 1991 thirty-six of the College alumni were honored as Distinguished Alumni (Table 4).

Table 4.   Distinguished Alumni

1991	Howard O. Beaver, Jr.	Metals Science and Engineering
1991	Warren M. Washington	Meteorology
1989	Frederick C. Langenberg	Metals Science and Engineering
1986	Norman J. Rubash	Petroleum and Natural Gas Engineering
1985	Victor G. Beghini	Petroleum and Natural Gas Engineering
1985	James J. Tietjen	Fuel Science
1984	Thomas M. Krebs	Metals Science and Engineering
1984	George E. Trimble	Petroleum and Natural Gas Engineering
1982	Paul B. Barton, Jr.	Geosciences
1981	Dennis J. Carney	Metals Science and Engineering
1975	G. Montgomery Mitchell	Petroleum and Natural Gas Engineering
1974	William Bellano	Mining Engineering
1973	John W. Hanley	Metals Science and Engineering
1968	* David R. Mitchell	Mining Engineering
1967	* George H. Deike, Jr.	Mining Engineering
1967	* Edward Steidle	Mining Engineering
1966	Jesse F. Core III	Mining Engineering
1966	* George S. Rose	Metals Science and Engineering
1965	George J. Bair	Ceramic Science and Engineering
1964	Max W. Lightner	Metals Science and Engineering
1964	* James L. Mauthe	Metals Science and Engineering
1964	* Roger W. Rowland	Ceramic Science and Engineering
1964	* Jerome W. Woomer	Mining Engineering
1963	Fletcher L. Byrom	Metals Science and Engineering
1962	* Livingston P. Teas	Geosciences
1961	John T. Ryan, Jr.	Mining Engineering
1960	* James C. Gray	Mining Engineering
1959	* Van H. Leichliter	Metals Science and Engineering
1958	* Luther C. Campbell	Mining Engineering
1956	* Edward G. Fox	Mining Engineering
1956	* William A. Haven	Metals Science and Engineering
1955	* William W. Sieg	Metals Science and Engineering
1954	* Jesse B. Warriner	Mining Engineering
1952	* George H. Deike	Mining Engineering
1952	* John V. Forbes	Mining Engineering
1952	* Lewis E. Young	Mining Engineering

*Deceased.

ALUMNI FELLOWS

In 1973 Penn State President John W. Oswald and the Alumni Association president, Larry Foster '48, conceived the Alumni Fellows Program to tap the generosity and talents of Penn State's greatest reserve, its graduates. Since then the Alumni Association, the President's Office, and the colleges have sponsored the three-to-five-day visits of those eminent alumni. While welcomed back as honored guests—with banners stretching from elm to elm across the campus mall—Alumni Fellows quickly find themselves immersed in the work of the Fellow programs, sharing their many gifts with the University community. Through classes, seminars, and informal meetings, Fellows offer students their viewpoints, philosophies, expertise, and advice.

The students are most receptive to such advice as "how to make it in the working world" and to the revealing of developments in their field. Fellows invariably stimulate students to think, and how even to expand their college careers, and they enjoy rolling up their sleeves to work in the program. Amid the lectures, seminars, interviews, and classes, Fellows have the opportunity to participate in campus tours, renew old acquaintances with friends, mentors, and professors, and build new relationships with students and faculty. Fellows are also entertained at luncheons and dinners and presented with a special memento of their visit. Between 1973, when William Bellano became the first Alumni Fellow of the College of Earth and Mineral Sciences, and 1991, twenty-one EMS alumni have been honored (Table 5).

Table 5.   Alumni Fellows

1991	Kee-Hyong Kim	Ceramic Science and Engineering
1990	Richard J. Janda	Geosciences
1990	Steward S. Flaschen	Mineralogy
1990	Richard F. Wesner	Mineral Processing
1989	Warren M. Washington	Meteorology
1989	Frank Rusinko	Fuel Science
1988	John C. Redmond	Geophysics
1988	King Wu	Mining Engineering
1987	H. Douglas Dahl	Mining Engineering
1987	Richard E. Hallgren	Meteorology
1986	George J. Demko	Geography
1986	Thomas V. Falkie	Mining Engineering
1985	Donald F. Stock	Ceramic Science and Engineering
1983	John W. Hanley	Metals Science and Engineering
1982	Adolph J. Lena	Metals Science and Engineering
1979	Paul B. Barton, Jr.	Geosciences
1977	Frederick C. Langenberg	Metals Science and Engineering
1976	John C. Calhoun	Petroleum and Natural Gas Engineering
1975	George J. Bair	Ceramic Science and Engineering
1974	Fletcher L. Byrom	Metals Science and Engineering
1973	William Bellano	Mining Engineering

THE FUTURE

The relevance of the research and education programs of the College of Earth and Mineral Sciences in solving challenging scientific problems and in attacking urgent societal issues continues to be increasingly apparent. There is worldwide recognition that human activities are changing the global environment, that voracious demands for energy will pose serious national and international difficulties, and that technological progress provides wide-ranging opportunities for the creation of new materials and their use. There is a fundamental need to renew productivity based on the knowledge that stimulates technological progress. These are challenges that present not only new responsibilities for the College, but also unprecedented opportunities.

The College of Earth and Mineral Sciences is embarking on a new and exciting journey in attempting to amplify the relevance of research and scholarship in the traditional disciplines by integrating them in multidisciplinary centers that will foster and stimulate comprehensive understanding of the Earth's complex physical and human system. In this approach the fundamental and applied research will be combined to provide paradigms that can be used to comprehend and assimilate the complexity of the world today.

The current developments in the earth, energy, and materials science are intimately linked and pose opportunities and challenges that arch across all the endeavors and disciplines of the College. The global environment through utilization of fossil fuel resources; modern material developments; demographics; and profound policy issues of state, national, and international importance in the sciences and economics of energy and minerals are all inherently interrelated. Few organizations in the world can match the broad scope of the College of Earth and Mineral Sciences in developing improved understanding of the complex issues related to the Earth and its resources in foreseeing the implications of policies that may be proposed to ameliorate the difficulties, or perhaps even crises, that lie in the future.

Chapter 4 | Interdisciplinary Research

The College has always recognized that many problems must be approached from an interdisciplinary perspective. The benefits to be gained from "cross-fertilization" among the basic disciplines became a major theme of EMS scientists in the 1950s. This was reflected by many government research-sponsoring agencies, which encouraged faculty to prepare more interdisciplinary, problem-oriented research proposals and to organize interdisciplinary research groups for a more effective attack on such problems as coal characterization and utilization, environmental impact, and structure of materials.

To provide the evolving specialized instrumentation necessary to support minerals research in the College, the Mineral Constitution Laboratories were organized in 1952 as an interdisciplinary research section of the Mineral Industries Experiment Station (Bates, 1952). At that time it was difficult to acquire equipment for individual programs through government grants, and university funding was minimal. To provide equipment for the College, the analytical tools were moved into a single laboratory, specialists were hired to operate it, and the laboratories were available to students and faculty on an hourly-rate basis, chargeable to research contracts or departmental budgets.

In 1956 the Mineral Conservation Section, the Coal Research Section, and the Mass Spectrometry Laboratory were organized. The Materials Research Laboratory was organized in the College in 1962 and transferred in 1964 to the University's newly created Institute for Science and Engineering, an intercollege research organization. In 1967 a Mine Drainage Research Section was developed, followed by the Ore Deposits Research Section in 1969. This interdisciplinary approach to research continues today with the three most recently created interdisciplinary research organizations: the Earth System Science Center, the Center for Advanced Materials, and the Center for Energy and Mineral Policy Research.

These special interdisciplinary units draw on expertise from across the University, as well as the College faculty. They are sometimes very broad in perspective, such as the Earth System Science Center, or more limited in scope, such as the Ore Deposits Research Section. It is in these units that the holistic nature of science becomes readily apparent. The investigators in these units are considering some of the most complex problems envisioned by scientists and engineers today.

THE EARTH SYSTEM SCIENCE CENTER

The establishment of the Earth System Science Center in the College of Earth and Mineral Sciences is a normal outgrowth of the College's long-established research traditions. Over the years the College's academic departments have developed a strong tradition of multidisciplinary cooperation in the investigation of environmental and energy problems. The Earth System Science Center involves faculty and students in the Departments of Geography, Geosciences, and Meteorology, augmented as required by new appointments and associations with others inside and outside the University. Eric J. Barron, associate professor of geosciences, was appointed as the first director of the Center in 1986.

The traditional approach in the earth science has been to study such individual components as the atmosphere and ocean, the geologic mantle and crust, or the land surface. Because these make up an integrated whole, it is now recognized that each individual component has a profound effect on the others. The physical and biological evolution of the Earth is controlled by these complex interactions. Although the integrity, unity, and interrelationships of all processes that occur on the Earth are intuitively evident, only now does science have the rudimentary knowledge and the prospect of adequate technological capability to attempt a formal understanding of change on the global scale.

Besides the need to study the natural processes that create the physical world, there is a present-day compelling urgency to understand these processes. Human activities, such as increasing the carbon dioxide content of the atmosphere or depleting the ozone in the stratosphere, may be altering the course of natural events on Earth. Evolutionary changes in the Earth's surface—some cyclical, some progressive, and some discontinuous—also impose long-term geologic modifications, including continental drift, sea-level fluctuations, and large-scale vulcanism. The frequency of these changes and the expected trends are now within the predictive reach of the earth sciences.

Dean John Dutton wrote in the *Earth and Mineral Sciences* bulletin (Fall 1985): "To determine whether the fears of human-induced adverse effects are justified, to separate such effects from variations due to natural causes, and to ascertain whether corrective actions could be effective, it is necessary to know much more than we do about the diversity of the interactions that occur within the earth system." He continued: "The current interest in formulating and fostering a science of the earth system thus arises for both practical and intellectual reasons. The need for a new approach coincides with advances in our scientific and technological capabilities. Modeling and other investigations concerned with the physical subsystems of the Earth are ready to incorporate more realistic considerations of subsystem interactions and are ready to cope with the implications of attempting to resolve and predict variations over wider bands of time scales. The observational, experimental, and computational resources necessary to support these efforts are becoming available. The global observations required to characterize important planetary processes are being assembled, or are contemplated, in space-based Earth observations. The needs and the opportunities thus converge to stimulate the creation of an earth system science."

The specific goals of the Penn State Earth System Science Center reflect the need for university-based national and international leadership in fostering a science of the Earth and in catalyzing the interdisciplinary communication essential for considering the issues of global changes (Barron, 1988). Three themes of investigation have evolved. These research themes are based on areas of common interest within the college, providing natural avenues of communication and interaction. A common interest has brought together a diverse faculty to focus on three of the major national and international priorities in the study of global change: The global water cycle, the interaction of global tectonics and solar-driven processes, and biochemical cycles.

THE GLOBAL WATER CYCLE

Water plays a major role in an enormous number of Earth processes and a central role in the world's ecosystem. The global water cycle is a fundamental component of biogeochemical cycles and plays a direct role in atmospheric and oceanic circulation, heat transport, and atmospheric chemistry. Clouds, ice, snow, and surface moisture act as major elements of the Earth's radiation budget. As well as being a vital resource, water is the major weathering, erosion, and transport agent in the sedimentary system, and water pollution, water quality, and hydrologic events such as floods and drought present major social issues.

Despite such significance, knowledge of water as part of the global interacting system is meager. At an earlier time hydrology largely involved classic problems of water supply and natural hazard reduction. It is now recognized that there must be the emergence of a global-scale

Computer-automated electron probe analyzer that can perform in minutes chemical analyses that formerly required hours is operated by Leland B. Eminhizer, center, electroprobe analyst in the College's Materials Characterization Laboratory. Assisting him is John Hunt, left, graduate student, while Derrill M. Kerrick, professor of mineralogy, looks on.

hydrology. There is a growing need to understand how the water cycle will respond to global changes and how these changes will influence other elements of the Earth's systems. The Earth System Science Center has projected studies that concern almost all of the different aspects of the global water cycle, and its expertise encompasses the areas necessary to achieve a perspective of the global water cycle as a part of a coupled, interactive system.

Soil Moisture and Surface Energy Fluxes

Surface turbulent energy fluxes provide the driving force for atmospheric motions. Soil moisture availability is the single most important factor in governing the partition of available radiant energy at the surface into sensible and latent heat fluxes. Latent heat flux, which is called evapotranspiration when it originates from both plants and ground, plays a vital role in the functioning of plants and is of major importance in the substrate water budget. Knowledge of the distribution and intensity of the heat fluxes at the lower boundary is crucial for describing the Earth's effect on regional and global-scale atmospheric motions. Toby N. Carlson is a leader in research on this aspect of the water cycle. He is working toward a long-term record of surface fluxes and soil moisture measurements from surface stations, using techniques to determine surface fluxes from remote sensing data, and developing sophisticated models of these important quantities.

Cloud Processes in the Hydrologic Cycle

Clouds are an integral component of the global water cycle and the climate system and play a critical role in regulating the energy and moisture budgets of both the surface and the atmosphere. A portion of the water condensed in clouds returns to the surface in the form of precipitation, while the portion that remains in the atmosphere continues to modulate the radiation budget of both the atmosphere and the Earth's surface.

Because most cloud processes occur on scales that cannot be explicitly resolved by climate models, it is necessary to parameterize or represent those effects as a function of the resolvable fields. There is still considerable uncertainty as to how to achieve this, and consequently the effects of clouds on the climate system and on the global water cycle are still not well understood. This uncertainty diminishes confidence in models currently used for simulating perturbations in climate due to either man-made or natural forces. Bruce A. Albrecht leads the Center's research forum on cloud processes through the investigation of observed data and modeling studies.

The Earth's Radiation Budget and Climate

From the perspective of climate theory and climate change, there is no more pressing problem than understanding the hydrologic cycle and its interaction with changes in the forcing of the climate systems. For the present-day climate, water vapor is the single most important greenhouse gas in the atmosphere, due to its extensive rotational and rotational-vibrational absorption bonds and the so-called absorption in the thermal window. The dominant control on the amount of solar radiation reflected from the planetary system is the fraction of cloud cover. High clouds also control the amount of thermal radiation lost from the system. One of the main mechanisms for moving excess solar energy from the tropics to high latitudes is through evaporation, the transport of water vapor, and condensation. From the perspective of past climates, it is essential to understand the hydrologic cycle in atmospheres that have markedly different pressure and temperature regimes, including the role of water vapor under conditions of very high CO_2 amounts at very warm surface temperatures, as well as such obvious factors as cloud amount and location during glacial maxima and minima. Thomas P. Ackerman, who joined the faculty from NASA, is analyzing data to determine global cloud properties and the statistics of the Earth's radiation field, with a focus on these critical climate and water-related problems.

The Cryosphere

The cryosphere forms one of the major reservoirs in the global water system. While the proportion of total water held in snow and ice fields is actually very small (approximately 2 percent), those fields do hold most of the world's supply of fresh water. Most of this water is held in the form of glacial ice, which at the present time covers about 10 percent of the Earth's land surface. Approximately 96 percent of this ice forms the ice sheets of Greenland and Antarctica, and only about 4 percent occurs as mountain glaciers.

There are several areas of major concern for current research with regard to the role of the cryosphere in the global water system. The first is to establish the size of the cryosphere reservoirs and their annual variability. The second concern is to decide how each component of the system would respond to possible future atmospheric and oceanic forcing due to climate change. One problem for all aspects of cryospheric research is data acquisition. Primary data is most likely to be derived from various remote-sensing platforms. The Earth System Science Center's efforts, led by Robert G. Crane, will contribute to research on the cryosphere in a number of significant ways, particularly in the interaction of the cryosphere with other components of the earth system.

Ocean-Atmosphere Interactions

In the traditional view of the coupled ocean-atmosphere system, the ocean is driven by a momentum flux from the atmosphere and by the latitudinally dependent radiational heating of the upper ocean. In turn, the atmosphere is driven by the surface heat and moisture fluxes, particularly from the ocean, and by the gradient of latent heating that arises in a coupled manner with the atmospheric dynamics from the surface fluxes. Within this scheme, the hydrologic cycle plays a relatively passive role, merely modulating the surface radiation budget through cloudiness.

Research within the Earth System Science Center and the Department of Meteorology, led by Peter Webster, suggests a more significant role for the hydrologic cycle in the coupled ocean-atmosphere system. Instead of a passive role, a hypothesis that the hydrologic cycle possesses a zero-order influence on the interaction of the two spheres is being investigated. A central theme of this hypothesis is that cloud and precipitation are zero-order contributions to the total diabatic heating and the body force structure of the ocean and the atmosphere.

Regional Hydrologic Consequences of Global Change

Changes in the environment for life, and changes in significance to societies, are rarely considered at the global level. Changes at the regional and local levels that are products of the global system are most readily detected. However, much of the current work on predicting planetary change involves the use of coarse-resolution global models. The resolution of the models used to predict global change does not match the needs for regional predictions.

Earth System Science Center work on these problems is led by Robert G. Crane and Brenton M. Yarnal in the Department of Geography. For some time this department has conducted research in synoptic climatology.

The Human Significance of Changes in the Global Water Cycle

Problems associated with water and water supply have always challenged humans, yet this close interaction between humans and water has not resulted in substantial efforts in overall planning at a societal level. At the same time, changes in the global water cycle create a new set of human demands and stress on water resources and an even greater need for planning. Significant changes from natural variations in the past are known, and significant alterations in the global water cycle are expected to accompany human-induced climate change in the twenty-first century. One goal of the Earth System Science Center is to evaluate the significance of the changes in the global water cycle on society.

INTERACTION OF GLOBAL TECTONICS AND SOLAR-DRIVEN PROCESSES

The second major theme of research in the Earth System Science Center focuses on an already identified international research priority: the interaction of global tectonics and solar-driven processes. The Center's research focus on the global hydrologic cycle has a number of links to the past and to efforts directed toward an understanding of Earth's history as well as to the future consequence for societies.

The study of global changes in the recorded history of the Earth provides, first, an opportunity to consider directly the interplay between the two major heat engines: an internal heat engine manifested in plate tectonics, and the external solar engine. Second, because there is abundant evidence of global change, the study of Earth's history provides an opportunity to reconstruct replicas or do case studies of past conditions that will provide clues to how the global system works. And third, the history recorded in rocks reveals past variables in temperature and/or pressure.

In the past the reconstruction of Earth's history has been primarily inductive, starting with individual events and attempting to reconstruct the larger picture. The opportunity now exists to combine models based on physical principles and observations and to unify earth disciplines in order to achieve much greater insight into how the system evolved at its present working.

Evolution of Mountain Belts

Tectonics activity and mountain-building have long been recognized as major components of the evolution of the continental lithosphere, and the role of critical tectonism in changing the basic structure of the continents is incorporated in today's plate-tectonic models. Another factor that is only now beginning to be recognized is the important coupling of this tectonic activity with other components of the dynamic earth system. None of the individual components of the Earth's changes can be understood without an understanding of the entire system.

In investigating the coupled system, the first aspect to consider is the role of uplift mechanisms in the evolution of mountains. The objective of the Earth System Science Center's research in this area, led by Kevin P. Furlong in conjunction with Thomas W. Gardner and Rudy L. Slingerland, is to develop a fully coupled model of uplift and basin formation that explicitly includes such processes as erosion and transport, which are needed to provide realistic time evolution. Based on available data, the model will focus on specific case studies—first the Appalachian system, then other mountain areas. The longer-term goal is to develop a tested dynamic model that can be applied to reconstructing global topography. These models will have important implications for climatic modeling.

Paleoclimate Models and the Global Water Cycle

The first-order goals in paleoclimatology and paleo-oceanography are to discover how the global climate has changed over geologic time. These goals coincide with a growing interest in the relationships between climate and the sedimentary record. The key element is to blend the expertise and accomplishments of the atmosphere and ocean sciences with those of the geologic sciences. Eric J. Barron is investigating these relationships, with a major focus on the role of geography and topography in climate change and the variations in precipitation-evaporation patterns.

Chemical Denudation and Biochemical Cycles

Chemical weathering rates are the result of a strong coupling among climate, orography, and the chemical composition of exposed rocks. On a global scale this coupling may be an important factor in the regulation of atmospheric composition, and it certainly is a major factor in the biogeochemical cycles of the elements, in the development of soils, and in the filling of sedimentary basins.

To understand the nature of this coupling more clearly, Lee R. Kump and Eric J. Barron have initiated a modeling study of the interactions between geochemistry and climate. Three aspects of the study include the evolution of the influences of the geographical distribution of exposed rock types on global chemical weathering rates, the development of coupled models of geochemical cycles and climate to investigate the integration among rock types, climate, and atmospheric CO_2 levels, and, finally, the inclusion of tectonic processes in the model so that the evolution of mountain ranges can be realistically represented.

Surface Hydrology, Sediment Transport, and Geomorphology

The next link in the interplay of global tectonic and solar-driven processes is made up of the processes that control surface hydrology, sediment transport, and geomorphological evolution. The key elements are to quantify the hydrologic cycle for a variety of watersheds by incorporating physically based and statistically driven equations into a predictive landscape evolution model. Remote-sensing systems are being utilized to characterize properties and hydrology in specific studies. Thomas Gardner is leading the research effort on these problems.

Predicting Sediment Characteristics Through Hydromatic Modeling

The sedimentary basins of the world contain a record of basin development, sediment supply, source of sediment, morphologic evolution, source climate, adjacent hydrology, and physical circulation within the basin. The basin contains an integrated record that reflects the sum of coupled global tectonic and solar-driven processes. The aim is to develop a model that simulates sedimentary characteristics and distributions and that is capable of making successful predictions in key case studies. The Center's research, led by Rudy L. Slingerland, aims at improving the capability to predict sediment forces by adding a numerical modeling capability, so that the processes that distribute sediments within basins can be examined.

BIOGEOCHEMICAL CYCLES

The solar-driven atmospheric circulation, and particularly the hydrologic cycle, drive the weathering and erosion processes that modify the continental surface, degrade the topography, and transport and deposit sediments within the Earth's fluid environments. In turn, the nutrient cycle, the chemical evolution of the oceans and the atmosphere, and many of our material resources are intimately tied to the sedimentary system. Nutrients, including carbon, nitrogen, sulfur and phosphorus, water, and sunlight are the fundamental limiting factors in life. Climate, nutrients, and the characteristics of the Earth's surface define the environment of life. Biologically regulated fluxes, fluxes from the Earth's interior, and the sedimentary cycle regulate the atmospheric and oceanic composition. These biogeochemical cycles are critical in maintaining climate, through the importance of radiatively active atmospheric components such as CO_2, CH_4, CO, N_2O and O_3. These important processes are a major focus of the Center.

William H. Brune, an expert on observing changes in atmospheric chemistry, and James F. Kasting, whose interest is the modeling of atmospheric chemistry throughout early history, are leading these projects. In conjunction with the ongoing meteorology research in acid rain, the geographic research in human-induced global change involving variation in atmospheric chemistry, and the strong geochemistry program in the Department of Geosciences, the College is expected to become a leader in these areas.

THE CENTER FOR ADVANCED MATERIALS

The Center for Advanced Materials (CAM) was established in June 1986 when the Gas Research Institute (GRI) awarded a research contract to The Pennsylvania State University for a multiyear program involving more than twenty interrelated projects. The Center was created to serve as a bridge between the advanced materials supplier community and user industries and to act as a mediator and performer in longer-term high-temperature materials research and development.

The Gas Research Institute recognized the need to apply new materials to industrial processes. In order to implement this research, it conducted a national competition to select an institution for a Materials Technology Center. The mission was to serve the materials research and development needs of industries that use natural gas. Richard E. Tressler, founding director of the Center, states: "The reasons for Penn State's success in the original competition included Penn State's willingness to provide some seed money, a commitment by the Ben Franklin Partnership Program to provide significant Center of Excellence funding, and, most important, Penn State's outstanding international and national reputation in ceramics and high-temperature materials research."

THE LAUNCHING OF THE CENTER

In the initial implementation of the Center, Dr. Tressler states, "the most challenging aspect was to organize and orient the faculty to pursue industrially sponsored research with well-defined objectives and milestones. The Gas Research Institute, particularly the Industrial Utilization

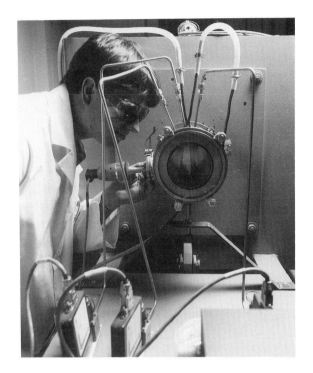

Vacuum furnace for simulation of heat treatment in low oxygen partial pressure environments. The system was designed and built in the Center for Advanced Materials for evaluating the long-term durability of nonoxide ceramics in atmospheres typical of a variety of metallurgical heat-treating processes.

Department, was a nontraditional sponsor of university research, and thus we had to devote considerable effort to understanding our 'customer' and reporting our results in the most effective way."

Two principal organizational features were incorporated into the Center's operation. According to Dr. Tressler, "First, staff positions were included in the GRI program to handle the important function of information dissemination, analytical, and engineering service to other GRI contractors, and overall administration of the day-to-day activities of the Center. Second, an interdisciplinary team of project directors was assembled from faculty in the Department of Engineering Science and Mechanics, Mechanical Engineering, Chemical Engineering, and Materials Science and Engineering. Faculty with principal appointments in Penn State's Materials Research Laboratory and Applied Research Laboratory were also included. The program was to incorporate the Center's research efforts into the existing departmental and graduate degree structures to form a truly integrated interdisciplinary program."

In order to implement these programs, the Center is divided into three groups: the Gas Research Institute Funded Projects, the Cooperative Program in High Temperature Engineering Materials Research, and the Individual Research Projects for Industrial Sponsors.

THE GAS RESEARCH INSTITUTE

The Gas Research Institute (GRI) is concerned with gas-fired technologies for industrial applications, which account for approximately 40 percent of the natural gas used in the United States. The Center for Advanced Materials tests and develops new materials for such applications as heat recovery systems, advanced gas-burner systems, indirect-fired heating equipment, and gas-fired engines. These projects also include assessments of appropriate uses for these new materials, plus development of a materials properties data base, that enable engineers to apply advanced systems design concepts to their application. Because of the Center's objective to commercialize the results of this research, a system for interactive communication with industry has been built into the program. This system serves a mechanism for focusing the Center's resources on critical problems and priority technologies and as a vehicle for disseminating research results to the industrial community. The Gas Research Institute topics at the Center for Advanced Materials are organized into three interrelated project groups: Research, Engineering and Analytical Services, and Technology Assessment and Transfer.

The Research project group specializes in the development, characterization, and application of advanced materials in high-temperature, gas-fired equipment. The projects in this group are concerned with degradation and corrosion, high-temperature mechanical properties, and tribology of structural ceramics, along with the fabrication of new materials. Projects have included such topics as test methodology for tubular components, performance verification of new low-cost ceramics, chemical surface interaction, and the mechanical behavior of fibers and of cellular ceramics. Many of the projects are designed to yield short-range results that can be applied in a commercial environment.

The Engineering and Analytical Services project group is designed to provide rapid technical support for the application of advanced materials to industrial processes. Representative projects include radiant tube technology-component test and design verification, failure analysis, and material characterization and evaluation.

The Technology and Assessment Transfer project group is designed to meet the applications and material development needs of advanced material suppliers, equipment manufacturers, and industrial end-users of natural gas. Projects in the technology assessment group include study of the potential for using natural gas in ceramic and powder metal sintering technology; identification of important research and development issues in high-temperature tribology of advanced ceramic and alloy materials; the definition of issues and opportunities in the development and implementation of a natural properties design data base; a classification of industrial practice in the aluminum remelt industry; an assessment of the current practice in the joining of nonoxide structured ceramics; and an assessment of the potential for implementary gas-fired boosting technology in the glass-melting industry. In addition, a number of technology transfer activities take place within this project group, publication of a quarterly newsletter and brochures, and organization of workshops, short courses, and conferences.

THE COOPERATIVE PROGRAM IN HIGH-TEMPERATURE ENGINEERING MATERIALS RESEARCH

The Cooperative Program in High-Temperature Engineering Materials Research is concerned with critical fundamental issues in the development and characterization of new classes of materials in high-temperature applications. Its objectives are to establish an interdisciplinary research program for the design, fabrication, characterization, and application of high-temperature materials; to provide a mechanism for member companies to invest in generic, fundamental research without initiating a major in-house research program; to provide for the timely exchange of research findings between Penn State faculty and the scientists and engineers of the member companies; and to improve the supply of advanced-degree candidates with a modern education in advanced engineering materials. Current projects involve the design and processing of advanced composites, the development of composite ceramics with both high-fracture toughness and creep resistance, and studies of long-term reliability of high-temperature structural materials.

RESEARCH PROJECTS FOR INDIVIDUAL SPONSORS

The Center for Advanced Materials encourages private industry to sponsor individual research projects. This makes it possible for the sponsoring company to utilize the expertise of the Center's staff to solve some of its own problems, develop long-range projects that require specialized facilities and equipment not available within the company, extend the company's own research, develop and engineer programs, obtain a fresh perspective, implement long-range planning, and interact with potential employees.

Industrial research at the Center is encouraged by Penn State's Office of Industrial Research, which helps companies obtain supplemental funding from such sources as the Ben Franklin Partnership Program, a nationally acclaimed $50 million program that helps support industry/university research and technological innovation. The State Program for Small Pennsylvania Companies, available to companies doing less than $30 million worth of business annually and employing fewer than 1,000 people, and the federal Small Business Innovation Research Program are possible sources of leveraged funding for the Center's sponsor.

Private individual research projects undertaken at the Center for Advanced Materials include fabrication science for ceramic tapes, fundamental studies of corrosion of monoxide structural ceramics, mechanical properties and fatigue behavior of metallized glass-bonded alumina ceramics, and fabrication and characterization of ceramic matrix composites for high-temperature structural applications.

In the fall of 1990 Dr. Tressler stated: "The dynamic nature of projectors and investigators originally envisaged for the Center for Advanced Materials is being realized." Two new programs are now under way at the Gas Research Institute. Wayne Huebner and Vladimir S. Stubican offer their collective expertise in ceramic processing, electrochemical behavior of ionic and mixed conductors, and mass transport in materials issues in solid-state fuel cells. In the second project, the team of David J. Green, Robert N. Pangborn, Bernard Tittmann, and Joseph C. Conway, Jr., have taken a multifaceted, multidisciplinary approach to studying the processing, microstructures, and behavior of three-dimensional interconnected metal ceramic composites.

In the Cooperative Program in High-Temperature Engineering Materials Research, two new assistant professors competed successfully for support of their projects: "Improved High-Temperature Joining" by Altaf H. Carim, assistant professor of ceramic science and engineering, and "Processing of Nanocrystalline Ceramics" by Merrilea Mayo, assistant professor of metals science and engineering.

CAM ACCOMPLISHMENTS

In 1991 Dr. Tressler summarized the accomplishments of the Center: "From the University's viewpoint we have succeeded in establishing an internationally recognized center for engineering materials research which attracts visitors and requests for data from all areas of the U.S. and abroad. We have many visiting researchers sent by their organizations to obtain advanced degrees or to develop expertise here." (Between June 1986 and June 1991, Penn State's CAM faculty granted twenty-eight graduate degrees, of which twelve were Ph.D.'s and sixteen were M.S. degrees.) He continued: "From the viewpoint of our research sponsors (our customers), I think we are viewed as being very responsive and excellent performers on research projects." At the 1991 Advisory Board meeting, members stated their views of CAM's progress: "There is an excellent interaction between experiment and theory throughout this program. Each experiment is well modeled and analysis feeds back into further experiments. This attitude prevails throughout each and every task and sets this program apart from many institutions where researchers either do experimental work or theoretical work, but seldom interact with each other. . . . It is gratifying for us to see the increasing dovetailing between research and application."

According to Dr. Tressler, "We've met our goals, and we're generally recognized at Penn State as a major success in building a significant effort with very little University funding. From the GRI's standpoint, I think we've met their expectations, and they are continuing to fund us beyond the initial five-year period with a core contract and through specific project support."

As a result of accomplishments within the first five years of operation, the Center has had a significant impact on the development and applications of advanced engineering materials in industrial processes. It is recognized within the academic community for its active role in transferring technology to researchers and engineers working in private industry. It is also recognized nationally and internationally for research and educational innovations in the field of advanced materials for newer environments. For example, the Center's research has provided a fundamental understanding of the corrosion and degradation, and thus safe-use regimens, of nonoxide silicon-based ceramics which are critical materials for high-temperature gas-fired industrial equipment. The Center's research on the application of ceramics and radiant tubes has provided mocking designers with a sound methodology for designing with these brittle substances.

In 1991, when Dr. Tressler became head of the Department of Materials Science and Engineering, Digby D. Macdonald was appointed director of the Center for Advanced Materials and professor of materials science and engineering. Dr. Macdonald's research is in electrochemistry, corrosion, and thermodynamics, with particular interest in the growth of oxide particles on metal surfaces, novel electrochemical techniques for studying charge transfer reactions, and high-temperature aqueous systems. One current interest is modeling the corrosion of materials in the cores of water-cooled nuclear reactors.

MINING AND MINERAL RESOURCES RESEARCH INSTITUTE

The Pennsylvania Mining and Mineral Resources Research Institute (MRI) at Penn State is one of thirty-two such institutes established in as many states under a federal program mandated by the Surface Mining Control and Reclamation Act of 1977. The states' governors chose the universities at which the institutes are located on the basis of the outstanding research and graduate programs in mining and mineral resources at those universities. The idea of establishing the Institute originated with Elburt Osborn when he was director of the U.S. Bureau of Mines. Dr. Osborn worked for several years to convince the federal government that federal support of mineral resources research was as important as federal support of agricultural research.

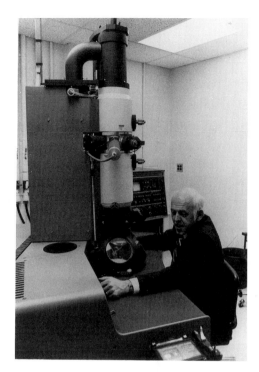

The Philips EM 420T analytical electron microscope acquired in 1983 by the College at a cost of $476,000 greatly enhances research capabilities in the materials and geological sciences. A grant of $200,000 from the NSF, along with alumni gifts and other University funds, made its purchase possible. Here it is operated by Peter A. Thrower, professor of materials science.

Penn State is the only Pennsylvania university with an outstanding research and graduate program in mining and mineral resources. In 1980, Z. T. Bieniawski was appointed director of the Mining and Mineral Resources Research Institute, succeeding Arnulf Muan, associate dean for research in the College, who had guided the Institute in its first two years.

The institutes are supported by congressional appropriations administered by the Bureau of Mines of the U.S. Department of the Interior. This support involves activities under an annual base of funding that has varied from $110,000 to $150,000. Between 1978 and 1988 a total of $1,203,161 was received, which provided support for 98 research initiative grants for faculty, 107 fellowships, and 49 scholarships. In addition, there was $430,200 for competitive research grants for faculty. The base allotment funding provided support for graduate research in mining engineering, mineral processing, ceramics, metallurgy, fuel science, petroleum and natural gas engineering, mineral economics, and the geosciences.

The general goals of the program are to stimulate and support mining and mineral industries research and to stimulate the training of engineers and scientists through their participation in research. The long-term specific goals include: defining the most promising mining and mineral resource challenges in Pennsylvania; developing and maintaining excellence in the field of mineral engineering and technology by providing a thrust in areas of particular potential, such as surface mining and strata control; encouraging greater use of computers for operational research and systems engineering; increasing the scope of mineral economics research; strengthening capabilities in mineral processing; and bolstering research in metallurgy, ceramics, and fuel science.

"Seed" money to initiate research was made available to many professors—for example, Kwado A. Osseo-Asare (Metallurgy), for new initiatives in hydrometallurgy research; H. Reginald Hardy (Mining Engineering), for new initiatives in applying microseismic techniques to mineral resources research; Turgay Ertekin and Mark A. Klins (Petroleum and Natural Gas

Engineering), for establishment of a data bank for Pennsylvania oil fields and for a laboratory investigation of the applicability of steam injection in Pennsylvania oil fields; James F. Keeney (Mining Engineering), for reviewing mining regulations for the use of small mine operators; George H. K. Schenck (Mineral Economics), to establish an input-output balance for mineral-based activities in Pennsylvania; Robert L. Frantz (Mining Engineering), for a detailed study to assess the mining and mineral resource needs for Pennsylvania; and Peter T. Luckie (Mineral Processing), to strengthen mineral-processing research and improve instructional programs. Some of these research initiatives resulted in obtaining large amounts of federal funding that far exceeded the total amount spent on research initiative grants.

A major purpose of the MRI program is the scholarship/fellowship fund administered at each institution for the purpose of aiding undergraduate and graduate students of exceptional ability in the areas of mining and mineral resources. Awards for fellowships are based primarily on the potential of the applicant for original research related to the mineral industries.

The research grants have been widely distributed in most areas of the mineral industries. Typical examples include control of blackwater in coal preparation plants by Frank F. Aplan (Metallurgy and Mineral Processing) and Richard Hogg (Mineral Processing); design procedures for coal-mine tunnels by Z. T. Bieniawski (Mining Engineering); removal of pyrite from coal by leaching, by Lawrence M. Cathles (Geosciences); point defects in hydrometallurgical processes by K. Osseo-Asare and George Simkovich (Metallurgy); development of procedure for land use potential evaluation for surface-mined land, by Raja V. Ramani and Richard Sweigard (Mining Engineering); factors controlling the generation of acid mine drainage, by Eugene G. Williams and Richard R. Parizek (Geology); processing of dolomites for refractory applications by Gary L. Messing and Richard C. Bradt (Ceramic Science and Engineering); cobalt behavior in ammonia leaching systems by K. Osseo-Asare and Howard W. Pickering (Metallurgy); and a handbook for state and local taxation of minerals by George Schenck (Mineral Economics).

Future objectives of the Mining and Mineral Resources Research Institute include strengthening understaffed individual programs that show particular promise. This includes helping new faculty get started and helping senior faculty reorient their research to the objectives of the program. Other efforts directed to improving the quality of programs in the mining and mineral resources field will include supporting innovative new approaches in research and teaching, and enriching the academic climate through seminars, invited speakers, and outstanding visiting professors. Finally, the problem of the availability of sufficiently advanced instrumentation and equipment for conducting research as efficiently as possible will continue to be addressed.

THE COAL RESEARCH SECTION

The Coal Research Section, created in 1957, has played a major role in establishing the College of Earth and Mineral Sciences as one of the foremost coal research institutions in the world, and a number of individual faculty members are internationally recognized coal experts. But what makes Penn State unique is the willingness of the individual experts to work as part of a team in truly multidisciplinary research programs. The scope of research activities covers the entire spectrum of possible endeavors, from the origin of coal to the environmental impact of its utilization. This includes coal geology, paleobotany, chemistry and mineralogy, exploration, mining, beneficiation, all major utilization technologies, and economic, environmental, and social impacts. The Coal Research Section helped foster interdisciplinary efforts within the College and with other colleges and provided administration and service for the faculty engaged in these efforts.

A unique feature of the Penn State coal program was its early recognition of the importance of the heterogeneous character of coals. This was particularly significant for industrial processing. William Spackman, Jr., director of the Coal Research Section from 1957 to 1985, was a pioneer in the advancement of this concept, with the result that many College researchers conducted their studies on the same well-characterized coal samples. Eventually this led to the development of the Penn State Coal Sample Bank, a collection of more than 1,100 samples collected by University sampling crews from around the United States. Donald L. Krebs is the photographer, and Ruth Krebs drafts illustrations of coal samples for publication, slides, and theses. In addition, a Penn State Coal Data Base of computerized information is available for more than 1,400 samples. Also conceived was the *Catalog of Fossil Spores and Pollen,* a forty-four-volume compendium of systematic information on fossil polynomorphs intended primarily for nomenclatural-taxonomic use. In addition to the above achievements, Dr. Spackman will be remembered for his studies on modern organic sediments of the Everglades and the Okefenokee Swamp as analogs of the materials that could have contributed to coal formation.

In 1979 the Cooperative Program in Coal Research, one of the first cooperative industrial-affiliates programs at the University, was initiated. The goal of this initiative was to formalize the strong but informal ties that College faculty had established with the coal-producing and coal-utilizing industries. Under the program, member corporations are entitled to send two representatives to each of the biannual Information Transfer Sessions, at which University faculty and graduate students report the results of research in topical areas. With such faculty members as William Spackman, Peter H. Given, and Philip L. Walker, Jr., who were all responsible for the promotion and operation of the Coal Co-op, it was an immediate success. Other faculty now participating in the program are Alan Davis, Peter T. Luckie, Alan W. Scaroni, and Harold H. Schobert. Their enthusiasm and appreciation of the value of the co-op program to the College's graduate programs in coal have helped keep it viable during some lean years in the coal industry.

In 1986 Dr. Davis, assistant director of the Coal Research Section under Dr. Spackman since 1973, became director. Then, in 1988, a new Center for Energy and Fuels Research was created to broaden the scope of activities of the Coal Research Section into a wider spectrum of energy-related research endeavors.

THE CENTER FOR ENERGY AND FUELS RESEARCH

The Center for Energy and Fuels Research focuses its research activities on a broad spectrum of energy resource and fuel utilization areas. Alan Davis, professor of geology, is director of the Center, which incorporated the College's well-known Coal Research Section. Dr. Davis states: "Coal will continue to be an important focus of the new Center, but we also plan to expand our activities to include aspects of petroleum, natural gas, and oil shale. In fact, the Center for Energy and Fuels Research will cover the entire spectrum of fossil fuel science, technology and utilization. We are particularly concerned with ameliorating some of the environmental problems that occur with the use of fossil fuels. We also plan to carry out studies of such new fuels as coal-water slurries, which allow coal to be stored, transported, and burned much like oil. Petroleum generations and migration is another area of interest to us. However, the basic chemistry and geology of fuels also will be emphasized. Areas to be focused on include the thermal and burial histories of sedimentary basins, the molecular structure of coals and kerogen, and the chemistry of changes that accompany the transformation of plant materials into the various ranks of coal."

The Center primarily involves faculty from the Departments of Geosciences, Mineral Engineering, and Materials Science and Engineering. Its goal is to foster interdisciplinary research projects, to stimulate undergraduate and graduate students to focus on energy-related problems, and to provide a point of contact among faculty, industry, and government agencies. The new Center assumed administration of the Penn State Cooperative Program in Coal Research that has been sponsored by major U.S. corporations since it was established in 1979.

The Center for Energy and Fuels Research offers a number of specialized services for energy researchers, including the sampling, analysis, and testing of fuels; a series of more than one hundred special reports detailing the results of Penn State research in energy-related areas, and the *Catalog of Fossil Spores and Pollen;* access to the Penn State Coal Sample Bank, the largest bank of well-characterized coals in existence; the Penn State Coal Data Base (which includes a remote-access Data Base of Pennsylvania Coals); and a variety of research support services, including drafting, photography, and report preparation. In fact, one of the well-known strengths of the Center, and its predecessor, the Coal Research Section, has been the quality of the illustrative materials it has produced. Donald and Ruth Krebs, photographer and draftswoman, respectively, who have been largely responsible for this artwork, have been part of much of the history of the Coal Research Section and the Center for Energy and Fuels Research, working in Ihlseng Building from 1958 before the move to Deike Building in 1966.

THE CENTER FOR ENERGY AND MINERAL POLICY RESEARCH

The Center for Energy and Mineral Policy Research was established in the fall of 1987 to facilitate interdisciplinary studies on energy and mineral policy. It seeks to maintain the long Penn State tradition of producing important scholarly but practically relevant studies of energy and minerals. This work utilizes the strengths of the Department of Mineral Economics and allied disciplines in the College and other parts of Penn State.

The Center was founded on the premise that energy and mineral developments and the public policies that affect them are issues of enduring importance. Policy debates generally are distorted by preoccupation with spectacular problems. The evidence suggests that, in practice, programs initiated to deal with crises that were terminated long ago exercise a good deal of influence, and that certain policies persist because only a few specialists examine them in detail and politicians see no urgent need to make changes.

Energy and minerals provide striking examples of how all the major market policy problems considered by economists are treated in practice. The issues are how to stimulate promising new ventures, react to severe deteriorations of market positions, respond to monopolies (or at least the perception of monopoly), control environmental impacts, regulate worker health and safety, and decide how to divide up the costs and benefits of adjusting to changing mineral market conditions.

A continuing issue is the perception that mineral production is an excellent source of tax revenue, which leads to tax policies that often force up mineral prices. Yet fears of high prices have influenced other policies aimed at controlling the prices of minerals, particularly such fuels as oil and natural gas. While policy impacts may be greater in some sectors, such as agriculture, they tend to involve fewer basic issues. Farm policies of industrialized countries, for example, are concerned only with increasing farm incomes.

The Center seeks to devleop a sustained program that can foster recognition that important policy problems in energy and minerals persist. Critical issues will be identified, studied, and discussed in reports directed at interested nonspecialists in government, industry, and the rest of society. Developing new sources of funding is critical to attainment of this goal. The Center has been given the task of seeking foresighted organizations willing to support a sustained effort. Traditionally, research in these areas has been conducted on a project-by-project, investigator-by-investigator basis, but the Center seeks to promote systematic involvement of specialists in relevant fields of social science, natural science, and technology.

An integrated approach is necessary to gain an understanding of the complex issues of the mineral world. The Center's goal is to initiate innovative approaches to research. Development of the greatest possible breadth of expertise in academic disciplines and in subject matter is sought. No other organization presently studying mineral problems systematically employs people from all relevant disciplines. John Dutton, dean of the College of Earth and Mineral Sciences, says: "Establishing the new Center is a logical step in focusing Penn State's expertise in the area of public policy. In view of the recent impact of global economic changes on mineral commodities and basic industries, it is vital that we develop sound and consistent policies in these areas."

Richard L. Gordon, professor of mineral economics and director of the Center, along with an advisory board, has selected two broad initiatives to study: the policy implications of new technologies in energy and the policy implications of changes in the world steel industry. While the energy technology initiative could ultimately range over many fuels and technologies, primary emphasis is presently on coal-related problems. The difficulties of the Pennsylvania coal industry are receiving particular attention. A preliminary review of U.S. coal market trends has already been completed, and work is proceeding on expanding the discussion. Another element of the new technology is consideration of how trends in electric utility regulations are profoundly altering industry investment decisions.

The steel initiative seeks to analyze the tendency to greater international trade in steel and steel-making raw materials, the changing nature of steel consumption, and the role of policy in these evolutions. Dr. Gordon notes: "Patterns of world steel production and trade have shifted profoundly since World War II. The steel industry of the United States has been altered by lower steel demands and rising import competition. In this economic climate the large integrated steel mills have declined in relation to the mini-mills with a more limited product line and reliance on scrap rather than pig iron as the raw material for steel. The steel industries of Western Europe face similar problems. Japan, which rose to be a leading steel producer, no longer enjoys steel output growth." He adds: "Policy deficiencies in leading steel-producing countries have had an important deleterious impact on market evolution. Excessive faith in steel production as an engine of progress has encouraged overly optimistic expansion plans and, in some notorious cases, extraordinary poorly conceived developments. As often occurs, the overhang of excess capacity has stimulated protectionist policies. In Western Europe the Economic Community has acted systematically to control competition while the United States has tried to protect the industry by imposing import controls."

The goal in this area is to produce a comprehensive objective study of developments in the steel industry around the world. Efforts are being divided into various parts, and several are at various advanced stages. Earlier research on the world iron-ore market and the Korean steel industry is being updated, and several new projects were initiated when the Center began operations. Timothy J. Considine is preparing a study of steel markets. While an econometric model is being used to develop the basic results, his objective is to introduce a discussion accessible to a more general audience. Several papers dealing with steel demand have been accepted for publication, and Dr. Considine is working on the topic of steel supply.

Two doctoral theses have been financed by the Center. The first, by a student employed by the principal Brazilian steel company, considers prospects for increased U.S./Brazilian trade in semi-finished steel. His data indicate that a combination of the availability of modern plants, spare capacity, low labor cost, and proximity to low-cost iron ore allow Brazil profitably to provide about 10 million metric tons of semi-finished steel to U.S. steel mills. The thesis was completed in 1989 and is available as a Center report. The other thesis treats the problems of the West German steel industry. Work is also being undertaken in the evolution of the world metallurgical coal market, with particular emphasis on changing business practices. A third new project involving developments in stainless steel began in the fall of 1989.

The insights already gained from this work and other research by Center participants has inspired a third Center initiative: studies in changing energy and mineral market organization. The organization of markets and firms in energy and minerals has changed radically, and there has been extensive reorganization of firms. Moves to create diversified energy and mineral companies by adding coal, uranium, and metals to major oil companies have largely failed. Some oil companies (and some metals companies, construction firms, and electric utilities) have succeeded in coal; others have had disappointing experiences. Oil company experience in diversification to areas other than coal has been even less satisfactory.

Dr. Gordon says: "Interesting issues and the material to study them continue to emerge faster in the energy and mineral realm than does the ability to undertake research. . . . We have a richer menu of ideas than when we first started. I expect this situation to continue for many more years. We have developed a clear vision of where we want to go and what it will take to get there. The challenge was and is to persuade others of the validity of our vision. A concerted effort by the Center's associates, the College's administrators, and the Penn State Development Office is needed to implement this task. The ultimate test of the wisdom of our vision will be our success at this task."

THE ORE DEPOSITS RESEARCH SECTION

The Ore Deposits Research Section was established in 1969 as one of the College's interdisciplinary research units. Its long-term goals are to stimulate research on the genesis of and exploration for mineral deposits and geothermal systems, to aid in the training of exploration and minerals research scientists, and to develop cooperative research practices with industries. Ancillary studies on the disposal of radioactive wastes have also been carried out. The Section consists of a voluntary association of interested faculty, typically about ten, from the College, together with graduate students, postdoctoral scientists, and supporting staff. Hubert L. Barnes, distinguished

Electron Microprobe operated by students in the Department of Materials Science.

professor of geochemistry, has been director of the Section since it began. More than a dozen countries are among those who have carried out the research mission of the Section.

For many years the Section maintained a close relationship with industrial representatives by holding a series of yearly conferences called "The Mineral Research Review for Industry" (Cathles, 1982). The purpose of these reviews was to provide a forum for communication of research results of potential value to mineral exploration; to generate state-of-the-art discussion of ongoing and needed research; to foster work in problem areas of major concern to the mineral industry; to stimulate cooperative research programs with industry; and to foster development of nongovernment support for graduate research and training programs, especially in areas of interest to industry.

Each year the review was designed to acquaint participants with new research trends related to ore deposits. In order to respond directly to industry needs, the previous year's participants were asked to fill out a questionnaire to help determine their current interests. The 1982 program, for example, was designed around three concerns of the 1981 participants: types of ore deposits formed by mineral precipitation from hydrothermal systems that were expelled from magmas during cooling, the concentration and occurrence of heavy minerals, and diamonds.

C. Wayne Burnham, emeritus professor of geochemistry and former head of the Department of Geosciences, led the discussion on ways the chemistry of silicate melts controls the chemistry of the fluids that the magma expels and the kind of ore deposits produced. For example, iron, copper, zinc, and gold are transported in high-temperature aqueous solutions of chloride complexes. For these metals, the chloride content of the magma is important. In other magmas the ore minerals are compounds of sulfur, and iron, copper, or zinc. These types of combustions provide guidelines for exploration.

Hiroshi Ohmoto, Arthur W. Rose, and H. L. Barnes, professors of geochemistry, led the discussion of scientific prospecting for gold. Dr. Ohmoto prepared a new system of gold deposits to be classified according to the oxidation site of the igneous rock with which they are associated. Dr. Rose reviewed the existing knowledge about rock alterations around gold deposits, and Dr. Barnes discussed the zoning of gold and associated mineralization observed in presently active geothermal systems. David P. Gold, professor of geology, presented a discussion on diamonds with a review of research on the origin of diamondiferous kimberlites.

Because of the virtual collapse of corporate exploration for ore deposits, these conferences were discontinued after 1982. In their place, topical written reports are prepared annually on selected mineral deposits, with an emphasis on gold, the principal objective of most exploration endeavors.

The Ore Deposits Research Section has also sponsored several technical meetings on scientific subjects related to its goals. These included, in 1976, a workshop on Research Frontiers in Exploration for Non-Renewable Resources, funded by the National Science Foundation and attended by representatives of the principal exploration companies. A report from that workshop remains a standard reference.

In response to the low level of mineral and geothermal activity in the United States in the 1980s, the Section shifted some of its emphasis from industrial applications to the more purely scientific aspects of mineral resources. This change is illustrated by the organizing and sponsoring of several international meetings. These efforts were strengthened because of the respect the Section has earned for its research on mineral resources and related sciences. In 1985 the Section administered the Second International Symposium on Hydrothermal Reactions, held at University Park under the sponsorship of five international societies and the National Science Foundation and with participants from ten countries. Responding to a request from the North Atlantic Treaty Organization, and with the help of NATO funding, the Section organized an Advanced Study Institute in 1987 on the geochemistry of hydrothermal ore-forming processes, based on lectures and field studies on the mineral deposits of Spain. In May 1988 the Section organized the first international V. M. Goldschmidt Conference on Geochemistry, Mineralogy, and Petrology. The meeting, held in Baltimore, was sponsored by seven societies and attended by several hundred participants.

Such activities will continue into the future. Strong funding continues from a variety of sources, including industry stemming from a focus of exploration efforts on deposits of precious metals. Because of shrinking or closing of the less-strong university and federal programs for research on mineral deposits during the 1980s, the country's expertise has dwindled. As industrial exploration efforts continue to expand, a major shortage of trained scientists in this field is anticipated. Consequently, there will be an acute demand not only for research but also for trained scientists. The goal of the Ore Deposits Research Section is to supply the future mineral industries with both.

THE MINERAL CONSERVATION SECTION

The Mineral Conservation Section was established in 1956 as a subdivision of the Mineral Industries Experiment Station. Its principal objectives were to initiate, encourage, and assist investigations of the mineral resources of the state of Pennsylvania; to integrate the program of investigation with graduate education wherever such integration appears to be mutually advantageous; to promote cooperation between faculty members of different departments and cooperation with branches of government in attacking mineral resources problems; and to collect, interpret, and disseminate available information and the results of research.

MacKenzie L. Keith, of the Department of Geochemistry and Mineralogy, served as director of the Mineral Conservation Section from 1956 to 1978 (Keith, 1963). In 1978 Arthur Rose was appointed director, serving until 1984, when the functions of the Section were assumed by the departments. Over the years many faculty were associated with the Section, and a significant percentage of their time was devoted to Section research activities, the balance being given to teaching and other academic responsibilities.

In his article in the June 1963 issue of *Mineral Industries,* Dr. Keith stated the objectives of the Mineral Conservation Section: "The primary objectives of a university are to contribute to knowledge and to produce graduates who are educated in a sense which includes, in proper proportion, an appreciation of the great ideas of the past and of the present frontiers of knowledge. In many fields, including science and engineering, there is an additional objective, namely, to provide the fundamentals of professional training. There is no common agreement as to the relative emphasis which should be placed on these several objectives, but experience has shown that graduate students gain inspiration, initiative, and self-confidence, as well as professional training, by participating in an active research project."

Research was supported in two different ways. In one procedure the Mineral Conservation Section provided funds to support investigations proposed by faculty members in any of the departments of the College. A second procedure involved programs of continuing research and long-range surveys carried out by staff members whose appointments and primary responsibilities were directly associated with the Section.

The long-range projects were those considered critical to Pennsylvania. As an example, in 1961 the Section initiated work in groundwater geology at Penn State under the supervision of Richard Parizek. Not only was research developed, but courses in groundwater geology were introduced. Funds were also provided for geochemical prospecting and for the initiation of operations research in mining. These and other fields were recognized as important in their future impact on the educational programs of the College.

Research proposals of individual faculty members were reviewed annually by the Mineral Conservation Committee and funds were assigned on the basis of their relevance and probable contribution to mineral resource development and knowledge. Requests for renewal of support were considered each year, but they had to compete with all other proposals submitted. This selection procedure was regarded as necessary for keeping the program flexible and for providing funds for developing new ideas. It was also considered an important source of "seed money" for basic research and for testing new methods of investigation, as well as a source of support for more direct kinds of investigation for which immediate practical results could be anticipated.

One function of the Mineral Conservation Section was to promote collaboration and consultation among faculty members in different departments with interests related to mineral resources. Collaboration proved fruitful in providing solutions to interdisciplinary problems. The Section also contributed to graduate education by providing graduate students with funds and facilities.

When the Mineral Conservation Section was established in the College of Mineral Industries, there was some concern that its activities would duplicate some of the activities of the State Geological Survey. That concern proved to be inaccurate. The Section and Survey projects generally were supplementary, and cooperative work was undertaken in several fields.

TYPES OF INVESTIGATIONS

A variety of technical investigations were completed under the supervision of the various staff members of the College. Many of the research studies resulted in M.S. or Ph.D. theses, in addition to published reports. The investigations were published not only in the *Mineral Conservation*

Bulletin issued by the Mineral Industries Experiment Station, but also in such professional journals as *Economic Geology,* the *Journal of the American Ceramic Society, The Annals of the Association of American Geographers, Mining Congress Journals,* the *Journal of Sedimentary Petrology,* and the *Journal of Paleontology.*

Two comprehensive statistical studies were prepared by John J. Schanz. The first—"Historical Studies of Pennsylvania's Mineral Industries, 1759–1955"—provided the first comprehensive view of the development of mineral industries in the state. The second volume, providing statistics from 1956 to 1960, was a continuation of the first. A major contribution was a coal atlas in two volumes, one on the bituminous fields (1959), the other on the anthracite fields (1963), prepared by George F. Deasy and Phyllis R. Griess. These two authors published more than half a dozen studies describing and analyzing the coal industry of Pennsylvania. A series of papers—including papers on limestones and dolomites by Frank M. Swartz and Richard R. Thompson, on an iron-bearing sandstone bed by Frank Swartz and H. J. Hambleton, and on the distribution of sand and gravel in a stream floodplain by A. A. Adler and Laurence H. Lattman—are examples of research by faculty and students from the geosciences. While the general distribution of nonmetallic minerals was known, much remained to be done on detailed stratigraphy and chemical analysis. For example, as a result of research on limestone deposits, millions of tons were added to the reserves of high-calcium limestone, and detailed information was obtained on the extent and chemical variability of limestone sequences in central Pennsylvania.

A number of studies on high-temperature reactions of clay mineral mixture and on quantitative determination of the clay content by x-ray diffraction were carried out by George W. Brindley and his co-workers in ceramic science. These studies of prepared clay mineral mixtures provided a foundation for understanding and predicting the properties of natural clays. It was demonstrated that mineral proportions and physical properties control the firing behavior and the phases developed at low temperature, but that the bulk chemical composition becomes the predominant controlling factor at higher temperatures.

Many types of geological studies were sponsored by the Mineral Conservation Section, including stratigraphic studies by Eugene G. Williams, Richard P. Nickelsen, and J. C. Ferm on a continuing basis. These studies were fundamental to the economic development of coal, clay, limestone, and other bedded deposits because they provided detailed information on the recognition and correlation of particular beds in one area with those of another area.

The regional folding and fracturing of the rocks was also studied by Dr. Williams and others, and the investigations of Dr. Lattman and Dr. Nickelsen demonstrated that some of the regional fracture patterns could be seen and mapped on aerial photographs. It was shown that fracture mapping could assist in locating oil and gas structures and proved to be one of the best methods for locating productive water wells in limestone formations. Since the 1960s, new wells for the University have been located by this method.

Research for the development of improved methods of stratigraphic and geologic mapping was also supported. In many rock sequences, fossils are scarce or absent and it is difficult to differentiate between rocks formed in the ocean and those formed on the continents of past times. The work of E. T. Degens, Eugene Williams, and M. L. Keith showed that trace elements and isotope ratios provide a means of recognizing marine and freshwater sedimentary rocks and mapping the extent and the shorelines of the ancient seas.

The Section supported some of the earliest studies of sulfur in coal. Dr. Williams and Dr. Keith found that sulfur in coal was related to the marine or freshwater character of the overlying roof beds. It was also shown that these studies provided a useful key to the regional distribution of refractory and plastic clays and to areas of possible oil and gas reservoirs.

Besides stratigraphic and geologic mapping techniques developed for prospecting, the Section supported work on direct search procedures, including the use of electrical measurements in the search for clay and limonite deposits by G. W. Gross and E. James Moore of Geosciences. Various geophysical tests were conducted by Christopher Crowe and co-workers in the search for iron ores of the Cornwall type.

As another example of exploratory techniques supported by the Section, Eugene Williams and John Griffiths developed an effective method for prospecting for high-alumina refractory clays, which occur in the Mercer beds of the Pennsylvanian formation. The problem here was that the clay weathered to a soil aggregate and did not develop recognizable outcrops. Dr. Williams discovered that an associated sandstone that did crop out in ledges on the hillsides was recognizably different in clay areas and in nonclay areas. A single measurement of the shape and roundness of separate sand grains was found to indicate areas in which an overlying bed of refractory clay was likely to be present.

The Mineral Conservation Section supported a number of projects in mining methods. Among the early projects were those in angle drilling, blasting, and open-pit mining machinery by Boris J. Kochanowsky. There were also studies of hydraulic fill materials by Howard L. Hartman and D. L. Mickle. And Charles B. Manula and Howard Hartman made major contributions in operations research methods, which improved efficiency resulting in cost reduction in mining.

A number of investigations to improve the grade of mineral raw materials were sponsored by the Section. These include the separation of iron oxide from ferruginous sandstone by Harold L. Lovell and J. W. Leonard, and the extraction of china clay from impure white clays by S. C. Sun. Working with H. Beecher Charmbury, F. J. Lerznar investigated the beneficiation and reduction of low-grade iron ores, and Harold Read, of the Department of Metallurgy, completed a study of the electrolytic production of manganese from low-grade manganese ores.

Under this category of studies, John J. Schanz and W. G. Jaworek of the Department of Mineral Economics, and George Deasy and Phyllis Griess of the Department of Geography, published studies on coal consumption, changeability of fuels, fuels used in power plants, and the competitive capabilities of Pennsylvania's electric generating plants.

MAJOR SCIENTIFIC ADVANCES

The scientists supported by the Mineral Conservation Section have made major scientific contributions. These include:

1. Development of the fracture trace method of prospecting for groundwater (Richard Parizek and Laurence Lattman). This technique, using aerial photographs, greatly increases the percentage of high-yield water wells and has many other applications to flow of water and pollutants and underground excavation in the crust of the earth.

2. Development of the "living filter" concept for disposal of municipal wastewater and sludges into fields (Parizek and co-workers in agronomy). The Environmental Protection Agency now mandates the use of this technique where tertiary wastewater treatment plants are being designed.

3. Demonstration of the degree and control of pollution from sanitary landfills in humid regions by the use of plastic liners to control seepage (Parizek and graduate students). These concepts are now widely used in the design of landfills.

4. Development of methods for the control of acid mine drainage by dewatering and by covering spoil banks with limestone (Parizek and students). Some of these methods are now used by the mining industry.

5. Development of thermal methods of prospecting for groundwater by using infrared remote sensing methods (Parizek and students). It has been proven that this method has extensive applications in glacial outwork and karst aquifers where groundwater approaches the surface.

6. Demonstration of the importance of small amounts of carbonate in overburden of coal seams as a major control of acid mine drainage (Parizek, Williams, and students). This concept is now being used in regulation of strip-mining of coal.

7. Demonstration of isotopic analysis of carbonates and the elements (boron, gallium, and rubidium) that can be used to determine the marine vs. nonmarine origin of shales and limestone (Williams and Keith). This approach has wide applications in predicting the presence and quality of coal, oil, clays, uranium, and other minerals in sedimentary rocks.

8. Studies revealed that regional variations in the sulfur content of coal are related to ancient topography and the distribution of marine and nonmarine deposits and can be predicted from reconnaissance geologic observations of the rocks enclosing the coal (Williams and Keith).

9. Demonstration that the location of deposits of high-alumina clay, bloating clay, loddle-brick clay, and other special-purpose clays was controlled by disconformities in deposition of the enclosing sediments (Williams and students). This information is used to find additional deposits with a minimum of effort.

10. Developed hydraulic equivalent concepts to determine whether sandstones were deposited by water or by wind and whether the transport was by turbulent or laminar flow (Williams, Slingerland, and students). This method has been applied to placer gold deposits, to demonstrate a windblown contribution to soils, and in many other applications worldwide.

11. Development of accurate methods for determining the direction of currents that deposited ancient sandstones (Williams and Slingerland). The way sandstones were deposited provides an important key to exploration for petroleum, uranium, and other deposits in sedimentary rocks.

12. The discovery that coal-bearing sediments in western Pennsylvania were deposited in deltas (Williams and Ferm).

13. Application of statistical regression techniques to remove the effects of geological variables in trace element control of stream sediments, so that weak anomalies from ore deposits can be clearly recognized (Rose, Keith, and students). This method is widely used in mineral exploration.

14. Development of techniques for separating and determining the amount of trace elements in clay, iron oxide, organic matter and other components of soils, stream sediment, and similar materials (Rose). These methods have been used in mineral exploration and pollution studies.

15. Demonstration that important amounts of mercury are being incorporated from the atmosphere into surface soils (Rose and students).

16. Recognition that copper is highly soluble in chloride solutions at room temperature and that important copper deposits around the world occur in association with salt deposits and other sources of chloride (Rose). This association is being used in evaluating the regional favorability for copper deposits.

17. Demonstration of radon in groundwater was an effective method of detecting uranium deposits (Rose and students). This method is now in extensive use in industry and government surveys.

18. Demonstration that uranium prospects in eastern Pennsylvania are similar to major deposits in Wyoming and that similar criteria can be used when searching for them (Rose and students).

19. Development of isotopic methods for determining the source of carbon (atmosphere, soil, organic matter, limestone) in groundwater (Deines and Langmuir). This method has greatly improved understanding of the chemistry and flow paths of groundwater.

20. Demonstration of the effects of pH, oxide state, and especially crystallinity of soluble iron oxides in groundwater, acid mine drainage, landfills, and other near-surface environments (Langmuir and students). This experiment has allowed a much-improved prediction of the behavior of iron in a wide variety of environments.

21. Demonstration that solubility and ion exchange concepts explain the concentration of both major and trace components in groundwater, and the application of these techniques to developing optimum quality of groundwater and minimizing pollution (Langmuir and students).

22. Discovery and delineation of a new commercially important belt of high-calcium limestone in southern Pennsylvania (Swartz and students). This limestone is being used in iron-making.

23. Development of knowledge about the chemistry and mineralogy of portland cement, allowing the design of improved high-strength hydraulic cements (Della Roy).

THE MATERIALS CHARACTERIZATION LABORATORY

The Mineral Constitution Laboratories, as the present Materials Characterization Laboratory was previously known, were organized by Thomas F. Bates and Elburt F. Osborn in 1952 (Bates, 1952). As Dr. Bates put it, "There is a direct link between . . . instruction and fundamental research on the constitution of matter. It is apparent that the expensive tools of the laboratories and the information they yield should be equally available to all. For this reason these instruments have been placed together in one area. The centralization of the laboratories prevents duplication of personnel and equipment and promotes safety, efficiency and economy." Dr. Bates went on to say: "The function of each laboratory is threefold. The main purpose is to provide instruction. The second function of the laboratories is to carry on research, the continuous accumulation of data and standards, [and] active technique research directed toward the improvement of instrumentation, sample preparation and interpretation and availability of results. . . . The third function of the laboratories is service. By this is meant the routine rapid and accurate qualitative evaluation of samples."

On the whole, the philosophy and structure of the laboratories in the last forty years has not changed, but there has been a shift in emphasis. In 1952 the laboratories were in a School of Mineral Industries, and the emphasis was on mining and minerals. Since then, however, a strong Materials Science and Engineering Department has emerged, and the emphasis has shifted from the geological toward materials, such as ceramics, metals, and polymers. This shift in emphasis has brought about the acquisition of instrumentation needed in materials research. Thus, in the last decade instruments such as a secondary ion mass spectrometer (SIMS), a scanning electron microscope (SEM), a scanning transmission electron microscope (STEM), and Fourier transform infrared spectrophotometers (FTIS) have been acquired.

From a modest beginning, when the laboratories consisted of two electron microscopes, an electron diffraction unit, five x-ray diffraction machines, two emission spectrographs, an infrared absorption spectrograph, and a spectrophotometer, the laboratories have grown appreciably. The major equipment and facilities are listed in Table 6. In order to reflect the changes which have occurred in the type of research and service performed, the name of the laboratories was changed in 1989 to the Materials Characterization Laboratory.

Table 6.   Equipment and Facilities Available in the Materials Characterization Laboratory

Atomic Absorption Spectrophotometry
Perkin-Elmer Models 3030B and 703. The 3030B is equipped with an HGA 500 graphite furnace and automatic sampling. An array of HCLs and EDLs are available, as well as a hydride generator.

Electron Microprobe
Etec Autoprobe, Model SA-3, equipped with a Kevex energy dispersive spectrometer, automated data acquisition, vistascan, high-speed reader terminal, and computer.

Scanning Electron Microscope (SEM)
International Scientific Instruments (ISI) SX-40 and SX-40A. Kevex energy dispersive spectrometers.

Scanning Transmission Electron Microscope (STEM)
Philips EM420T, fully equipped with Link energy dispersive spectrometer.

Secondary Ion Mass Spectrometer (SIMS)
Cameca IMS 3F for surface analyses. Can perform chemical and isotopic analyses of small areas, in-depth profiling, and ion microscopy.

Emission Spectroscopy
Jarrell-Ash Wadsworth Spectrograph with usual auxiliary equipment. Also a Spectrometrics Spectraspan III d.c. plasma emission spectrometer completely updated with Spectra Hardware computerized data acquisition system.

Infrared and Raman Spectrometry
Perkin-Elmer 283B infrared spectrometer covering the 4,000–200 cm^1 – range. Digilab, Fourier Transform Infrared, and Ramanor HG-24 Raman Spectrometer.

Spectrophotometry
Perkin-Elmer Lambda 9 for UV-visible-near IR (185–3,200nm) with integrating sphere and absolute specular reflectance accessory.

X-ray Diffraction
Two Rigaku units for powder x-ray diffraction analysis. One unit is automated.

X-ray Fluorescence
Philips PW1480 sequential microprocessor controlled x-ray spectrometer, Rh-target source for qualitative and quantitative analysis.

Carbon, Hydrogen, Nitrogen Determinators
LECO CHN-600 for determination of C, H, and N in various samples.

CO_2 Coulometer
Coulometrics Inc. apparatus for total, organic, and carbonate carbon determinations.

"Proximate" Coal
Fisher model 490 for the determination of moisture, ash content, volatile matter, and fixed carbon in coals.

Chemistry Laboratory
Primarily devoted to inorganic analyses of various types. Emphasis is on nonroutine determinations, solution techniques, and separations. Standards are also prepared for the different instrumental techniques.

Robert Schmalz in his office talking with a geology student.

Adam field ion microscope, Howard Pickering Laboratory in Metallurgy.

Students at work in outdoor and indoor laboratories of the College.

PART TWO | PROGRAMS OF THE COLLEGE

Student awards presented at the College of Earth and Mineral Sciences student-faculty awards dinner each spring are supported by endowed funds established by college benefactors or made possible by annual gifts. Recipients of the 1982 awards are shown here with Dr. C. L. Hosler, left, dean of the College, and Dr. John Cahir, right, associate dean for resident instruction. *Back row, left to right:* Kevin Crupi, Jerome N. Behrmann Award to outstanding seniors in meteorology; Keith R. Elwood, E. Willard Miller Award to a geography graduate student; Paul Heppner, Behrmann Award; John W. Zwick, third place in William Grundy Haven Memorial Award student paper competition; Barry Mikucki, Robert Lindsay Award in metallurgy; Michael Weber, Arthur P. Honess Award in geosciences and Ellen Steidle Achievement Award. *Front row, left to right:* Dennis Dunham, first place in Haven Award competition; Richard Eckman, Behrmann Award; Mary Lew Kehm, Miller Award to a geography undergraduate; Bernard R. Serina, second place in Haven Award competition; Joseph Sychterz, Lindsay Award. Not present for the photo were Daniel Armbrust, George W. Brindley Award for undergraduate excellence in crystal chemistry; and Daniel J. Skrovanek, DuPont Award to the outstanding junior in polymer science.

Chapter 5 | The Department of Geography

In the development of the first agricultural program of The Pennsylvania State University the study of geography was recognized as an important subject. This reflects a tradition that has evolved over centuries that an "awareness of place" is important in human endeavors. The study of physical geography provided practical information for agricultural students. In order to provide this needed knowledge about the earth, the first catalog in 1859 offered a course called "Geography and Meteorology." The course description read: "Embracing the general principles and the special application to agriculture, involving questions of the influence of temperature, rainfall and the general outline of the earth upon the production power of the soil for different vegetable substances."

At this early time it was known that physical patterns varied from place to place and that an understanding of these areal variations was essential to the agricultural development of the state. In 1860 the title of the course was changed to "Physical Geography" and remained a required course in the scientific and agricultural program until the late 1870s. During these early years geographic training was also required for admission to what was then known as the Pennsylvania State College.

Although the practical aspects of geography dominated the course offerings during these early years, it was also recognized that geography was an ancient discipline that had flourished during the height of Greek civilization. As a result, the study of ancient geography, focusing on how Greek philosophers and others viewed the world, was considered an appropriate focus for nineteenth-century college training. From time to time a course embracing these ideas appeared in the catalog. This course was taught by a faculty member, usually in philosophy or history, who had an interest in the ancient world.

Administration
Geography

In Charge

Raymond E. Murphy	1931–1945

Division of Geography

E. Willard Miller	1945–1954

Department of Geography

E. Willard Miller	1954–1963
Allan L. Rodgers	1963–1970
Wilbur Zelinsky	1970–1976
Ronald F. Abler	1976–1982
C. Gregory Knight	1982–1989
Ronald F. Abler	1989
Rodney A. Erickson	1990–

Little, if any, geography was taught at Penn State between 1880 and 1917, when the subject was reestablished in the School of Mines. The first two courses in geography's revival were entitled "Physical and Commercial Geography" and "Geography of Mineral Resources."

The importance of geography as a subject was recognized by Deans Elwood S. Moore and Elmer A. Holbrook, who taught geography on a regular basis. Throughout the 1920s Geography of Mineral Resources was a required course in the freshman year for students in the School of Mines and Metallurgy. Other geography courses were Physiography, introduced in 1922, and Geography of North America, coming in 1926. Both were taught by C. W. Robinson, associate professor of geology. During the summer session, geography courses were available for teachers in Pennsylvania's public schools.

The geography courses of this period were primarily descriptive in nature. Their major goal was to impart information, and they did not have any distinctive disciplinary philosophy. Consequently, the instructors required little or no formal training in a geographic approach to knowledge.

ESTABLISHMENT OF THE DISCIPLINE

During Dean Edward Steidle's restructuring of the School of Mineral Industries he wrote: "Since the study of geography, with its emphasis upon correlations and interrelationships between the physical and cultural aspects of the world, is the intellectual bridge or catalyst between technical earth studies and human institutions, it becomes imperative that continued advancements be made both in the field of geographic research and in the field of mass dissemination of geographic knowledge through our institutions of higher learning."

Dean Steidle was well aware that geographic patterns are constantly changing and that these changes could affect every aspect of society:

> Examples of the ways in which technological progress might conceivably remake the geography of the world by the year 2000, and rend asunder existing patterns of human institutions, are fantastic in their potentialities. It is well within the range of possibility that the end of the century will witness not the evolution of an "atomic age" but instead the full-blown blossoming of a "solar age" in which energy derived from the sun will be the overwhelmingly dominant source of industrial power. The human implications of such a development will be cataclysmic and will radiate through every facet of every individual's life. The seat of world power will shift from the present coal-rich, middle-latitude nations, like the United States and the Soviet Union, to sun-rich tropical lands. Industrial pygmies, such as the Sahara and Australian deserts, may well evolve into the gigantic workshops of a nearby tomorrow. . . .
>
> It behooves the educational and political leaders of our nation to ponder long and well the possibilities of economic, social, and political repercussions to its technological advances, and to engage the most competent personnel available to analyze and predict the effects upon the future geography of the world of probable advancements in the physical sciences, so that this country may foresee and plan for such contingencies long in advance of possible adversaries dedicated to a way of life inimicable to the democratic tradition. Furthermore, instruction of the masses of the people, in both the present and possible future geography of the world, is essential in order to obtain an intellectually alert and receptive citizenry who will understand and support social, industrial, and political policies that will enable our nations, our way of life, and our very people themselves to exist and thrive in a rapidly changing world. (Steidle, 1952)

In order to provide geographic instruction on a permanent basis, Raymond E. Murphy was appointed assistant professor of economic geography in the fall of 1931 in the Department of Geology, Mineralogy, and Geography. Dr. Murphy thus became the first professionally trained geographer to serve on the faculty at Penn State. In the fall of 1932 a regular program of college geography was offered for the first time (Murphy, 1932). The first courses given were Geography of the World, North America, Europe, South America, and Pennsylvania; Geography of Mineral Resources; Principles of Geography; Geography Laboratory; Climatology; Physiography; and Physiography of the United States. C. W. Robinson continued to teach physiography, but Dr. Murphy was responsible for all other geography courses. A normal teaching load was four three-credit courses per semester.

A major in geography was not yet developed, and geography courses were elected by students desiring a geographic perspective. During the 1930s, the world geography course attracted a large number of students seeking an elective course. By 1935 a minor and major in geography were established for education students under the science requirements in the School of Education. It was a weak program, requiring only four courses in geography. Although not a single geography course was listed as elective or required in the physical or social science program for teachers in the School of Education, many education students took geography courses as a general subject.

The program in geography grew during the 1930s, and in 1937 a second geographer, John R. Randall, was hired. Dr. Randall taught the geography of North America, Latin America, and

Raymond E. Murphy teaching a geography class in 1933.

Europe, and regional climatology, as well as the lower-level courses but in 1940 he resigned to take a position in geography at Ohio State. He was replaced by Henry Bruman, a specialist in Latin America. Dr. Bruman remained at Penn State for four years, leaving in 1944 to take a position in the Department of Geography at the University of California at Los Angeles.

In 1937 a master of education degree program in geography was approved. The program was offered to public school teachers during the summer session, and the first M.Ed. degree in geography was granted in 1939.

In the World War II years, geography was a required course in the Arms Specialized Training Program (ASTP). In order to provide instruction for the hundreds of students in this program, geography was taught by many nongeographers. During this period, Phyllis R. Griess, a secretary to the dean of the graduate school but also a trained geographer with a master of arts from Wellesley College, entered the department and remained a faculty member until she retired in 1966. Hugh Spittal, a geographer who had acquired a master of education degree, was also hired to teach in the ASTP program, but in 1946 he resigned to take a position at the U.S. Army Map Service.

The course offerings in geography were expanded during the 1930s and 1940s, so that by 1944 the catalog listed eleven lower-level and eleven upper-level and graduate courses, and three courses at the graduate level only. Besides the regional courses, the program included such topical courses as Political and Cultural Geography, and Regional Climatology, and such methodology courses as Navigational Aids, Cartography, and Field Methods in Geography. These courses were elected by students in teacher training programs and as general education courses. During World War II a special course for one credit, Geography of the War Zones, was offered by Phyllis Griess. This course attracted hundred of students each semester, for it discussed the geography of the areas of immediate interest in the then-current world conflict.

EARLY RESEARCH ENDEAVORS

A research program that has been a continuous integral part of the geography program was initiated by Raymond Murphy as soon as he arrived at Penn State. In the December 1933 issue of *Mineral Industries* he outlined a program for the study of the geography of Pennsylvania: "Pennsylvania, until now, has remained a frontier insofar as geographic field work is concerned. With one or two minor exceptions, neither state-supported nor private work has been done on the geography of Pennsylvania. . . . No exact detailed and quantitative information is available. For some time the geography division of the School of Mineral Industries has been planning a series of field surveys which, when carried out, will make available a complete and accurate picture of the geography of Pennsylvania."

The initial step in this project was to determine the important geographic regions of the state. By December 1933 Dr. Murphy had tentatively defined the regions. The next step was to describe and analyze the geography of each region. Dr. Murphy stated: "The reports resulting from the geographic survey of a region or subregion will cover such topics as the following: the natural environment of the area; the distribution of population throughout the area; population trends; the principal economic activities together with their geographical bases and trends; other adjustments which people have made to the natural environment in the area; undeveloped resources and industries for which these resources might form a basis."

The geographic survey of the state culminated in publication by Dr. Murphy and his wife, Marion Murphy, of the regional *Geography of Pennsylvania* in 1937. The approach taken by this book was copied by authors of most state geographies in the next thirty years. The text remains of historical value today for the information it provides on the state for the 1930s period.

As a response to the intensive field studies of Pennsylvania, Dr. Murphy concentrated his work on a number of urban areas, and therefore became one of the pioneer geographers in the study of urban centers. Two of his articles, "The Geography of Johnstown, Pennsylvania: An Industrial Center" (Murphy, 1934) and "Johnstown and York: A Comparative Study of Two Industrial Cities" (Murphy, 1935), are considered classics from the 1930s. The detailed analysis of land utilization presented a new approach to the study of urban areas.

Studies of minerals were also important research endeavors. For example, in 1938 Dr. Murphy wrote an article published in *Economic Geography* entitled "The Anthracite Region of Pennsylvania," describing the spatial pattern of anthracite mining, analyzing the decline of the industry, and discussing the region's prospects for the future.

GEOGRAPHY PROGRAM ESTABLISHED

In the 1930s and early 1940s, the geography program was part of the curriculum of the earth sciences along with geology, geophysics, and meteorology. While it was possible to secure a major in geography within the geology program, no students elected to do so. With the reorganization of the School of Mineral Industries in 1945, geography became a separate program offering B.S., M.S., and Ph.D. degrees. E. Willard Miller became the first chief of the Division of Geography in

E. Willard Miller and Ruby M. Miller studying volcanism at the Parícutin volcano, Morelia, when it was erupting in 1949.

the Earth Sciences Department. He held this position until 1954, when a Department of Geography was established, and then he continued on as head of the department until 1963.

When the Division of Geography was established the program had two major objectives (Miller, 1952). The first was to train professional geographers to meet the needs of the period. These demands came from three areas of work. First, the demand for geographers in the federal government continued after World War II, not only in the military but in such civilian agencies as the Soil Conservation Service, the Weather Bureau, the Library of Congress, the Department of State, and others. There was also a growing demand for geographers in the business, commercial, and industrial world. Airlines, railroads, heavy and light industry, book and magazine publishers, and foreign trade companies employed geographers. Finally, there was a growing demand for instruction in geography at the collegiate and secondary levels. Geography programs were expanding rapidly in colleges and universities across the nation.

The second major objective of the Division was to provide a wide range of service courses for students at Penn State. As Dr. Miller wrote in a November 1952 *Mineral Industries* article: "Never in the history of the World has there been a greater need for an understanding of the ways in which different peoples live. Modern communications and transportation have made it possible for all people to be in close proximity. Getting to know one's neighbors, however, is a difficult and strenuous task which takes a great deal of time and much mental effort. At present much of the information of the average citizen on world relations is superficial and frequently based on false impressions. We need to spend more time in giving the average citizen sufficient information to discuss present-day world problems intelligently. So let us be assured of this, that the Russian question, the natural resources question, the South African race question, will never be solved until *all* people know a lot more about such basic matters."

FACULTY DEVELOPMENT

Research and teaching by the faculty have evolved over the years as the discipline has developed. Initially, the faculty was small and little known in the profession. After the establishment of the degree programs in 1945, faculty research concentrated in the branches of economic geography, although teaching responsibilities were much wider. The research emphasis on economic geography developed a critical mass of publications in this single area. Only by this means could a national and international reputation be developed.

In 1945–46 the only faculty member with a professional rank was E. Willard Miller. In the late 1940s and 1950s he carried out a research program in the fields of minerals and manufacturing. These early endeavors culminated in the first book published in the United States in the field, *The Geography of Manufacturing* (1962). This book used both a topical and a regional approach to the study of manufacturing. The factors of localization and causal relationships that influenced the locational patterns were emphasized.

After World War II, Phyllis Griess continued on as a faculty member, receiving her Ph.D. from Penn State in 1949, the first doctorate granted in geography. She was particularly interested in the world flow of commodities and how this flow affected the economy of the Third World nations.

A growing student enrollment brought the first opportunity to build the program in 1947, when George F. Deasy joined the program. Dr. Deasy was an economic geographer with an emphasis on agricultural and mineral problems. He taught a course on physical geography that had as many as 250 students a semester. Dr. Deasy also taught cartography and developed one of the first aerial photography courses given in the United States. A number of his papers analyzed the problems of the bituminous coal and anthracite industries of Pennsylvania. In 1957 he, along with Dr. Miller and Dr. Griess, wrote *The World's Nations: An Economic and Regional Geography.*

Allan Rodgers was the fourth economic geographer to join the staff. His teaching and research focused on economic development with a regional concentration on Italy and the Soviet Union. Dr. Rodgers states: "My general philosophy is that research and teaching complement each other. I believe that one cannot become a good teacher without extensive field and library research." Because his work required field investigation, he carried out fieldwork in Italy and the Soviet Union. One of his major studies evaluated the commodity flow, research potential, and regional economic development of the Soviet Far East as a response to the construction of the Baykal-Amur Railroad. His interests in economic development led to the publication in 1979 of *Economic Development in Retrospect: The Italian Model and Its Significance for Regional Planning in Market Oriented Economies.*

Frederick L. Wernstedt, whose teaching and research interests were Southeast Asia, regional climatology, and economic geography, joined the faculty in 1953. His field experience in Southeast Asia led to such publications as *The Philippine Island World: A Physical, Cultural, and Regional Geography* (1967, with Joseph Spencer of the University of California at Los Angeles) and *Philippine Migration: The Settlement of the Digos-Padada Valley* (1971, with Paul Simkins). In the 1970s and 1980s one of his major efforts was devoted to advising and counseling undergraduate students. Dr. Wernstedt is also known worldwide for his compilation of climatic data.

These five faculty members formed the core of the department for many years. They were aided by one or two junior faculty members—Frank Seawall, Roger Heppell, and Mark Chesnutwood—who were instructors working toward Ph.D.'s. Teaching and research were given equal priority. The faculty were particularly prolific in developing research in the 1950s as a foundation for a strong graduate program. As a consequence, each year seven to ten professional articles appeared in such leading geographic journals as *Economic Geography, Geographical Review, Professional Geographer,* and the *Journal of Geography.* At every national and regional meeting the faculty presented professional papers. During the 1950s a national recognition was achieved. In the peer evaluation of graduate geography programs in the Roose-Anderson report of 1962, the department was ranked eleventh in the nation. A solid foundation of professional attainment had been achieved in a very short period of time.

By the late 1950s the undergraduate and graduate program and service load had grown enough that the faculty needed to be increased. Although Penn State had gained national recognition for its work in economic geography, major changes in the field of geography which required a change in the philosophy of faculty recruitment were occurring. The topical specialties in human geography were becoming increasingly important, and methodological courses utilizing quantitative techniques were becoming essential for a well-rounded research and teaching department.

In 1958 Peirce Lewis joined the faculty. His focus has been "the American scene," and his fundamental goal is to teach students how to interpret landscapes and to understand how the basic framework of vernacular landscapes came to be through these evolutionary processes since colonial times. In two studies, "The Unprecedented City" (1979) and "The Galactic Metropolis" (1983), he argued that Americans have been creating an urban morphology that is unique on the face of the earth. The new morphology is "galactic"—that is, composed of bits and pieces that in preautomation times were necessarily concentrated around a nuclear downtown. But no more— residential, commercial, industrial, and recreational functions now float in space, held together by thin mutual attraction for people who travel in automobiles.

Arriving a year later in 1959, Paul Simkins began devoting much time to the study of changing patterns of population distribution and characteristics and the effect these changes have on human conditions. Of special interest to Dr. Simkins is how recent trends in residential preference and lifestyles have significantly altered traditional demographic patterns. A second interest focuses on how different developing countries have attempted to adjust their inherited systems of organization to cope with rapidly changing world conditions. Dr. Simkins pursues this field of study by analyzing the impact of the expansion of Europeans, and their ideas and institutions, on Third World cultures, with special emphasis on Latin America, where regional variations in the nature and intensity of change is especially marked.

Wilbur Zelinsky, coming to Penn State in 1963 as a "Red Star" professor, has spent his time thinking about, teaching, and carrying out research on the cultural, social, and population geography of North America. He says: "It has been exciting to be a member of the trailblazing generation to begin exploring the many unexplored facets of our continent's human geography, including such topics as the spatial aspects of religion, town morphology, house types, popular regions, free and slave Black populations, rural depopulation and repopulation, memberships in voluntary organizations, place names, and personal names." His 1973 book *The Cultural Geography of the United States* has become one of the classic studies in the discipline. In the demographic community he is best known for his 1970 study *The Hypothesis of the Mobility Transition*. A second major interest of his has been the ethical, social, and ecological responsibilities of the geographer.

E. Willard Miller on the banks of the Yukon River in 1950, where he was conducting environmental studies in Alaska for the U.S. Quartermaster Corps.

Peter Gould, who came to Penn State in 1963, has been closely involved with the development of quantitative methods in geography. He has worked closely with mathematics on an algebraic topological "language of structure," a methodological perspective that challenges the transfer of rather constrained mathematical structures from the physical to the human sciences. Traditional mathematics describes the physical world adequately at classical scales, but it may be much too limited to describe the structural complexity of the human world. Dr. Gould conducts joint studies with colleagues in physical education, archaeology, and mathematics. In 1987 he became the first Evan Pugh Professor of Geography, the highest academic distinction the University can bestow on a faculty member.

Peter Gould in the classroom.

Peter R. Gould
Evan Pugh Professor of Geography

You Mean I Get Paid Too?

Seeing where you came from is easier than knowing where you are going. Neither is easy to explain to others. The future brings surprises—answers to questions that were not asked—while the past has threads so tangled that they resist neat and orderly braiding. Any coherence in a professional life is imposed and apparent. A lot of it is luck, despite all the plans made. The best-laid schemes. . . . Gang aft a-gley, as Burns knew so well. As always, the poets are the truthsayers. Soothsaying is left to science. At least that is the claim the scientist makes for prediction.

Geographers are strange people, alternately bemusing and exasperating their academic colleagues by failing to fit neatly into one of the many specialized boxes that spun off from the core of philosophy during the last three hundred years. No one really chooses to be a geographer. You are either called or not. So I make no excuses; I had no other choice; it was not my fault. That I actually get paid for following my calling is an ever-renewed and still puzzling delight.

Many colleagues I know across the University feel the same. We are privileged: a *privus lex*, a private law, marks our lives. It also drives us. Of those who do not feel this I am suspicious. So, quite rightly, are the students. Whether a teaching style is sober or histrionic, students know whether a teacher takes delight in a calling that is a compelling privilege.

A calling? All very well for priests and poets, but what about geographers? Or material scientists? Or meteorologists? Or geochemists? Or any of those who form the rich intellectual fabric of the College? Very well, if you discard the notion of a calling, explain to me why a fourteen-year-old boy, birdwatching on the cliffs of South Devon, decided to become a geographer. There were, of course, many who helped on the way. A devoted schoolteacher who shared such a fascination for the beauty of classical physics that it remains an amateur delight to this day. A grandfather who had the rhythms of English poetry so much a part of his being that he could pass his joy on to another. A professor of philosophy who opened up the questions that are posed again and again over the two-and-a-half millennia of our Western heritage. A geographer who let me go my own way when I was numbed by the sad banality that formed part of graduate work thirty years ago. And colleagues here at Penn State and around the world who gave more than they ever realized.

Privileged? Spoilt rotten more likely.

The first path taken was methodological—a path toward a path (*hodos*) toward (*meta*) knowledge (*logos*). Even now there are no regrets: those who took the same path, and cleared away some of the underbrush, were given a joyful freedom to move in "problem space." The way was mathematical, often made practical by the soaring power of computation. But the mathematics had grown over centuries from the longing to describe with fidelity the physical world of things. It often did so with a beauty that was shattering, a beauty that brought tears to your eyes when you lay there thinking in the quiet of the night. But what happened when you mapped the human world, the world of the human geographer, onto those mathematical structures devised for celestial *mechanics*, statistical *mechanics*, continuum *mechanics*, quantum *mechanics* . . . ? Could the human world be anything but mechanical? Would the "language" employed allow it to be anything else? Was artificial intelligence all we had left, when we so desperately needed real intelligence? Was there a gentler, less tyrannical mathematics capable of describing the allowing, forbidding, but not requiring structures that make up the human world and its daily interaction with the world of physical things?

So it was back to the beginning again, back to mathematics and back to those who still wished to keep thinking open. If you had told me that I would spend sixteen weeks on forty-five pages considering a dozen words of a fragment of a Greek text I would have said you were mad. But Anaximander became the entry to thinking about the constitutive grounds of being human. Not a bad place for a "human scientist" to start. But the questions and texts are difficult. You need help— teachers, colleagues and students. Teachers and colleagues who *are* students. And in this university you can find them, and also in the words and thoughts of "best brothers"—an old Swedish mode of academic address—at other universities. It is a privileged world. We are privileged to learn, and privileged to use our learning to help others to learn. We even get paid for doing it.

Privileged?

Spoilt rotten.

Anthony V. Williams, associate professor of geography, giving instruction for the preparation of graphics on a computer.

In 1966 Anthony Williams added strength to the quantitative aspects of the departmental program with his work in computer mapping—the application of techniques for handling large-to-very-large geographic data bases. These areas have wide practical applications, as shown by his contact with the Los Alamos Scientific Laboratory, where he carried out studies to enhance their offshore oil-leasing data base. An interest in interaction computer mapping led to his development of a pilot system written in the computer language APL (A Programming Language). Dr. Williams spent a year in the Department of Geography of the University of the Cameroons, where he was influential in establishing a computer system. In addition to his expertise in computer mapping, he teaches political geography.

Ronald Abler came to Penn State in 1967 and has been conducting pioneering research on the interplay of interpersonal communication techniques (postal, telegraph, telephone, etc.) and other relationships to the changing locations of economic activities. His studies have provided a useful perspective on the role of technology in society. He has also been interested in the development of cartographic techniques to display spatial variations. As a result of these efforts, he designed and edited a comprehensive atlas of America's twenty largest metropolitan regions. The atlas provided an innovative comparative study by using standard sets of variables across metropolitan regions that documented and explained the similarities and differences among American cities. From 1984 to 1988 he served as director of the Geography and Regional Science Program at the National Science Foundation. A major accomplishment during his term there was to expand the program to include physical geography. In 1990 he became executive director of the Association of American Geographers.

Roger M. Downs, arriving at Penn State in 1970, has had a major commitment to understanding the use and origin of maps. He has a longtime interest in the development of cartographic understanding by children. He is also interested in the nature of human wayfinding, with attempts to understand the creative use of space, graphics, and visualizations, and he is considering procedures to develop spatial thinking. He makes geographic learning a distinctive approach not only in acquiring knowledge but also in applying it to problem-solving.

C. Gregory Knight, a member of the faculty since 1971, carries on research and teaching on the human use of the environment with an emphasis on African studies. He states: "The sustenance and survival of human society depends on its organization and use of natural resources. Each society brings to that challenge its own perceptions, technologies, and aspirations. My research interest has focused on how societies appraise and utilize resources, seeking frameworks with which to view human-environment interactions." In developing these concepts he utilizes the field of "ethnogeography," through which a society's knowledge and beliefs are described and analyzed. In addition, his work has extended to the industrialized world, still asking the question of how we best assess, manage, and use resources. Because his work straddles the nebulous boundary between human and physical geography, he has brought to his teaching of physical geography an emphasis on implications for human society of environmental processes. In 1989 Dr. Knight became dean of undergraduate instruction and vice provost.

In 1977 Rodney A. Erickson and Lakshman Yapa, both economic geographers, were added to the faculty. Dr. Erickson's teaching and research involve theories and empirical applications relating to the transmission of economic growth impulses both within and among regional economies; regional economic forecasting and impacts analysis; industrial location and location change using a product life-cycle and other theoretical frameworks drawn from economics and business administration; the evolution of geographic development patterns, particularly among economic activities in large metropolitan places; spatial patterns of economic welfare among minority groups in large cities; and the role of geography in international trade and business management.

About his teaching Dr. Erickson states: "I think that my greatest accomplishment has been to attract and interest a significant number of students from across the University and help them learn to 'read' the city around them, to develop the analytical concepts to make order out of the urban mosaic, and to be better informed about contemporary public policy discussions dealing with urban problems."

Besides his geographic interests, Dr. Erickson has made major contributions in the public service arena as director of the Center for Regional Business Analysis in the College of Business Administration. His research and ideas have been a part of state government policy-making on several occasions, and he has had the opportunity to advise and brief members of the state legislature, governors, and other senior administration officials. He has also worked closely with business and civic leaders across the state, and in the process demonstrated the value of the geographer's approach and analytical skills.

Lakshman Yapa's interests lie in the applications of quantitative geography and the economic development of the Third World. In quantitative geography he addresses the issues of areal sampling and the special problems of adapting bivariate multivariate techniques to geographical distributions. In his course on economic development he treats such aspects as underdevelopment as part of the historical process in a global system of international trade and commerce, the problems of transfer of technology from the developed world, and the role of appropriate technology in the production and provision of basic human necessities. The goal of his research is to demonstrate that countries of the humid tropics, where much poverty is present, contain a variety of resources that can provide the material and energy resources for the provision of basic goods. Dr. Yapa has carried out field research in many areas of the world, including Bolivia, Thailand, and Sri Lanka. From these experiences, he developed the use of microcomputers in regional planning. The concept was to develop a system of user-interaction programs so that Third World regional planners could use the computer without extensive prior training.

In the past the cartography program of the department was directed by Ronald Abler and Ronald Eyton (now at the University of Calgary). Alan M. MacEachren was appointed in 1984 to develop the cartography and remote-sensing program of the department. He is director of the George F. Deasy GeoGraphics Laboratory. In 1989 David DiBiase was appointed the first full-time cartographer in the laboratory.

Dr. MacEachren has primary interest in cartography and geographic information processing. This includes human cognitive processing of spatial information and related computer-processing associated with computer mapping and geographic information systems. In his teaching he utilizes a more conceptual-theoretical approach with an emphasis on map design and symbolization. His research has taken him into the study of historical applications of maps and the implications of the use of strip format maps. As a long-range project his research addresses the role of maps in spatial understanding. He is particularly interested in how people use maps in developing or altering regional images. A related project considers the more basic question of how maps convey geographic information.

With the development of the Earth System Science Center in the College, Brenton Yarnal and Robert Crane, both arriving at Penn State in 1984, became associated with this program. While maintaining strength in human geography in the department, the new Center provided the opportunity to strengthen physical geography. Dr. Knight states: "It seemed that there was a splendid opportunity to rebuild the department's role in the college by emphasizing a component of physical geography."

Dr. Yarnal has been developing an instructional and research program in climatology on a global scale. This includes the observation and dynamical theory of global teleconnections, especially El Nino/Southern Oscillation events, the relationships between the ocean-atmospheric system of the North Pacific and cyclonic distributions, relationships between the tropical atmospheric circulation and the deposition of snow in tropical mountains, and the methodological problems in the use of computers to evaluate climate patterns objectively.

Geography students study the raised relief map of central Pennsylvania in Walker Building.

Robert G. Crane has concentrated his work on the use of microwave remote-sensing for studies of polar sea ice and a problem associated with Arctic cloud cover. He has been particularly concerned with the analysis of ice melt using remotely sensed data and a comparison of satellite-observed Arctic cloud cover with the cloud generated by the Goddard Institute for Space Studies General Circulation Model. In his teaching he is concerned with image analysis classes, with an emphasis on satellite systems and environmental applications. He has introduced a new course on satellite climatology in connection with his work at the Earth System Science Center. This course concentrates on satellite applications to large-scale climate experiments.

In the 1980s the field of geographic information systems evolved, as a result of advancements in the computer areas. In order to be at the cutting edge of this new advancement, Donna J. Peuquet was welcomed to the faculty in 1985. Her pioneer work in geographic information systems is widely recognized in the geographic profession. Apart from her own research in artificial intelligence techniques and new methods of representing information that can be applied to remote-sensing and other geographic problems, she has had a major impact in the upgrading and reorganization of the computer and graphics facilities in the department's research program.

Upon the retirement of Wilbur Zelinsky in 1987, Deryck W. Holdsworth joined the faculty to continue work in human geography. Before coming to Penn State he had a distinguished career in Canada, where he made major contributions to the 1990 *Historical Atlas of Canada*. His research and teaching focus on the historical and cultural geography of North American cities, and he is particularly interested in the roles of social and economic forces in the production of the built environment. Frequently reflecting his experiences in Canada, his teaching greatly increases student awareness and appreciation of our important northern friend and neighbor.

The urban and social environments provide the laboratory for Glenda Laws' research. Coming to the department in 1989, she brought her particular focus on the impact that changes in social policies have on local communities and the ways local communities might influence those social-policy changes. But to understand the evolution of policies, attention must be given to the broader economic environment that constrains government action. Dr. Laws' research on such topics as deinstitutionalization in Canadian cities, homelessness in New York City, and women's employment patterns, and her educational background from Australia, bring to her teaching varied insights into the social geography of urban areas.

Diana Liverman, in collaboration with Penn State's faculty in the Earth System Science Center, studies the effects of drought and climatic changes on agriculture and water resources. She has conducted research on global warming, famine prevention, and technological hazards in the Americas and Africa. Focusing especially on Mexico, she seeks to understand how technology and political economy make agriculture and people vulnerable to environmental change and variability, as well as to study the relations among environmental issues, development, security, and international relations. New courses on physical geography, human environment relationships, and Latin America communicate her concern about the social causes of environmental changes and the interplay between environmental change and sustainable development.

Alan Taylor came to the department in 1990 with biogeography as a research and teaching focus. His primary research interests are the effects of natural and human disturbance on vegetation dynamics. This research theme has led to work in China, Rwanda, and the western United States. Recent research has included an applied wildlife conservation component, as the forests he studied were homes of the endangered giant panda, mountain gorilla, and spotted owl. Preservation of biological communities and wild landscapes are underlying concerns that generate research questions.

THE UNDERGRADUATE CURRICULUM

With the establishment of geography as a separate discipline in 1945, there were increased efforts to develop the undergraduate major. In the April 1946 issue of *Mineral Industries,* Dr. Miller stated:

> In any field of science, knowledge must be organized into systems, so that in attacking and solving problems the knowledge of facts, general concepts, and principles that bear on the problems are readily available. In geography, knowledge is organized into systems in two quite different ways—that of systematic geography and regional geography.
>
> The organization of geographic knowledge in terms of individual phenomena of areal differentiation is called systematic geography of which physical and human geography are the two main branches. Physical geography deals with the components of the natural landscape and such special branches as physiography, climatology, geography of soils, biogeography, and cartography are developed. The field of human geography deals with the cultural landscape and is divided into four main branches, each of which has several subdivisions. Of the four, economic geography is without doubt the most important and has such subdivisions as industrial geography, mineral geography, agricultural geography, and geography of transportation. Political geography considers also military geography and geopolitics. The geography of peoples includes urban geography, rural geography, and studies of population distribution, and the fourth major subdivision is cultural geography, which has as its specialties social and anthropo-geography. . . . It can be demonstrated by even a random observation of the literature that the greatest emphasis, either in systematic or regional geography, consists of a combination of physical and human geography.
>
> The integration of all or selected branches of systematic geography, focused on a particular place on the earth, is regional geography. Almost all geographers agree that the clearest view of geography is to be obtained in regional geography when the geographer observes, describes, and interprets the relationships between the natural environment and man's activities in a given area.
>
> At the present time, there are two dominant developments in geography that are complementary. The first is philosophical and scientific and calls for the intensive study of regions involving the recognition, mapping, classification, interpretation, and comparison of areas. The second is social and practical in character and grows out of an active interest in economic and social problems, such as the wise utilization of natural resources and land.
>
> In order to grasp and solve the many problems of the present-day world, the preparation of geographers calls for much greater accuracy and clearer thinking than in the past. A greater concentration on the exact sciences will introduce new types of measurement, will clarify present methods of interpretation, and will give us results quantitatively exact as well as qualitatively true. The interest of geographers must be directed more and more into the scientific aspects of the field in order to establish sound thinking.

In the initial planning of the undergraduate major it became evident that, although a wide variety of courses had been developed during the Murphy era, there were no courses in the field of economic geography, except mineral geography. Because economic geography had developed as the leading systematic field in the 1940s, this was a major deficiency, which literally prevented development of a modern curriculum: an agreement with the College of Liberal Arts prevented the establishment of courses in economic geography. Dr. Miller immediately protested to Dean Edward Steidle, indicating that the development of the new program had been stymied. Dean Steidle and Dr. Miller met with Dean Charles Stoddart of the College of Liberal Arts to resolve the problem. After less than an hour of discussion it was recognized that the Geography Department must have the responsibility of developing the field of economic geography. Initially, courses were established at the undergraduate level in economic geography, agricultural geography, and industrial geography, and at the graduate level an economic geography seminar and a research course were established.

The initial undergraduate curriculum in geography consisted of 37 credits in geography. The distribution among the different branches of geography reflected the philosophy of curriculum-building of the period. There was a balance of systematic, regional, and methodology courses with 12 credits in regional, 15 credits in systematic, and 10 credits in methodology courses. The course in aerial photogrammetry, taught from a geographic perspective, was one of the first, if not *the* first, course of this kind in the United States. The initial curriculum leading to the bachelor of science degree had a strong physical emphasis, with 8 credits in mathematics, 10 credits in chemistry, and 10 credits in physics. The other earth science fields—meteorology and the geological sciences—were also strongly represented.

In 1960 a bachelor of arts degree in geography was established in the College of Liberal Arts. This development reflects the fact that the field of geography has major components in the social sciences as well as the physical sciences. The B.A. program was devised for students who wanted a stronger human emphasis. The geography faculty in the College of Earth and Mineral Sciences advises students in the Liberal Arts program.

A major change in the philosophy of structuring the curriculum came in the 1960s with the development of human geography and particularly with the influence of the quantification "revolution" in geography (Miller, 1982). The emphasis shifted to topical and methodological courses, which included such new topical geography courses as population geography, the geography of manufacturing, cultural and anthropo-geography, regional physiography, and the geography of transportation and communications. New methodological courses emphasized spatial analysis, computer mapping, digital terrain models, remote-sensing, and cartographic symbolization and design.

The undergraduate majors grew steadily in the 1950s and the early 1960s to about fifty students, but in the late 1960s and early 1970s enrollment declined to as few as fifteen. The department recognized that a sound undergraduate enrollment was necessary if geography was to flourish on the campus. In order to strengthen the undergraduate program, Frederick Wernstedt was appointed undergraduate officer in the early 1970s. A major responsibility of his was to coordinate the advising of students in the department. Students began to recognize that the geography program had advisers who were concerned with their welfare.

To make the geography major more attractive to students who wanted to concentrate in a particular branch of the field, options were created in 1981. In the B.S. program three options were approved. The general option is designed to serve the needs of students who want to learn about the various topics and perspectives that comprise the discipline. This option is appropriate both for students who intend to pursue postgraduate degrees and for students who want to emphasize a topic for which no option exists. For students who want to pursue positions in public and private mapping agencies and firms, an option in cartography, remote-sensing, and geographic information systems has been prepared. Finally, the physical geography option is designed for students who seek a broad understanding of the earth and environmental sciences. This option

Student computer laboratory in the Department of Geography.

is designed to develop competence in the description, analysis, explanation, and management of problems arising from human use and exploitation of the natural resources and natural systems.

For the B.A. program in the College of Liberal Arts, two options have been developed. The general option ranges across a diversity of topics that comprise the disciplines of geography, and the economic and development option is especially appropriate for students who intend to pursue careers in business and industry in the economically developed nations and in the Third World.

Besides the continued updating of the undergraduate geography programs and the introduction of an effective system of advising geography students, several special programs have been inaugurated to enhance the undergraduate program. During the summer a number of students work in planning offices as interns, an opportunity that provides practical training. Special geographic field trips are planned periodically to provide experiences in studying spatial problems. Special readings and research courses are available for advanced undergraduate students. The department has a career placement service that aids students in finding a position upon graduation. Enrollment has grown steadily to between 115 and 130 in recent years.

THE GRADUATE PROGRAM

Programs leading to the M.S. and Ph.D. degrees were begun in 1946. The first M.S. was granted in 1947, and the first Ph.D. was conferred in 1949. Between 1947 and 1963 forty-three master of science degrees, one doctor of education, and seven doctor of philosophy degrees were granted. The overwhelming percentage of these degrees were in the field of economic geography, with mineral and manufacturing geography dominating. By 1961 on a peer evaluation of geography graduate programs in the Roose-Anderson survey in the United States, Penn State stood in eleventh position. The quality of the program has continued to improve, and in 1983 the Jones Lindsay survey ranked the graduate program second in the nation—convincing evidence of a productive faculty and exceptional students over a long period of time.

In order to attract geography students, there is a need for adequate financial aid as well as for outstanding faculty. Initially this aid came through graduate teaching assistantships. The assistants taught in physical geography laboratories and led human geography recitation sections.

The number of graduate students grew from two in 1946 to thirty-four in 1960 to a peak of fifty-nine in 1970. The significant growth in the 1960s was largely attributable to graduate student aid received from the National Defense Education Act, the National Science Foundation, and university fellowships. Graduate students were attracted from the most prestigious American universities, but there was also a major influx of foreign students, particularly from Great Britain and the Commonwealth nations. These people came because the graduate program combined quality instruction not only in the traditional facets of the field but also in the newer, quantitative branches that blossomed in the 1960s.

Cartography laboratory in the Department of Geography.

The graduate program continues to be a major endeavor of the faculty. Since 1970, enrollment has varied between forty and fifty students each year. The theses and dissertations reflect modern geographic trends. Recent titles include "Modeling the Evolution of Suburbanization in a Metropolitan Region," "Two-Variable Mapping: A Practical Case for the Soil Map," "Equity of Bus Transit Subsidies: A Case Study of Dayton, Ohio," "Spatial Development and Internal Spatial Organization of the Southeastern Pennsylvania Plain Dutch Community," and "Geomorphology of the Fall Stretch of the Potomac River."

The graduate program functions under a set of regulations set by the graduate school and the department. A graduate officer coordinates the selection of new students. While a faculty committee makes certain that each graduate student has achieved the minimal level for graduate work, a major feature of the graduate program is that each student has a program that is developed specifically for him or her. An important facet of the graduate program is a seminar in which each faculty member presents his area of research and becomes acquainted with the new graduate students. Discussions on new concepts and trends in the field are also planned. In the spring semester the students present proposals for their theses research to faculty and other graduate students. These meetings become lively sessions that hone a student's geographic understanding of his research program.

The graduate program is enriched by a number of special programs. In the 1960s a tradition of inviting distinguished American, British, and Swedish scholars to present lectures and develop seminars in the graduate program began. Throughout the academic year a Friday coffee hour brings outstanding speakers to the department. These coffee hours are attended by undergraduates and the general public as well as by graduate students. To encourage scholarship at both the undergraduate and the graduate level, the department established the E. Willard Miller Award in geography. Given annually, the award consists of a monetary gift and a plaque. The recipient must prepare a paper that is judged by a faculty committee. In order to maintain relations with both graduates and undergraduates who have been students in the department, the *PSUDOG* series— the departmental newsletter—has become a hardy perennial.

IDEOLOGICAL DIALOGUE

The field of geography has been dynamic in its attempts to provide an ideological framework for understanding spatial distributions on the earth. These include such approaches as environmental determinism, human ecology, and regionalism among other major themes. At Penn State the basic philosophy has been to be at the cutting edge of the development of the discipline. Beginning in the late 1950s the field of geography experienced a "quantitative revolution" that advocated a rigorous scientific approach to the subject. Faculty were recruited accordingly to develop these new concepts.

As a result, in the Department of Geography, as throughout the nation and even the world, an ideological controversy ensued between the newly arisen so-called "quantifiers" and the more traditional practitioners, many of whom subscribed to a more humanistic philosophy. Teaching and research were polarized along these lines. These two approaches raised fundamental questions that could not be resolved in a short time. The debates in the department extended well over a decade. Discussions occurred among individual faculty members as well as at times during faculty meetings. From these debates it became evident that a monolithic ideology did not exist. The study of spatial distribution, for example, could be carried on from a variety of methodological and philosophical approaches. As professors presented a case for their particular approaches to the discipline, they sharpened their concepts, which made each member of the faculty a better teacher and researcher. The geography program may have suffered some slight setbacks during the early stages of the ideological debates, but the department made remarkable gains throughout the middle and later stages. Enrollment in the undergraduate and graduate programs increased, and research productivity grew. Although the debates were rigorous, there was an overriding philosophy that the unity of the program must be preserved. During these dynamic times the skillful administration of the department heads was extremely important in holding the department together. The department heads not only kept the department functioning but also provided guidance for its continuing growth.

GEOGRAPHY AND GENERAL EDUCATION

The geography faculty has always recognized that general education is an avenue for providing students with a geographer's perspective. The unique perspective of geography makes it the only discipline that has as its core the study of the spatial dimensions of a problem. Because physical geography is part of the physical sciences, and human geography is part of the social sciences, general education courses have been developed in both of these major branches.

General education courses provide students with a geographic perspective by using a number of different themes. One traditional approach of the geographer is to describe, analyze, and interpret spatial patterns and to compare and contrast these patterns found in nature as well as those formed by the work of men and women. A student approaches the study of geography with three basic questions: *Where* are the patterns on the earth located? *Why* are they located there? *What* are the consequences of their locations? Although the first question is fundamental to the geographic approach, scholars recognized centuries ago that *where* simply defines the location to be analyzed and interpreted. If the study ends there, geography becomes a sterile field of memorization. The vitality of the discipline lies in the attempt to explain the existence of incredibly complex geographic patterns. The answers are rarely obvious, but seeking to solve these puzzles makes the geographic approach exciting.

Theoretical as well as empirical approaches to knowledge are used to provide students with an understanding of the spatial aspects of the physical, economic, cultural, and political systems existing on the earth. The study of the functions of regions, also long established in geographic work, gives students an understanding of spatial structures that involve both patterns and linkages in complex interrelationships. Approximately 1,800 to 2,000 students who are not geography majors take geography courses each year to satisfy a part of the general education requirements.

Students learn that a geographic approach to knowledge is exciting for its own sake. It provides a way to interpret some of the events that are happening in the world every day. It provides a framework for raising such issues as why different densities of people exist on the earth, why some regions are important to us and other regions are of lesser importance, why industry is concentrated in a few places and why the location of industry is dynamic, why some people are poor in material goods while others are rich, and why there are differences in agricultural productivity from place to place. There is a spatial perspective to such questions. The geographer's approach provides the student with the methodology to view problems. The geography general education course can thus open for students vistas that can enrich their lives.

As the general education requirements of the University have evolved since the 1950s, the Geography Department has prepared courses to meet the changing trends. The most recent changes occurred in 1987 with the development of the concept of "breadth" courses. A student can no longer satisfy the general education requirement by taking only the beginning-level courses. Students must take at least one breadth course in each distribution category, and then they can complete the category with breadth or depth courses. The geography faculty has prepared courses for the breadth and depth levels to meet the new requirements.

THE GRADUATE PROGRAM FOR TEACHERS

The graduate program in geography began in the 1930s during the summer sessions. Public school teachers who wanted to improve their geographic knowledge in the classroom took the courses. A master of education degree could be earned when 30 credits were completed over a series of summers. The first M.Ed. degree in geography was awarded in 1938. The department continued to offer courses for teachers during the summer sessions until the mid-1970s. Many of the courses were taught by visiting faculty from such universities as Illinois, Ohio, Bowling Green, Texas, and Michigan State. In the 1970s the program was discontinued as in-service programs developed in the public school systems.

The D.Ed. degree program was begun in the early 1950s. This program, primarily during the academic year, was always small, but its graduates secured positions in institutions where teacher training was emphasized, such as Bloomsburg University and Frostburg College. In the 1960s the

Tami Mistrick, a graduate student in geography, inspects a map film separation.

National Defense Education Act programs recognized the importance of geographic training in the public schools. In 1967–68 Peirce Lewis and Frederick Wernstedt developed an academic year program for fifteen public school geography teachers. The program was devoted entirely to the development of geographic concepts and the teaching of geography to students at the junior and senior high school levels. Although the program was not a degree-granting program, more than half the students wrote an acceptable paper, and M.Ed. degrees were awarded.

THE GEOGRAPHY LABORATORIES

The Department of Geography has established two major laboratories for teaching and research. These are the Deasy GeoGraphics Laboratory and the Advanced Geographic Information Systems Laboratory.

DEASY GEOGRAPHICS LABORATORY

The Deasy GeoGraphics Laboratory was established in 1984 to support the research and teaching activities of faculty and graduate students in the University. Alan MacEachren is director of the laboratory, and on January 1, 1989, an associate director, David DiBiase, was appointed to consult with students and supervise a staff of student cartographers. The staff is familiar not only with geographic techniques but also with the geographic arts, the psychology of visual perception and cognition, statistical methods, computer graphics, and the theories and techniques of spatial information display. The Deasy GeoGraphics Lab offers the technical capability to manage data of various formats and scales, and the expertise necessary to judge the appropriateness of various techniques in the context of a particular problem. The maps and diagrams in the laboratory have been published in numerous professional journals and books, some of which have been recognized in national design competitions.

The laboratory consists of several components for instruction and research. A classroom is available for cartography and remote-sensing courses, including a fully equipped darkroom facility for use by students and faculty. A second component of the laboratory is the computer facility, which contains both an instructional lab and a research lab. For research, there are two DEC MicroVax computers devoted to image analysis and geographic information systems; two IBM ATs, each equipped with a vectrix color graphics system; and an IBM PS/2 model 60. On the MicroVax, in addition to standard programming languages and related software, the NASA Goddard Land Analysis System, which makes use of the laboratory's Raster Technologies monitor as a color-image display device, has been acquired. The laboratory also has 9,600-baud direct lines to the University IBM mainframe, Vax and Sun computers, allowing access to a variety of software as well as to the computer center's monochrome and color electrostatic plotters. An instructional computer laboratory contains an additional five IBM ATs with color graphic capabilities. Three digitizers are available for data input, and there are several printers and plotters for hardcopy output.

A third component is the cartographics production laboratory, which contains a separate darkroom facility with a large-format vertical process camera as well as a microcomputer system with both black-and-white and color displays. A dot-matrix printer, Apple LaserWriter Plus, HP Paintjet, and HP plotter are available for output, and a variety of geographic and text-processing software is installed on the system.

THE ADVANCED GEOGRAPHIC INFORMATION SYSTEMS LABORATORY

The Advanced Geographic Information Systems Laboratory is a state-of-the-art, high-level workstation laboratory specifically designed to provide an integrated teaching and research environment for the study of Earth-related phenomena. The laboratory provides sophisticated cartographics, image-processing and geographic information systems, software integrated in a multiprocessor local area network where the operating system is also specially configured for the special operational requirements to this application.

The laboratory includes eight SUN 4/65FGX (SPARC station 1+) desktop workstations converted to a SUN 4/490-S file server. Each workstation has a 16-inch color monitor with accelerated graphics, mouse, 4MB central memory, two 100MB local hard disks, and a 3½-inch floppy drive. The server has 32MB of main memory, a 1GByte IPI, and a two-cartridge tape driver. Graphics hard copy within the laboratory is provided by an Apple LaserWriter and a page-size QMS color plotter.

Application software supported in the laboratory includes geographic information systems, maze-processing systems, and other software needed to support advanced spatial data analysis and graphics directly. It is intended that the Advanced Geographic Information Systems Laboratory provide a public access resource for faculty and students in all disciplines within the University that have a need for this specialized environment. The laboratory is directed by Dr. Peuquet.

Because of the work of this laboratory in the Department of Geography, The Pennsylvania State University is in a unique position to become the lead university in North America in geographic information systems instruction and research. These facilities provide a threefold opportunity for training students in modern, computer-assisted spatial analytical techniques, a service to industry and the community in offering training opportunities for current professional staff in the use of new analytical techniques, and a continuing source of relevant expertise and research in the area of geographic information systems.

COMMUNITY SERVICE

Many members of the geography faculty have been participants in community activities. Peirce Lewis has long been active in State College borough planning in both official and unofficial capacities. In the early 1970s he protested a proposal to remove trees from a number of streets by actually climbing a tree to prevent its removal. Ronald Abler served for a number of years on the borough council. Gregory Knight served and chaired the Ferguson Township Planning Commission. Roger Downs was a member and chair of the Borough Planning Commission. E. Willard Miller has been active in the development of the Heritage Museum in Boalsburg. All these services have a spatial dimension to them, and the geographer brings a particular perspective to the solving of community problems.

DEPARTMENTAL FUNCTIONS

The coffee hour at 4:00 P.M. on Friday afternoons has become a major tradition of the Department of Geography. The lead-off speaker in the fall semester is the dean of the College of Earth and Mineral Sciences. Speakers during the year are not only from the University Park campus but also from all over the nation and occasionally even from other countries. There is no theme to the topics, which vary from art to zoology. Attendance is voluntary, but the room is packed every Friday, with people even standing in the hall. The audience is from all over the campus, not just geographers. To be asked to speak at the Friday coffee hour is now considered an honor.

The department also prepares a newsletter, *PSUDOG*, to provide information about the faculty and students, both present and past. Faculty and students are asked to write about their life during the past year. *PSUDOG* provides a nostalgic view of the present but also—and perhaps even more important—news about past graduates.

FACULTY AWARDS AND HONORS

The geography faculty has received numerous awards and honors both from within and from outside the University. Five—Anthony Williams, Paul Simkins, Roger Downs, Frederick Wernstedt, and Peirce Lewis—have received the Matthew J. Wilson Award presented annually to an outstanding teacher in the College of Earth and Mineral Sciences. Peirce Lewis received the Christian R. and Mary F. Lindbach Award for distinguished teaching (the highest teaching honor given to a faculty member at Penn State) and the Distinguished Achievement Award of the National Council for Geographic Education. Peter Gould was honored with the Faculty Research Medal, the highest honor for research in the University, and has been further honored by being made Evan Pugh Professor of Geography, the most distinguished professorship in the University. In 1983 he received an honorary doctorate from the Louis Pasteur University of Strasbourg, France. E. Willard Miller, Wilbur Zelinsky, and Peirce Lewis received the Honors Award from the Association of American Geographers. E. Willard Miller is one of the few geographers listed in *Who's Who in the World* for his work on international affairs. In 1990 the Penn State Alumni Association made Dr. Miller and his wife honorary alumni. Ronald F. Abler was awarded the Centenary Medal of the Royal Scottish Geographical Society in 1990.

The faculty has played an active role in the geographic profession. E. Willard Miller was secretary and president of the American Society for Professional Geographers, and he was a founder of the Pennsylvania Geographical Society, serving as president and a member of the council for nearly forty years. In 1983 he received the Meritorious Service Award from the Society, and in 1988 he was made a life member of the Council. Dr. Miller also served as president of the Pennsylvania Academy of Science. In 1982 and 1986 the Academy presented its Distinguished Service Award to Dr. Miller. Wilbur Zelinsky, Peirce Lewis, and Ronald Abler have been presidents of the Association of American Geographers. George F. Deasy was treasurer of the American Society for Professional Geographers and the Association of American Geographers. Rodney A. Erickson is a councilor of the American Geographical Society.

A number of organizations have honored the faculty. E. Willard Miller received the Distinguished Service Award from the Office of Strategic Services. Ronald Abler was honored by the Geographical Society of Chicago for being editor of the *Comparative Atlas of America's Great Cities*. Dr. Miller was given a citation from the governor of Pennsylvania as well as Pennsylvania's Department of Commerce Secretary's Meritorious Service Award for contribution to the Commonwealth. Alan M. MacEachren has received the Andrew McNally Award presented by Rand McNally Company. Wilbur Zelinsky received the Distinguished Service Award from the North American Cultural Society.

The faculty has received a number of grants to pursue their professional careers. Allan Rodgers, Wilbur Zelinsky, and Peirce Lewis have held Guggenheim Fellowships. Rodney Erickson has been a Fulbright Senior Research Scholar and a Simon Senior Research Fellow. Gregory Knight has been an honorary visiting scientist at the International Institute of Tropical Agriculture at Ibadan, Nigeria. Frederick Wernstedt has held a Fulbright grant as external examiner at the University of Malaysia. Paul Simkins and Fred Wernstedt have held National Science Foundation grants for study in the Philippines.

A number of faculty members have served as editors of professional journals and books. Gregory Knight has been the editor of the *Resource Publications of the Association of American Geographers*. Roger Downs and Gregory Knight have been members of the editorial board of the *Annals of the Association of American Geographers*. E. Willard Miller has been contributing editor to *Producers Monthly, The Pennsylvania Geographer,* the *Journal of Geography,* and is an

---

George J. Demko
Alumni Fellow

George J. Demko (Alumni Fellow 1986; Ph.D. Geography 1965) has had a distinguished career in academic and government service. After earning his doctorate at Penn State, he began his career in the Department of Geography at Ohio State University, where he spent the next two decades rising through the ranks to professor of geography. He began government service as director of the Geography and Regional Planning Program at the National Science Foundation and then became director of the Office of the Geographer of the U.S. Department of State. Presently he is director of the Rockefeller Center for Social Sciences at Dartmouth College. Of his college days at Penn State, he writes:

I will remember the departmental sense of community. The students and faculty had an informal and respectful interaction, socially and intellectually, which had important impacts on our lives and program. The graduate program was rigorous, research-oriented, and relevant to problem-solving. The graduate students showed a sense of loyalty and healthy competitiveness. The most memorable course was clearly George Deasy's seminar on crop ecology. Any good student of those years always compares notes with others on "his experience" in crop ecology.

editor of the Pennsylvania Academy of Science books. Peter Gould was appointed a member of the editorial advisory board of the international journal *Environment and Planning* and a consulting editor of *Geographical Analysis*. Allan Rodgers has served on the editorial board of *Economic Geography*, and Roger Downs has served on the editorial advisory board of *Environment and Behavior*. George Deasy and Phyllis Griess have been editors of *The Professional Geographer*.

THE DEPARTMENT'S MISSION

The mission of the Department of Geography is to maintain the highest creativity and excellence in geographical research, scholarships, teaching, and public service at several scales of spatial resolution.

THE GLOBAL LEVEL

At the world level the mission of the Geography Department is to remain one of the major centers of innovation and training in human geography and geographical methodology. The crisis of underdevelopment in the Third World, as well as in lagging areas of the industrialized world, has created significant employment and research opportunities for geographers in regional and interregional development. These factors are already affecting Penn State geography through demands for faculty and graduate expertise in development-related issues. Several faculty members serve as consultants to the World Bank and to American and United Nations development institutions.

A growing awareness of a singular global environmental system signals a change from a broad recognition of the unity of the biosphere to a commitment to detailed scientific investigation of global processes. A plethora of international research programs, including current efforts of NASA, the Department of Energy, and similar groups, is evidence of this trend. Important in this research is both fundamental physical understanding of global environmental processes and understanding of the implications of and for human activities. Technical skills of geography (cartography, remote-sensing, spatial analysis, geographical data systems), basic research interests in physical geography (climatology, biogeography, water resources, geomorphology, glaciology), and a continuing human/environment focus within human geography (resource management, cultural ecology, environmental impact assessment, environmental perception, spatial organization) all point to significant opportunities for geography to play a focal role in the study of global environmental systems.

THE NATIONAL LEVEL

Geography's fundamental role in public education and current affairs is being increasingly recognized. Important initiatives are under way to improve secondary-level geographical education in the United States. College and university faculty positions in geography are increasing, particularly in the areas emphasized at Penn State—geographical methodology and human geography.

There are significant opportunities for B.S.-level employment for students who are more technically oriented, with work in spatial analysis, geographical data systems, cartography, computer mapping, and remote-sensing. Recent experience has shown that U.S. military and civilian governmental agencies rank Penn State's department of geography as among their most important recruiting sites. Similarly prepared graduates going to the private sector are now receiving entry-level salaries usually associated only with the physical sciences, engineering, and computer sciences. Regional planning agencies remain an important source of employment for B.S. degree students. Job opportunities in these areas are enhanced when the student has undertaken an internship during his student days.

Kevin Kolb digitizing a computer-based map.

THE STATE LEVEL

Environmental quality and economic development are two critical imperatives in the state of Pennsylvania. Issues in these areas offer substantial opportunity for geographical research, and some employment opportunities, with direct benefit to the state. There is also a significant need to improve the quality of geographical education at the elementary and secondary level. This challenge requires a more active role of the University and College geography faculty in cooperating with state and local authorities in curriculum design and with colleagues in education in preparation of future educators.

UNIVERSITY-WIDE

A renewed Penn State commitment to general education represents, in the view of the geography faculty, an important reaffirmation of the basics of a liberal education. Geography is clearly a focal subject in general education courses. A steady upward trend in enrollment and number of majors is anticipated. This trend, although modest, possesses significant challenges to maintain a quality program.

William Duke, assistant professor of geology, operating his wave machine.

In specialized geographical courses there is a demand for traditional and digital cartographic research and teaching as well as for related areas of computer graphics, geographic information systems, spatial data analysis, and digital terrain modeling. Science and research opportunities in these areas have the potential to increase the scope and quality of research across the different disciplines, not just within geography. Similarly, students experienced in the activities of the Deasy GeoGraphics Laboratory can provide important career development for B.S. and graduate students.

Geography has an important role in interdisciplinary research units and instructional programs. Among these are area study programs (e.g., Black studies, Russian area), environmental programs (e.g., ecology, land, and water), and the programs focused on research methods and techniques (e.g., operations research). Faculty must be encouraged to participate in these activities and to foster interaction in newly emerging areas of interest.

THE COLLEGE LEVEL

The quality of research and graduate programs in the College of Earth and Mineral Sciences in disciplines related to geography (e.g., meteorology, geosciences, mineral economics) suggests opportunity for research collaboration within the College. A College focus on global environmental systems provides an excellent avenue for development of such collaboration. It also significantly enhances recruitment efforts in physical geography.

Chapter 6 | The Department of Geosciences

The teaching of geology at Penn State began in 1859 with the first class at the Farmers' High School. In the study of agriculture it was recognized that a knowledge of geology was necessary. President Evan Pugh gave high priority to geology and mineralogy, and one of the school's first faculty members, J. S. Whitman, professor of natural science, taught geology as one of his courses. In the period between 1860 and 1890, geology was taught by a number of faculty members from the biological sciences. In 1867 the catalog listed Henry James Clark as professor of zoology, botany, and geology. He was followed by J. Trimble Rothrock, professor of human anatomy and physiology, botany, and geology, and later by William A. Buckhout, professor of geology, zoology, and botany. The early faculty also included Albert H. Tuttle, professor of geology and physiology. The catalog first mentions a Department of Geology and Zoology in 1882, but there is no evidence that a true program in geology was developed. In 1889 Franklin E. Tuttle joined the faculty as instructor in chemistry and mineralogy.

When the bachelor of mining engineering degree was established in 1890, geology assumed a more important role. Magnus C. Ihlseng, head of the new mining department, was also professor of mining engineering and geology, and Thomas C. Hopkins was appointed instructor in geology. The teaching of mineralogy also appears to have been located in the mining program. The 1894–95 catalog shows that the degree of engineers of mines was offered with a specialty in geology and petrology.

The mining engineering program encountered many problems in the following years, and the growth of the geosciences was tied closely to progress in mining. In 1896 geology was listed as a

Administration
Geosciences

Mining Geology

Elwood S. Moore	1909–1921

Department of Geology

Elwood S. Moore	1921–1922
Chesleigh A. Bonine	1922–1927

Department of Mineralogy

Arthur P. Honess	1921–1927

Department of Geology and Mineralogy

Chesleigh A. Bonine	1927–1929

Department of Geology

Chesleigh A. Bonine	1929–1933

Department of Geology, Mineralogy, and Geography

Chesleigh A. Bonine	1933–1941

Department of Mining and Geophysics

W. R. Chedsey	1934–1939
David R. Mitchell	1939–1941

Department of Earth Sciences

Chesleigh A. Bonine	1941–1945
Herbert Insley	1945–1946
Elburt F. Osborn	1946–1953
O. Frank Tuttle	1953–1954

Division of Geology

Frank M. Swartz	1945–1954

Division of Mineralogy

Paul D. Krynine	1945–1954

Division of Geophysics

Sylvain J. G. Pirson	1945–1948

Division of Geophysics and Geochemistry

Benjamin F. Howell, Jr.	1949–1954

Department of Geology

Frank M. Swartz	1954–1961
Lauren A. Wright	1961–1963

Department of Geophysics and Geochemistry

Benjamin F. Howell, Jr.	1954–1963

Department of Mineralogy

Paul D. Krynine	1954–1955
John C. Griffiths	1955–1963

Department of Geochemistry and Mineralogy

John C. Griffiths	1963–1968

Department of Geology and Geophysics

Lauren A. Wright	1963–1971

Department of Geochemistry and Mineralogy

Arnulf Muan	1968–1971

Department of Geosciences

Arnulf Muan	1971–1973
C. Wayne Burnham	1974–1985
Shelton S. Alexander	1985–1990
Michael A. Arthur	1991–

department in the newly established School of Natural Science. The program was not developed and soon disappeared due to a lack of funds.

As the mining program gained status, the importance of the geological sciences was recognized by a statement in the 1906 catalog: "By means of a series of electives, the student is further allowed to prepare himself more particularly along the line of prospecting or searching for valuable materials, a life work in itself (Geology or Economics or Mining Geology)." At this time courses in geology and mineralogy were included in nearly all the curricula of the College, including the philosophy, classical, Latin, scientific, and modern language curricula. Three faculty members—Dean M. E. Wadsworth, L. B. Smith, and H. J. Smith—were responsible for the geology instructional program.

Geology grew in importance, and in 1909 Dean Walter R. Crane established mining geology as a separate major in the School, with Elwood S. Moore, professor of geology, in charge. The first B.S. graduate was Stuart St. Clair, in 1912. The first M.S. graduate was Lloyd B. Smith, who worked under Professor Moore, in 1913. Stanley S. Cathcart, who obtained his B.S. in metallurgical engineering in 1912, earned his M.S. degree in geology in 1916. During his graduate days he was listed in the catalog as a teaching fellow in geology. He later had a distinguished career with the U.S. Geological Survey, various oil companies, and as state geologist of Pennsylvania from 1947 to 1953.

In the second decade of the twentieth century the geological sciences gained status. New faculty were added, and the course offering was expanded. Arthur P. Honess, mineralogist and crystallographer, joined the faculty in 1917, and Chesleigh A. Bonine, an economic geologist, joined in 1918. As the program developed, an administrative structure gradually evolved. In 1921, with the reorganization of the School of Mines, two separate departments were created, with Dr. Moore as head of geology and Dr. Honess as head of mineralogy. The geosciences continued as separate departments until 1927, when they were combined into a single Department of Geology and Mineralogy under Dr. Bonine. In 1927 there was a faculty of six: Dr. Bonine and Dr. Honess, Clair W. Robinson, and three instructors, one of whom was Frank M. Swartz, who later became head of the Department of Geology. In 1930 Clark F. Barb, a petroleum engineer, and George H. Ashley, a geologist, were added, along with two instructors: Paul G. Shelley in oil and gas production, and Emil F. Williams in geology and mineralogy. Oil and gas production was an option in the geology curriculum in 1930, but in 1931 it was made a separate major. In 1933 Petroleum and Natural Gas Engineering became a separate department and the geology program was renamed "Geology, Mineralogy, and Geography" to include the interests of the recently appointed geographer, Raymond E. Murphy.

The instructional program developed rapidly in the 1920s (Bonine, 1939). By 1928 there were twenty geology courses listed in the catalog, of which three were graduate courses: Geology Seminar, Stratigraphy, and Geological Investigation. In addition, there were ten courses in mineralogy, one of which—Physical Mineralogy—was at the graduate level. All students in the School of Mines and Metallurgy in 1928 were required to take Physical Geology, General Geology, and either Historical Geology or Descriptive Mineralogy.

A mineralogy laboratory class in the 1890s.

By the 1920s the study of geology had broadened to meet the shifting demands of industry, science, and education. As a result, a B.S. in geology was offered in 1928, replacing the B.S. in Mining Geology. As Dr. Bonine wrote: "When the sciences of geology and mineralogy first began to develop in Europe before much practical use was made of them, a classical foundation in college was considered essential. Later, engineering and technical subjects were stressed and a period of mass production of mining and petroleum geologists ensued. At present, emphasis is being placed on thorough training in the fundamental sciences, such as chemistry, physics, and physical chemistry as well as on cultural subjects in order that the student may continue his training in a graduate school and eventually be well prepared for a research, teaching or industrial career. It is desirable for students in geology to supplement their undergraduate training with graduate work in order to have a maximum of opportunity for success."

Geology majors had to take 45 credits in geology and mineralogy, including a summer practicum. The evolution of the geology major from the mining-metallurgy program was evident in the course structure, with 15 credits of work required from those fields. The catalog description indicates that the geology program equipped "students for such fields of work as those of the Federal and State Geological Surveys, for the geological survey work of mining and oil companies, for prospecting, for the teaching profession, and ultimately, after gaining considerable practical experience, for the position of consulting geologist."

THE DEVELOPMENT OF GEOPHYSICS AND GEOCHEMISTRY

In the development of the academic structure of the School of Mineral Industries, Dean Edward Steidle indicated: "[The] Earth Sciences—geology, mineralogy, geophysics and geochemistry, meteorology and geography—are basic sciences dealing with those problems covering the origin, constitution and utilization of the earth's materials." In this statement he laid the foundation for the development of the modern branches of the geosciences, geochemistry, and geophysics, which provided significant new techniques for mineral exploration. He continued: "For our future development, we must know what rock structure and types underlay the surface to a depth of several miles. This we can find out with the laying out and execution of a wise and broad research program in geophysics. During the course of the program, new techniques would inevitably be developed to accelerate the work. By the year 2000, extensive geophysical work will have been done in Pennsylvania if we do what a progressive state should do" (Steidle, 1950).

Formal instruction in geophysics began in 1931, when W. R. Chedsey offered a one-credit course in geophysical prospecting. Interest in the field grew so rapidly that in 1934 the name of the department was changed to Mining and Geophysics, a name that existed until 1941. In the fall of 1934 Helmut Landsberg, formerly assistant director of the Taunus Observatory of Geophysics and Meteorology at the University of Frankfurt, joined the mining faculty as the first instructor in geophysics (Landsberg, 1941). The announcement of his appointment in *Mineral Industries* read: "He will teach the regular courses in geophysical methods of prospecting, climatology, and physics of mining. His duties in the beginning will have to do with the general application of geophysical principles to ground movement, subsidence, roof support and the development of instruments for measuring accumulated stresses which cause strain and ruptures in rocks during mining operations. Along with his research, which is of prime importance to the mining industry of Pennsylvania, will be the development of a meteorological and seismological laboratory, including a seismograph for recording earthquakes."

In the fall of 1934 a horizontal component seismometer was built in the central wing of the Mineral Industries Building (now Steidle Building) in the School of Mineral Industries. The recording and timing equipment was provided by the U.S. Coast and Geodetic Survey through the support of N. H. Heck, then head of the Division of Seismology and Terrestrial Magnetism. The first seismological bulletin, listing the times of twelve earthquakes, was issued in 1935.

Dr. Landsberg taught five courses in 1934–35: two on the physics of the earth, two on the physics of the atmosphere, and one on "ground movements." By 1937, enrollment in the courses had grown so large that additional faculty were needed, and Hans Neuberger of the University of Hamburg, Germany, was appointed, to be followed a year later by Victor Conrad of the University of Vienna, Austria, after whom the "Conrad discontinuity" in the earth's crust is named. In 1939 Dr. Conrad left to join the faculty of Harvard University, and in 1941 Dr. Landsberg went to the University of Chicago. Dr. Neuberger headed the geophysics program from 1941 to 1945.

As petroleum reserves of the United States were rapidly depleted during the World War II period, the emphasis in geophysics began to shift toward prospecting for petroleum. This shift was stimulated by Sylvain J. G. Pirson, then head of the Department of Petroleum and Natural Gas. In 1945, in a reorganization of the School of Mineral Industries, the Department of Earth Sciences was created, with Dr. Pirson becoming chief of the Division of Geophysics and Dr. Neuberger becoming chief of the Division of Meteorology (Pirson, 1946). Dr. Pirson started research on well-logging and, through his interest in geochemical prospecting, taught the first geochemistry course at Penn State. In a November 1942 article in *Mineral Industries*, he reflected that, although geological studies had long been utilized in petroleum exploration, new techniques were needed. For drilling to be successful, there was a need to "make available large scale reconnaissance prospecting surveys such as subsurface geological maps, convergence maps, isopach maps, and geophysical maps, magnetic, gravimetric and seismic surveys."

In 1948 Dr. Pirson resigned, leaving geophysics with no regular faculty members. Two senior graduate students, John C. Cook and Lloyal O. Bacon, kept the research and teaching going until Benjamin F. Howell, Jr., arrived on July 1, 1949. Although there had been bachelor degree candidates in mining and geophysics and in earth science with an emphasis on geophysics, the first degrees specifically granted in geophysics were a B.S. in 1948 to David J. Stuart and an M.S., also in 1948, to Lloyal Bacon.

In 1946 E. F. Osborn joined the faculty as professor of geochemistry, the first in the United States to have this title. He initiated a program in high-temperature experimental geochemistry bearing on phase relations among oxides, applicable both to the origin of igneous rocks and to ceramics, and he developed and taught a graduate course in geochemistry.

SOME EARLY GEOLOGISTS

The following profiles represent more than half a century in the evolution of the geology program at Penn State.

Arthur P. Honess came to Penn State in 1917. He is best known for his research in the fields of crystallography and petrology. At the time he came he was one of the outstanding mineralogists and morphological crystallographers in the United States. He was also the first scientist to make microscopic petrographic studies of the oil sands of Pennsylvania. His research standardized the methods used for decades in porosity studies, but his major contribution may have been in the area of etching. By using reagents to develop etch figures, he developed physical concepts concerning crystal structure symmetry. He also employed photography to prove his contention that when acids eat wet crystals they leave a symmetrical molecular structure. In 1927 he wrote his classic study, entitled "The Nature, Origin, and Interpretations of the Etch Figures on Crystals." In recognition of this work he was elected to the Royal Mineralogical Society of Great Britain; only seventeen other Americans had been so honored.

Dr. Honess was an enthusiastic and inspiring teacher. To his former students he was known as "Doc," and his office was the gathering place for students and old grads. The toughness of his quizzes was the subject of innumerable stories, but his reputation as a teacher was so great that the most prestigious universities, such as Harvard, M.I.T., and Yale, granted fellowships to any of his students upon his recommendation.

Chesleigh A. Bonine was a leader of the geological sciences at Penn State from the time of his arrival in 1922 until his retirement in 1945 and provided a fine foundation of teaching and research during his long tenure. He was among the early geologists to establish a research program at Penn State. Through his research, he proved in 1942 that the bentonite in Pennsylvania was genetically related to that found in the southern Appalachian states. Not only a renowned geologist, he was also an archaeologist who earned the respect of his colleagues. He directed the archaeological excavations at Lewes, Delaware, that resulted in the discovery of the first Dutch settlement founded in 1631.

Dr. Bonine was a devout Christian and published a book entitled *Christ and the Gospel Record,* focused on the Gospel of John. He once wrote: "The most rewarding experience of my life has been a five-day trip through the Holy Land." He was actively engaged in the Moral

Arthur P. Honess and students in a mineralogy laboratory in the 1930s in Steidle Building.

Rearmament movement, a name the movement acquired after President Theodore Roosevelt declared that the underlying strength of the world consisted of the moral fiber of its citizens. Dr. Bonine supported the movement by asking his colleagues to join him in efforts to help the student body be more morally responsible and to practice their faith by following the simple standards of honesty, purity, unselfishness, and love in their daily lives. Dr. Bonine often welcomed students into his home as part of the Oxford Group—students and faculty from Oxford, Cambridge, Penn State, Harvard, Yale, Rutgers, Princeton, and other leading American universities—whose aim was "to bring America under God's control."

In a postscript to *Christ and the Gospel Record*, Dr. Bonine wrote that as a scientist and teacher of geology, and after a lifetime of studying and teaching the Bible, he was often confronted by students with questions about the relationship between science and religion. His answer was "that where science said that something was a matter of the laws of nature, faith said that something was a matter of the divine power which gives form and meaning to everything."

Frank M. Swartz came to Penn State in 1927 and retired in 1961. For the last fifteen of those years he was head of the Geology Department. His special interest was the geology of central Pennsylvania, with an emphasis on the sedimentary rocks of the Silurian and Devonian periods. He was particularly interested in paleontology, with emphasis on ostracods. These fossils were important because their short stratigraphic ranges made them excellent zonal fossils. In a 1932 paper, "Revision of the Ostracod Family Thlipsura," Swartz wrote: "Their importance to geologists is enhanced because they will aid in the recognition of the Shriver (formation of the Lower Devonian) both in surface outcrops throughout central and eastern Pennsylvania and in wells in northern and western Pennsylvania. In further study they will also help to clarify the unsettled correlation of the Shriver chert of western Maryland and central Pennsylvania."

Dr. Swartz identified many new species of ostracods. In 1935, for example, at a presentation before the Paleontological Society of America, he described twenty new species of these animals. Dr. Swartz was also a collector of rocks. In his study and office, rocks were piled on the table, on the floor, and even on top of cabinets. Besides being a first-rate researcher, he was a practical geologist. In 1944 he investigated an area of approximately 1,200 square miles for the selection of

Four scientists in the geochemistry laboratory in the mid-1950s. Left to right are Lesley Glasser, Della M. Roy, Charlotte Warshaw, and Hildegarde Hoss. Lesley Glasser is operating a single crystal gonimeter machine that shoots x-rays at crystals to obtain diffraction patterns.

a new limestone mine for the National Gypsum Company. He located the quarry and plant at Pleasant Gap that was operated by the Standard Lime and Stone Company. Dr. Swartz received praise from his students for his enormous amount of patience and his ability to bring complex concepts down to levels of simple understanding.

Paul D. Krynine came to Penn State from Yale University in 1937. At the time, he was already recognized as one of the world's leading sedimentary petrologists. He continued this work at Penn State, concentrating on the characteristics of the state's oil sands. In order to expand his research, he enlarged the Krantz Collection of the College, which contained more than 12,000 thin sections of sedimentary rocks from all over the world.

Through his research, Dr. Krynine evolved a new fundamental concept of the genetic and descriptive classification of sedimentary rocks. He showed that not only the texture but also the mineral composition of a sediment was directly related to the amount of tectonic deformation in the source area and in the basin of deposition both before and during sedimentation. Specifically, he divided sedimentary rocks into three major classes, characterized mineralogically by quartz, quartz and rock fragments, and quartz and feldspar. These three classes, named the quartzitic, graywacke, and arkose types, are related respectively to low, moderate, and intense structural deformation and are characteristic of regions of quiesence, geosynclinal subsidence, and intense orogeny. In addition, Dr. Krynine demonstrated the probable existence of a direct relationship between regional structure, regional mineral composition, and the development of certain types of oil fields.

The new classification was presented by Dr. Krynine in December 1941 at the meeting of the Geological Society of America in Boston and at the April 1942 meeting of the American Association of Petroleum Geologists in Denver. In 1943, at the invitation of the Distinguished Lecture Committee of the American Association of Petroleum Geologists, Dr. Krynine presented a series of lectures on "Diastrophism and the Evolution of Sedimentary Rocks" to more than 1,100 petroleum geologists.

The new concepts were recognized as a major advance in the study of sedimentary rocks. It was now possible to study sediments in the same logical and systematic way as igneous rocks were studied. Furthermore, the suspected relationship between a certain evolutionary stage of sedimentary differentiation and the presence of a certain type of oil deposits promised to develop into a valuable tool for oil exploration. Dr. Krynine's research established the pattern of the study of sedimentary petrology for more than a quarter of a century, and today his classification is recognized as one of the major breakthroughs in geologic classifications.

Dr. Krynine was a dedicated scholar. In his March 1948 *Journal of Geology* article entitled "The Megascopic Study and Field Classification of Sedimentary Rocks," he opened with a quotation from Edgar Allan Poe: "The necessary knowledge is that of what to observe." This reflects Dr. Krynine's philosophy that the essence of science is to know *how* to look at things. On the topic of research methods Dr. Krynine wrote: "The object of scientific research, whether it be pure or applied, is to arrive at the truth, which generally means solving certain specific problems. Depending upon the complexity of the problem and the number of variables involved such solutions may be produced by trial and error (so call "hit or miss") methods or by an orderly reasoning and stating of the problem beforehand. . . . Professional men, however, must discover at all costs how their problems are to be solved theoretically since in their future work they will have to try to produce similar discoveries on the basis of analogies."

Dr. Krynine's writing, even at its most technical, often reflected a literary and philosophical flair. In another article, in the *Bulletin of the Geological Society of America* (November 1960), entitled "On the Antiquity of Sedimentation and Hydrology" subtitled "With Some Moral Con-

Rustum Roy with his wife, Della Roy.

Rustum Roy
Evan Pugh Professor of Solid State Science

In looking back on my career, I can see that the role of chance in scientific research (indeed, in any system as complex as life) has become much clearer to me personally, as it has to the scientific world in general. I am struck by the fact that it was by chance that I landed in the research group that was to become Penn State's "big bang" entry into big-time research. As E. F. Osborn's first Ph.D., and first postdoc, working on the University's first major government contract (with the Office of Naval Research) of the modern kind, I was certainly in on breaking new ground.

That became one theme of my career, taking the first counterentropic step to start, literally to create new "patterns"—in matter, in process, in local or national institutional arrangements. The University clearly had the responsibility both to organize and to pass on to the next generation the wisdom of the past, but also literally to create the future human response to the intrinsic evolutionary context we call the universe. The other major theme was *synthesis* across artificial boundaries. I took the "Uni" prefix in "University" to stand for unification or integration. "Disciplines" or "departments" were obviously shifting lines drawn on the seamless garment of knowledge. "Interdisciplinarity" should be clearly *more* central to the mission of a *Uni*-versity than an emphasis on disciplines, which militate against what *uni*-versities are supposed to be about. I deal with these two themata in my career in turn: newness and unification.

The following are some of the new things in which I was involved. I was a part of the initial research in phase equilibrium as a core experimental area under the direction of Dr. Osborn. In 1948 we began high-pressure research in the College under an Office of Naval Research contract. In this research we redesigned the Tuttle-Roy high T/P furnaces and started systematic p-t-x geochemistry. We also did experiments on alternative routes to diamond synthesis. Although this research was unsuccessful, the research on "super-pressures" (above 20kb) with anvils laid the foundation for Frank Dachille and I to synthesize more new high "p" phases than all other labs specializing in anvils. We also developed a new approach to synthesizing new materials, such as ferromagnets, phosphors, and glasses. I was also involved in the development of a number of new processes, including solution sol-gel process, the development of fine powders, the applications of rapidly cooled ceramics by splattering and sputtering, and the development of the Derjaguin process to reach the highest-pressure phases.

My work on "unifying" or crossing disciplinary divides has been important in my career, as my research in chemistry and the geosciences shows. I have been instrumental in developing a number of interdisciplinary programs. I organized and chaired the Solid-State Technology Program. I also started the Materials Research Laboratory and was the director for twenty-three years. This is the largest interdisciplinary lab on campus and in the nation. I also organized the Science, Technology and Society Program for undergraduates, covering the widest spectrum of disciplines. I was the founding editor of the *Materials Research Bulletin* and organized the first meeting of the Materials Research Society. Since 1970 I have been active in getting women and minorities into science at the Materials Research Lab. I was the first person of Indian descent to be elected to the U.S. National Academy of Engineering and the first to be elected to two major national academies. In 1987 my wife, Della M. Roy, and I became the first couple in history to be elected to the National Academy of Engineering.

clusions," he reflected, "The ancient Greeks held very modern views on sedimentation . . . [and] some leading modern physicists have rediscovered the fruitfulness of certain basic principles of early Greek scientific thought, perhaps geologists should look into it."

Dr. Krynine was active in local affairs. He wrote often to the *Centre Daily Times*, praising teachers and stating his views on local matters of education. In one discussion, about whether money should be used to build a new school, he commented, "Bricks are not brains." He liked to quote from Greek philosophers who shared his own attitude: "It is advisable to lay no claim to strict originality of one's own ideas or hypotheses."

Thomas F. Bates, who came to Penn State from Columbia University in 1942, specialized in the application of x-ray diffraction, electron diffraction, and electron microscopy to mineralogical problems. He was particularly interested in using these and other techniques in detailed investigations of the clay minerals. One of his early endeavors was the development of a large collection of x-ray diffraction photographs of crystalline materials. In 1947 he was placed in charge of the high-magnification laboratory of the School, established to meet the needs of faculty who required the investigation of minute particles and structures of materials. Through the use of the electron microscope, he advanced the field of clay mineralogy. For example, he identified and characterized the clay mineral illite as a major component of slate in the deposits of northeastern Pennsylvania. Where illite is found in a typical shale, the individual shreds are difficult to resolve even under magnification up to 100,000 diameters. Dr. Bates was the first to use the electron microscope to reveal and explain how the clay mineral halloysite, and some varieties of asbestos, could crystallize in the form of minute cylindrical crystals.

Benjamin F. Howell, Jr., came to Penn State in 1949 as head of the geophysics program. When he arrived there were only fourteen students in the geophysics program—six graduates and eight undergraduates. He writes, "Throughout my administration as division chief and department head a principal goal was to expand the program to be viable in numbers. In 1959, enrollment had risen to thirty-seven graduate students and forty-eight undergraduates. I originated five new undergraduate and three new graduate courses in geophysics, and built the faculty from myself and E. F. Osborn in 1949 to twenty-four in 1962." Dr. Howell is the author of two textbooks in general geophysics and in 1990 published his *Introduction to Seismological Research: History and Development.*

Dr. Howell's research interest was seismic-wave transmissions, especially the absorption of seismic waves. He took part in a series of North American crustal structure experiments and around 1970 Carl Stepp, one of his graduate students, got him interested in problems of the statistical evaluation of seismic risk. Besides his teaching and research, Dr. Howell was interested in the moral fiber of his students. For example, he wanted an honor system in geophysics for all examinations. He writes: "The individual thing that has given me the most personal satisfaction was obtaining Senate approval of the idea that a formally constituted honor system satisfied University rules for supervisory classroom honesty." He operated such a system in his advanced geophysics classes.

John C. Griffiths came to Penn State in 1947 as assistant professor of petrology to work with Dr. Krynine, of whom Dr. Griffiths states: "Dr. Krynine was (and still is) in my opinion the world's outstanding sedimentary petrologist and therefore the leader in my special field." Dr. Griffiths's research in the initial years was in sedimentary petrology with special application to the oil industry. Beginning about 1951 Dr. Griffiths became a pioneer in the application of statistics and computers to solving geosciences problems. In a February 1966 article in *Mineral Industries* he wrote: "This emphasis on mathematics now permeating all the geosciences began with the adoption of the classical procedures of measurement as used in physics and enumeration as applied in chemistry. The flourishing of the borderline disciplines of geophysics and geochemistry acted as a catalyst in this difficult transformation." In the later years of his career Dr. Griffiths taught graduate courses in scientific methods and the development of general systems research as applied to geoscience problem-solving. He raised a fundamental question: What determines when and where exploration becomes important in mineral discovery? In retirement, he continues to study geological diversity and mineral resource assessment.

In addition to making outstanding research contributions in his field of expertise, Dr. Griffiths was an outstanding classroom instructor. His basic philosophy of teaching was "to take the less fortunate student and raise him/her at least to the average level of his/her limit. I was extremely fortunate in this practice because I had a really fine and highly successful group of graduate students throughout my career. They are still my friends."

William Spackman, Jr., came to Penn State in 1949. His research work centered on problems in the fields of coal petrology, palynology, and modern organic sediments. With G. O. W. Kremp of the University of Arizona he served as co-editor of the *Catalog of Fossil Spores and Pollen,* a standard reference work of some twenty volumes. He was also author and co-author of a variety of papers, including studies of teak substitutes for battleship decks, the effect of wood preservatives on paints, fossil woods, modern coal-forming sediments, and the effects of coal composition on the quality of metallurgical coke. In 1956 he became director of the Coal Research Section of the Mineral Industries Experiment Station, a position he held until retirement.

Robert Scholten was born in the Netherlands and received his undergraduate degree from the University of Amsterdam. After coming to the United States, he did his graduate work at the University of Michigan, then joined the Penn State faculty in 1951. His research interests were in the areas of gravity tectonics, the mechanics and dynamics of thrust-faulting, and the stratigraphic-tectonic evolution of the northern Rocky Mountains. Another major field of teaching and research for him was the origin, migration, and occurrence of oil and gas.

Frank Dachille was a geochemist and did fundamental work in his high-pressure laboratory. His most exciting work may have been his studies of meteoritic impact. Dr. Dachille believed that meteoritic impact had dramatically altered the physical, chemical, and biological history of the Earth. His interpretation was not based on a Velihovsky-like catastrophe but on careful studies of crater sites. He and a geologist colleague, Alan O. Kelly, spent months searching in South Africa, Germany, and other countries for identifiable high-pressure phases of silica found in craters. In later years Dr. Dachille duplicated these phases in his high-pressure laboratory. Dr. Dachille's theories long preceded NASA's landings on the moon, but they were based on the assumption that the very large craters resembling the surface of the moon were the result of large meteorites (about 5,000 of them) that had hit the moon over the course of 5 billion years.

Dr. Dachille pursued a distinguished career in the field of geochemistry while disregarding the arrows many scientists shot while he pursued one of the great geological mysteries of the influence of meteoritic impact on the Earth. He once remarked, "Trust in your own scientific training and ignore nothing. There can be great advantages to working alone, and even when you stand alone in your interpretation do not fear aloneness. If you are near the truth, proper recognition will come in due time."

C. Wayne Burnham came to Penn State in 1955 to continue his research, begun at Cal Tech, on the nature of the magmatic fluid phase and its role in the formation of contact metamorphic ore deposits. Concerning his acceptance of a position at Penn State, he states: "Penn State—owing to the leadership of E. F. Osborn and O. F. Tuttle—was the only university in the United States that was extensively engaged in experimental research under the very high temperatures and pressures of the magmatic environment. Hence, I was fortunate to have been offered a faculty position at the university that already had in place the necessary physical and technical support facilities."

Lauren Wright focused his teaching on the geology of North America and was interested in developing techniques in field geology. During most winters he did fieldwork in Death Valley, California. His objective was basically to study the geology of this region, its historical development, dating from the pre-Cambrian period to the present. Of particular importance were the structural events that produced the present fault system. These faults created the present landscape and may have occurred in historical time. Dr. Wright states: "The work we have done purely out of scientific interest has become of considerable interest to people because it is a proposed site for the permanent storage of high-level radioactive wastes. There is concern about whether the site will be disturbed by faulting or volcanic activity in the next few thousand years.

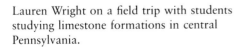

Lauren Wright on a field trip with students studying limestone formations in central Pennsylvania.

This geologic work is, thus, a case in point where purely scientific work may eventually have a very practical application."

Eugene Williams taught in the area of stratigraphy, sedimentology, and sedimentary petrology and the history and foundations of science. He says: "While recognizing the advantages of specialization in geology, I felt it was one of my main roles at Penn State to illustrate, both in research and teaching, the unity of the science and to explain why such unity was essential not only to geology as a science but to those individuals who practiced it. My most important course was, therefore, the History and Foundations of Geology, which had been taught by my predecessor, Paul Krynine. In studying the classics in geology (as well as related sciences) and an analysis of my own research, I attempted to illustrate the variety of approaches that had been used in successful scientific work and thereby to develop a tolerance and respect for all sciences."

Dr. Williams believes he undertook research "partly in order to become a better teacher, which may account for the fact that my research interests covered a wider range of problems and were of an applied nature as well as of a basic nature." He continued: "My main research was in demonstrating the many factors that controlled the properties of coals and related sediments, and translating them into criteria that could be used in the exploration, mining, and utilization of coals, clays, and associated rocks."

MAJOR RESEARCH THRUSTS

Four major long-term research themes illustrate the types of research in the geosciences: the high-pressure and high-temperature research of the geochemistry faculty; the seismology research of the geophysics faculty; the study of palynology; and the application of geomathematics to geological problems. Other traditional research themes include stratigraphy and petrology.

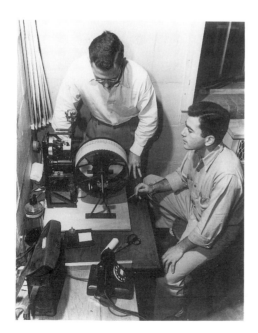

Joseph W. Berg, Jr., Ph.D. student, left, and Keeva Vosoff, an M.S. student, are shown in 1954 with the original seismic visible recorder that was installed in the Mineral Sciences Building in the early 1950s.

HIGH-PRESSURE AND HIGH-TEMPERATURE RESEARCH

Penn State has a long history of interdisciplinary experimental studies on the effect of high pressure and high temperature on the physics and chemistry of materials. Work in these areas is expanding with the addition of new faculty and the initiation of new research projects (Kerrick, 1987).

The Beginning: The 1940s

The high-pressure and high-temperature (high P/T) research was initiated in the fall of 1946, when Elburt F. Osborn joined the faculty as professor of geochemistry and head of the Earth Sciences Department. Before coming to Penn State, Dr. Osborn was interested in the application of high P/T research in both earth sciences and material sciences. Supported by industrial grants in his early years at Penn State, Osborn focused on experimental phase equilibrium studies related to industrial problems—especially blast furnace slags, steel plant refractories, and glass. In 1948 a grant from the Office of Naval Research provided support for studies directly in the geological sciences. These involved studies on "dry" (anhydrous) systems at one atmosphere pressure, and "hydrothermally" in Morey-type pressure vessels that operated to maximum pressures of a few hundred atmospheres. Penn State professors Della Martin Roy, Rustum Roy, and Arnulf Muan were graduate students working under Dr. Osborn in this research. Illustrating the interdisciplinary nature of this research program, Della Roy's Ph.D. was in mineralogy, Rustum Roy's was in ceramics, and Arnulf Muan's was in geochemistry and materials.

Rapid Growth: The 1950s

There were major advances in high P/T research in the 1950s. In 1950 MacKenzie L. Keith joined the faculty as associate professor of geochemistry. His geological experience and experimental phase equilibrium studies at the Geophysical Laboratory (Carnegie Institution of Washington) provided a basis for his collaboration with Dr. Osborn on his high-temperature phase equilibrium studies (system $MgO-Cr_2O_3-SiO_2$) and Rustum Roy's work on crystal chemistry of synthetic crystals.

In the 1950s Dr. Osborn and his students continued the studies on phase equilibria. Particularly noteworthy were the studies of Arnulf Muan on iron oxide-silicate systems and Robert DeVries's and Kenneth Gee's studies on the phase relations in the system $CaO-MgO-Al_2O_3-SiO_2$. Dr. Muan's work using oxygen partial pressure as a variable was not only of fundamental importance to an understanding of steel plant refractories but also led to Dr. Osborn's basic concept of the role of oxygen in the crystallization and differentiation of basaltic magma. From these studies basic principles were developed for estimating the optimum composition of iron blast furnace slags. In 1965 Dr. Muan and Dr. Osborn co-authored the book *Phase Equilibria Among Oxides in Steelmaking*.

Dr. Muan used these background studies to continue work into high-temperature phase equilibria. He developed a novel experimental technique for controlling the composition of gas mixtures used in high-temperature experimentation, a method subsequently adopted by such major research facilities as the Geophysical Laboratory of the Carnegie Institution of Washington.

In 1951 Rustum Roy began a major effort in hydrothermal research and materials synthesis. His research in the 1950s accordingly involved extensive studies on systematic phase equilibria

Geophysics students measuring the pull of gravity in field work in the early 1950s.

and the synthesis of layer silicates and hydrous minerals (clays and zeolites). His experimental studies on these and other mineral groups were paralleled by a growing interest in systematic crystal chemistry. His training in ceramics provided a very strong link between geochemistry and materials.

In the 1950s Frank Dachille and William B. White studied under Rustum Roy, attempting to extend the pressure range of experimentation in crystal synthesis. Dr. Dachille constructed several "opposed anvil" devices that extended the pressure range of experimentation to more than 100,000 atmospheres. Dr. White's work involved synthesis and crystal chemistry of a variety of oxides, an effort that included pioneering experimental research under high oxygen pressures.

When Dr. Osborn became dean of the College, his work was continued by O. F. Tuttle, whose research focused on hydrothermal experiments related to geological phenomena. Of special interest were phase relations in silicate melts containing water as a component and the implication of such data to the then controversial issue of the origin of granites. This hydrothermal research led to several now-classic papers bearing on the pressure-temperature conditions of metamorphism and the origin of granites. In 1955 C. Wayne Burnham began studies on ore-forming processes associated with silicate magmas. He joined Dr. Tuttle in developing large-volume internally heated pressure vessels for their studies.

In 1950s the equipment at Penn State was entirely "homemade" by machinists in the College; there were no commercial producers. Because demand for this type of equipment was growing, Rustum Roy, O. F. Tuttle, and Patrick H. Licastro (a geophysics graduate student) formed Tem-Press, a commercial enterprise involving the construction and sale of high P/T experimental equipment.

Livingston P. Teas
Distinguished Alumnus

Livingston P. Teas (Distinguished Alumnus 1962; B.S. Geology 1916) began his geological and mining work at Jerome, Arizona, and later worked in Colorado, Wisconsin, Louisiana, Texas, Ohio, New Mexico, and Mexico. After serving as an army lieutenant in World War I, he became assistant state geologist of Georgia. In 1941 he opened his own firm of consulting geologists in Houston, Texas. He has contributed articles on geological subjects to many professional publications and has also provided the Teas Scholarships through a generous endowment fund. His citation read:

> To Livingston P. Teas, for distinction as a geologist; for his success in establishing and directing his professional practice; for his many philanthropic activities, particularly in behalf of his alma mater; and for his genuine modesty in connection with his achievements.

Continued Growth: The 1960s

The 1960s witnessed many changes in personnel in the high P/T program, particularly in the geological sciences. Beginning in 1960 Richard H. Jahns joined Dr. Burnham in the study of volatiles in magmas, particularly on pegmatites, the volatile-rich produce of late-stage crystallization of magmas. When Dr. Jahns left Penn State in 1965 to head the School of Earth Sciences at Stanford, he was joined by O. F. Tuttle. Today the high P/T facility at Stanford is named "the Tuttle-Jahns Petrology Laboratory." Penn State faculty thus had an important role in developing the experimental P/T program at Stanford University.

In the 1960s Dr. Burnham established a major experimental research program on hydrous silicate melts and magmatic volatiles. Initially these experiments were hampered by the lack of thermodynamic data for water in the pressure-temperature realm of igneous processes. In order to overcome these limitations, two graduate students—Nicholas Davis and John Holloway—constructed a novel experimental apparatus to measure the volumetric properties of water as a function of pressure and temperature. These studies culminated in the milestone paper of 1969 on the thermodynamic properties of water and the thermodynamics of hydrous silicate melts. Other studies by Dr. Burnham and his students dealt with the chemistry of aqueous fluids and the role of water and oxygen in the crystallization of magmas and provided the foundation for geochemists throughout the world to construct theoretical models. The data provided the experimental basis for Dr. Burnham's construction of a unified thermodynamic model of aluminosilicate melts (magmas). This model was first presented at the Nobel symposium in Karlskoga, Sweden, in 1979, and published in the proceedings in 1981.

During the same period, Hubert L. Barnes began his studies on the relationship of high pressure and high temperature related to ore deposits. He designed large-volume hydrothermal vessels for experimentation on the solubilities of ore minerals. These vessels were subjected to mechanical oscillation to provide mixing within the sample container and to assure homogeneity and maximum reactivity. The so-called "Barnes-type Rocking Autoclave" became one of several types of hydrothermal high P/T equipment.

Peter J. Wyllie was on the geosciences faculty at Penn State for several years, working especially with Dr. Tuttle, before going to the University of Chicago. Ian Harker was also an important member of the faculty, working with Dr. Tuttle. He left to join Tem-Press, and later the faculty at the University of Pennsylvania.

Arthur L. Boettcher did his Ph.D. research under Peter Wyllie at Penn State and later did postdoctoral research with Wyllie after his transfer to the University of Chicago. Dr. Boettcher returned to Penn State as a member of the faculty in 1967. He was interested in the genesis of melts within the Earth's upper mantle, and he set up a piston cylinder apparatus to allow him to experiment in the pressure range of 10–60 kilobars. Dr. Boettcher and research associate Robin Hull carried out pioneering research on the role of carbon dioxide in mantle-derived silicate melts.

In 1969 Derrill M. Kerrick came to Penn State from the University of Manchester. His initial research at Penn State involved setting up a cold-seal laboratory to investigate metamorphic reactions at pressures up to a few kilobars and temperatures up to 700° C.

During the 1960s, Rustum Roy was actively involved in an effort to establish a multidisciplinary laboratory focusing on state-of-the-art research on solids. In 1962 the Materials Research Laboratory (MRL) was officially established within the College and was awarded the first National Science Foundation block grant for large-scale multidisciplinary research. A year later the MRL separated from the College, becoming an intercollege research program involving scientists with a wide range of department affiliations in the College of Earth and Mineral Sciences, Engineering, and Science.

The 1970s: High-Pressure Geophysics and Volatiles in Experimental Petrology

In contrast to the 1950s and 1960s there were few new faculty added in the 1970s, but high-pressure and high-temperature research advanced. The development of the plate-tectonic theory of the late 1960s required additional laboratory measurements to yield equations of state for minerals subjected to mantle pressure and temperature conditions. Earl K. Graham conducted high-pressure research on the elastic properties of the Earth's mantle. To develop these concepts

---

Paul B. Barton, Jr.
Distinguished Alumnus

Paul B. Barton, Jr. (Distinguished Alumnus 1982; Alumni Fellow 1979; B.S. Geosciences 1952), deputy chief for scientific programs for the U.S. Geological Survey's Office of Mineral Resources, returned to research in 1983. Noted for his research on the chemical processes that create mineral deposits, he was inducted into the elite National Academy of Sciences in 1978. Frequently honored for his accomplishments, he has had a mineral, bartonite, named for him. In 1982 he received Penn State's Distinguished Alumnus Award. The citation read:

> To Dr. Paul B. Barton, Jr., geochemist, for earning continual acclaim for his achievement and contribution to the understanding of the earth sciences, and for serving the needs of youth and his community.

cooperative research continued with the Materials Research Laboratory. Dr. Graham and Dr. Barsch, a physicist, developed an internally heated pressure vessel to measure the elastic properties of selected minerals.

In 1969, when rocks from the manned lunar landings were brought back to Earth, there was intense interest in the mineralogy, petrology, and genesis of the lunar rocks. Because Arnulf Muan and his students had carried out a considerable amount of laboratory experimentation under the low-oxygen partial pressure conditions existing during the formation of lunar igneous rocks, Penn State became an important center for the study of lunar rocks. Dr. Muan was the director of the project.

In 1976 David H. Eggler, a former postdoctorate fellow at Penn State, joined the faculty and continued the experimental programs on mantle-derived magma. Later his work was directed to the role of volatiles in the genesis of magmas in the earth's crust. During the same period, James G. Blencoe began developing experimental data to be used in deriving the thermodynamic properties of geologically relevant solid solutions.

In 1971 the geochemistry faculty received a large grant from the National Science Foundation to support experimentation related to the extraction of hot dry-rock geothermal energy. Studies were made of interactions between water and rock at pressures corresponding to different depths. The Penn State investigators also carried out an experimental study on the chemistry of geothermal fluids. In order to carry out the research, an experimental apparatus was constructed in which water was pumped through a rock specimen.

New Directions in the 1980s

High-temperature and high-pressure research remains at a strong level with new directions as the field advances. With the acquisition of such equipment as a cube anvil device and a tetrahedral anvil, the work of Earl K. Graham has been extended to higher pressures representative of deep Earth conditions. It is now possible to measure the elastic properties from 10 kilobars to about 100 kilobars. These anvil devices for measurement have helped Penn State stay in the forefront of high P/T research.

In the fall of 1980 Terry Engelder joined the faculty and has now constructed an apparatus to measure the mechanical properties of rocks to a temperature of 200° C and pressures of 1 kilobar. These instruments obtain in-situ measurements related to fracture and crack propagation in rocks subjected to stress. Susan L. Brantley, who joined the faculty in 1986, is studying water-rock reactions with particular emphasis on the geochemistry of aqueous solutions. Stephen J. Mackwell, who came to Penn State in 1987, is working on the effects of fluid on the rheology of rocks of the Earth's lower crust and mantle.

The Future

Penn State is recognized as a world-renowned center of high-pressure and high-temperature research. Since William Counts earned the first master's degree in 1948, more than 125 advanced degrees in experimental high P/T research have been granted. Over time, the initial high P/T research efforts emphasizing the synthesis, phase equilibria, and reaction kinetics of silicate and oxide systems have expanded to include physical property studies such as thermoelasticity, equations of state, brittle and ductile deformation, and spectroscopy, as well as a wider range of materials and observations (Graham, 1987).

Benjamin Howell, professor of geophysics, supervises installation of the seismograph, early 1950s.

Dr. Graham writes: "The unusually large number of faculty and staff with broad interests and backgrounds in high P/T research, coupled with our particularly extensive variety of experimental equipment, provide a climate where collaborative efforts are easily initiated and performed, on either a large scale or a small scale. Indeed, our numbers and diversity in both research staff and equipment suggest an overall capability that is probably unique."

SEISMOLOGY

Teaching and research in seismology was one of the earliest endeavors in the geophysics program. The equipment for the program has been continuously upgraded (Howell-Alexander, 1981). In 1938, when the central wing was added to the Mineral Industries Building (now Steidle Building), a small subbasement in which a separate seismometer was set directly on bedrock was included. Unfortunately, because the galvanometer that amplified the ground motion sensed by the seismometer was located on a shelf near the basement elevator door, the seismic system also recorded the opening and closing of the door. New springs on the door helped but never cured the problem.

In 1944 the seismographic system was rebuilt, and in 1946 a second horizontal component instrument was added, both recorded photographically. Development of a vertical-component system was begun in mid-1948 and completed in 1950 using a pen-and-ink recorder. In 1952 a visible recorder, operating initially from the north-south horizontal component seismometer, was installed on the second floor of the Mineral Industries Building. The first large earthquake recorded by this instrument was of magnitude 7.7. This was the Kern County, California, earthquake of July 21, 1952. In 1954 the system was rebuilt again, with an improved recorder providing photographic seismograms of all three components.

With the arrival of Benjamin F. Howell in 1949, teaching and research were expanded. Dr. Howell was interested in pursuing his interest in the propagation of seismic waves. Because of his work in earthquake seismology, one of his initial efforts was the introduction of a general geophysics course. This led to work in tectonophysics long before the processes associated with seafloor spreading were widely investigated during the late 1960s. Dr. Howell also introduced a course in instrumentation.

The early seismographic instruments were too crude for accurate calibration, and the seismograms presented little more information than timing the arrival of the principal wave pulses from large earthquakes. But through dedicated effort in these early years the faculty managed to record and study hundreds of earthquakes annually with cooperation from other seismic observatories. In the early 1960s Penn State was selected as one of the locations for a new global network of high-quality seismic observatories, the Worldwide Standard Seismographic Network funded by the Department of Defense's Advanced Research Project Agency (DARPA). The purpose of this state-of-the-art global network of seismic stations was to stimulate the study of earthquakes and man-made (nuclear) explosions at a time when establishing a reliable means of identifying and locating underground detonations as part of an anticipated ban on nuclear blast detonations was an important national objective. This station began operations in 1962 with equipment provided by the national program and has recorded continuously twenty-four hours a day ever since.

In 1981 the station was upgraded to include digital recording of vertical and horizontal components of ground motion, and this became part of the Digital Worldwide Standard Seismographic Network (DWSSN). In addition, during the summer of 1981, a very sensitive new borehole seismometer system was installed in a seismically quiet location about twenty-five miles southwest of State College, Pennsylvania, on University forestry land.

An expanded monitoring system has become part of the National Earthquake Hazards Reduction program. The program includes a thirteen-station network of seismic stations located throughout Pennsylvania and extending into Maryland and West Virginia. The data from the stations are telemetered using telephone lines to a central recording site in Deike Building at Penn State. This Pennsylvania Seismic Monitoring Network is part of the Northeastern U.S. Seismic Monitoring Network funded jointly by the U.S. Geological Survey and the U.S. Nuclear Regulatory Commission. The function of this network is to monitor earthquake activity in the northeastern United States in order to assess earthquake hazards. These data are especially important for the siting and safety of nuclear power plants, because approximately 80 percent of all U.S. plants are east of the Mississippi and heavily concentrated in the Northeast.

Research in seismology has continued to be a major endeavor in geophysics. The addition of Peter M. Lavin in 1962 and Robert Watson in 1963 significantly increased the geophysics capability in exploration seismology. Subsequently, other faculty who are interested principally in the solid-earth seismology were added, including Shelton S. Alexander, Charles A. Langston, and Roy J. Greenfield. The recent addition of John N. Louie in high-resolution seismology continues this emphasis. These faculty have carried out basic research relating, for example, to earthquake sources, the structure of the Earth's interior, and discrimination of earthquakes from explosions, a capability needed to monitor a comprehensive nuclear test ban treaty.

PALYNOLOGY

Penn State has had a long tradition in the field of palynology, dating from the tenure of Anton Kovar, a pollen analyst in the Department of Biology. The appointment of William Spackman in 1949, a paleobotanist from Harvard University, marked the beginning of the palynology program in the College of Earth and Mineral Sciences. Dr. Spackman established close ties with the Department of Biology and began courses in palynology. His primary interests in the origin and formation of carbonaceous substances defined the initial focus of the program and led him to establish the *Catalog of Fossil Spores and Pollen,* a compilation of standardized descriptions and illustrations of palynological literature.

In 1955 G. O. W. Kremp joined the College to edit the *Catalog.* In the 1960s first W. G. Chaloner and then Alfred Traverse continued the traditional focus of the palynological program. Dr. Traverse, who holds a joint appointment with the Department of Biology, served as editor of the *Catalog* from 1966 to 1977. Dr. Traverse has contributed widely to the field of palynology. These studies include the basis of palynofloras and the understanding of a geologic-stratagraphic link between the Triassic-Jurassic basins of eastern North America and the buried Triassic basins of Georgia and Texas, stages in the separation of North America from Africa and South America. Dr. Traverse's recent text, *Paleopalynology,* is the only comprehensive English-language text on the subject available.

Other faculty in the College involved in palynological research included the late Peter Given, a coal scientist who for many years made valuable contributions to investigations in the organic geochemistry of coal, especially the study of sporapollenin compounds. In 1989 Patrick Hatcher joined the faculty to continue the study of organic matter in marine sediments and the organic geochemistry of coal, and humus substances.

GEOMATHEMATICS

By the 1950s, statistics applied to problems in many geological areas had become so massive in number that computers became necessary to analyze them. John C. Griffiths was one of the early leaders in the application of computers to geological problems. He was the adviser for the first Ph.D. thesis using the University's IBM 604 computer. In this study a regression analysis to determine the length and breadth of 9,950 quartz sand grains was developed. In the late 1950s and early 1960s, studies on oil sands relating grain size to permeability were completed. For example, it was found that in West Virginia in a secondary recovery effort the water was passing through the coarse-grained sands that were already depleted of their oil. The oil that remained was located in the fine-grained sand lenses, and in order to produce the remaining oil, measures had to be developed to move water through these sands. Computers have greatly expanded the understanding of the permeability of oil sands, and the result has been an increased percentage of oil recovered from secondary recovery efforts. Without the computer, modern petrographic analysis could not occur (Griffiths, 1966).

Dr. Griffiths also uses geomathematics as a major tool in the search for new mineral wealth. He says: "The developments in search procedures have now passed through stages in which geology, geophysics, geochemistry, and finally geomathematics become integral parts of the tactics and strategy for location of natural resources. . . . To optimize search strategy or tactics, it is necessary to be able to specify the objectives and the degree of achievement as a means of success of the effort. . . . One future development that holds great promise is construction of a simulation model of the entire system with physical and economic constraints and then, by gaming, deciding what the optimal strategy requires, and how it may be modified, to maintain an optimum recovery rate under changing environmental conditions." He continues: "The application of mathematical modeling and simulation of exploration programs, using past results as a test of their success, suggests that some commercial success may be attained under a wide variety of conditions. . . . If the United States of America is taken as an example, then the total value of nonrenewable material resources already produced in the period 1880–1963 for the coterminous United States and Alaska is $459,619 million. The area of this region is 3,608,787 square miles. As a first approximation it may be claimed that any 1,000-square-mile area has an expected value of $127 million. This can form the basis for investment decisions for exploration for nonrenewable natural resources." Dr. Griffiths gives another example: "Again, given an area such as the United States with a roughly rectangular outline of 3,000 by 1,000 miles, suppose this area were to be drilled on a square grid with spacing of 20 miles, then 7,500 wells would be required to complete the grid. . . . Wells of this kind could be drilled in the United States for about $250,000 (1963) each, leading to a total drilling cost of $1.875 billion. Selecting any five very large targets (oil and gas fields or ore deposits) would lead to a return of some $15 billion, so that if five such targets are located the search would be eminently successful in a commercial sense."

The importance of geomathematics as a tool in the geosciences at Penn State is now recognized. Its application to solving geoscience problems is assured. Says Dr. Griffiths: "In the next decade the problems with greatest public impact will receive greatest emphasis and support. This will require that the geosciences comprehend exceedingly complex probabilistic systems and then, in turn, demand the use of operations research, cybernetics, and system analysis. Such a development may well lead to a change in the paradigms underlying geoscience. They will certainly include more realistic models in the "real-world" systems, and the tool of simulation with cybernetic models may well become the basis for rejuvenating experimentation in the geosciences."

CURRENT FACULTY RESEARCH CONCENTRATIONS

In 1990 there were thirty-nine members of the faculty and ten active emeritus professors representing such branches of the discipline as geology, geophysics, geochemistry, mineralogy, petrology, paleontology, and palynology. The following profiles reveal the current areas of teaching and research.

GEOSCIENCES FACULTY

Michael A. Arthur, who came to Penn State in 1990 as professor and Head of the Department of Geosciences, has focused his research on the ways in which chemical and physical variables in the oceans are reflected in the geochemistry of marine sediments and their modification by subsequent processes such as burial and/or weathering; on the nature and causes of temporal evolution

Wayne Burnham, professor of geochemistry, in his high-temperature/high-pressure laboratory.

of ocean chemistry and circulation as studied through the marine sedimentary record; and on evidence for substantial changes in the global carbon cycle in the geologic past and consequent variations in atmospheric CO_2 and the earth's climate. In particular, he continues to examine the production of organic matter in modern marine environments and processes that influence its subsequent incorporation into sediments as a way of understanding past episodes of very widespread "black shale" deposition—prolific hydrocarbon source beds—as well as developing stable isotope methods for tracing geochemical cycles.

Eric Barron, director of the Earth System Science Center, is interested in the topic of global change. He is involved in research incorporating numerical models of the climate system and the study of change throughout earth history.

Susan Brantley investigates problems involving water-rock interaction, emphasizing the kinetics of mineral dissolution and precipitation and the effects of these processes on permeability in rocks. Her work ranges from high-temperature and high-pressure laboratory experiments to low-temperature experimental and field studies of natural water systems.

Terry Engelder's interest in rock mechanics began early in his graduate school days. He has become nationally known for his studies of the regional tectonics of the Appalachian Plateau. By taking careful stress measurements, he has shown that part of the Appalachian Plateau was overpressured during the Alleghanian orogeny. In a series of papers since the late 1970s, he has presented some well-documented examples of residual stress and time-dependent relaxation in rocks. Recent studies in the area of hydraulic fracture have shown that remnant stress affects the in-situ stress data.

Donald Fisher, whose interest is in the interaction of metamorphism and deformation, has concentrated on the structural and tectonic evolution of accretionary prisms. In ongoing research on convergent margins and collisional mountain belts, he focuses on such areas as fold-and-thrust kinematics and metamorphism during cleavage development.

Terry Engelder operating high-pressure equipment.

Kevin Furlong uses computer simulations and modeling analyses to investigate the thermal evolution of the lithosphere. His work has focused on the evolution of the plate boundaries, the development of sedimentary basins, and thermal and compositional evolution of the continental crust.

James Kasting hopes to gain understanding of the different evolutionary pathways followed by Venus, Earth, and Mars by developing theoretical models to investigate atmospheric evolution on the terrestrial planets. He has focused on developing climate models for studying the "greenhouse effect" in present and past terrestrial atmospheres, but his interests range from photochemical modeling techniques to the study of the origins of life.

Lee R. Kump's goal in teaching is to introduce interdisciplinary approaches to his students. A new undergraduate course he developed in the earth system science stresses the interactions among Earth's major components—the biosphere, the geosphere, the atmosphere, and the oceans—and how these interactions act to regulate the Earth's surface conditions. His research centers on studies of oceanography, sedimentary, and marine chemistry. Specific research themes include global biochemical cycles and their role in the regulation of atmospheric oxygen, trace metals in sea water, the marine chemistry of pallodium, the global cycle of phosphorus, and the diffusion of solutes in water. Dr. Kump writes, "I believe that my most significant research has arisen through interactions with others, especially with those outside of my field."

John Louie is interested in the acquisition, processing, inversion, and interpretation of high-resolution seismic data. His work focuses on the physical nature of lithospheric structures and their relation to tectonic processes.

Stephen Mackwell studies the mechanical, physical, and chemical properties of geological materials under lower-crustal or upper-mantle conditions. He uses laboratory experiments to measure the rates of transport of fluid components in mantle and crustal rocks and the effects of such components on the properties of the rocks.

GEOLOGY FACULTY

William Duke's professional interests are in clastic sedimentary structures and stratification sequences, especially those involving wave-generated flows. In the field, he studies spatial fossil arrangements in the deposits of ancient epicontinental seas. In the laboratory, he models wave-generated flows with oscillatory- and combined-flow water tunnels.

Thomas Gardner teaches geomorphology and photogeology. He uses field techniques and remote-sensing to quantitatively investigate questions of fluvial and tectonic geomorphology, watershed hydrology, and quarternary geology.

David Gold teaches economic geology, remote-sensing, structural geology, and structural analysis of metamorphic tectonics, and his research efforts are concentrated on fracture analysis using remote-sensing techniques, the tectonic deformation of ore deposits, and fission-track dating. Dr. Gold has been an active participant in the data collected by the earth resources satellite programs. In addition, he has been interested in the use of satellite imagery to recognize tectonic regimes that are favorable hosts to certain types of ore deposits, particularly the niobium, rare earths, and apatite associated with carbonatites and diamonds in the peculiar kimberlitic and lamproitic intrusions. Laurence Lattman, Shelton Alexander, Richard Parizek, and David Gold led the development at Penn State of the use of multispectral scanner data for lithographic mapping, as well as spatial mapping for structure and geomorphic features. From this work, procedures for characterization of lineaments, fracture traces, and other important structural features have evolved.

Albert Guber's interests have centered on problems rather than disciplines in both teaching and research. Research contributions have been made in the functional morphology of Early Paleozoic ostracods, the distribution of pyrite in coal-bearing rocks and its environmental causes, the deep-water origin of the Kuroko massive sulfur deposits, the compaction model for barrier island migration, and the sedimentary geochemistry of salt marshes.

Richard Parizek's research interests include the study of hydrology, the hydrogeology of coal mines, the relationship between land-use planning and groundwater quality and availability, and the treatment and isolation of liquid and solid wastes. He is co-developer of the fracture-trace method of groundwater prospecting and co-director of the living-filter concept for treating liquid wastes and sludges. He offered the first graduate-level environmental geology course in the United States in 1962.

Rudy Slingerland has taught classes in the fields of coal and petroleum geology, field geology, and clastic depositional environments. His research focuses on numerical modeling of fluid circulation, the resulting sediment transport, and deposition and basin subsidence, especially in basins filled by ancient continental seas. Traditionally, models of the sedimentary and stratigraphic relationships in sedimentary basins were descriptive. With the development of simulation models, they now assume a form that fosters quantitative inferences about the stratigraphy of a basin and its origin. In the development of a model, Dr. Slingerland starts with the known paleobathymetry and paleogeography of the basin and then assumes a tidal forcing action at the entrance to the open ocean, wind stresses, and a starting grain-size distribution. The model then calculates the fluid circulation field, the sediment transport rates of the various-size fractions, and the amount of erosion or deposition of the bed. In the development of this basic research, Dr. Slingerland measures stratigraphic sections in the Appalachian foreland basin, studying quantitative dynamic strategy of fluvial systems.

Robert F. Schmalz's principal interest is chemical interactions between modern sediments and natural waters. He has concentrated on carbonate and evaporate systems, which is the basis for his research visits to tropical reefs in January and February. Dr. Schmalz states: "Academic research has afforded me an excuse to pursue my own interests, to satisfy my urge to teach and my curiosity about the world. This explains why we enter the academic world, and why it is so rewarding. For thirty years I have explored my surroundings with the freedom to investigate any problem that piqued my interest. I have enjoyed the stimulation of imaginative colleagues, and above all I have had the opportunity to work closely with hundreds of students from diverse backgrounds and disciplines. The excitement they shared with me, and the pleasure I derived from watching them mature, are (for me) the real reward of a life in the university community."

Barry Voight's first contact with geology came when he was a student at Notre Dame, when, he says, "I had the good fortune to stumble into the office of Ray Gutschick. His enthusiasm for geology and zeal for discovery were made obvious to me from our first meeting." With a dual major in engineering and geology, Dr. Voight began his career by drawing on engineering fundamentals in order to solve geologic problems. His teaching and research have always been centered on problems of mass movements and various topics in rock mechanics. In 1968 he taught his first course on finite element analysis at Penn State, and he continued to do so until engineering mechanics made it a part of their curriculum.

Dr. Voight has spent many years pursuing his goals in distant places all over the world. His studies of Iceland, mapping fracture and stress fields, took place over a series of years, and on one visit the northeast rift zone erupted "in a remarkable fashion before our eyes." He says: "These were memorable times. At summer's end the high cliff lines were etched in snow, and green aurora veils, driven by magnetic currents, slowly shifted in a dark night sky. A simmering lamb and tomato goulash warmed the proudly timbered Heidarhus, our mountain retreat halfway between the Skirnir Jonsson family warmth at Skard farm in Dalsmynni and the unforgettable rustic charm of Orn and Erla, in Brettingsstadhir on the very edge of the Arctic Ocean. The rocks told a story of enormous transform strain and oroclinal flexure, the dike swarm twisted to a right angle along the length of the peninsula, and the virtual gas-magnetic poles of the lavas and dikes bent with them. Yet even now I can scarcely believe it. In all respects, magnetism dominated our thoughts."

The eruption of Mount St. Helens in April 1980 provided Dr. Voight with the opportunity to study a massive movement of rock material. He was invited to assist the U.S. Geological Survey in evaluating the landslide hazard. He immediately recommended a monitoring program because it was evident that a massive rock movement would occur. As he predicted, a massive rock failure occurred in May 1980. During the next several years, Dr. Voight studied avalanche deposits and offered several solutions to control the mass movement of rock and the hazards associated with these events. His focus continues to be on predictive methods for eruptions and slope failure and on aspects of disaster prevention.

GEOCHEMISTRY FACULTY

Hubert L. Barnes's principal objective, in addition to his work with graduate students, has been to investigate by field, theoretical, and especially experimental methods the dominant problems of hydrothermal geochemistry. This work started in 1961, when Dr. Barnes offered the first graduate course in the subject, now recognized as one of the principal specialties in geochemistry.

Peter Deines's interests lie in the study of stable isotope variations of the light elements hydrogen, carbon, nitrogen, oxygen, and sulfur in natural materials. His stable isotope studies have made many contributions in such diverse fields as archaeology, biochemistry, cosmochemistry,

Peter Deines, professor of geochemistry, in the isotope laboratory.

geosciences, hydrology, and meteorology. The work includes the study of natural variation as well as the laboratory calibration of requisite isotope fractionation factors. This information is then used in conjunction with geologic and chemical principles to formulate computer models that will replicate the variations observed in the natural materials. Dr. Deines indicates that this approach has provided unique information on natural processes as diverse as the formation of meteorites, diamonds, ore deposits, the dissolution of limestone, or the movement of groundwaters in Pennsylvania soils and karst waters.

Michael Machesky has developed a research program investigating the complexities of mineral-liquid interfacial processes. His research focuses on colloidal geochemistry, groundwater chemistry, and early diagenetic processes.

Arnulf Muan, who died in 1990, had a joint appointment in the Department of Geosciences and the Department of Materials Science and Engineering. He coordinated an extensive research program investigating heterogeneous phase equilibria and their applications to petrological and technological problems.

Hiroshi Ohmoto is an expert in stable isotope mass spectrometry. He pursues genesis of mineral deposits and the chemical evolution of the oceans and atmosphere. His work includes field geology, laboratory and theoretical analysis, and high-temperature and rock-water experiments.

Arthur W. Rose's main approach in teaching and research has been to apply basic scientific principles to the solution of real problems and to teach students to apply basic concepts to these problems. He considers one of his greatest accomplishments to be the publication of his 1979 book entitled *Geochemistry of Mineral Exploration*, which emphasizes the scientific basis for geochemical techniques and has become the leading textbook in the field.

Rustum Roy, former director of the Materials Research Laboratory, is director of the Science, Technology, and Society Program. He has wide-ranging interests in crystal chemistry and mineral synthesis. His recent work has focused on radioactive waste composites, chemical vapor deposition of diamonds, and diphasic gels.

Norman Suhr was director of the Materials Characterization Laboratory. He supervised several chemists and maintains an analytical laboratory for measurement of chemical and spectroscopic properties of rocks and minerals.

William B. White's research interests range from spectroscopy of silicate melts to the hydrogeology of karst terrains. Because of his wide interests he could be called a mineral physicist or a low-

Hubert L. Barnes
Distinguished Professor of Geochemistry

No one plans to become a professor of geochemistry. Only a long series of career choices, perceived at each time to be optimized, leads to such a fulfilling endeavor. By my ancestry, I was preordained to be something else.

My family, dominated by careers in commerce, valued practicality. Consequently, a degree from the Massachusetts Institute of Technology was considered appropriate. When graduate studies extended into a postdoctoral fellowship, however, their enthusiasm dimmed, with veiled observations about the hazards of graduating directly to Social Security benefits. Their doubts became crystallized when the title of "professor" arrived, and they could only offer sympathy to closer relatives at my enthusiasm for the appointment.

However, with the station of "professor" came engrossing new opportunities. The geological sciences had just begun the transition from a qualitative, descriptive science to a science emphasizing the quantification of natural processes. By adopting geochemistry as a specialty, one could move freely among field, experimental, and theoretical methods to attack the multitude of open, major questions on the evolution of the earth. Even the simplest of theoretical or experimental insights brought magnified dividends in improved understanding as the advances of other fields were assimilated into the geological sciences.

At this pell-mell frontier, it was easy to produce acutely embarrassing blunders as well as successes. The only insurance against such inadvertent lapses is unrestrained reviews by talented critics. They were present at each stage of my career as blind luck continued to provide me with close association early with developing (or, later, with recognized) leaders of geological sciences, the eagles of the field whose attitudes and expertise were contagious.

These associations catalyzed for me fascinating research. Opened were the pure pleasure and awe of exploring virgin truths, where flashes of insight instantly compensated for months of worrying a problem and carried over to extra impetus for new quests. My own excitement was amplified by sharing with students the elation of discovery as we contributed to the resolution of long-standing puzzles. Boredom was never a problem. Instead, enthusiasm for the search for understanding carried interpretative discussions long past civilized hours. Self-discipline was needed not to go *to* the office but to control impatience with mundane impediments to our activities in geochemistry.

Like other professors captivated by research and teaching, clearly we have been among the world's most fortunate.

temperature aqueous geochemist. His special interests include infrared and Raman spectroscopy, crystal field theory, mineral luminescence, dissolution kinetics, carbonate geochemistry, and environmental geochemistry of metals and radioactive wastes.

GEOPHYSICS FACULTY

Shelton S. Alexander is interested in a wide range of geophysical problems, including seismology, plate tectonics, remote sensing, space science, and geophysical exploration for energy resources.

Shelton Alexander, professor of geophysics, demonstrates a seismic recording machine, mid-1970s.

His work in seismology ranges from the use of modes of Rayleigh and Love waves to determine lateral variations in crustal structure and source parameters for earthquakes, to the nature of the Earth's core-mantle boundary. He has developed numerous signal-processing techniques to extract diagnostic information from single and array seismic observations of earthquakes and explosions. His work on seismic hazards includes the operation of the Pennsylvania Seismic Monitoring Network and a probabalistic-hazard methodology for assessing risk in the eastern United States.

Earl K. Graham's research interests include an emphasis on pressure and temperature dependence of elastic properties on primary earth-forming silicates and oxides and their application to the compositional aspects of planetary interiors; elastic properties of porous ceramics and glasses; experimental synthesis and characterization of high-pressure and high-temperature phases and composites of engineering ceramic materials; experimental and theoretical evaluation of equations of state appropriate for the prediction of the compression of silicates and oxides; and the calculation and evaluation of compositional models of Earth and terrestrial planets in terms of observable geophysical data.

Roy Greenfield works in the general area of exploration geophysics using electrical and magnetic field techniques. His other research interests include theoretical seismology and acoustic gravity waves. A special interest of Dr. Greenfield is the locating of miners trapped underground.

Charles A. Langston's teaching and research program at Penn State reflects a continuing commitment to the goals of scientific research. His concentration on the application of quantitative seismology to the solution of problems in wave propagation and source parameterization began as a graduate student at the California Institute of Technology. His philosophy of teaching emphasizes the usefulness of the subject matter toward the solution of real research problems. Several techniques developed in his research program have been put to use throughout the seismological community. These include inversion of source parameters using wave-form data, determination of crustal and mantle structure through the receiver-function technique, and calculation of synthetic seismograms for complex wave fields.

Peter Lavin's general interests in exploration and engineering geophysics have led him to pursue the use of gravity and magnetic data for interpreting the crustal structure and tectonics of the eastern United States.

Charles Langston in the seismic laboratory.

PALEONTOLOGY-PALYNOLOGY FACULTY

Roger Cuffey teaches in the area of historical geology, paleontology, stratigraphy, evolution, and paleoecology with an emphasis on the systematics of colonial invertebrates, principally bryozoans. Three different but related emphases serve to focus his research. A major area of interest has been to develop biologically realistic species concepts and to apply these concepts in repeatable fashion to fossil and related living bryozoans. This has required careful examination and measurement of morphologic variability at all levels from colony form to wall microstructure. These studies have resulted in the discovery of a number of new species and genera.

As a second area of interest Dr. Cuffey traces evolving lineages of bryozoans on different time scales. Such tracing employs the species concepts in order to trace the various evolutionary patterns, taxonomic and systematic implications, and potential uses in precise biostratigraphic age-dating. Especially interesting is the tracing of the evolution of Paleozoic groups into surviving living types. Other research focuses on the contributions made by bryozoans to the geologically important sedimentary environments, particularly reefs and bioherms and extending for comparison to carbonate platforms, mixed-sediment shelves, and detrital coastlines.

Alfred Traverse developed his research interest as a graduate student in paleopalynology and in 1951 prepared the first thesis on the fossil types found in North America. He wanted to begin his career in an educational institution, but there were no positions available and he was not able to begin his career in academia until he came to Penn State in 1966. His course, Introduction to Palynology, was one of the first of its kind developed in the nation.

Major field experiences in Dr. Traverse's research included work in the Black Sea region, first with the Woods Hole Oceanographic Institution and later with the Deep Sea Drilling Project (Glomar Challenger). The research revealed expansion and contraction of the typical forest in central and southern Europe for millions of years before the present. A second area of interest has been the rift basins of eastern North America. Evidence collected in his palynological laboratory placed the dating of the rocks on a sound basis. Further work has demonstrated time-coordinated sedimentary rock in basins, predating the opening of the Atlantic between Africa, South America, and North America about 230 million years ago. In a study of central Pennsylvania, it was

Roger Cuffey, professor of paleontology, studying molar teeth of a mastodon, about 15,000 years old, from a site near Hollidaysburg, Pennsylvania.

revealed that the first land plants were producing resistant-walled spores and primitive plant tissues as long ago as 440 million years. This represents one of the high points in evolution. Dr. Traverse states: "It is exciting that some of the best rocks in which to study these events are within a short ride from our laboratory." The information banks represented by samples, slides, and literature are the best in the nation.

PETROLOGY-MINERALOGY FACULTY

Alan Davis, director of the Energy and Fuels Research Center, coordinates a research program investigating the geology and petrology of coal deposits. He is particularly interested in the origin and optical properties of coal and their relation to coal metamorphism and utilization.

David Eggler, using traditional field techniques as well as high-pressure-laboratory experiments, studies the compositions and genesis of continental igneous rocks. Recently focusing on xenolith composition and petrography, his fieldwork complements piston cylinder experiments aimed at understanding melt generation and mass transport at mantle conditions.

Derrill Kerrick, a metamorphic petrologist, is recognized for his theoretical, experimental, and field work on metamorphic rocks. The major emphases of recent research have included the $Al_2Si_2O_5$ polymorphs, the origin of gold in the mother lode of California, and thermal modeling of contact metamorphic aureoles.

Deane K. Smith is a mineralogist whose research interests have been in the crystal chemistry of uranium in minerals and nuclear ceramics, including waste forms. He has been active in the International Center for Diffraction Data and has conducted pioneer studies in the development of theoretical modeling of powder diffraction. Dr. Smith was one of the original organizers of the international journal *Power Diffraction*. In recent years he has been developing computer programs for x-ray analysis of minerals and inorganic materials.

Charles Thornton's contribution to the geosciences lies in his teaching of mineralogy and in his responsibilities as associate head for undergraduate programs in the department. He is particularly interested in volcanic rocks, eruptions, landforms, and structures, as well as granites and related ore deposits. He is also chair of the undergraduate program in earth science.

Richard J. Janda
Alumni Fellow

Richard J. Janda (Alumni Fellow 1990; B.S. Geosciences 1960) joined the U.S. Geological Survey in 1963 and within a few months was named leader of a project, Geomorphological Studies of the Sierra Nevada, California, which focused on weathering, transportation, and disposition of sediment. In 1968 this work was extended to the coastal area of Oregon and also to the Hawaiian Islands. These studies were notable for their pioneering use of satellite imagery and ultrahigh altitude photography.

In 1973 he was named project chief of a special interagency task force organized to advise the secretary of the interior on the potential effects of environmental degradation in forested areas adjacent to Redwood National Park, California. His findings provided the rational basis for answering many of the complex management problems facing the park. Dr. Janda received a meritorious award for this work and was cited by the secretary of the interior as an outstanding scientist.

Following the eruption of Mount St. Helens, Dr. Janda, together with Barry Voight (Penn State) and Harry Glicken (University of California), in 1984 carried out joint research on eruption-related debris and sediment emplacement that brought them the George Stevenson Gold Medal and the Case History Award. As an internationally acclaimed expert on volcanic disaster prevention, volcanic sedimentology, and erosion processes in coastal drainage basins, Dr. Janda is frequently called on to assess hazardous situations around the world.

TRENDS IN GEOSCIENCE EDUCATION

Shelton Alexander notes some trends in geoscience education: "The geological sciences were traditionally much more descriptive than today, with heavy emphasis on field mapping. This reflected a national interest. For instance, the U.S. Geological Survey spent a good deal of time in the early years making geologic maps and describing surface or near-surface geologic phenomena. At one time a student could get an M.S. and even a Ph.D. thesis approved just by making a good geologic map of an area that had not been previously mapped and by qualitatively interpreting the geologic relationships observed." But, he continues, over time "the whole field of geological sciences has evolved and become much more quantitative. Emphasis on geophysics and geochemistry, two fields that have risen to the fore in the past twenty-five years, required strong background in physics, chemistry, and mathematics. Major advances in digital computing made it possible to simulate actual three-dimensional geologic problems including time-dependent behavior. With improvements in the ability to make quantitative analyses and realistic models of geologic processes, there has been a natural evolution toward a much more quantitative treatment of geological problems. As a consequence, students in classical geology, as well as geochemistry and geophysics, now must have a much stronger background in mathematics, physics, and chemistry than in earlier days. All students graduating today must be well versed in the physics and chemistry of the Earth. However, field experience is still considered a vital part of geologic training."

With regard to recent developments he says: "Because of unifying concepts of global geological processes, such as plate tectonics, developed over the last two decades, and because of the current strong emphasis on the Earth as a system, we are much closer to understanding how the Earth works today and in turn how it worked in the past," and adds: "Modern geoscientists must be generalists in the sense of being able to synthesize and interpret diverse types of information, but at the same time they must be able to work at the frontiers of their specialty. In recent years there has been an explosion of knowledge in earth sciences. To cope with such rapid advances over their careers, our graduates must be well-grounded in the fundamentals, which are strongly emphasized in our academic programs at both the undergraduate and the graduate levels."

THE GEOSCIENCES GRADUATE PROGRAM

The graduate program in the geosciences at Penn State got a late start, compared with many state universities. The first Ph.D. was not granted until 1951, but annual growth after that point was rapid. The number of doctorates granted each year increased irregularly, from 2 in 1951 to 12 in each of 1958 and 1959. In the first 10 years (1951–60) 58 Ph.D.'s were granted. In the next five years (1961–65) there were 60, or a total of 118 in the first fifteen years.

In 1964 the American Council on Education evaluated the graduate geology programs of major universities. In *An Assessment of Quality in Graduate Education* by Allan M. Carter, published in 1966, the leading geology departments were rated by "quality of graduate work," and "leading departments by rated effectiveness of graduate programs." In the first category, Penn State was eighth on the list. Only Harvard, California (at Berkeley), Cal Tech, Columbia, Princeton, M.I.T., and Stanford, in that order, were ranked higher, but of the state universities only California ranked higher. In the second category the results were very similar: Penn State was rated ninth and Yale became eighth. The growth of the graduate program was truly remarkable.

From the beginning of graduate work until 1989 the graduate degrees were granted in the subbranches of the field: geology, geophysics, geochemistry, and mineralogy (Alexander, 1981; Kerrick, 1981; Gold, 1981). In 1989 a single degree in geosciences was established. The change reflects the changing nature of the geological sciences at the national and international levels. A growing number of sciences approach problems on multidisciplinary and global scales, so that subdiscipline labels, such as geophysics and geochemistry, can no longer encompass the breadth of research entailed in existing projects.

The merged program places less constraint on students and faculty who want to pursue research or coursework that crosses current program boundaries. This change is especially relevant because newly hired faculty nearly always cross program boundaries. Students are expected to reach academic goals of professional training in breadth and depth. The faculty believe that under the new plan students will achieve extended goals of breadth of outlook and a multidisciplinary spirit that will be important for future careers in the geosciences.

The geosciences graduate program has about 125 students. From 1965 to 1980 the number of students grew by about 50 percent, and in the 1980s the graduate enrollment was steady. The quality of the students has always been high, and this is an established goal to be maintained. There are more than three hundred applicants for the program each year, many of whom come from foreign countries.

The large size of the geosciences faculty has unique advantages. The diversity of the faculty makes it possible for graduate students to have a wide selection of research topics and courses.

The breadth of the faculty interests has made it possible to develop excellent laboratories and other research facilities in a number of specialties. Furthermore, students working in one specialty have contact with students in other branches of the field, and at the same time the faculty provides students with a wide range of expertise. This has made it possible to tailor each student's program according to his or her interests and to give individual faculty attention to each student.

Steward S. Flaschen
Alumni Fellow

Steward S. Flaschen (Alumni Fellow 1990; Ph.D. Geochemistry and Mineralogy 1953) received his doctorate in geochemistry and mineralogy at Penn State in 1953 and subsequently held positions in research and development with Bell Telephone Laboratories and Motorola. In 1964 he joined ITT as director of materials and components research. Two years later he was named vice president and deputy technical director, and in 1969 he became general technical director responsible for the worldwide technical activities and investments of the corporation. From 1982 until his retirement in 1988 he was senior vice president, general technical director, and a member of the ITT management policy board. In this capacity he managed the more than $1 billion a year in research and development investments of the ITT corporation in a network of some 250 companies worldwide and directed the ITT companies in converting technology into new products and markets. He was directly involved in the technology transfer activities of ITT's research and engineering centers in twenty-four countries and has personally received awards from Chilean government for his assistance in industrial technology transfer to the private sector.

He is an adviser to the president of Penn State, to the Office of University Development, and to the Materials Research Laboratory. He is also a member of the board of directors of the National Retinitis Pigmentation Foundation and the National Voice Foundation and a Fellow of the American Association for the Advancement of Science and the American Institute of Chemists.

THE UNDERGRADUATE PROGRAM

The Department of Geosciences participates in two undergraduate programs: the geosciences program, for which it has sole responsibility, and the interdisciplinary earth science program, coordinated by a committee of faculty from the Geosciences, Meteorology, and Geography Departments.

Until 1990, when a single geosciences major was developed, the geosciences major consisted of three options. The traditional program was the geology option, the geophysics option dated from the late 1940s, and the biogeology option dated from the 1980s. Over the years the number of required courses increased and the number of electives decreased. Charles P. Thornton, associate head for the undergraduate program, states: "In order to correct this situation, to increase the flexibility of the program, to integrate the field aspects of the geosciences more thoroughly with its laboratory aspects, and to involve the undergraduate students with the research being carried out by our faculty, a rather drastic revision of our undergraduate program was undertaken."

Geosciences faculty and students in 1954.

The goal of the undergraduate program is to introduce students to the study of the Earth's physical and chemical makeup, its history, and the physical, chemical, and biological processes that cause the surface and interior of the Earth to change. For example, students develop an understanding of how the Earth and other planets were formed and evolved to their present state; of what causes the continents to move and mountains and seas to disappear; of how minerals and oil and gas were formed and emplaced; of what causes destructive earthquakes, volcanic eruptions, and other natural hazards, and how their effects can be mitigated; and of how global, regional, and local environmental changes are caused by and affect human activities.

One of the more important philosophical concepts involved in the revision of the undergraduate program is that, as they progress through their undergraduate years, students should be encouraged to take on more and more responsibility for deciding what courses they should take. The logical end is that, for most students, in the senior year the only required course will be the senior project. The aim is to graduate well-educated geoscientists who are competent in modern quantitative techniques, have good communication skills, have a strong grounding in the fundamentals of chemistry and physics, and have an excellent background in the specialty of their choice.

In the late 1950s and early 1960s the undergraduate enrollment rose from about 25 to 30 students to about 125 in the early 1970s, reaching a peak of about 250 in the early 1980s. During this long period of a rising student body, the principal employer of graduates was the petroleum and natural gas industry. In the 1980s, with the decline in the petroleum and natural gas industries, employment opportunities shrank and the undergraduate enrollment declined. A modest but significant increase has occurred in recent years, in part because of new jobs in groundwater and environmental areas.

Because the earth science program is interdisciplinary, the student receives a broader background in the earth sciences, with a concentration in one of the three disciplines that the student chooses as his or her "area of concentration." The majority of these majors are in the geosciences area of concentration, but a number of students concentrate their work in geography or meteorology. The program has a distinct environmental character, with courses in ecology and environmental resource management. One distinctive feature of the program is the requirement of a senior thesis. The enrollment in the earth science program has grown from about thirty-five students in the late 1960s to more than one hundred in 1991.

GENERAL EDUCATION

The study of the physical Earth, in contrast to the biological world, has played an important role in the general education of students at Penn State. Since the beginning of the program, geoscience courses have been offered for the nonmajor. These include "Planet Earth," "Earth History," and "The Sea Around Us." Because the department has always considered these courses for the nonmajor important, the most experienced professors teach them.

Laurence Lattman—who was at Penn State from 1957 to 1970 and is now president of the New Mexico Institute of Mining and Technology—remembers his experiences as an instructor in Geological Sciences 20, "Planet Earth," which he developed at Penn State: "Shortly after I arrived at Penn State in 1957 I was asked to teach the geology course for nonmajors in addition to advanced geomorphology and photogeology courses. Of all the courses I taught over the years, my major teaching contribution was in Geological Sciences 20, which in later years reached an enrollment of about 1,800 each term. This involved back-to-back lectures to 900 students in

John C. Redmond
Alumni Fellow

John C. Redmond (Alumni Fellow 1988; Ph.D. Geophysics 1962) has since 1965 been vice president for research and engineering of GTE Corporation and president of GTE Laboratories Inc. He was previously vice president for research and development of GTE Communication Systems Corporation, a major component of General Telephone and Electronics. GTE Laboratories is the principal research and development resource for about one hundred individual GTE telecommunications, lighting, and precision materials operations around the world. Dr. Redmond directs the laboratories' seven hundred scientists, engineers, and support staff in leading research programs in electronics and photonics, telecommunication, computer and intelligent systems, and materials science. During his career he has been particularly active in the Institute of Electrical and Electronic Engineers (IEEE). He is Senior Member and past Outstanding Lecturer of the IEEE, and former president of the IEEE Geoscience Electronics group, now the Geoscience and Remote Sensing Society. In 1984 he was awarded the Distinguished Service Award from the Oceanic Engineering Society and also the IEEE Centennial Medal.

Schwab Auditorium." He continues: "Teaching at Penn State was a most rewarding if not thrilling experience. The quality of a university is measured really by only two things—the quality of its faculty and the quality of its student body. A lot of people today talk only about the quality of the faculty as being a measure of the quality of the school, but if you don't have a top-quality student body, there's no way the faculty is going to turn out a quality product. Penn State's student body was excellent."

The personal satisfaction Dr. Lattman got from his experiences as an instructor was significant: "I derived a great deal of personal satisfaction out of teaching GSci 20 because the students who took the course were not majors. They approached anything with a scientific name with fear and trepidation, and they would resist any effort to get solid scientific information unless it was made pleasant, understandable, and challenging. And because I was dealing with a rather high quality of student, it was fairly easy to meet this challenge. At the beginning these students had in their minds 'I am no good in science,' and when they left the course they were certainly not scientists but they had some appreciation of the physical Earth. They had the ability to look around them when they traveled and recognize some of the things they had been taught, and because the course concentrated on the surface features of the Earth they could see it in their everyday life and find it a continual source of enjoyment. Over the years I have had cards and letters from students who would write 'I saw a landform that looked exactly like the picture you showed in class,' and so the course remains a living part of their life rather than a dead memory of having taken a test on landforms and forgotten everything they had learned, which is so commonly the case."

SUMMER FIELD CAMP

The study of the geological sciences was furthered when in 1937 the U.S. Department of Agriculture provided camp buildings on about 4,000 acres of submarginal farmland. This facility was located about thirteen miles south of State College in wide, rolling Stone Valley (Bonine, 1941).

The development of the geological field camp provided an education in the earth sciences comparable to the instruction of laboratory practice in chemistry and physics. As Chesleigh Bonine said, "Geological field work offers exceptional opportunity to develop the investigative powers of students, leading as it does to semi-original work and in some cases to actual research and discovery. No one can deny that such work is exceedingly valuable not only for professional training, but also for general educational development."

To provide students with a wider geological perspective, the local field camp was discontinued in the early 1960s and the geology students were required to spend a summer at Red Lodge, Montana, in the Rocky Mountains Field Camp. In recent years a segment centered in the Rocky Mountains at Alta, Utah, was added. The field experience begins at University Park, for on the way to the field camp the geology across the United States is studied to show students as great a variety of geologic features as possible. Not only are the geologic aspects studied, but also the social features that occur enroute. For example, the geologic aspects of waste disposal have been investigated for many geology students will eventually be employed in this kind of endeavor.

The Red Lodge Field Camp is situated in an area of open plains and nearby high mountains, and Alta is in the Rocky Mountains (Gold, 1976; Kerrick, 1980). In these areas the student can see living geology. During the summer the student moves through a series of six to seven independent

The Mineral Industries Camp in Stone Valley, central Pennsylvania. Paul Krynine is on the right side of the photo.

exercises during three to seven days. The first problem is to prepare a structural geologic map of the sediments of the area. After this, each exercise presents a more complex problem, ending with a two-hundred-mile trip to a hot spring area where there is a collapsed caldera. This volcanic field provides a series of difficult mapping problems. Says David P. Gold, "I don't know of any field camp in the country that shows the students this variety of features, from pre-Cambrian terrains to recent volcanic sediments. The object is to show the types of geologic terrains and techniques that are used to map and interpret each of these particular types of terrains."

THE MARINE SCIENCE PROGRAM

The Marine Science Program, an interdisciplinary program located at field stations at Lewes (Delaware) and Wallops Island (Virginia), became possible in April 1971, when the University joined the Marine Science Consortium Inc. (Guber, 1973). This is a consortium of sixteen colleges and universities with a common interest in marine education and research. The first co-chairs of the program were Eugene G. Williams and Albert L. Guber from the geosciences, and William A. Dunson from the Department of Biology.

The Wallops field station provides a nearly ideal environment for students interested in coastal environments. The nearby environmental features of barrier bars, tidal flats, salt marshes, tidal channels, and shallow brackish bays are characteristic of most of the Atlantic and Gulf seaboards.

Geoscience students studying mountain structure in the Rocky Mountains of Montana.

The brackish waters of Chincoteague Bay are only a mile from the station, and the open ocean barrier beaches of Assateague and Wallops Island are only a ten-to-fifteen-minute drive. Not only is this environmental complex representative and accessible, it is also relatively unpolluted. Furthermore, the station is located in a rural setting so that students are not distracted by the social activities of a town or city. The students soon form a cohesive group that provides a unity of purpose and camaraderie.

The program includes courses in methods of oceanography, marine biology, and coastal geology. The coastal geology course focuses on the chemical and physical processes operative in each of the systems of the coastal supersystem. The ocean system, the marsh-tidal flat system, and the bay-tidal channel system are sampled, mapped, and analyzed. The older deposits of the mainland are examined and interpreted on the basis of the student's knowledge of modern coastal processes. In a final report, the students synthesize their knowledge of the present-day systems and the past evolution of the systems and then predict the systems' future course of evolution.

A student at Wallops Island takes only one course at a time, so there is "total immersion" in a single activity. Consequently, the course content is discussed while eating, working, and playing, and some students even dream about the course. A number of the geosciences faculty take part in the field experience. The ratio is normally about one faculty member to twelve students, and the faculty member is always available to discuss problems. The potential for independent research is good. Dr. Guber states: "My teaching philosophy, that the lab and field experiences are the most meaningful, was most fully realized in Penn State's off-campus Marine Science Program at Wallops Island. I consider myself extremely fortunate to have been put into a situation at Wallops Island where one could bring his educational philosophy to fruition with the complete support and cooperation of the participating faculty and higher administrators. We seized the opportunity, eliminated exams and deemphasized grades, and concentrated on problem-solving and presentation of research results. The enthusiasm the students showed for independent original research was fantastic."

GEOSCIENCES FACULTY RECOGNITION

The geosciences faculty have been honored for their teaching and research abilities at both the University level and at the College level. Albert Guber and Robert Schmalz have received the University's Christian R. and Mary F. Lindbach Award for Distinguished Teaching. Drs. Robert F. Schmalz, David P. Gold, Eugene Williams, Charles P. Thornton, Peter M. Lavin, Kevin P. Furlong, and Richard R. Parizek have received the College's Matthew J. and Anne C. Wilson Outstanding Teaching Award. Hiroshi Ohmoto received the Faculty Scholar Award for Outstanding Achievement at Penn State. In 1990 Barry Voight received the Matthew J. Wilson Research Award for a series of contributions to the understanding of catastrophic failures in natural materials associated with volcanic eruptions, rock slides, and snow avalanches.

At the scientific level, the faculty have received many national and international honors. A few typical examples follow. E. F. Osborn received the Roebling Medal of the Mineralogical Society of America in 1972, the highest honor given by the Society. He and Rustum Roy have been elected into the National Academy of Engineering. Eric J. Barron received the 1988 Excellence of Presentation Award of the Society of Economic Paleontologists and Mineralogists. Hubert L. Barnes was awarded a Senior U.S. Scientist Award by the Alexander von Humboldt Foundation in recognition of his research achievement in the geochemistry of ore deposits. In 1989, Arnulf Muan received the prestigious Alexander von Humboldt Foundation Senior U.S. Scientist Award. And several faculty members have minerals named after them: Rustum Roy, Rustumite; Della Roy, Dellaite; and George Brindley, Brindleyite.

Many of the faculty have not only been honored by professional organizations but have also served as officers and chairs of programs. In 1986 Roger C. Cuffey was elected president of the International Bryozoology Association. In the same year, Shelton S. Alexander was elected to a three-year term on the board of directors of the Seismological Society of America and became vice president in 1987 and president in 1988. In 1984, William Spackman received the Reinhardt Thiesain Medal of the International Committee for Coal Petrology. He also has served as chair of the Paleobotanical Section of the Botanical Society of America and president of the Society for Organic Petrology; he was also editor of the *International Journal of Coal Petrology* for several years. David Gold received the Barlow Memorial Medal from the Canadian Institute for Mining and Metallurgy. Arthur Rose has been a member of the National Research Council's Board on Mineral and Energy Resources. E. F. Osborn served as president of the Mineralogical Society of America in 1960, of the American Ceramic Society in 1964, of the Geochemical Society in 1967, and of the Society of Economic Geologists in 1972.

Richard Parizek was the sixth Birdsall Distinguished Lecturer of the Hydrogeology Division of the Geological Society of America. Hubert Barnes has served as vice president and president of the Geochemical Society. Robert Schmalz has served as a distinguished lecturer for the American Association of Petroleum Geologists. Alfred Traverse has been president of the International Commission for Palynology. C. Wayne Burnham was honored by the Society of Economic Geologists. Benjamin F. Howell served in 1963–64 as president of the Seismological Society of America.

In 1988 Susan L. Brantley was among twenty faculty members selected nationwide to receive sciences and engineering fellowships from the David and Lucille Packard Foundation. The fellowship provides $500,000 over five years for research expenses, such as scientific instruments, supplies, and scholarships for graduate students. Dr. Brantley states: "It's pretty exciting as a geologist to get the recognition and the opportunity to continue my work. This will enable me to work with more graduate students to continue researching the ideas I'm interested in." In 1987 she was selected by the National Science Foundation as a Presidential Young Investigator. Richard Alley was named a Presidential Young Investigator in 1990.

Chapter 7 | The Department of Materials Science and Engineering

In the evolution of civilization, metals have characterized eras, such as the Iron Age and the Bronze Age. The future can be appropriately termed the Age of Materials. In addition to the traditional engineering applications of metals, ceramics, and polymers, new materials and composites must be developed by materials scientists to aid human progress. These new materials will help meet the demands of society for improved effectiveness and reliable performance under severe conditions.

The Department of Materials Science and Engineering at Penn State, as presently organized, was formed in 1967. Its evolution, however, was unlike most such departments across the nation that were initiated and dominated by one of the classic materials science disciplines. At Penn State the roots of the Department of Materials Science and Engineering are firmly planted in the College of Earth and Mineral Sciences, a college with a fine established tradition in mineralogy and the earth sciences. Strong academic programs were established in metallurgy in 1907–8 and in ceramic technology in 1923. Fuel science, another subject with a rich history at Penn State, was first offered as a major in 1934. These three disciplines were the nucleus of the newly formed Department of Materials Science and Engineering in 1967. The addition of the polymer science program in 1972 and the interaction with the multidisciplinary solid-state science program completes what is today one of the finest and best-balanced departments of materials science and engineering in the United States.

The department is organized into four separate programs: ceramic science and engineering, fuel science, metals science and engineering, and polymer science. Each program offers undergraduate (B.S.) and graduate (M.S. and Ph.D.) degrees. An interdisciplinary graduate program, solid-state science, is administered through the graduate school.

The department is large and diverse, affording students the opportunity to interact with faculty and postdoctoral and graduate students from a wide spectrum of disciplines. There are 40 full-time faculty members, some 200 graduate students, and about 300 undergraduates currently in the department. Materials science courses that cut across disciplines are offered in addition to those offered by the individual programs, and students are encouraged to broaden their horizons by taking these and other University-wide courses.

Administration
Materials Science and
Engineering

Philip L. Walker, Jr.	1967–1979
Richard C. Bradt	1979–1983
Michael M. Coleman	1983–1991
Richard E. Tressler	1991–

Faculty members in the Department of Materials Science and Engineering have many responsibilities, including teaching and advising of students, undertaking research and disseminating results, maintaining academic standards, and performing other services for the University. The department's faculty members have consistently been rated well above average as teachers by students and alumni. Eight of the current faculty have won college-wide teaching awards. Research productivity of the faculty as a whole is outstanding, as measured by the national and international recognition of their peers, the number and quality of papers published, and the amount of research dollars generated (in excess of $5.4 million in outside research funding in 1990–91).

CERAMIC SCIENCE AND ENGINEERING

Factories for the production of glass and other ceramic products developed long before the Farmers' High School received its charter in 1855. The well-known Stiegel glass was produced at Manheim, Pennsylvania, between 1765 and 1774, and production was discontinued only because of the difficult economic conditions during the Revolution.

In 1898–1900 Thomas C. Hopkins, assistant professor of geology at the Pennsylvania State College, published a comprehensive three-part study entitled *Clays and Clay Industries of Pennsylvania*, the first evidence of ceramic research at Penn State. This study was followed in 1915 by a bulletin entitled *Thermal Conductivity of Refractories*, by Boyd Dudley, Jr., an instructor in metallurgy. This scientific study of high quality set the tone for future work. A third publication, by E. S. Moore and T. G. Taylor and entitled *The Silica Refractories of Pennsylvania,* appeared in 1924.

The first reference to ceramics appeared in the 1911–12 college catalog. It stated: "On account of the great importance of the ceramic industry in the State of Pennsylvania, it is deemed advisable to develop a course in Ceramics in conjunction with the course in Mining Engineering." Three courses were listed: Elementary Ceramics, General Ceramics, and Cement Materials. It was indicated that a four-year program was not developed at this time due to the lack of laboratory facilities. The courses were offered by geology professors and thus were geologically oriented. Because ceramic products (refractories) are used in the metallurgical industry, some informal instruction was given in courses in the Department of Metallurgy by Harry B. Northrup, C. E. McQuigg, and others.

Philip Walker studying xenon absorption on carbon black, 1965.

Philip L. Walker, Jr.
Evan Pugh Professor of Materials Science

Carbonaceous solids are of great importance in the real world, yet this importance is not reflected in the level of research activity on these solids in universities. In some small way I tried to correct this imbalance of organizing a significant research program in the carbon area at Penn State.

Fortunately there are an infinite number of naturally occurring and abundant precursors that can be used for the production of carbons. The most prominent precursors are coal, petroleum, and natural gas. At room temperature these precursors are a solid, a liquid, and a gas, respectively. The precursors have in common that they all contain a significant amount of carbon, but they also contain some heteroatoms (H,O,N, and S). Each of the precursors is composed of a number of organic structures (compounds) of different molecular weight and configuration. These compounds, in the case of coal and petroleum, interact with each other through strong and weak chemical and/or physical bonding. My colleagues and I studied how these organic precursors could be converted, through thermal treatment in the absence of oxidizing gases, to carbons of varying structure and properties. We found that the chemical and physical structures of the precursors determine to an important extent the structures of the carbons formed. When organic precursors are processed thermally (heated) to elevated temperatures of about 1,000° C they lose most of their hydrogen and oxygen. Small graphite-like crystallites are formed, exhibiting a crystallite size distribution and a degree of crystallite alignment. We found that it is primarily this crystallite size and alignment which determines the properties of the resulting carbon.

To simplify our research on the connection between organic and carbon-formed precursors, we ran a parallel research program that elucidated the fundamentals of the conversion of single, pure organic compounds of variable and selected structures to carbons. We discovered that different organic compounds have markedly different rates of losing hydrogen upon thermal treatment, condensing into larger entities, and eventually forming carbons. Also, each organic compound leads to a carbon of different structure and, hence, properties. By judicious selection of organic compounds or their mixtures, we found that we could produce essentially a continuum of carbons. These carbons have many applications, such as for molecular sieves, catalyst supports, and absorbents.

Once we were able to produce carbons of varying structure, we were interested in understanding the relationships between their structure and their properties, such as reactivity to gases, electrical conductivity, and mechanical strength. In particular, we studied the interaction of oxidizing gases (oxygen, carbon dioxide, and steam) with carbons, because these reactions are of great commercial importance in the production of energy and metals from their oxides. We showed quantitative correlations between the concentration of active sites on carbons and their reactivities. Further, since we previously showed that we could produce carbons of varying structure (and active sites concentration) by appropriate selection and processing of organic precursors, we are able to produce carbons of different reactivities.

Over the thirty-five years of conducting research on carbon, we trained about 150 M.S., Ph.D., and postdoctoral students. Now they are located over the world and form an important nucleus of the "carbon community" contributing to our understanding of such important areas as carbon composites and production of synthetic diamonds.

In addition, our efforts resulted in the starting of the advanced series entitled *Chemistry and Physics of Carbon*, now in its nineteenth volume, and the international journal *Carbon*, now in its twenty-fifth volume. We also took an active part in the formation of the American Carbon Society.

CREATING A DEPARTMENT

By the 1920s the ceramic industry was one of the major mineral industries of Pennsylvania. As the industry became more developed technologically, it was recognized that personnel skilled in ceramic engineering were required. The Pennsylvania State College recognized this need by establishing a Department of Ceramic Engineering in 1923 with a program leading to the bachelor of science degree. The 1923 general catalog stated: "Ceramic Engineering, which deals with the

---

Administration
Ceramic Science and Engineering

Department of Ceramic Engineering

Joseph B. Shaw	1923–1932
George J. Bair	1932–1933
Nelson W. Taylor	1933–1943
Edward C. Henry	1943–1945

*Department of Mineral Technology
Division of Ceramics*

Edward C. Henry	1945–1953

Department of Ceramic Technology

Floyd A. Hummel	1953–1955
George W. Brindley	1955–1962
Floyd A. Hummel	1962–1967

*Department of Materials Science and
Engineering, Ceramic Science Section*

Floyd A. Hummel	1967–1969
Guy E. Rindone	1969–1978

Ceramic Science and Engineering Section

Guy E. Rindone	1978–1980

Ceramic Science and Engineering Program

Richard E. Tressler	1980–1986
Karl E. Spear	1986–1991
David Green	1992–

---

clay-working and allied industries, recently has been made a separate department, offering a course intended to prepare men for engineering, administrative, or research positions in the brick, tile, pottery, refractory, cement, glass, and allied industries. Pennsylvania is second among all of the states in the value of ceramic products, and this school, situated in a region where there is a diversity of ceramic plants, offers a favorable location for the training required by the Ceramic Engineers."

The first head of the department was Joseph B. Shaw, who had a degree in ceramic engineering from Ohio State in 1908 and many years of industrial experience. Eight resident courses— including Ceramic Materials, Drying and Burning, Manufacturing Processes, Ceramic Technology, and Ceramic Calculations—were offered to junior and senior ceramic students. The program required 13 hours of recitation and 27 hours of laboratory work a week. Also required as part of the curriculum were a senior thesis, a field trip of two weeks duration, and several inspection trips to local ceramic plants.

The initial development of the ceramic curriculum reflected the ceramic education philosophy of the period. Nelson W. Taylor, head of the Ceramic Engineering Department from 1933 to 1943, wrote: "Just as in metallurgical education of an earlier decade, it was thought best to teach the plant practices of the ceramic industry rather than the scientific principles, perhaps because these principles appeared to be insufficiently developed, and to have the student operate pilot or semi-pilot scale experiments. The difficulties of this type of instruction are that such experiments usually have many uncontrolled variables, that they are time-consuming and expensive, and that

Ceramic science laboratory in the Steidle Building (Mineral Industries Building) in the early 1930s.

Robert Insley, a graduate student in 1952, working on a high-temperature phase equilibrium and silica system.

in most colleges they are done too frequently with outmoded equipment which industrial concerns have donated after it has ended its usefulness to the donor. A more serious criticism, however, is that such 'apprentice' instruction tends to narrow the outlook of the student rather than to provide that adaptability which every technical man needs for a successful career. One consequence of this philosophy in the ceramic department was that very few pieces of apparatus for process control were acquired until 1931–32, when a new course, 'Ceramic Process Control' was introduced. Consequently, the ceramics instruction did not keep pace with the technical advances which many branches of the industry were making. The need for training men was such, however, that nearly all the graduates were able to find employment in their chosen profession."

The student enrollment in the ceramic program grew from three in 1923 to twenty-seven in 1931. The program itself also expanded greatly to twelve undergraduate, six undergraduate and graduate, and six graduate courses. In 1925 Walter Preische, a graduate in ceramic engineering from Alfred University, became an assistant to Professor Shaw. After Preische resigned in 1927, George J. Bair, a 1927 Penn State graduate in ceramic engineering, was appointed instructor in his place; he received his M.S. degree from Penn State in 1930. In 1932 Shaw resigned, and during the 1932–33 year the entire work of the department was handled by Bair and a part-time assistant.

In the late 1920s Professor Shaw wrote a number of informative publications. One of these, *The Fire-Clays of Pennsylvania,* presented the results of laboratory studies of the plastic properties and the firing behavior of clays. A second publication, *The Ceramic Industries of Pennsylvania* (Mineral Industries Experiment Station, Bulletin 7) described the various branches of the industry and listed the names of manufacturers in the state in each branch. These publications were supported almost entirely from industry funds. Penn State was then primarily a teaching institution, and research funds were not considered important by the administration.

THE EVOLUTION OF THE DEPARTMENT UNDER NELSON TAYLOR

With the resignation of Professor Shaw, Dean Edward Steidle wanted to develop the ceramic teaching and research with a more scientific viewpoint. The first task was to get the proper leadership. In the appointment of Dr. Taylor to head ceramic education, Dean Steidle noted: "My original ideas of ceramic education were influenced by Dr. Alexander Silverman of the University of Pittsburgh, a nationally known glass scientist and a person that I looked upon as an 'igneous physical chemist.' When the occasion arose to select a new head for our ceramics department in the School of Mineral Industries, I first consulted Ross Purdy, general secretary of the American Ceramic Society. Ross agreed that there was too much 'cookbook' teaching of ceramics in this country and urged me to take the 'igneous physical chemistry' approach and to find a more properly educated and trained person to furnish the leadership of our ceramic department. He said he knew of one young man who could do the job, namely Nelson Taylor, then teaching physical chemistry at the University of Minnesota. On two or three occasions Taylor had presented papers at meetings of the American Ceramic Society, and Ross advised that I talk to Dr. A. V. Bleininger, U.S. Bureau of Standards, and Dr. A. L. Day, director of the Geophysical Laboratory in Washington, D.C. Both men backed up Ross Purdy, but with the comment that Penn State alumni and other schools teaching ceramics would not approve of the break with tradition. I immediately wrote Dr. Taylor of our plan, invited him to visit with us, and offered him the job, which he accepted. He was thrilled with the opportunity to do something constructive in the way of ceramic education in the U.S.A. at both the undergraduate and graduate levels" (Hummel, 1969).

George H. Brindley discusses the structure of clay minerals with students.

One of the first endeavors of Dr. Taylor when appointed department head was to acquire equipment (Taylor, 1940), because without modern equipment, a scientifically oriented ceramic program could not be developed. Initially a sum of $2,000 had been saved in the salary budget of the department in 1932, and this was made available for new equipment. Shortly after Dr. Taylor's arrival, homemade x-ray equipment was constructed for identification of crystal phases by the powder diffraction method. A petrographic microscope was purchased, an instrument for measuring the thermal expansion coefficient of refractory and other ceramic bodies was built, several wire-wound electric furnaces were made, and equipment of a process-control type was acquired. The laboratories were renovated so that modern experimentation could proceed. Between 1933 and 1940 about $8,500 worth of new equipment and supplies was secured. Without these acquisitions, not only the research program but also the instructional efforts would have been severely handicapped.

Because College funds for research were minimal during these depression years, Dr. Taylor prepared proposals and received a number of grants from organizations and government sources. The first was a grant of $2,500 from the Geological Society of America for an investigation of reactions between solids in the system $CaO-MgO-SiO_2$. Another grant of $400 was obtained from the National Research Council to study certain solid phase reactions. The larger part of this was used for equipment that later became available for undergraduate instruction. Many firms donated commercial products in various stages of manufacture.

The department also benefited through Works Progress Administration and General Services Administration construction on the campus in the late 1930s. One darkroom for spectroscopic and other optical work was built, as well as a new laboratory for advanced glass research. With new apparatus and laboratory changes, Penn State's ceramic department was now among the best equipped in the United States.

During the 1930s the ceramic undergraduate curriculum was completely revised. Most of the descriptive, empirical courses were replaced by those that tested principles and theories. A new basic course, Fundamentals of Ceramics, was developed. Its objective was to relate the student's training in chemistry and physics directly to high-temperature phenomena. A number of other courses established new directions in ceramic instruction.

"The Theory of Ceramic Processes," taught by Dr. Taylor, considered high-temperature reaction of silicates and allied materials from the thermodynamic, kinetic, and atomistic viewpoints, emphasizing the structural changes of materials caused by heating and the concomitant changes

Kee-Hyong Kim
Alumni Fellow

Kee-Hyong Kim (Alumni Fellow 1991; Ph.D. 1961) is chairman of the Korean Advanced Institute of Science and Technology. After receiving his doctorate in ceramic science and working in the United States for six years as a research scientist with Airco-Speer, he was called on by Korean president Park to assist in planning Korea's scientific and technological base. He served as Korea's first minister of science and technology from 1967 to 1971 and on the Economic-Scientific Council from 1971 to 1979. He has served as president of the Korean Ceramic Society, director of the Korea Energy and Resources Research Institute, president of the International University in Seoul, and president of Korea's National Science Foundation. He is a fellow of the American Ceramic Society, an honorary member of the Japanese Material Research Society, and has received a number of awards, including Korea's presidential Highest Services Award and the Presidential Citation.

in physical and chemical properties. Woldemar Weyl introduced ceramic petrography in 1939–40 through a course in mineralogy where the subject matter comprised "a study of sediments with reference to the classification of clays and other ceramic materials." He advanced the study of ceramics under the petrographic microscope, which included examining refractory products at various stages of their thermal history and after they had been corroded by slags and molten glass. The microscope was applied also for defects in glass, the interface between enamel and metal, and other relevant phenomena. Samuel Zerfoss, supported by a Bethlehem Steel Company research grant, aided Dr. Weyl in developing the microscopy course. Penn State had now integrated the study of refractories into its ceramic curriculum. Dr. Taylor, in noting the value of studying refractories during ceramic education, stated: "The quality of the refractories course is illustrated by the fact that one of our recent graduates, on entering the employ of the world's largest refractory company, was able to complete his special training in two weeks instead of the two months usually needed by graduates of other colleges or universities" (quoted in Hummel, 1969).

Between 1933 and 1943 a number of internationally recognized faculty joined Dr. Taylor to create a modern ceramics program. The appointment of Dr. Taylor to the ceramics faculty had indeed given a new direction to both instruction and research. S. R. Scholes wrote: "Nelson really brought physical chemistry into ceramics as few teachers had done before. We were glad to send

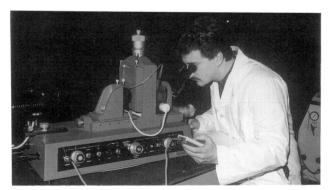

Electrophoretic mobility apparatus for determining the optimum processing procedures for ceramic matrix composites.

Secondary ion microscope for interfacial studies in high-temperature composites.

men from Alfred to him for their graduate work. As an experimentalist, he was quite original." In 1969 Floyd A. Hummel wrote of Dr. Taylor: "The key phrase 'igneous physical chemist' appears in both memorials (memorials written by Dean Steidle and Frank Preston, president of Preston Laboratories) and indicates that it was imperative in 1933 to draw chemists and physicists within the field of oxides and silicates, high temperature, and eventually high pressure, so that fresh approaches could be taken to constitution vs. property relationships in solids. It is probably very difficult for the present generation to understand the complete significance of the break with tradition. Perhaps it is sufficient to point out that, as late as 1933, the teaching of ceramics in the universities was dominated by men who had highly specialized interests in a limited number of natural minerals, such as clay, feldspar, silica and a few others, and the products made from these minerals, especially clay products. This is in sharp contrast to the present-day nonmetallic inorganic ceramist who is interested in the nuclear, electronic, electrical, magnetic, optical, mechanical, and chemical properties of oxides and compounds of almost every element in the periodic table."

In the biennium 1937–39 the state of Pennsylvania provided some funds for research, as long as they were matched by industry. This arrangement made it possible to inaugurate a research program on the beneficiation of ceramic raw materials by using froth flotation. This project offered significant economic potential for the state because there were widespread low-grade mineral deposits that would find a ready market if an inexpensive method of purification could be developed. Donald W. McGlashan was employed to carry out this project because he had been successful in reducing the iron oxide content of glass sand to 0.016 percent, which made the sand available for the best quality glass.

Henry Mauzee Davis began his career at Penn State as a research assistant in ceramics in 1936. In 1938 an agreement was made with the Bethlehem Steel Corporation by which Dr. Davis would carry on a series of investigations on slags and refractories. Besides his research, he taught one advanced course in ceramics.

In 1937 Edward C. Henry, who had received his Ph.D. in ceramics at Penn State, became an assistant professor. In 1940 he proposed a classification of dinnerware to the American Ceramic Society. He was particularly interested in the manufacture of ceramic products. In 1945 Dr. Henry became chief of the Division of Ceramics in the Department of Mineral Technology, and in 1953 he resigned to join the General Electric Company.

Woldemar Weyl, who for several years had been in charge of all investigations on glass at the Kaiser Wilhelm Institut für Silikatforschung in Berlin, Germany, accepted a position as associate professor of glass technology in 1938. He had directed many advanced students and had acted in a consulting capacity for glass manufacture in Germany, Czechoslovakia, France, Belgium, and England. His scientific work, particularly in regard to gases in glass and colored glass, was known throughout the world of glass technology. He came to Penn State in August 1936 and remained until June 1937, when he went back to Germany to complete some work there. In January 1938 he returned to Penn State and was appointed professor of glass technology. He later was made an Evan Pugh Professor.

Woldemar Weyl in his home planetarium.

Woldemar Anatol Weyl
Evan Pugh Professor of Glass Technology

Woldemar Anatol Weyl will be remembered principally for two major periods of scientific research, which culminated in his modern theory of the constitution of glass. Born in Darmstadt, Germany, he completed the dangerous research of glass melting under high oxygen pressure at the Kaiser Wilhelm Institute for Silicate Research (now the Max Planck Institute) in Berlin-Dahlem (1926–36), which led to the definitive monograph entitled *Coloured Glasses,* published by the British Society of Glass Technology in 1936. This was the first connected, critical review of modern theories on the structure and constitution of glasses.

The second period evolved over thirty years of research as professor of glass technology and later as Evan Pugh Professor in the College of Earth and Mineral Sciences at Penn State (1938–68). Weyl's dream of a glass research institute for the

United States materialized hopefully in 1944 with the formation of "Glass Science Inc.," an organization established at the University by the cooperative efforts of five leading companies (American Optical Co., Eastman Kodak Co., Bausch & Lomb Optical Co., Corning Glass Works, and Pittsburgh Plate Glass Co.) through George Wells, Kenneth Mees, Carl Bausch, and Eugene Sullivan. Because of the threat of antitrust action by the government against some of the firms, however, Glass Science Inc. had to be dissolved in 1947, but all research results were fully published, and the resulting patents were assigned to the public.

During 1948–57, government aid through a contract with the Office of Naval Research supported major research on glass structure and properties. Research on the surface chemistry of glass and the role played by polarization, anharmonicity, defective structures, and asymmetrical units in crystal chemistry led to the formulation of the screening theory—all of which was published in 1962 and 1967 in a multiple-volume treatise entitled *The Constitution of Glasses: A Dynamic Interpretation,* by Weyl and Evelyn C. Marboe.

While in Germany, Dr. Weyl had as his mentors some of the greatest scientists in crystal chemistry and glass research: Wilhelm Eitel, Hermann Salmang, Lothar Wohler, Franz Weidert, Fritz Haber, Herbert Freundlich, W. E. S. Turner, G. Gehlhoff, E. Berger, and V. M. Goldschmidt. Dr. Eitel recalls: "In this unique, stimulating atmosphere, Woldemar enjoyed a period of ripening which molded his personality to that of an independent investigator."

Dr. Weyl loved research and teaching and could direct his thinking with such an intense passion that his students and colleagues were always on a "scientific high" in his presence. The essential question Dr. Weyl was always posing was "What are the specific conditions of glass formation?" He was devoted to the education of his undergraduate and graduate students and was a spellbinding lecturer. Graduate students from all over the world (Finland, Japan, India, Germany, Norway, England) came to work in his laboratories at Penn State, and during emergency hard times, he personally helped finance some of them. He valued the spending of money for the education of an individual above all else. Having survived the devastating inflation and debauch of the Hitler era, he always preached "Put your money into education—no one can ever take your brains away from you!" His complete lack of interest in money as a reward product or status symbol is reflected in one of his basic philosophies: "Any problem that can be solved with money is no problem at all!"

Dr. Weyl's workday began at 4 A.M., when in the quiet atmosphere of his beautiful home he would begin writing his scientific "memoirs" in longhand and then walk to his campus office, arriving by 7:30 A.M. to beat the traffic. He always wrote everything in longhand, detesting dictation to secretaries or machines.

Dr. Weyl had the capacity to reduce the most complicated scientific problem to its lowest common denominator—the most basic scientific theory—and by conducting "test tube" experiments he could propound simple solutions and explanations. Some scientists have accused him of "solutions by intuition" rather than by a more quantitative approach involving complicated, sophisticated experimentation that might produce "hard, quantitative data." Weyl's answer was that his "intuition" was molded from hard thinking, no enslavement to the status quo, and a lifetime of accumulated knowledge in many scientific fields.

Aside from his scientific genius, the most profound memory Dr. Weyl's friends will have of him is his fascination and love of nature's beauty. His home contained tanks of exotic, beautiful fish; pictures of nature scenes (some of them painted by him); a backyard filled with flowers, fruit trees, berried bushes, bird feeders, and a large secluded "hole," which he dug and landscaped to provide a natural setting for relaxation and thinking.

Evelyn C. Marboe
Guy E. Rindone

Dr. Weyl's appointment to the ceramic faculty illustrates Dean Steidle's search to find the best-qualified persons available in the world and bring them to Penn State. The February 1938 issue of *Mineral Industries* contains the following comments by various educators and industrialists about Dr. Weyl:

It seems to be the unanimous opinion that Dr. Weyl is a great asset, not alone to the Pennsylvania State College, but to American ceramics.

I have a very high regard for his personality and scientific ability and think you are to be congratulated.

The best research man in the field of glass in Germany.

Based on my personal knowledge, I consider Dr. Weyl to be an outstanding glass technologist.

I have the highest regard for his work.

I have followed Dr. Weyl's work for several years and have a high regard for it.

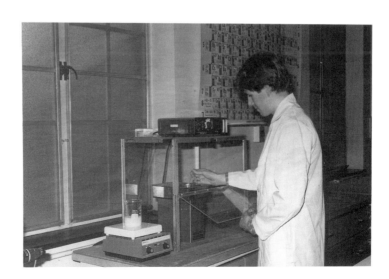

Sol-gel synthesis of ceramic-matrix composites.

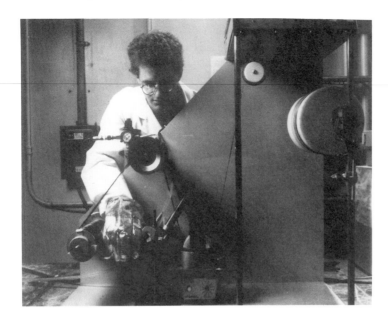

Continuous fiber winding, used in the fabrication of ceramic fiber preforms.

In 1938 Dr. Weyl and his assistant, A. G. Pincus, published four papers on the role of gases in glass. Dr. Weyl had studied this subject experimentally for some years at the Kaiser Wilhelm Institut. These were the first of a long series of papers that Dr. Weyl prepared during his career at Penn State until his death in 1975.

The first paper, published in July in *Glass Industry*, detailed the role of oxygen in glass melting. It was a well-known problem that the decolorization of glass results from the unavoidable iron content of glasses, and is related to the equilibrium between FeO and Fe_2O_3. With prolonged melting, the iron tends to acquire a lower state of oxidation, giving rise to a relatively dark bluish-green color. Ordinary oxidizing agents will not change these colors. It is therefore necessary to add to the glass batch certain components, such as oxides of arsenic and cerium, that are able to retain their oxygen at high temperatures and have it available for the oxidation of the ferrous iron to the less-colored ferric state.

In the production of colored glasses containing such elements as chromium or manganese, the oxygen balance is important. In glasses that contain more than one element capable of existing in different valance states—for instance, arsenic and manganese—interactions that make it impossible to predict the color can take place. To solve this problem, Dr. Weyl developed a series of experiments that indicated the stability of different polyvalent oxides and made it possible to predict the reactions that occurred in colored glasses.

In the second paper on this subject, published in the September 1938 issue of *Glass Industry*, Dr. Weyl discussed the reactions during the formation of glass. As most of the alkali and alkaline earths are introduced as carbonates, carbon dioxide evolution plays an important role in the rate of melting. Dr. Weyl described a new method that permitted recognition of the exact temperature at which glass formation started. Such a method was of general interest in the field of ceramics as glass formation also plays a role in many ceramic processes other than glass manufacture itself.

Water plays a similar role to CO_2 in glass-making. Its complete removal is the aim of the glass-maker, for it leads to the same defects in the glass that carbon dioxide causes. Dr. Weyl discussed the removal of water from glass in the November 1938 *Glass Industry* in a pioneer paper on the

Tape casting, used in the fabrication of whisker-reinforced ceramic-laminate preforms.

subject. He recognized the need for the additional studies, which he undertook in the following years. In the December 1938 *Glass Industry* Dr. Weyl examined the reaction between glass and sulfur dioxide and miscellaneous gases. This fundamental research laid the foundation for the study of the surface of glasses.

George J. Bair
Distinguished Alumnus

George J. Bair (Distinguished Alumnus 1965; Alumni Fellow 1975; B.S. 1927 and M.S. 1930, Ceramic Engineering) is a ceramic scientist who, although retired from Corning Glass Works, is still called on to share his expertise with the industry as a research consultant. Dr. Bair directed Corning's technical staff services until his 1970 retirement, and he added to his long list of professional services a term as president of the American Ceramic Society in 1966–67. He has been an active alumnus, serving a term as Alumni Association president. Florence Bair writes of their Penn State days: "We had a wonderful time as a young couple at Penn State. George had been a president of Alpha Sigma Phi and I was a Theta Phi Alpha. We were always asked to be chaperones at Alpha Sigma Phi, and believe me there are many stories I could tell about that. It was Prohibition times, so you can imagine! We were as young as most of the students." His citation for Distinguished Alumnus read:

> To George J. Bair, for a career marked by great professional achievement of benefit both to his company and to science generally; for imagination and inventiveness in the field of ceramics; for leadership in industry and the community; and for energetic and wise guidance of alumni activities.

The papers noted above also laid the foundation for Dr. Weyl's long career at Penn State as a worker on some of the most fundamental problems of glass production.

Norbert Kreidl came to Penn State in 1939 with a splendid industrial background, having been engaged in research on and the manufacture of glass for ten years in Czechoslovakia. As associate professor of glass technology he worked with Dr. Weyl. One of his earlier projects, sponsored by the Monsanto Chemical Company of St. Louis, was to study the uses of phosphates in glasses, porcelain, and other ceramic bodies. He introduced an advanced course in glass technology.

THE GLASS SCIENCE RESEARCH FOUNDATION

In order to encourage relationships between the College of Mineral Industries and companies, Woldemar Weyl established the Glass Science Research Foundation in May 1944 (Weyl, 1944). During the first year the sponsors included the Pittsburgh Plate Glass, Eastman Kodak, Bausch & Lomb Optical, American Optical, Kopp Glass, and Armstrong Cork companies. Faculty from other institutions were made collaborators of the foundation. These included H. Mueller of the Department of Physics at the Massachusetts Institute of Technology and R. E. Powell of the Department of Chemistry at Princeton University.

The Glass Science Research Foundation not only sponsored research but also acted as a clearinghouse for developments in the glass industry. Many meetings, both formal and informal, of leading glass scientists and industrialists were held at Penn State.

A wide variety of research topics were being investigated. Dr. Weyl and Helen S. Williams studied the reactivity of alkali in glass-making and the possibility of withdrawing alkali from the glass surface. H. H. Kellogg employed a method used in ore flotation to determine the adsorption on glass surfaces of ions from aqueous solutions. The surface chemical work also called for a method to determine the presence of free metals on a glass surface. This problem was solved by

Roger W. Rowland
Distinguished Alumnus

Roger W. Rowland (Distinguished Alumnus 1964; B.S. Electrical Engineering 1917; B.S. Ceramic Engineering 1948) had a driving ambition to make Penn State one of America's great universities. He began his long service on the Board of Trustees in 1939, where as chairman of finance and business he played a major role in the $75 million residence halls building program of the 1960s. He served on essentially every committee and task force of the Board of Trustees. Besides his University obligations, he became president of New Castle Refractories in 1929. His citation read:

> To Roger W. Rowland, for a notable career in the business world; for untiring efforts as a member of the Board of Trustees to make his alma mater a great university; and for his quarter-century of wisdom and counsel in trustee and administrative affairs which have helped and continue to help Penn State achieve the objective he assisted in formulating.

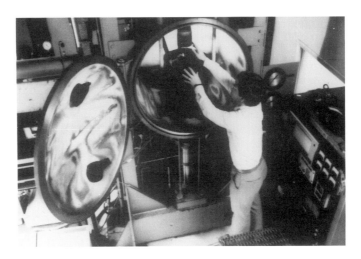

Hot pressing to consolidate metal and ceramic matrix composites.

Evelyn C. Marboe through inducing the physical development of the metal nuclei by means of a copper tartrate solution in the presence of formaldehyde.

When the Mineral Sciences Building was approved, Dean Steidle asked Guy E. Rindone and Evelyn C. Marboe to design glass research laboratories for the entire third floor. Before the building was completed, however, the glass companies withdrew support from the Foundation because they feared antitrust suits. Although the Foundation existed for only a few years, it provided an environment for research in the department and thus allowed the faculty to build a national reputation.

THE PENNSYLVANIA CERAMIC ASSOCIATION

The Pennsylvania Ceramic Association was founded in 1947 (Coxey, 1947). Its main goal was to foster education in ceramics because of a strong need for ceramic graduates at a time when very few students were entering the field. High school counselors were not aware of the demand for these graduates and were frequently misinformed, thinking of ceramics only as an art form. Representatives from the association gave lectures in high schools to acquaint students with the opportunities. To encourage students further, the companies provided individual scholarships, which at that time were large enough to pay the full tuition.

The Pennsylvania Ceramic Association continues to function, sponsoring and providing scholarship money and soliciting funds from other organizations. The task of informing students of opportunities in the ceramic field is never-ending, and the association continues to provide high school students with basic information about the field.

ELECTRON MICROSCOPY AND CERAMICS

In the early 1950s the College of Mineral Industries acquired an electron microscope. While the electron microscope was a tool used in a number of fields, its application to the study of ceramic microstructures provided a major advance. Guy E. Rindone reflects: "One of the projects that I

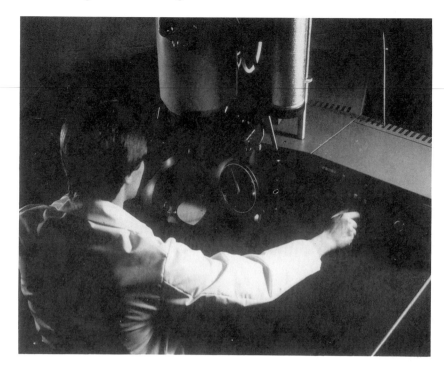

Scanning transmission electron microscope for microstructural analyses of engineering materials.

was first involved in was the use of the electron microscope to study the microstructure of opal glass. At that time very little electron microscope work was being done in the ceramic field in the country. So I think that Penn State really got a pretty good head start on a lot of universities. The electron microscope was used not only in the graduate program but also in the undergraduate program, in the attempt to develop a better understanding of the relationships of microstructure to properties" (Rindone, 1981).

DEVELOPMENT OF THE CERAMIC FACULTY

With the continued growth of the ceramic program, the faculty continued to expand. In the 1940s Floyd A. Hummel, Guy E. Rindone, Frederick R. Matson, Samuel Zerfoss, Roy G. Ehman, and William H. Earhart became members of the faculty. Roy Ehman joined the faculty in 1948 and was primarily involved in extension teaching, but he also lent his industrial experience in glass technology to the program. Frederick Matson joined the faculty in 1948 with a background in ceramics engineering and archaeology. In 1953 he transferred to the archaeology faculty, from which he retired in 1978. In 1952 Wilhelm R. Buessem, who had been associated with Dr. Weyl in Germany, joined the staff and developed work in electroceramics, a newly emerging field of ceramics.

With the resignation of Edward C. Henry in 1953, Floyd Hummel became the acting head of the Department of Ceramic Technology until George W. Brindley was named head in 1955. Dr. Brindley came from the University of Leeds, England, and had a specific interest in clay-mineral crystal chemistry and structures, an area in which he gave Penn State an international reputation. In 1962 he chose to return to full-time teaching and research. Dr. Brindley retired in 1973, but he continued to conduct an active research program until his death in 1986. Dr. Hummel, known particularly for his contributions to ceramic phase diagrams, to linear and oxial expansion of thermal-shock-resisting materials, and to luminescence and inorganic pigments, succeeded Dr. Brindley as head of the program. He remained head until 1969, when Dr. Rindone, who had been teaching ceramics and coordinating research in glass science and technology, became chairman of what had become in 1967 the Ceramic Science Section in the Department of Materials Science.

The ceramic program underwent many changes under the direction of Dr. Brindley and Dr. Hummel, keeping pace with the continuing advances both in the traditional fields and in increasing use of modern ceramic materials in electronics, communications, and transportation. This period also saw the beginning of faculty participation with the Materials Research Laboratory, which included Herbert A. McKinstry, Robert E. Newnham, Leslie E. Cross, James V. Biggers, Rustum Roy, and Della Martin Roy.

In 1959 William O. Williamson joined the staff, adding his experience in colloidal chemistry in the rheology of ceramic systems, as well as knowledge gained during twenty-two years of close contact with the ceramic industries of Great Britain, South Africa, and Australia. In addition, he had authored or co-authored numerous papers on the petrology of natural and artificial materials. Vladimir S. Stubican, originally from Yugoslavia, became a faculty member in 1961, adding expertise in thermodynamics of high-temperature ceramics. In 1967 Richard C. Bradt joined the ceramics faculty and contributed significantly to the current strength of Penn State in the area of mechanical properties in which Wilhelm Buessem had already been active.

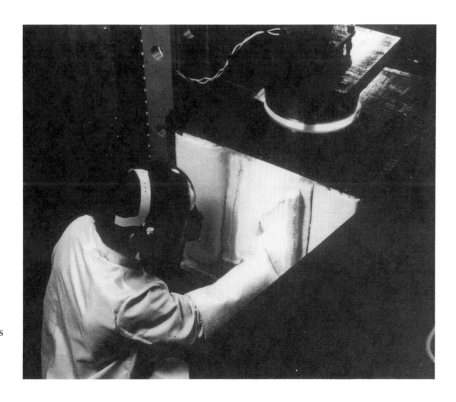

High-temperature tube-burst tester, designed and built at the Center for Advanced Materials for verifying mechanical test methodologies for tubular components.

RECENT FACULTY RESEARCH THEMES

Of the present twelve members of the ceramic science and engineering faculty, four—Vladimir S. Stubican, Robert E. Newnham, Karl E. Spear, and Herbert A. McKinstry—joined the group in the 1960s and 1970s. Each does research on distinctive elements of the field.

The research of Dr. Stubican is directed to the determination of phase equilibrium and ordering in zirconia and hafnia systems. His interests also lie in the study of the influence of point defects on grain boundaries and surface diffusion in ionic compounds of eutectic solidification of ceramic materials.

Herbert McKinstry investigates x-ray analysis; diffraction and fluorescence; the relationship of physical properties and structure, thermal expansion, and elastic constants; ceramic micro-structure and properties and mechanical strength; computer simulation of structure and properties; and computer graphics.

Robert Newnham came to the College of Earth and Mineral Sciences as a graduate student in 1954. He was Dr. Brindley's first Penn State American student, and together they carried out the first single-crystal structure analysis of a clay mineral, using a well-crystallized specimen of dickite from the Schuylkill Mine in eastern Pennsylvania. In 1966 Dr. Newnham returned to Penn State to work with Rustum Roy and Leslie E. Cross at the Materials Research Laboratory. In addition to affiliation with the ceramic science program, he also heads the intercollege solid-state science graduate program. At the Materials Research Laboratory, Robert Newnham and Eric Cross have developed one of the world's premier groups studying electroceramics and composites. Among their discoveries is a large family of composite transducers made from polymer and ferroelectric ceramics, with extremely high sensitivity to weak pressure waves. Other areas of research in-cluded multilayer capacitors and electrostrictive actuators, composite thermistors, and chemical sensors and pyroelectric sensors made from polar glass-ceramics. Most recently, they extended their studies to the microwave and optical frequency ranges by miniaturizing and integrating materials into nanocomposites and integrated electroceramic packages.

The research program of Karl E. Spear focuses on the modeling of thermal and plasma-assisted vapor deposition processes, the corrosion of materials at high temperatures, the interface reaction between solids, and the thermodynamic modeling of phase diagrams. Dr. Spear transferred to ceramic science and engineering in 1975 after spending his first five years at Penn State as a solid-state science faculty member. He was part of the Materials Research Lab team at Penn State to develop techniques for thin diamond films. Later he teamed with Michael Y. Frenklach, a professor in fuel science, to develop techniques for the homogeneous nucleation and growth of diamond powders.

Three of the present ceramic science and engineering faculty joined the staff in the 1970s. In addition to Karl Spear, Richard E. Tressler came in 1972 and Carlo G. Pantano came in 1979. Dr. Tressler has research interest in the creep, creep-rupture, and crack growth behavior of ceramics, fibers, and composites; the degradation and corrosion of structural ceramics; point defect and impurity diffusion in silicon; and the effect of oxide and oxynitride insulating films on silicon. He was the original director of the Center for Advanced Materials.

Carlo Pantano maintains an interest in understanding the surface chemistry and structure of glass and the development of methods to study and characterize them. His early work showed that typical silicate glasses undergo a surface reaction in the ambient atmosphere to produce an alkaline reaction product zone at their surfaces. This zone is responsible for the hygroscopicity of many glasses, long-term weathering, and hazing. He has extended these studies and concepts to the development of surface treatments that would passivate "real" surfaces. His more recent efforts are fundamental studies of surfaces created during the fracture of glass, the electronic and ionic particle emission which accompanies this phenomenon, and interfaces in glass matrix composites.

In the 1980s the scientific and engineering advances of ceramics—such as the advanced techniques for determining chemical synthesis and surface composition, the mechanisms that toughen ceramic products, the dielectric materials development, the powder synthesis of thermal reactions, the development of composite electroceramics, and numerous other advances—have made the use of ceramic products a powerful competitor in the new materials field. As a consequence the number of students studying in the field has reached an all-time high, but, equally important, research funds are available for these new endeavors. In the field of materials, ceramics is on the cutting edge of new uses of materials. As a response to these endeavors, six new faculty members have come to the program in the 1980s. Gary L. Messing came in 1980, David J. Green and John J. Mecholsky came in 1984 (Mecholsky resigned in 1990), Wayne Huebner came in 1985, John R. Hellmann and James H. Adair came in 1986 (Adair resigned in 1990), and Paul W. Brown came in 1987.

David Green came to Penn State to combine his research on the mechanical behavior of ceramics with teaching. This research emphasizes the mechanical behavior of ultralightweight ceramics, the surface modification of ceramics, and toughening mechanisms. Before coming to Penn State Dr. Green spent five years with the Rockwell International Science Center studying the relationship between the fabrication, microstructures, and properties of ceramic materials. His research included microcracking in ceramics, analysis, micromechanical theory, fabrication and evaluation of transformation-toughened ceramics, and the reliability of ceramics for aerospace application and structural design. He was particularly involved in experimental and theoretical research regarding the ceramic tiles used on the thermal protection system of the space shuttles.

The general theme of Gary Messing's research program is the development of a comprehensive and fundamental understanding of all facets of ceramic processing; the synthesis and fabrication of composite, lightweight ceramics via controlled powder synthesis; epitaxial nucleation of ceramic reactions; sol-gel processing, and densification by pressure enhanced or pressureless sintering and hot isostatic pressing.

John R. Hellmann received his B.S. and Ph.D. in ceramics from Penn State and after working at a national laboratory returned to Penn State as assistant professor of ceramic science and engineering and assistant director of the Center for Advanced Materials. Dr. Hellmann's work varies from organizing mechanisms for the dissemination of research findings, to implementing research and analytical service activities that assist various industrial concerns in their development of advanced high-temperature systems.

Paul W. Brown conducts research on chemically bonded ceramics, bioceramic composite materials, multicomponent phase equilibria, and thermodynamics.

Altaf H. Carim, who came to Penn State in 1990, has research programs that focus on the microstructure and microchemistry of interfaces in materials. Some topics of special interest include the joining of ceramics, interfacial phases in composite materials, and thin films in superconductor and semiconductor systems. He and his group make extensive use of transmission electron microscopy (TEM), prompting him to characterize himself as "basically, a high-tech photographer." Although that is a bit of an oversimplification, the high resolution of the TEM does make it possible to directly take pictures of atomic arrangements at magnifications of over 1,000,000 x. Armed with an understanding of defects and interfaces at this level, one can

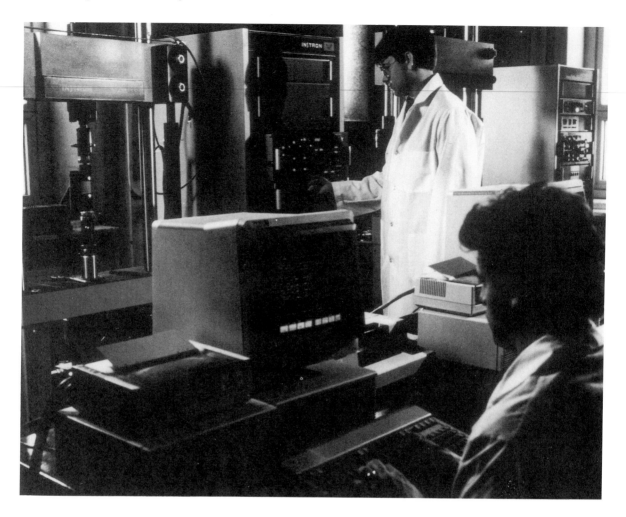

Computerized mechanical test facilities.

intelligently tailor material properties by carefully controlling the processing conditions so as to obtain the best possible microstructure.

Wayne Huebner's research involved the formulation and characterization of new dielectric materials and the phenomenological theory of feroelectricity and piezoelectricity.

John J. Mecholsky was interested in crack/microstructure interactions in the fracture of optical, electrical, and structural ceramics. This included studying the properties and processing of reinforced metal and tape-cast inorganic, brittle matrix composites. Fracture in brittle materials was modeled as a fractal process.

The research interests of James H. Adair were directed to the application of colloidal and physical chemistry in ceramic powder processing. The use of surface chemical modification techniques, including metalorganic coupling agents and graft polymerization to modify particle-particle interaction, was of particular interest. The development and application of techniques to synthesize complex silicates, titanates, and niobates was the focus of his particle synthesis work.

CURRICULUM DEVELOPMENT AND JOB OPPORTUNITIES

The field of ceramic science and engineering is developing rapidly, so there is a constant need to review the program. As a result, besides minor annual changes, major curriculum revisions occurred in 1987 and 1988. Traditionally ceramic graduates were employed in the glass, whitewares, refractories, and structural clay products industries. These are mature industries and job opportunities are somewhat limited. In recent years the job opportunities have been in what is now called "high-tech" ceramics, in which the structural, electronic, and optical properties of materials are investigated.

In the structural properties field, students are now working on heat exchangers, turbine blades, and even whole engines made out of ceramics. About the undergraduate program, Dr. Spear states: "Students need to understand more science than in earlier years if they are to understand the structure of materials, processing, characterization, and finally the electronic, optical, mechanical, and chemical properties. Our undergraduate curriculum has long moved away from memorizing recipes for products such as whitewares to understanding their applied physics and chemistry and then the applied math that goes with the program. We have a much stronger bent toward a basic understanding and much less toward the operation of specific kinds of equipment, such as tunnel kilns, that we used to learn how to build. Now we have to understand the basic principles behind the different kinds of heat treatment, and if somebody works with a refractory company and has to operate a tunnel kiln, that person can acquire the engineering a lot quicker than the basic science of the operation can be acquired. In response to this training, the students are learning how to analyze and attack problems that are occurring in industry, whether a modern silicon carbide engine is involved or a brick to line a steel-making furnace. The same kind of thinking is used to understand a chemical interaction as is used in solving a processing problem. It is the same thinking, the same logic, just a different application. Thus, we are going toward learning how to think and to apply the logic behind solving problems."

Donald F. Stock
Alumni Fellow

Donald F. Stock (Alumni Fellow 1985; B.S. Ceramic Technology 1949), after graduation from Penn State, joined Harbison-Walker as a research engineer. In 1954 he became laboratory manager at the former Hays Laboratory in Pittsburgh and later at the Garber Research Center in West Mifflin. In 1968 he joined the planning group at the Pittsburgh headquarters, and in 1971 he was appointed manager of product development and planning; he also served for two years as director of research. In 1980 he was appointed president of Harbison-Walker Refractories, U.S. Division, Pittsburgh. He is a fellow of the American Ceramic Society and a member of the North American Society for Corporate Planning, the National Institute of Ceramic Engineers, and the Pennsylvania Ceramics Association. He is a board member of the St. Clair Memorial Hospital, Pittsburgh. He says: "Penn State gave me a broad background in chemistry, math, physics, and engineering, and more specific teaching in areas related to ceramic science. In the latter, I particularly remember Dr. Tom Bates and Fred Matson in mineralogy/petrology, Woldemar Weyl in glass technology, and Floyd Hummel in ceramic glazes and whitewares. . . . How could a poor boy from a farm go that far? I must give the bulk of the credit to Penn State and its push for excellence."

EQUIPMENT AND EDUCATION

The most modern equipment is essential for training ceramic graduates who are about to enter companies that already have it. If students are not trained to use modern equipment, they are at a disadvantage. New equipment needs are both a blessing and a problem. With modern equipment, materials can be investigated even at the atomic scale, and data can be secured thousands of times faster than in the past. At the same time the cost of modern equipment has risen phenomenally. The minimum cost for a piece of processing or characterization equipment is at least $100,000, and with a great many pieces of analytical equipment, such as the electron microscope, the cost is more than $500,000. Even when the equipment is secured, there must be trained people to operate it and keep it working. A piece of equipment is outmoded in as little as five to ten years and must be replaced. In spite of all these problems, the importance of modern equipment has always been recognized in the ceramic program, and the department is now equipped with first-rate equipment.

Although the faculty and students recognize that a first-rate program cannot exist without first-rate equipment, interpretation of the data provided by the equipment is still a fundamental part of the educational program. Dr. Spear states: "In spite of the modern equipment, the critical step in developing understanding is interpreting the data. No matter how fast the computers are, developing models that simulate the behavior of materials and can help in interpreting what the data really means is essential in University training."

HONORS AND AWARDS

The ceramic faculty have received many honors and awards in the past half century.

George Brindley was known worldwide for his work on the crystal structures of clay minerals, studies on thermal and chemical effects on these structures, and work on the complexes between clay and organic minerals. In 1969 he was honored with the Roebling Medal, the highest award the Mineralogical Society of America gives. In 1978 he became one of only five Americans who were elected into honorary memberships in the French Society of Mineralogy and Crystallography. This honor reflects the fact that in all his research his concern was with the precise structure of natural and synthetic minerals. Dr. Brindley was active long after his retirement. In fact, three years after his retirement he was invited to give the opening paper at the seventh conference on clay mineralogy and petrology in Czechoslovakia.

Robert Newnham was named Alcoa Professor in 1987. This professorship was made possible by the generosity of the Aluminum Corporation of America. In recognition of his teaching, the College of Earth and Mineral Sciences presented him with the Wilson Teaching Award. He is a Fellow of the American Ceramic Society and the Mineralogical Society of America. In 1987 he was president of the American Crystallographic Association and distinguished lecturer for the Institute of Electronic and Electrical Engineers. He was elected into membership into the National Academy of Engineers in 1989.

Floyd A. Hummel received many honors and awards during his career at Penn State. In 1951 he received the Ross Coffin Purdy Award of the American Ceramic Society for outstanding contribution to ceramic literature, and in 1961 he was given the S. B. Meyer, Jr., Award for the most creditable paper in the field of glass technology. In 1983 he was honored with the Victor Albert

Bleininger Award of the Pittsburgh Section of the American Ceramic Society. He has held a number of positions in the American Ceramic Society and the Pennsylvania Ceramics Association.

In 1988 Richard Tressler received the prestigious I-R 100 Award for developing one of the year's most significant new technical products. Guy Rindone received the Frank Forrest Award in 1963 from the American Ceramic Society for papers in the field of glass technology. He also received the Victor Albert Bleininger Award in 1988 for distinguished achievements in ceramics, and in 1984 the Philadelphia Section of the American Ceramic Society presented him its Founders Award, and the Northwest Ohio Section gave him the Toledo Glass and Ceramics Award. The Karl Schwartzwalder Award for professional achievement in ceramic engineering, presented by the American Ceramic Society and the National Institute of Ceramics Engineers, went to Dr. Tressler in 1982 and John J. Mecholsky in 1984. Carlo G. Pantano received the Matthew J. and Anne C. Wilson Outstanding Teaching Award of the College of Earth and Mineral Sciences in 1984, as Dr. Bradt, Dr. Brindley, Dr. Newnham, and Dr. Williamson had done in earlier years.

Ceramic faculty members have also served on many state and national committees and organizations. Until 1987, Guy Rindone was director of materials processing in the space program of the Universities Space Research Association. Dr. Tressler has served on the Education Panel in Materials Science and Education. Dr. Stubican was elected in 1985 to the editorial board of the new international journal, *Reactivity of Solids*, published by Elsevier Press in the Netherlands. In 1985 Dr. Tressler was appointed a member of the National Research Council's National Materials Advisory Board Committee on Ceramic Technology for Advanced Heat Engines. In 1985 Gary Messing was appointed editorial co-chairman for the *Journal and Bulletin of the American Ceramic Society*. In 1983 Dr. Spear was elected chairman of the Gordon Research Conference on High Temperature, and then in 1984 he was elected to a three-year term on the Committee on High Temperature Science and Technology of the National Research Council's Commission on Physical Sciences, Mathematics, and Resources. Dr. Tressler was elected a Fellow of the American Ceramic Society.

THE FUTURE

The development of the ceramic program at Penn State is related to the fact that Pennsylvania, by virtue of its raw and processed materials, is a leader in inorganic technology. This technology includes a diversified ceramic industry of great national importance. Indicating future directions of the ceramic program, Dr. Tressler recently stated: "The total undergraduate enrollment in ceramics is at an all-time high, with a strong demand for graduates from the traditional employers and, in recent years, increasing demand from the electronics (particularly semiconductor) and automotive industries. Our graduate enrollment too is at an all-time high. Many research projects conducted in conjunction with other departments, such as electrical engineering and geosciences, and interdisciplinary laboratories, such as the Materials Research Laboratory, support students in ceramic science." He continued: "Societal needs in the areas of efficient energy usage and conservation, in which ceramics are finding increasing applications, argue for continuing interest from prospective students, from prospective employers, and from potential research sponsors. These pressures and the fact that University support has not kept pace with the increased costs of everything are putting a strain on facilities and faculty." Dr. Tressler stressed the support of the community: "By various means, the assistance of industry and individuals is being sought to modernize our educational facilities, particularly in the area of automation of equipment and the use of interactive computation for problem-solving. The continuing support of the community we serve is essential in maintaining the high quality of education and research that has been the hallmark of the Department of Ceramic Science and Engineering at Penn State."

Ceramic science is playing an ever-increasing role in supplying materials for a wide variety of uses. Says Guy Rindone: "The habits and needs of modern society have been revolutionized by the solid-state ceramics involved in all types of electronic devices, including calculators, computers, telephones, and copy machines, to name a few. Fiber optics are replacing wires to update our telephone communications by using laser light pulses carried through glass fibers that will eventually stretch across continents and under seas. Space exploration relies on high-temperature-resistant, high-strength ceramics, in addition to the multitude of electronic devices with ceramic components that are used in the spacecraft. Nuclear energy is not feasible without ceramic fuel elements, control rods, and insulation, and the nuclear waste problem is being alleviated by ceramic encapsulation of spent radioactive waste. Ceramic engines and components for automobiles are a reality and will play a strong role in utilizing our energy resources most efficiently. As important as these new uses for ceramics are, there are many more uses for the traditional ceramics. High-strength and highly insulating glass and crystalline ceramic structural products, harder ceramic abrasives, more durable and temperature-resistant consumer products, and improved refractories are but a few examples." He continues: "Ceramic raw materials are, in most instances, in abundant supply as a natural resource. Twenty-five percent of the earth's crust consists of silicon, which in combination with oxygen and other elements is the backbone element of most ceramic materials. And as we expand our habitat into outer space, the question of what building materials are candidates for constructing space stations, and eventually housing whole cities in space, is likely to be in the forefront. The answer is glass and crystalline ceramics, in all probability, because of the availability of their raw materials on the moon and from asteroids. The products of our endeavors—ceramic materials—continue to increase in quality and to be long-lasting and endure virtually forever. We anticipate that ceramic science and engineering education and research at Penn State will do likewise."

FUEL SCIENCE

The study of fuels began in Europe in the late nineteenth and early twentieth centuries. The demands of the synthetic gas industry required a thorough understanding of the scientific principles underlying the processes of manufacturing. Consequently, in Germany, the famous "Gazinstitut" was founded in 1904. Three years later, a department of fuels and metallurgy, the first of its kind among British universities, was established at the University of Leeds. This department had the support of the West Yorkshire coal owners as well as the Institute of Gas Engineers. The scope of its curriculum is suggested by the name: Coal, Gas, and Fuel Industries with Metallurgy. Somewhat later a department of fuel technology was established at the University of Sheffield.

In the United States the study of fuels was offered in a number of universities in the nineteenth century but was associated with such departments as chemistry, mechanical engineering, or metallurgy. At Penn State, coal-working was an important subject in the mining engineering curriculum as early as 1893. This was the beginning of processing materials in order to achieve a more desirable fuel.

In the 1894–95 general catalog a "gas producer, regenerator, and furnace for investigation into the economical use of fuels" was described. By 1906 the importance of the technology of fuels was recognized with courses in the mining curriculum in coal-working for preparation in the market, including a ten-week summer practical course in coal-working. A course in mining was concerned with mechanical treatment and preparation of anthracite and bituminous coal, a course in mining geology included the origin, occurrence, distribution, and properties of coal, and courses in metallurgy involved the study of gas production as well as fuel characteristics and fuel testing.

In the 1908–9 catalog the Department of Mining offered a course called "Mechanical Preparation of Coal and Dressing of Ores," which suggests that there must have been a consolidation of courses. The course included a practicum. Under "Metallurgy" a course in Principles of Metallurgy, Fuel Testing, and Calorimetry was offered. The following year, however, a separate course in fuels and fuel testing again appeared in the catalog. From 1910 to 1920 the courses relating to fuel technology remained substantially unchanged. During the 1920–30 decade, however, there was growing recognition by the faculty of the importance of advanced instruction and research as well as undergraduate instruction. This is evidenced by the introduction of graduate courses in coal carbonization in 1921 and in the utilization of fuels in 1922 in the Department of Metallurgy.

ESTABLISHMENT OF A FUEL TECHNOLOGY DEPARTMENT

When Edward Steidle began to organize a School of Mineral Industries, one of his first endeavors was the establishment of a Department of Fuel Technology. He wrote: "Fuel technologists deal with the problems of origin, constitution, processing, and utilization of those materials which are useful for the production of heat energy and industrial raw materials. America, the most highly industrialized nation in the world, has a per capita coal, oil, and gas consumption equivalent to 250,000,000 Btu's and provides reserves of these fuels sufficient to last about 1,000, 10, and 35 years, respectively. New oil and gas reserves will undoubtedly be discovered as a result of the extensive exploration now in progress. . . . Nevertheless, the present wasteful practices of using quality fuels for inferior applications will have to be eliminated if this country is to remain self-sufficient. . . . Because of the importance of mined fuels in the present economy of the country, specialists in the technology of processing and utilizing these raw materials are urgently needed."

As an integral part of mineral industries education, the Board of Trustees established a separate curriculum in fuel technology in 1932, the first in an American college. Alfred W. Gauger, who had joined the faculty as professor of fuel technology and director of mineral industries research in 1931, became head of the new department.

In the 1934–35 year the new curriculum admitted its first freshman class of seven. By this time the coursework had been organized, a teaching staff had been assembled, and facilities and equipment for instructional work in the practicum course had been secured. A most capable staff in fuel technology was built in the early 1930s. Soon after Dr. Gauger arrived, George Brady came to take charge of the analytical work for the Experiment Station and was in charge of courses offered in advanced fuel testing. In 1932 Calvert C. Wright came initially as a National Research Council Fellow for the study of the hydrogenation of coal, a process whereby coal can be converted into liquid fuel. He stayed on as assistant professor of fuel technology. The laboratory Dr. Wright set up at Penn State was the first coal hydrogenation laboratory at a public institution in the United States.

Administration
Fuel Science

Department of Fuel Technology

Alfred W. Gauger	1932–1945

Department of Mineral Technology
Division of Fuel Technology

Calvert C. Wright	1945–1954

Department of Fuel Technology

Philip L. Walker	1954–1959
Howard B. Palmer	1959–1966

Department of Fuel Science

Peter H. Given	1966–1967

Department of Materials Science and
Engineering, Fuel Science Program

Peter H. Given	1967–1969
Howard B. Palmer	1969–1976
Philip L. Walker	1976–1983
Robert G. Jenkins	1983–1988
Harold H. Schobert	1988–

In December 1933 Harlan W. Nelson was hired as a research assistant in the Experiment Station. The next year he was made an instructor in the Department of Fuel Technology and was responsible for teaching several courses. Walter M. Fuchs joined the staff of the Experiment Station in 1935 as research associate and professor. Dr. Fuchs had wide experience in fuels research, having been an assistant director of the Kaiser Wilhelm Institute in Berlin. Author of *Die Chemie der Kohle* (1931), he had published a number of scientific papers dealing with organic chemistry and the chemistry of wood and coal. In addition to his research work, a portion of his time was devoted to teaching two graduate courses in fuel technology. Otto P. Brysch, a research assistant in the department who had had extensive experience working in various capacities in manufactured gas plants, was in charge of the course in gas manufacture.

THE SCOPE AND CONTENT OF THE FUEL TECHNOLOGY CURRICULUM

Because the fuel technology program was the first one established in the United States, there was no established pattern to draw on. Lengthy discussions occurred within the faculty of the department concerning the curriculum. It was recognized that the needs and trends within the industry should be considered, including technological but also economic factors, as well as the factor of social utility. Dr. Gauger (1939) expressed the following viewpoints on social utility: "In the history of science and invention the social consequences have been given little consideration. Now, however, mastery over material forces has far outdistanced the old moral and legal controls and the future welfare of society demands a type of scientific leadership that is fully awake to the importance of some type of moral or social control; whether this will or will not lead to further public regulation than exists at present is an open question. There seems no doubt, however, that the engineer of the future will have to consider factors of economic effects and social expediency to a much greater extent than the engineer of the past. Other factors that must be considered are ones concerned with changing consumer habits, as exemplified by the desire for fully automatic heat."

In order to meet these objectives, Dr. Gauger believed, "The difficulties of predicting the future make it imperative that any curriculum devote a large part of its program to the basic subjects that time has demonstrated to have lasting value—that is, mathematics, physics, chemistry, the earth sciences, and English. To these, then, will be added the general engineering subjects that are a part of every engineer's training, economics, and the professional courses in fuel technology, which will acquaint the student with the problems and terminology of the fuel industries and give them some training in design. It would also be desirable for the undergraduate program to contain general courses in such subjects as public speaking, the humanities, industrial management, and similar subjects, but we must keep in mind the four-year limitation."

Dr. Gauger added that within the specific field of fuel technology, the student must "be thoroughly versed in the properties of the different fuels and the relationships between them." He continued: "Then, with respect to coal, which is still the most important of the fuels, preparation and processing have become as important as mining and utilization. The fuel technologist must have a thorough understanding of the underlying principles of coal preparation and washing. This, in my opinion, involves some knowledge of the fundamental nature of coal, including the

Howard Palmer, professor of energy science, adjusting a visible ultraviolet spectrograph in the shock-tube laboratory for studying extremely fast gaseous reactions at high temperatures, about 1960.

types, composition, and physical properties of the mineral matter associated with coal substance and the effect of the mineral matter on coal utilization. Similarly, coking involves not only a knowledge of the different carbonization processes but, what is much more important, fundamental information concerning the physics and chemistry of the distillation of coal, the important properties of coal that affect in any way the coking process, as well as the recovery, processing, and treatment of the by-products recovered in carbonization." On combustion he stated: "The subject of combustion involves much more than boiler tests and standard combustion equipment. The fuel technologists must know the mechanics of combustion of solid, liquid, and gaseous fuels and the relation to equipment design, besides the properties of the fuel that influence its selection for various types of utilizations."

During the formative years of the fuel technology program at Penn State, Dr. Gauger remained head from 1932 to 1945. In 1945 he was succeeded by Calvert Wright, who remained head of the program until his untimely death in 1954. During this period, a number of outstanding faculty were in the program.

An early addition was Theodore S. Spicer, who received the first bachelor of science degree granted in fuel technology in 1934 and continued as a faculty member. He introduced coal combustion into the fuel technology curriculum. Dr. Gauger recruited Walter M. Fuchs, an eminent coal scientist from Germany, to develop the area of organic chemistry of coal. Corliss R. Kinney, who joined the faculty in 1944, was a world-renowned authority on organic geochemistry, coal characterization, and coal liquefaction. Other early members of the faculty included H. Beecher Charmbury, Theodore S. Polansky, James A. Taylor, Louis L. Newman, and Harlan W. Nelson. Philip Walker joined the program in 1952 and was head of the Department of Fuel Technology from 1954 to 1959, and again from 1976 to 1983.

GRADUATE STUDY IN FUEL TECHNOLOGY

In the establishment of the fuel technology program it was recognized that graduate study had to play a fundamental role in training students. Alfred Gauger wrote in 1933: "Graduate study and research are also important in modern education. To serve society adequately in the solution of the social and economic problems facing the mineral industries, our colleges must educate leaders by graduate as well as undergraduate instruction, and must supply leadership in the solution of technical problems by research. The two chief objectives in graduate study are to strengthen the student's grasp and to broaden his or her knowledge of his or her subject, and to develop the student's ability to apply existing knowledge in new directions. The primary approach in the first instance is made through supervised study, in the second, through original research. To accomplish these objectives, the student is advised to select courses in those fields of science and technology in which he or she is deficient. Specific courses in fuel technology are limited in number, but the student is required to devote a considerable share of time to research on some problems in this field. It is believed that 'learning by doing' offers the best method for research training. At the same time, the student is encouraged through seminars and individual conferences to read widely in the current literature in fuel technology."

The first master of science degree was granted in 1934 and the first Ph.D. in 1937. Since then more than 130 M.S. and over 160 Ph.D.'s have been granted. Graduate student enrollment averages about thirty each year. There are also usually a number of postdoctorals and visiting scientists in the program.

James J. Tietjen
Distinguished Alumnus

James J. Tietjen (Distinguished Alumnus 1985; M.S. 1958 and Ph.D. 1963, Fuel Science), after receiving his graduate degree in fuel science at Penn State, turned his research and technological genius into new ideas, new principles, new materials, and new products. In 1983 he became president and chief executive officer of RCA American Communication Inc. In 1990 he became president and CEO of SRI International. An Evan Pugh Professor at Penn State ranked Dr. Tietjen as one of the top five graduate students he had ever taught. Dr. Tietjen has been twice recognized with RCA Corporation's highest technical honor, the David Sarnoff Outstanding Achievement Award. He has been active in NASA's terrestrial application advisory committee and on the solid-state science advisory board of the National Academy of Sciences. His citation read:

> To James J. Tietjen, scholar, researcher, and corporate leader, for pioneering advances in electronic invention, for applying his technological genius to revolutionizing the world of communications, and for transforming scientific ideas into consumer realities.

STATE FUNDING OF FUEL SCIENCE RESEARCH

The decline in production of bituminous coal and anthracite in the 1920s and 1930s was considered to be largely the result of the technological advances made in the production, distribution, and use of competitive fuels—natural gas and petroleum. The coal industry had not kept pace with these changes. As a result, a report to Pennsylvania Governor John S. Fine from Secretary of Mines Richard Maize stated in 1938: "The overall effect upon the economy of the Commonwealth has been evidenced in unemployment, declining real estate values, loss in tax revenue by local and state government, and a general decline in business in areas dependent on the coal industry."

The Pennsylvania General Assembly recognized these conditions and, in 1939, passed Act No. 392 under the sponsorship of Senator R. M. Miller. This act provided for a program of research on anthracite and bituminous coal to be conducted in the School of Mineral Industries under the supervision of the Pennsylvania State Secretary of Mines. The act appropriated $50,000, but Governor Arthur H. James reduced the appropriation to $35,000 for the biennium. But at a meeting on July 14, 1939, called by John I. Thomas with representatives for the anthracite and bituminous industries, each group agreed to match one-half of the funds appropriated—namely, $35,000 for the biennium.

On July 27, 1939, a committee representing the anthracite industry met at Penn State, and after careful consideration of numerous suggestions offered by representatives of both industry and faculty from the School of Mineral Industries, a decision was reached to initiate the program with two specific investigations: the gasification of anthracite use and the production of carbon products from anthracite. Dr. Gauger, director of the project, instructed the faculty to prepare research programs for the two projects with an emphasis on gasification. Calvert Wright was in charge of the new research.

Two major delays were encountered before the research program began. The new wing of the Mineral Industries Building and the modernized laboratories were not complete by the time the research contract was approved. Electrical services had not been connected, and from December 1939 to April 1940, the work of electrical installations was spasmodically carried out, with resultant delays to the experimental work. It was further discovered that the heating system installed in the laboratory was entirely inadequate, and even after a heating stove was added the temperature of the laboratory often ranged in the low fifties. There was also a problem with a large canopy hood that was supposed to discharge smoke and fumes from the laboratory. This hood removed only a fraction of the fumes produced by the decrepitation furnace and stokers, and it was necessary to install individual hood systems for both furnaces. Construction of the hoods was delayed considerably because permission had to be obtained from the State Authority. The laboratory finally was in full use by April 10, 1940.

The major initial project of the anthracite program was to be plant-scale tests and experiments on water gas production. Negotiations were begun with the Central Pennsylvania Gas Company immediately after plans for the project had been completed. The extent and nature of the tests were discussed with the personnel of the gas company, and a tentative agreement was reached.

William C. Rovesti (Ph.D. Fuel Science 1970) studying reactions of sulfur dioxide with carbon.

On December 5, 1939, a publicity release from Harrisburg appeared in the newspaper, stating erroneously that Penn State had secured the Axeman Gas Plant for experiments on the gasification of anthracite. As a result of this publicity, the gas company directors reacted unfavorably to the entire program and asked that the College secure permission from the Public Utility Commission, secure permission from the various insurance companies covering the plant, and post a $1,000 cash bond before they considered the matter further. The staff of the projects complied with the first two requests as soon as possible. When this had been done, the gas company drew up a contract covering the work proposed. The attorney for the College advised against signing the agreement, however, on the grounds that (1) despite permission from the insurance companies, the wording of the agreement made the College liable for numerous possible claims that could not be attributed to anything the College staff had done during the tests, and (2) that the cost of a surety bond to cover the contingencies listed would be prohibitive. After extensive negotiations between the Central Pennsylvania Gas Company and the College, the use of the Axeman plant was dropped and efforts to find a suitable facility elsewhere were begun.

On January 18, 1940, negotiations to use the Carbondale Water Gas Plant owned and operated by the American Welding Company were begun. Modernization plans were developed, but on February 29, 1940, the company rejected the proposals of the College, indicating that conditions did not warrant the investment, and the future of the welding process for which the gas was to be used was in considerable doubt. The search for a new plant continued, and two sites were finally chosen and secured for experimental work: on May 9, 1940, the Carlisle plant of the Pennsylvania Power & Light Company, and on June 2, the Pottsville Gas Works.

With the completion of these two facilities the original research programs were initiated. During the 1940s and into the late 1950s the General Assembly appropriated funds to continue the research. For example, in 1941 and 1943 the sum of $60,000 was appropriated, provided the coal industry of the state matched this amount with an additional $30,000. In 1945, 1947, and 1949 the sum of $70,000 was appropriated, again with the provision that the industry provide an additional $35,000 each year. The coal industry of Pennsylvania supported this program, not only by matching funds from the state but also by active participation on a Research Advisory Committee, whose membership included representatives from the coal industry and labor.

ANTHRACITE AND BITUMINOUS COAL RESEARCH

Research on "new and improved uses for anthracite and bituminous coal" conducted under grants from the Pennsylvania legislature and the coal industry gradually was broadened and covered a wide range of projects in the 1940s and 1950s. The research was practical and largely empirical in nature. A basic consideration was how anthracite or bituminous would burn in a given situation.

Research on Anthracite

Gasification. Gasification, the conversion of coal into carbon monoxide and hydrogen, was a major research theme. This gaseous mixture is the starting material from which synthetic natural gas, liquid fuels, or chemicals could be manufactured. Laboratory studies were completed on the mechanism and speed of the major gasification reactions (steam-carbon) in order to supply fundamental data on which equipment could be designed for the synthesis gas process. Laboratory studies were also conducted on the high-speed gasification process in which incandescent fuel was blasted with air or oxygen at velocities of up to 10,000 feet a minute. These studies yielded information on the speed at which carbon could react with oxygen. Data were secured in full-scale plant tests at Trail, British Columbia, on the production of synthetic gas from rice and barley anthracite and from coke by reactions from oxygen and steam, and on the utilization of synthetic gas in the synthetic ammonia process. These data were calculated and reported in terms of the application of the above processes to synthetic liquid fuels manufacture. The results of these tests indicated the advantages to be gained by using relatively pure oxygen instead of air for the gasification process and the suitability of anthracite and anthracite synthesis gas. These studies did not lead to commercial development. The development of natural gas and petroleum in the world at much lower costs stifled all development of the use of anthracite in the production of synthetic gas.

Utilization of Fines.   Studies were conducted on the blending of small percentages of anthracite fines with bituminous coal for the manufacture of by-product coke. This practice was not only to increase the fuel supply but also to improve the quality of the coke. Specifications for the anthracite fines most suitable for use in this process were developed, and studies were completed indicating the usefulness of the anthracite fines in controlling the increasing pressure that develops when certain bituminous coal blends are carbonized. Detailed blending practices and experiences were recorded in a number of plants using anthracite fines. The use of anthracite fines, however, did not advance far beyond the experimental laboratory.

Mary Johnson (Ph.D. Fuel Science 1970) studying the devolitilization of coal using a laser mass spectrometer system. Such instrumentation for fundamental studies on coal reactions was pioneered at Penn State under the leadership of Francis J. Vastola during the 1960s and 1970s.

Beneficiation of Fines.   By the late 1940s there were huge piles of surface materials at the underground anthracite mines. The cleaning and recovery of anthracite fines that once were permitted to erode into streams and rivers was a major problem in the industry. Much of this fine-size coal was contaminated with appreciable quantities of mineral matter that needed to be removed before the product could be used as a fuel. Considerable research was conducted on the then current and proposed methods used for cleaning such fine-size coal. Studies indicated that for different types of coal certain cleaning processes were better than others. Ultimately the studies suggested the desirability of applying the various cleaning processes only to the fuel size range for which each was best suited, and then increasing overall recovery of the marketable product and improvised efficiency of operation. The cleaning of fine coals has made possible the extraction of the fines from anthracite culm banks over the years. This research has had wide commercial developments.

The possibility of "pelletization" of anthracite fines was also investigated. This process consisted of forcing wet fines under pressure through a die to produce spaghetti-like rods. After drying, these rods or pellets had a reasonably good strength. It was hoped that, because of high heat content and ease of igniting, they would be used as a household fuel. The project was never developed on a commercial scale.

Anthracite as Cupola Fuel.   Because of the scarcity of foundry coke, interest in the use of anthracite as a cupola fuel increased. An extensive research program was undertaken to determine the best conditions for its use in high-speed iron-melting operations and to evaluate the characteristics of the various anthracites available for this use. It was found that because anthracite tends to pack into a denser bed than coke of equivalent size, the resistance to the flow of gases through a cupola was increased when using anthracite. However, it was found that if a blower was utilized high-speed melting could be attained using an anthracite-coke mixture, and in some uses with anthracite alone. Although plant-scale tests were completed, the process was not accepted by the iron and steel companies because the operation was less flexible and generally less satisfactory because of higher pressures.

Other Studies.   Studies on the flow of gases through deep beds of fuel were carried out to determine how much of the gas admitted to the bottom of a fuel bed actually passes through the fuel and how much escapes along the walls and has little contact with the fuel. The investigations were made using a range of fuel sizes from buckwheat to anthracite pieces twenty-four inches in diameter. A relationship was found between the ratio of the diameter of the container to that of the fuel, and the percentage of gas bypassing. Theoretical studies on the effect of the stationary gas film surrounding each particle on the pressure drop through the bed were completed and proved of value in interpreting the mechanics of gas flow through beds of broken solids.

Data such as electrical and thermal conductivity, specific heat, thermal diffusivity, thermal expansion, specific resistance, and dielectric constant were also compiled on the physical properties of anthracite and bituminous coal. This information is valuable to organizations engaged in engineering calculations on design of drying bulk flow and gasification equipment.

Research on Bituminous Coal

Comfort Heating.   The development of an automatic ash-removal-type Pennsylvania stoker was pursued in order to secure additional data on mechanical defects that might arise from continuous operations over a period of years. Detailed tests were performed on the year-round use of the ash-

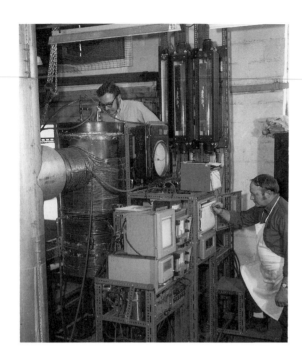

Richard Waibel (Ph.D. Fuel Science 1974) and Carl Martin, machinist, operating an early version of a fluidized bed combustor. This combustor has been supplanted by more modern and sophisticated units in the Combustion Laboratory.

removal stoker-type for service in producing not only heat but also hot water. These tests showed that the Penn State stoker was capable of furnishing trouble-free semi-automatic operation year-round, with a considerable saving of fuel over hand-firing methods, with no noticeable overheating of the home during the summer months, and with a lower cost than other methods of home heating plus hot water production. One of the leading stoker manufacturers was licensed to manufacture stokers incorporating the improvements developed in the College laboratories.

Commercial and Industrial Stokers.   A number of studies were conducted on the development and uses of commercial and industrial stokers. One major project involved the development of the single retort underfed stoker in the size range from 100 to 1,200 pounds per hour burning rate. Extensive tests using a variety of bituminous coals indicated that the lack of satisfactory combustion performance with most coal could be traced directly to the distribution of sizes of the fuels as actually delivered to the burning zone of the stoker rather than to the coking, caking, swelling, and plastic properties of the coals. In tests, when the coal was at the correct size, combustion performances were good. Because it was not possible to produce and sell coal at the ideal size, research shifted to producing a furnace to improve the burning performance. This led to studies of stoker retort design. A satisfactory baffle design was developed in which the burning rates nearly doubled, overall efficiency improved, manual attention decreased, and smoke products were reduced to negligible proportions.

Nonfuel Uses.   Investigations on the development of chemical uses for bituminous coal were begun on a laboratory scale. The faculty, notably Calvert C. Wright and Corliss R. Kinney, were pioneers in these endeavors. Emphasis was placed on the production of humic acids, the chemical nature of these acids, and the coals from which they could be prepared.

One early effort was the conversion of coal by the action of nitric acid into nitrohumic acids. By treatment with nitric acid, coal is oxidized and nitrated, and a product results that contains about 5 percent organic nitrogen in a form that is slowly made available to plants. Greenhouse and field tests indicated this product's suitability as an organic fertilizer. In order to make it a commercial source, emphasis was placed on reducing the nitric acid required and on shortening the processing operation. The development of nitrohumic acids became the basis for the early studies of the chemical properties and structure of coal. These studies of the constitution of coal led to the preparation of about a hundred different solvents and solvent mixtures.

Another early endeavor of the fuel technology faculty was the hydrogenation of coal at high temperatures and high pressures. The work concentrated on the chemistry of the process, with the creation of chemical compounds that were related in chemical structure to the coal molecule. Two products, pyrene and carbazole, gave promise for commercial development. With the increased oil supply in the 1950s the investigations were terminated.

Tars and Oils

A number of investigations of tars and oils were undertaken by the faculty. While most of these studies were practical, several had theoretical implications.

Tar Characterization.   The increased demand for tar chemicals by the plastics and synthetics resin industries provided the incentives to seek standard methods of separation and analysis. Studies on the developments of a characterization method were sponsored by the American Gas Association and resulted in a tentative classification.

Vacuum Distillation.   In dealing with high-boiling, heat-sensitive mixtures of compounds, such as those found in tars, the use of distillation at greatly reduced pressures is frequently employed. Because fundamental data on the efficiency of various types of fractionation were not available, an investigation was undertaken to determine the efficiency and general operating characteristic of a variety of packings at pressures from about 10^3 to 10^5 Pa. This investigation showed that the separating efficiencies of different column packings did not fall off at reduced pressures, as anticipated.

Peter Given analyzing a sample of coal-derived synthetic liquid fuels by gas chromatography. Dr. Given was another of the outstanding faculty members in fuel science receiving international recognition for research on the geochemistry of coal, the macro-molecular structure of coal, and the conversion of coal to liquid fuels.

Another project dealt with the chemical compounds present in water-gas tar. The inadequacy of the physical data, normally used for product identification, on the complex organic compounds found in tars necessitated employing tedious and time-consuming chemical methods of identification. A number of what were believed to be pure compounds were isolated, and methylstyrene was identified in addition to a number of more easily identified compounds that were known to be present.

FUEL SCIENCE AND EARLY INDUSTRIAL RESEARCH

In the 1950s a number of industrial companies sought help from the fuel science faculty that broadened the research endeavor of the department. One of those companies was the Stackpole Carbon Company of St. Mary's, Pennsylvania, who turned to the department for help. The company was having difficulty with some of the carbon blacks they were using, particularly in regard to their electrical properties. Philip Walker prepared a proposal to investigate and solve the problem.

The Consolidation Coal Company supported a number of research projects. One of the most important of these was the study of how to change a chemical reaction into an electrical current, important in fuel cell development. George Young came to Penn State from Carnegie Mellon to lead this investigation.

ESTABLISHMENT OF MODERN FUEL SCIENCE

The foundation for the present-day fuel science program developed in the 1950s from the work of Corliss R. Kinney, Howard B. Palmer, and Philip L. Walker. Each of these scientists had a deep interest in fundamental chemical processes and there was a desire to broaden the program from a coal science into gaseous combustion. Philip Walker was a chemical engineer by professional background but also a fuel technologist. His approach to research was a very constructive mix of practical orientation derived from his engineering training and a scientific depth from his scientific background. Dr. Walker developed a major research program focusing on carbons and established for himself an international reputation.

Corliss Kinney had an extensive background in organic chemistry. His interests were in such processes as carbonization and conversion of liquid fuels into coke. His work was thus a study of fundamentals, but with a practical orientation. Howard Palmer came to fuel science as a physical chemist. He had a particular interest in chemical kinetics and high-temperature chemistry, including flames and combustion.

By the 1950s there was a general thrust in fuel science toward a more scientific base for the study of fuels and combustion (Palmer, 1981). This included the initial stages of modeling. There were a number of interesting new thrusts in fuel science during this period. Basic questions were being raised, such as the type of reaction that occurred at a typical flame temperature of between 1,500 to 2,500 Kelvin. Another investigation centered on the emission of light from chemical reactions in a flame. The study of flames led to investigations of free radical species and eventually into some novel flame systems that could generate free radicals. These studies led to a number of papers that dealt with spectroscopy and molecular parameters of small species.

William Kinneman (M.S. Fuel Science 1983), project associate, and Ronald Wincek, research associate, operating a research boiler for combustion of coal/water slurry fuels. During the late 1980s, studies of coal/water slurry combustion became a major focus in the Combustion Laboratory under the direction of Alan W. Scaroni.

The scientific study of carbons of various types was fundamental to the research programs during the 1950s and 1960s. Carbon formation at high temperatures and high pressures, and the breakdown of the organic molecules under certain conditions, were important research themes. These studies began to measure quite accurately the deposition rate of carbon on surfaces in the presence of thermally decomposed gases. These initial efforts led to a series of studies that related deposition rates to gaseous processes and connected the kinetics of the deposition with the kinetics of gas phase pyrolysis.

In the 1960s a number of new faculty members extended fuel science research. Francis J. Vastola and Leonard G. Austin, both of whom completed their Ph.D. work under Philip Walker, were added to the faculty. Peter H. Given, coming from England, came to the program with a strong background in organic chemistry and with experience in geochemistry and coal. Robert H. Essenhigh came to fuel science in 1961 from Sheffield, England, and began construction of furnaces and other practical combustion devices for laboratory study. He liked to talk about applied research at the "fundamental level," a favorite phrase that he epitomized in practice.

In the period from about 1950 to 1970, fuel science was becoming more sophisticated technologically in terms of its measurement capabilities. The scientific approach to the problems created a deep interest in mathematical modeling. At the same time, although all these powerful new methods and techniques were being brought to bear on fuel science, it was done in a context of a very deep concern for the practical consequences and the ability to improve efficiency of practical equipment, combustion devices, fuel conversion systems, and fuel utilization methods.

CURRENT RESEARCH THRUSTS

The faculty in the Fuel Sciences are presently engaged in three broad research topics. One of long standing is the traditional study of combustion of coal. This work was begun by Alfred W. Gauger and Theodore Spicer in the 1930s, and studies are presently being continued by Alan W. Scaroni, whose research focuses on a number of topics that are important not only to the state of Pennsylvania but also to the nation and the world. The present studies include the combustion of coal-water slurries, which will provide a potential new market for coal, replacing oil in boilers that were originally designed to burn oil.

Another research area is techniques that are environmentally acceptable methods for the combustion of coal, particularly with regard to sulfur emissions. The studies are part of larger endeavors focusing on the question of how the properties of fuels affect the ways fuels can be used. These endeavors are attempting to solve some of the fundamental problems of fuel combustion. Another major thrust is the high-temperature and high-pressure organic chemistry of fuels. The major component of the program is the study of the liquefaction of coal. This work also has a long history at Penn State. Peter H. Given made notable contributions in this area during his long and illustrious career at the University, and since he retired, the work has been continued by F. John Derbyshire and, more recently, by Harold H. Schobert. The study of liquefaction has evolved from the conversion of coal into liquid fuel. The same basic chemistry, apparatus, and analytical approaches are used as in traditional research, but new initiatives are being emphasized. A major effort involves the liquefaction of coal in the presence of petroleum-derived fuels. This research is of great interest today because it permits the introduction of coal-liquefaction processes into existing oil refineries so that entirely new coal-liquefaction plants do not need to be constructed.

A new area of research of liquefaction has been introduced by studies of the thermal stability and other chemical reactions of jet fuels. Dr. Schobert states, "This research area is of particular interest now to the Air Force because there is a question about the use of very high-performance aircraft: What do we do with the heat that is generated in the structural framework of the aircraft while it is flying at high speeds? One answer is that we can use the temperatures that are generated to reform the fuel before it goes into the engine in order to convert it into a more efficient fuel form. But when we do that, it's crucial that we don't do some chemistry to the fuel that could cause it to form solid deposits in the fuel lines or other parts of the fuel systems, which of course

Frank Rusinko, Jr.
Alumni Fellow

Frank Rusinko, Jr. (Alumni Fellow 1989; B.S. 1952, M.S. 1954, and Ph.D. 1958 Fuel Technology) began his career as a scientist with Speer Carbon Company and Air Reduction Company. He has held a number of positions, including vice president and technical director of the Airco Speer Carbon, Graphite Division, from 1970 to 1976. Since 1976 he has been president of Electrotools Inc., a division of Uti Inc., and president and chair of Edimax Transor since 1983. His fields of research also include carbon and graphite, gas-solid reactions, gas absorption, coal carbonization, irradiation of coal and graphite, nuclear graphite, catalysts of heterogeneous carbon reactions, fuel cells, surface chemistry, research and development management, high-temperature materials technology, and electrical discharge machine technology.

would be literally a disaster. So, in addition to coal liquefaction and processing, we are starting a vigorous and expanded research program on the high-temperatures and high-pressure chemistry of jet fuels."

Yet another vigorous research area in fuel science is carbon reactions in a high-temperature combustion environment. This work, directed by Michael Y. Frenklach, began in the late 1980s with the fundamental study of the formation of soot in combustion flames. This study is based on two important facts: (1) the emissions of soot into the atmosphere are not desirable from an environmental point of view and (2) if soot is formed, fuel efficiency is low. Because Dr. Frenklach believes the common threads in this work are the chemical reactions, he is branching out from soot formation into areas relating to the depositions of films from the vapor phase. He is collaborating with faculty in ceramics and the Materials Research Laboratory on this research. This investigation has led to some esoteric research on the formation of carbon particles and carbon-containing materials in the atmosphere. In the study of the atmosphere of stars, Dr. Frenklach is now collaborating with faculty in astrophysics.

MODERN ANALYTICAL TOOLS

In the 1960s there was a major revolution in the field of analytical chemistry. A wide range of new kinds of analytical methods were developed in order to probe molecular structures and compositions. For a number of years the field of fuel science was peripheral to these events. Only with the energy crisis of the early 1970s was renewed attention given to research on the chemistry of fuels. Fuel scientists became inheritors of the tremendous development that had been carried out by the analytical chemists.

The definition of fuel science has consequently focused strongly on the composition of fuel at the molecular level, on the composition of fuel-derived materials, such as oil produced from coal, and on the deposits in boilers and other similar aspects. Peter Given was a pioneer in these endeavors through his work in the probing of the molecular architecture of coals. Leonard Austin was also a pioneer, playing a strong role in understanding the molecular behavior of the mineral constituents of coal and how each affects the utilization of coal.

Today the fuel science faculty is investigating such things as the structure of coal, the molecular composition of liquid products derived from coal, and the solid materials derived from coal and other sources, all in an effort to understand the molecular level of the processes that result in good carbon materials, and the processes at the molecular level that determine the activities of catalysts. An understanding of the molecular level of fuels makes it possible to control the reactivity of these processes. No longer would "shake and bake chemistry"—where chemicals are mixed and heated in the hope that something would happen—have to be relied on.

A second major change in analytical equipment and instrumentation that permits a more precise understanding of the structures of fuels is the use of the computers. Computer modeling of molecular structures has exhibited great advances, opening up an entirely new perspective on understanding the utilization of fuels.

While the computer has become a standard piece of equipment for all faculty, Michael Frenklach is a leader in setting up computer links between his research group and most of the mainframe supercomputers available in the United States. This is a tremendous intellectual revolution. Computers and advances in modeling have brought about a major advance in understanding the rate and mechanisms of chemical processes.

Changes in the discipline of fuel science—heavier reliance on analysis conducted at the molecular or atomic levels—require a different type of equipment. The traditional fuel science laboratory was not easily distinguished from a boiler room. Today, because much of the coal analysis relies on computers for data acquisition and data reduction, one laboratory in the program is totally devoted to computer use.

Students must be exposed to advanced techniques of organic and inorganic chemical analysis, depending on their research in progress. This requires advanced chemical laboratories. All students must be familiar with microcomputers so they can perform word-processing, spreadsheet calculations, and reasonably sophisticated data reduction.

Fuel science laboratories are therefore becoming more and more heavily instrumental, and microcomputers are readily available. Although these tools advance the field, the equipment is extremely expensive, and it is difficult for a small individual department to have all the necessary equipment. Consequently, the fuel scientists work closely with colleagues in other programs in the Materials Science Department, in other departments in the College, and even outside the College. For example, they use the Materials Characterization Laboratory and the supercomputer centers established by the National Science Foundation for computer-modeling chemical systems.

Garth Hassel (M.S. Fuel Science 1989) conducting studies of coal behavior in a specially designed high-pressure entrained flow reactor, a facility unique to Penn State.

RESEARCH FUNDING

Securing funds for research programs has always been a major objective of the fuel science faculty. Within recent years the U.S. Department of Energy has been a major funding source, but before this funds came from the Energy Research and Development Administration (ERDA) and its predecessor, the Office of Coal Research in the U.S. Bureau of Mines. In addition, the program has received some funding from the Department of Defense for its jet fuel research program.

Fuel sciences have traditionally had strong relationships with industry. Harold Schobert states: "We regard it to be very important in the fuel science program to maintain a strong interaction with the private sector, particularly the coal industry and the electric power generating industry. We certainly have good interaction on a number of levels. First, a number of industries and utilities have funded research programs in the fuel science program. Second, we have acted as partners with industry in obtaining funding for research from such state agencies as the Ben Franklin Partnership and the Pennsylvania Energy Development Authority. Furthermore, we have had a long and vigorous interaction with industry through the Penn State Cooperative Program in Coal Research, which is generally known as 'Coal Co-Op.' Through the Coal Co-Op program, we are able to obtain grant funding from industry, which allows us to support graduate students and conduct small-scale research programs." He adds: "In addition, we have representatives of industry come to Penn State twice a year for an information exchange meeting that allows industrial sponsors to learn the latest advances in fuel research at Penn State and at the same time provides a forum for those people in industry to tell us what they are thinking and what they see the future needs of their industry to be."

Dr. Schobert noted the importance of the interrelationship between industry and faculty: "Further, we have always had a long interaction and one-on-one relationship between various faculty members and counterparts in industry. In some cases that's an entirely informal occasional exchange of ideas by visits or phone calls, and in some cases it has been more formal, through an actual consulting arrangement with the company. But we try hard to ensure that the research and teaching in the fuel science program is directed toward the needs of industry and of society. These efforts help keep us from marching off into left field while the rest of the world is headed in the opposite direction. For practical reasons, it is also important that our graduates be trained for potential future employers so they will find employment."

THE COMBUSTION LABORATORY

The Combustion Laboratory, jointly financed by the College and the coal industry of Pennsylvania, was placed in service in 1948. This new facility of the Mineral Industries Experiment Station was the most completely equipped research laboratory in the nation for work on stokers. Boilers and stokers ranged in size from domestic units to the 178-horsepower boiler fired with a 6-by-6-foot underfeed stoker.

The Combustion Laboratory has been a major teaching and research unit in the fuel science program. In the mid-1980s the facility was modernized and located in the newly constructed Academic Activities Building. In addition to the basic combustion lab, supporting facilities include a machine shop, a room reserved for grinding and separating coal, and analytical laboratories, which researchers use for the analyses necessary to an understanding of the combustion

The Penn State Combustion Laboratory.

process. There are plans to expand the work on the desulfurization of coals. Past directors of the laboratory have been Robert H. Essenhigh, Robert G. Jenkins, and James J. Reuther. The present director is Alan W. Scaroni.

The Coal-Water Fuel Facility

The Coal-Water Fuel Demonstration project of the Combustion Laboratory, dedicated on September 15, 1989, demonstrates the technology for using coal slurries to fuel commercial boilers. The project is funded by the state of Pennsylvania as part of its effort to support the development of new uses and markets for Pennsylvania coal. The strong support of State Representative William R. Lloyd, Jr., and Edward J. Haluska was instrumental in the establishment of this project. Pennsylvania Lieutenant Governor Mark S. Singel stated at the dedication: "With the development of clean coal technology, coal will be one of the growth industries of the state in the 1990s. With the development of this facility, the technology is moved from the classroom to practical reality. Utilities, such as the one at Homer City, are interested in using this process."

The facility, an expansion of the Penn State Combustion Laboratory research on coal-water fuels from Pennsylvania coal, houses an industrial boiler with an output of 15 million Btu per hour, a typical size for heating a large apartment complex, a hospital, or a military facility. The boilers, originally designed for oil-firing, are modified for combustion with coal-water fuels—slurries of pulverized coal and water that are handled and burned much like fuel oil.

The major goals of the coal-water fuel project are (1) to demonstrate the future and environmentally acceptable combustion of coal-water fuels derived from Pennsylvania coals; (2) to demonstrate the feasibility of retrofitting existing oil-fired boilers for use with coal-water fuels; and (3) to evaluate the effect of long-term firing with coal-water fuel on boiler performance.

Pennsylvania Lieutenant Governor Mark Singel, center, at the dedication of the Coal-Water Fuel Facility. Dean John Dutton is on the left and David Schuckers, Penn State Director of Government Relations, is on the right.

THE INTERNATIONAL CHARACTER OF FUEL SCIENCE

Although the number of fuel scientists is small, they are truly an international group. Howard B. Palmer states: "One of the most enjoyable aspects of working in the field of combustion—and I think it's probably true of fuel science in general—is the international character of the activity. In the combustion field there are, worldwide, perhaps 4,000 people engaged in research. The group is thus so small that you can get to know a reasonable fraction of them. When I was president of the International Combustion Institute, I found that the coal researchers were a close-knit community throughout the world. This makes rapid and widespread dissemination of knowledge possible. It is a major advantage to a researcher to be able to have friends in the international laboratories where advanced research projects are ongoing."

GRADUATE STUDENT ENROLLMENT

Because there are few undergraduate programs in fuel science in the United States, fuel science at Penn State gets its graduate students predominantly from chemistry and chemical engineering. This relationship exists because, to a considerable degree, fuel science lies between chemistry and chemical engineering. Fuel science is a discipline that is somewhat more applied than the traditional chemistry curriculum at most universities, in that students in chemistry who are looking for an applied science as their graduate program find fuel science a good career choice. The practical aspects of graduate study in fuel science also appeal to students in engineering. In addition to chemistry and chemical engineering, students selecting fuel science for their graduate program come with undergraduate degrees from mechanical engineering, geology, and physics.

GENERAL EDUCATION

The course "Energy and Fuels in Modern Society," Material Science 101, has been taught since the late 1960s by a series of fuel science faculty including Francis J. Vastola, Robert G. Jenkins, Alan W. Scaroni, Ljubísa R. Radovic, and Harold H. Schobert. It provides basic information about energy utilization and technological developments and gives a scientific insight into factors that influence energy conversion. Problems and trends in the human use of energy are also considered. Enrollment has steadily grown to more than 600 students each semester.

HONORS AND AWARDS

Fuel science faculty have served their profession in a number of capacities and have been honored at national and international levels. The following sketches illustrate the wide ranges of these recognitions.

In 1969 Philip L. Walker, Evan Pugh Professor, received the American Chemical Society's Storch Award for contributions in coal research, and in 1971 he received the American Carbon Society's Skakel Award for contributions to carbon science. He has served as distinguished speaker for the American Ceramic Society, Sigma Xi, and as George Graffin Memorial Lecturer for the American Carbon Society. In 1983 he was awarded a citation by the British Joint Carbon Committee for extensive and fundamental contributions made to carbon science.

Peter H. Given was a member of the American Chemical Society, a Fellow of the Chemical Society (London), the Geochemical Society, and the Geological Society of America. He also served on a number of committees that bridged the chemical and geological fields. Between 1972 and

Dedication of the Coal-Water Fuel Facility in 1989 with coal/water mixture demonstration.

1973 he served as chair of the Organic Geochemistry Division of the Society, and in 1984 he received the Storch Award of the Fuel Chemistry Division of the American Chemical Society for his distinguished contributions to coal research. At that time, he was the only non-American ever to receive this prestigious national award.

The work of Howard B. Palmer has been closely associated with the Combustion Institute. He served as editor of its journal, *Combustion and Flame,* for fourteen years, guiding it through forty volumes with some 15,000 pages of topflight research papers. He also served the institute as vice president from 1984 to 1985 and as president from 1985 to 1988. For five of its biennial international Symposiums on combustion he has been a member of the program committee. Dr. Palmer states: "It is a superb worldwide group of researchers, and interaction with these distinguished colleagues has been one of the most happy aspects of my professional career. I am grateful to the College and the University for encouraging—indeed, for making possible—these and other very stimulating and fulfilling professional experiences, and I hope that the dedication to excellence so evident in the EMS college is reflected in my present role in the graduate school."

Leonard G. Austin has received a number of honors for his work. For his paper entitled "The Process Engineering of Size Reduction: Ball Milling" with R. R. Klimpel and P. T. Luckie, he received the 1983 Gaudin Award of the Society of Mining Engineers "for his contributions to the theory, design and optimization of comminution and the education of students in this operation." In 1986 he received the Babcock Award of the Institute of Energy (U.K.) for his work on upper wall slag deposits from American coals in utility boilers. This award was followed in 1987 by the Percy W. Nichols Joint Society Award of the Coal Division of the Society of Mining Engineers. The award was granted "for significant contributions to the understanding of slagging and fouling in coal burning utility boilers." Dr. Austin is a regional editor of the international committee of the international journal *Particle Characterization.*

Robert H. Essenhigh was chair of the Arrangements Committee for the fourteenth International Symposium on Combustion in 1972, sponsored by the Combustion Institute. He was also co-chairman of a colloquium on combustion in practical systems at the fifteenth International Symposium on Combustion in Japan in 1975.

Harold Schobert has edited a volume of symposium proceedings, *The Chemistry of Low-Rank Coals* (1984), and has written an introductory text on coal for the educated layperson entitled *Coal: The Energy Source of Past and Future* (1987).

METALS SCIENCE AND ENGINEERING

When the Agricultural College of Pennsylvania was founded, Pennsylvania was on the threshold of becoming a major industrial state. Although agricultural programs dominated for many years, the importance of industry was recognized by individual courses in the areas of mineral resources and the processing of the ores into metals. Many of the early bachelor's theses dealt with metallurgical topics, such as "On Some Zinc and Lead Ores from Columbia County," "On Slags and Scoriae Produced in Refining Iron by the Charcoal Process and by Puddling," "On Some Iron Ores of Penn and Nittany Valleys," and "Miscellaneous Chemical Analysis (Including Copper Ores and Limestone)." These early papers studied practical subjects and were primarily interested in observations of processes and in providing technical information.

Although the importance of metallurgy was recognized, formal coursework was slow to develop. Finally, in 1893, Magnus C. Ihlseng, professor of mining engineering and geology, and Harry Harkness Stock, assistant professor of mineralogy and metallurgy, offered a two-year option in metallurgy in the mining engineering program, but financial difficulties slowed development of the program. In 1902 M. E. Wadsworth, who succeeded Dr. Ihlseng, offered a two-year option in metallurgy with metallurgical courses aggregating 24 credit hours. In 1904 Clarence P. Linville, from Ohio State University, was made the first full-time instructor in metallurgy. In 1906 there was a considerable expansion of the metallurgy curriculum, and Frank A. Dalburg and Howard I. Smith were added as assistants.

THE INITIAL PROGRAM

The first metallurgy major was approved by the Board of Trustees for the 1907–8 academic year, in response to a special legislative appropriation in 1906 and the reorganization of the School of Mines into the School of Mines and Metallurgy. As a result of these administrative changes, Metallurgical Engineering attained departmental status. The 1907 catalog described the new major:

> Instruction in Metallurgy begins with the first semester of the junior year. There is first given a course which covers the general principles of Metallurgy, fuels, furnaces, fluxes, slags, and a short survey of the whole field. This is followed with a number of courses, which deal with the different phases of the subject.
>
> It is the purpose of the instruction in Metallurgy to give a thorough understanding of the principles which govern the different metallurgical processes, together with the study of the best and latest methods and apparatus for carrying them out, so that one may take up actual work in Metallurgy in an intelligent manner and combine theoretical with practical knowledge.

The catalog listed sixteen courses in metallurgy and thirty-four different laboratory sections. By 1908, however, the laboratory sections had been combined with the regular metallurgy courses. The emphasis was on the production and processing of metals and alloys, either individually or as a group. There was one course devoted to what is now known as "physical metallurgy." In 1911 the department installed a new Leitz metallograph, thus making Penn State one of the first educational institutions in America to lead in metallographic study. Because this branch of metallurgy was then in its infancy, Penn State was clearly at the cutting edge of new developments. The study of mechanical properties was, however, not developed by the metallurgy faculty, who relied on courses in mechanics, engineering materials, and the testing of materials in engineering to provide metallurgy students with the necessary information.

The major was initially under the direction of Clarence P. Linville, assisted by D. K. Bullens, assistant professor of metallurgy. In 1910 Hugh D. Pallister replaced D. K. Bullens as instructor in metallurgy, and in 1911 Harry B. Northrup, coming from Ohio State University, was added to the metallurgy staff as an instructor. In 1912 Charles E. McQuigg, also from Ohio State University, was made assistant professor of metallurgy, and Frank A. Fahrenwald was a teaching assistant. In 1913 Boyd Dudley, Jr., from the Missouri School of Mines and Metallurgy, took the place of

Administration
Metals Science and
Engineering

Department of Mining

Magnus C. Ihlseng	1893
Clarence P. Linville	1904–1907

Department of Metallurgical Engineering

Clarence P. Linville	1907–1912
Charles E. McQuigg	1912–1917
Harry B. Northrup	1917–1918
Harry B. Northrup	1919–1920

Department of Metallurgy

David F. McFarland	1920–1945

Department of Mineral Technology
Division of Metallurgy

John Low	1945–1948
Harold S. Read	1948–1949
Jay W. Fredrickson	1949–1952
Amos J. Shaler	1952–1953

Department of Metallurgy

Amos J. Shaler	1953–1960
Robert W. Lindsay	1960–1967

Department of Materials Science and
Engineering
Metallurgy Section

Robert W. Lindsay	1967–1969
William R. Bitler	1969–1973
Frank F. Aplan	1973–1975
Harold W. Pickering	1975–1980
John H. Hoke	1980–1985

Metals Science and Engineering Program

Donald A. Koss	1986–

Frank Fahrenwald, and the department staff remained McQuigg, Northrup, and Dudley until the entrance of the United States into the world war in 1917. At that time McQuigg and Dudley left to work in the army ordnance department, leaving Northrup in charge of the department until May 1918, when he too was called to army ordnance. In this capacity they rendered notable service. A large number of students enrolled in the metallurgy curriculum also entered military service or were engaged in other war work, and metallurgy instruction was carried on, with difficulty, by William R. Chedsey, head of the mining department.

Only Dr. Northrup returned to the metallurgy staff at the end of the war. He headed the department with instructors Oscar A. Knight, from Ohio State University, and Ogden B. Malin, a 1913 Penn State graduate with a B.S. degree. In 1920 Dr. Northrup resigned to take an industrial position. He returned to the faculty in 1931 to become director of the Mineral Industries Extension Division, which he guided through a period of extensive development until his retirement in 1947. In the months immediately preceding Dr. Northrup's resignation, the metallurgy courses and curriculum were considerably revised, their contents were improved and better coordinated with the needs of the metallurgical industry, and metallurgical laboratory equipment compatible with the evolving curriculum was purchased. New oil-fired assay and heat-treating furnaces, additional metallographics, hardness testing, and tensile-testing apparatus are worthy of specific mention.

THE McFARLAND YEARS

David Ford McFarland, who received his Ph.D. from Yale in 1909 and had been on the University of Illinois faculty for ten years, was appointed professor and head of the department in 1920. Dr. McFarland was to serve in that capacity for the next twenty-five years, always striving to strengthen and expand the program. Throughout his tenure the department gained increasing recognition from the metallurgical industry for its strong undergraduate program and established a reputation it continues to maintain (McFarland, 1939).

The faculty of the department was gradually built under the direction of Dr. McFarland. In 1926 Manley E. Brooks was made a graduate assistant in metallurgy. He was succeeded in 1928 by James R. Long, who was promoted to instructor in 1930 and was instrumental in the installation of a 35 K. W. Ajaz Northup high-frequency induction furnace. He also introduced various other improved equipment and laboratory procedures.

In 1934 Charles R. Austin, with a Ph.D. from the University of Wales, came to the staff from the Westinghouse Research Laboratory in Pittsburgh, replacing Oscar Knight. In 1937 Carl H. Samans of Yale and Maurice C. Fetzer of Harvard were added to the faculty. These professors engaged in both undergraduate and graduate teaching and research. Also during 1937 a new 600–60,000-pound double-range Baldwin-Southwork hydraulic testing machine was added to the instructional equipment.

The metallurgical major attracted students from its initial year in 1907, and by the 1920s the department had an enrollment of twenty to twenty-five undergraduates. In the 1930s the undergraduate enrollment grew surprisingly during the depression years. While employment declined in the metallurgical industries, the demand for engineers survived. In the year 1938–39 the enrollment consisted of 30 freshmen, 44 sophomores, 37 juniors, and 28 seniors, making a total of 139 undergraduates. All of the twenty-eight graduating seniors with bachelor of science degrees were

David Ford McFarland, head, Department of Metallurgy (1920–45), teaches a class in metallography.

placed in metallurgical positions. By this date, graduates from the metallurgy curriculum were occupying positions of great importance in the metallurgical industry of Pennsylvania and all over the United States.

With the establishment of a graduate school at Penn State in 1922, the faculty initiated a formal graduate program. During the first years, two master of science degrees were awarded in metallurgical engineering to R. M. Learn and J. A. Succop. The graduate program, however, developed slowly. In 1938–39 there were six candidates for advanced degrees. The first doctorate was awarded in 1940 to Bernard S. Norris.

A significant factor in the early development of the metallurgy program was the selection of metallurgy courses by students for other departments and curricula. Many of the courses were specifically planned to suit the needs of nonmetallurgy students. A large laboratory was equipped with microscope tables of special design, with twenty-four working places and microscopes and other facilities for accommodating 120 students working in five sections. During the year 1937–38 some 222 nonmetallurgy students were enrolled in twelve different courses.

Metallurgy Research Program Established

In the mid-1930s Charles R. Austin was responsible for establishing the first organized research program in metallurgy. His plan of research gained sponsorship, financial assistance, and technical guidance from several steel and allied industrial companies and came to be known as the Steel Companies Fund.

The two major projects investigated in the laboratories were (1) tensile deformation characteristics of alloys at elevated temperatures and (2) studies on reaction rates of carbon steels when subjected to quenching and tempering treatments. The results of these efforts were reported at a number of meetings and provided several publications. The scope of the research is revealed by the following research report titles: "Effect of Tempering Quenched Hypereutectoid Steels on the Physical Properties and Microstructure," presented at the 1937 annual convention of the American Society for Metals; "Temperature Gradient Studies on Tempering Reactions on Quenched High Carbon Steels," presented at the 1938 annual meeting of American Institute of Mining and Metallurgical Engineers; and "Comparison of the Tensile Deformation Characteristics of Alloys at Elevated Temperatures," presented at the 1938 annual meeting of the Iron and Steel Institute, London.

The general research program in metallurgy was outlined by Dr. Austin in the May 1938 issue of *Mineral Industries*. Research on high-temperature alloys included further study of the tensile properties of stainless steels and Kovar-type alloys; development of improved apparatus for multiple tensile test data, to be installed in a constant-temperature laboratory; fundamental studies to shed light on some of the controlling mechanisms of creep at elevated temperatures; and preparation of pure iron base alloys for the purpose of studying quantitatively the effect of certain elements on the resistance to deformation of pure iron. Research on reaction rates in carbon steels included further studies on the dissimilar reaction to heat treatments of carbon steels having "similar" chemical analyses; fundamental study of the structure of carbon steel obtained with intermediate cooling rates; and preparation of pure iron-carbon base alloys with specific additions of a third element for the purpose of quantitatively examining the effect of the third element on reaction rates obtained during heat treatments.

This program served to coordinate the postgraduate efforts of the staff, research assistants, graduate students, and even the thesis work of the more able undergraduate senior-year metallurgy students. Ten companies initially cooperated with the metallurgy faculty in developing the program. Contact between the department of metallurgy and the technical representatives of the various cooperating companies was obtained by arranging an annual research conference for the purpose of reporting the progress of the investigations and obtaining guidance in developing the next year's program. In this manner the company representatives had the opportunity to play an important role in the solution of the problems investigated.

Howard W. Pickering
Distinguished Professor of Metallurgy

People tend to label me as a corrosion scientist. It's a convenient term because much of my work has had direct application to the solution of corrosion problems. But my true interests are much wider and deeper than simply the problem of corrosion.

I'm fascinated by a world we cannot probe with our eyes—for example, the surface of metals at the atomic level. I want to know how and why changes take place there—discover how atoms react and move, understand chemical reactions and electrochemical processes at the scale of individual atoms. This nanometer world is, for me, totally absorbing.

I have been amazingly fortunate in my career. I came into metallurgy in the late 1950s at the time when the Russian space capsule *Sputnik* had galvanized American science and federal funding was focused on metals programs. I became involved in applying electrochemical techniques, a new area just emerging.

I had entered metallurgy by chance. After drifting through grade school and much of high school, far more interested in model aircraft and rebuilding cars than in schoolwork, I finally woke up to the fact that there was a future out there. I crammed every course in science I could find, with the general idea of doing something in science or engineering. Then a distant cousin, who was a chemist working in sales of metallurgical microscopes, visited my family and talked to me about metals. As a result, I entered the University of Cincinnati to study metallurgical engineering.

I was particularly lucky to have three outstanding mentors in my early career. My graduate adviser at the Ohio State University, Mars Fontana, a wise and broadly experienced corrosion engineer, introduced me to urgent problems in metal corrosion and gave me my initial focus. But the influence of Carl Wagner, a world-renowned physical chemist who directed my postdoctoral studies at the Max Planck Institute in Göttingen, was probably the most crucial. He taught me the ethics and practice of fundamental science.

I also owe a great deal to Larry Darken, an inspiring scientist who directed the U.S. Steel Edgar C. Bain Laboratory for many years, before joining the EMS faculty when his laboratory was disbanded. Working with him and others at the Bain Lab was intellectually stimulating while I honed my research skills.

My research has continued unabated for the past two decades in the College of Earth and Mineral Sciences. I have never regretted entering an academic career. You have great freedom in research. You are forced to learn how to interpret your work for many different audiences, and I believe scientists have a responsibility to do that. There is the added challenge of passing on knowledge to students and trying to inspire them. And there is the satisfaction of working with students and watching them develop and become enthusiastic.

I find myself enjoying teaching more and more as the years go by. I'm not by nature a spontaneous classroom teacher and I've had to work hard at it. Teaching has been especially important to me because I have always learned most readily by listening. As a young student, even in high school, the elation I felt in class when I finally understood a difficult concept was one of the things that led me to become a scientist.

Later, I discovered that there is also a special kind of freedom that accompanies sustained scientific investigation—an intellectual freedom. Once you've gained that and experienced the excitement of trying to solve a mystery, you never want to stop. For me, these things have made life very satisfying.

I've had some excellent students in EMS. Thanks to them and exciting new instruments we are finally beginning to answer some questions that were raised as long as thirty years ago. The fundamental studies we're doing in the College today have applications in some fascinating areas—highway deterioration, bridges, pipes—and many implications for taking care of the nation's infrastructure as well as for progressing into new types of materials.

Metallurgy has changed considerably during my career. New techniques using lasers and advanced microscopy, and sophisticated equipment like the atom-probe field ion microscope and the scanning tunneling microscope, have increased the range of our investigations. Our outlook is broader. We have, for example, whole new technologies of rapid solidification, powder metal alloys, and fiber reinforced metals that have developed from a painstaking study of the chemistry and physics of metals at the micro level combined with ingenious techniques for manipulating the microstructure of metals as they are melted and solidified. Metallurgy is an exciting discipline these days.

Metallurgical Conferences

The custom of holding an annual metallurgical conference at Penn State, as a part of the series of conferences held each year by the School of Mineral Industries, was inaugurated in May 1934. At this meeting the name of the Penn State Metallurgical Society was changed to the Penn State Chapter of the American Society of Metals, under a charter granted by the National Society. Membership in this chapter consisted largely of student members. The chapter, which continues today, enjoys certain financial and technical support from the National Society.

The meeting was so successful that the American Society of Metals voted to hold such a meeting at Penn State every other year. It was then decided that the School of Mineral Industries should hold a metallurgical conference during the intervening year. In 1935 the general topic of the conference was "The History and Present Development of the Blast Furnace in Pennsylvania." The note in the May 1935 *Mineral Industries* bulletin stated:

> Interest in this topic is prompted by the great importance which the charcoal iron industry occupied in Central Pennsylvania during the first half of the nineteenth century. This is kept in the memory of the present generation by the fifty or more old blast-furnace stacks which are still to be found in this region; and by these descendents of the old iron masters who are still prominent in the life of this community.
>
> A further reason for recognition of this topic is the large number of able blast furnace operations and executives who have gone out as graduates from Penn State and who have been powerful agents in developing the blast furnace to its present great efficiency.
>
> It is equally appropriate to dedicate our program to the pioneer iron masters of Pennsylvania and to these latter-day Penn State furnace men.
>
> The program has been developed with a view towards sharing the progress of this industry from the primitive furnaces with their hand-labor production of fifteen to thirty tons each, to the present highly mechanized and wonderfully efficient great furnaces capable of making from a thousand to fifteen hundred tons of iron per day.

These conferences were continued during the 1930s. The leading metallurgists in the eastern United States attended, many presenting scientific papers. In 1938 more than two hundred members of the American Society for Metals attended the May 20 and 21 conference. These meetings provided excellent opportunities to showcase the work of Penn State's metallurgical program.

World War II

During World War II the number of students in the undergraduate and graduate program of metallurgy declined drastically. The faculty, however, contributed in other directions by providing instruction for military personnel being trained at Penn State. The department also participated in a program sponsored by the Hamilton Standard Propeller Company. Two groups of young women were sent to Penn State to be trained in various fields, including metallurgy and chemistry. The aim was to provide education in such areas as heat treatment, metallography, mechanical testing, and pyrometry to prepare the women for assignments in the company's plants and laboratories. An interesting side effect of this program was the return of some of the female trainees to Penn State to pursue degrees after the war. One of these, Marguerite Grymko, who received her master's degree in 1949, was the first woman to receive a Penn State advanced degree in metallurgy (Lindsay, 1981).

McFARLAND THE MAN

Under Dr. McFarland's direction an active program that produced more than four hundred bachelor of science degrees was built during his tenure. Dr. McFarland was an authority on the iron industry of Pennsylvania. He made personal visits to United States plants for almost every kind of industrial chemical process and metallurgical treatment possible. His research centered on studies of copper, nickel, and tin alloys and the grain growth of metals.

A nationally recognized expert in his field, Dr. McFarland was honored by many of his colleagues. The David Ford McFarland Award was established at Penn State to achieve three goals: "To constitute a public recognition of an individual of merit, to serve as an inspiration to students and young graduates, and to honor the college by directing attention to her able alumni." Despite his national reputation, Dr. McFarland remained a humble man with a sense of humor about himself. His father was a cemetery superintendent, "which no doubt accounts," Dr. McFarland said, "for my cheerful disposition." Another of his favorite stories was of how he got his doctorate from Yale in 1909 four days after his wedding. He and his wife attended commencement exercises during their honeymoon, with the dean awarding the honorary degree of "master of hearts" at the ceremony to his new bride. When he retired and was asked what he intended to do he grinned and said, "Continue to be checking up on the Penn State mets."

FACULTY AND PROGRAM DEVELOPMENT

After David McFarland retired in 1945, John R. Low, Jr., became head of metallurgy. H. Mauzee Davis and Eugene P. Klier continued on the faculty while Robert W. Lindsay returned from a brief period in industry. Maxwell Gensamer, coming from the Carnegie Institute of Technology to head the newly created Department of Materials Technology, was a metallurgist (Gensamer, 1946). Revisions in the undergraduate program planned by Dr. Gensamer and Dr. Davis included the introduction of two courses designed to use metallurgical literature, films, and processes to sharpen the student's skills in observation and oral and written presentations. The intent of these courses has continued into the present program of study. New additions to the faculty were William J. Reagan and Harold J. Read. Professor Reagan taught steel production metallurgy and instilled enthusiasm in many students who went on to have successful careers in the steel industry.

Dr. Read was an excellent teacher and also carried on an extensive research program. Of his teaching, he states: "I stressed the importance of writing and oral presentations in technical life—whether that life be in research, production, sales, or whatever. I devoted much time and effort to careful criticism and annotation of written work and to working in oral presentation, using tape recordings made in seminar-type sessions. All this was worked into the framework of technical courses at both the undergraduate and the graduate level."

Dr. Read was a pioneer metallurgist in the field of electroplating. Research and development in this area had previously been the province of chemists who were primarily concerned with the appearance and corrosive resistance of the deposits. There was no realization that other important characteristics could be influenced by metallurgical structures and properties. Dr. Read, along with his graduate students, designed test equipment for assessing the properties of the very thin films of metal that are encountered in electroplating. Special mechanical tests, plus extensive use of electron diffraction and electron microscopy, both ordinary and scanning, resulted in many

Dr. Read and William P. Minnear ('68 B.S., '69 M.S., '75 Ph.D.) use the microprobe analyzer of the College in the late 1960s to study interdiffusion between electrodeposits and their substrates.

scientific advances in the field. Dr. Read considered consulting an important part of keeping in the forefront of metallurgical knowledge benefiting both teaching and research.

In the late 1940s Dr. Low accepted a position in industry. Dr. Read served as acting head of metallurgy for a year until Jay W. Fredrickson came from the University of Utah to join the faculty in 1949. During Dr. Fredrickson's tenure an attempt was made to reestablish the Steel Companies Fund, which had become dormant. Representatives were invited to a meeting in 1951, and enough support was generated to sponsor research by Thomas A. Prater on fatigue behavior in metals.

Dr. Fredrickson left in 1952 to work in industry, and Dr. Read again served as acting head for a year until Amos J. Shaler came from the Massachusetts Institute of Technology to direct the metallurgy program.

During the 1950s the metallurgy faculty participated in the Atoms for Peace program involving various university departments. Sponsored by the Atomic Energy Commission, this brought nuclear scientists and engineers from free-world countries to Penn State for studies related to the peaceful use of atomic energy. As a by-product of this experience, the Atomic Energy Commission provided a grant for equipment to each of the participating universities. As a result the department acquired a good deal of modern equipment, such as tensile-testing machines and special types of balances.

Also during the 1950s the metallurgy faculty were pioneers in the use of television instruction. The use of television in the metallography laboratory began in the early 1950s. In the traditional laboratory, the students used individual light microscopes to examine their own specimens, and the professor went from microscope to microscope discussing with each student what was in the field of the microscope. Obviously, this technique had disadvantages because different students couldn't view a single specimen at the same time. After experimentation, the idea of attaching a television camera to the metallograph on which you could then place one sample was developed. The image of the sample was then projected on a television screen, and the professor and students could discuss the microstructure of the sample as a group. This was a major advancement in the instructional program.

Howard O. Beaver, Jr.
Distinguished Alumnus

Howard O. Beaver, Jr. (Distinguished Alumnus 1991; B.S. Metallurgy 1948) had a career with Carpenter Technology that spanned nearly four decades. He began his work as a mill hand and progressed through a succession of executive positions to head the corporation as chairman and CEO. In 1981 he was awarded the Horatio Alger Award, which recognizes business leaders who have risen from humble beginnings to further the cause of American free enterprise. He has also been awarded the B'nai B'rith International Humanitarian Award and is a distinguished life member of the American Society for Metals, whose Penn State chapter awarded him the 1972 David F. McFarland Award. *Financial World* has given him its certificate of distinction and its bronze award, and the Berks County Chamber of Commerce named him 1982 Businessperson of the Year. Penn State has long been an object of his affection. He has not only headed the Berks Campus advisory board, but also led its successful capital campaign and earned its 1978 Loyal Penn Stater Award and its 1989 Outstanding Service Award. His citation read:

> To Howard O. Beaver, Jr., for rising from humble beginnings to a life of professional and civic accomplishment, for his financial management and leadership, and for his many years of service to his alma mater.

Frederick C. Langenberg
Distinguished Alumnus

Frederick C. Langenberg (Distinguished Alumnus 1989; Alumni Fellow 1977; Ph.D. Metallurgy 1955) spent most of his career as a steel industry executive in such companies as the Crucible Steel Corporation and the Trent Tube Division of Colt Industries. Since 1979 he has been with Interlake Inc., where he is presently chairman, chief executive officer, and chief operating officer. With company sales approaching $900 million, he has been the driving force in converting an ailing steel company into a multitudinal producer of a broad range of materials handling and packaging systems and engineering materials. A former president of the American Iron and Steel Institute, he was awarded a Distinguished Life Membership in the American Society for Metals in 1982. He has maintained his ties with the College and continues to be a regular visitor and valued adviser. In 1983 he received the David McFarland Award of the Penn State chapter of the American Society for Metals. His citation read:

> To Frederick C. Langenberg for distinguishing himself as a dynamic executive, for contributing to the global advancement of the metals industry, and for sharing his experience and enthusiasm with the youth of his community.

Thomas M. Krebs
Distinguished Alumnus

Thomas M. Krebs (Distinguished Alumnus 1984; B.S. Metallurgy 1949), after receiving his metallurgy degree, joined the firm of Babcock & Wilcox, where he rose to the position of senior vice president and group executive of the Tubular Products Group of the company. In 1975 he received the Penn State Beaver Campus Distinguished Service Award, and in 1981 he was honored with the McFarland Award for achievement in metallurgy, given by the Penn State chapter of the American Society for Metals. Of his college career he writes: "Unquestionably, my metallurgy classes were my most interesting studies, and they provided an excellent foundation for my thirty-five-year-long career in the steel industry business. Dr. H. M. 'George' Davis, Dr. Robert Lindsay, Dr. Harold Read, and Dr. John Low all contributed significantly to my metallurgical education. I particularly remember Dr. Davis's Metallurgical Problems course. In addition to being a dedicated and demanding teacher, Dr. Davis was an excellent musician and directed a church choir in which my wife was a soloist."

Thomas Krebs has a special relationship to Beaver County, having been active in the United Way, the Beaver Valley Chamber of Commerce, the County Medical Center, and the Allegheny Trails Council of the Boy Scouts. His citation read:

> To Thomas M. Krebs, metallurgist and industrial executive, for advancing to the pinnacle of his profession, for unstintingly encouraging Beaver Campus development, and for unselfishly sharing his energy and talents with his profession and his community.

Dennis J. Carney
Distinguished Alumnus

Dennis J. Carney (Distinguished Alumnus 1981; B.S. Metallurgy 1942) retired from United States Steel as vice president of research in 1974 and joined Wheeling-Pittsburgh Steel as vice president of operations, rising to the corporation's chief executive officer and chairman of the board in 1981. For his distinguished achievements in iron and steel production and ferrous metallurgy, he was presented with the 1978 Benjamin F. Fairless Award of the American Institute of Mining, Metallurgical, and Petroleum Engineers. He also received the McFarland Award in 1966. Outside the industry he has served as a director of Wheeling College and has been active in the Allegheny Trails Council, the Boy Scouts of America, and the United Way campaign in Allegheny County. His citation read:

> To Dennis J. Carney, industrialist, for distinguishing himself as an outstanding executive, for contributing to the worldwide advancement of the metals industry, and for providing progressive leadership to business and civic organizations.

Robert W. Lindsay inaugurated instruction of metallurgy via television with a course in ferrous metallography that he taught in the mid-1950s. Here he is shown with a TV camera attached to a metallograph.

Additions to the faculty in the 1950s included Charles Kropp, who supervised the laboratory instruction in the Metallurgy Science course for engineers, and Arnulf I. Muan, later professor of geochemistry and materials science and former associate dean for research in the College. John H. Hoke and Earle R. Ryba joined the metallurgy faculty in 1960. Dr. Hoke placed great emphasis on teaching physical metallurgy, particularly mechanical properties and behavior. Dr. Ryba specialized in x-ray investigation of metals and alloys, the determination of crystal structure, and properties of intermetallic components. George W. Healy joined the faculty in 1963, bringing with him interest in high-temperature calorimetry as applied to obtaining thermal data for solidification and solid-state changes in various systems. He retired in 1974.

In 1960 Robert W. Lindsay became the chairman of the metallurgy major, serving until 1969. Of his administration, Dr. Lindsay reflects: "My approach as an administrator was to build a strong undergraduate program that would prepare the students for two stems upon graduation: he would be prepared adequately for direct entry into an industrial position or for entry into a graduate program. As an adjunct to this, I felt it necessary to build an adequate and stable faculty in which the senior members would teach at both the undergraduate level and the graduate level. I felt it necessary, also, to maintain a strong connection with the metallurgical/materials industries, which has been done for years at Penn State through the Cooperative Program in Metallurgy. This served to maintain a strong contact between the faculty and the metallurgical industry. This also served to showcase our students and keep the faculty cognizant of what was new in the industry. I was much in favor of research for educational purposes. A faculty member should secure funds to maintain his ability to do research in the field of his choice, but not to the extent that it would interfere with teaching commitments."

In 1969 Dr. Lindsay was succeeded as department head by William R. Bitler, who served until 1973. Frank F. Aplan served as head from 1973 to 1975 when Howard W. Pickering took over. John H. Hoke assumed direction of the program in 1980 to his retirement in 1985.

William R. Bitler came to the faculty in 1962. He is a physical metallurgist with specific research interests in superconduction and magnetism, the thermodynamics of solids and interfaces, solid-state diffusion, and solid-solid reaction kinetics. One of the most interesting and perplexing problems in metallurgy that Dr. Bitler is working on is diffusion-induced grain-boundary migration. Grain-boundary motion has been subject to numerous investigations, but a generally acceptable model or explanation has not evolved. The object of Dr. Bitler's research is to develop such a model.

George Simkovich is primarily interested in the physical chemistry of materials, high-temperature oxidation, point defects in ionic-type solids, electrical conductivity, and thermodynamics. Current research includes the study of high-temperature oxidation of materials, with and without dispersed phases, the mechanism of hot corrosion, refractory metal oxidation properties, and coatings applications.

Howard W. Pickering established an internationally recognized teaching and research laboratory in the area of electrolytic corrosion and corrosion prevention and developed a state-of-the-art atom probe field ion microscope laboratory that is one of only a few found in a materials or engineering department. This tool can be used to study materials at the atomic level. In 1988 Dr. Pickering constructed a scanning tunneling microscope that may be the first in a materials department in the United States.

Peter A. Thrower supervises the College's electron microscopy facilities and is the graduate student coordinator for the Department of Materials Science and Engineering. His research interests lie in carbon and graphite materials. Kwado Osseo-Asare is a hydrometallurgist. His research activities are concerned with the study of interfacial, colloidal, and transport phenomena associated with separation processes in aqueous and organic solvent systems in membrane systems and with the thermodynamic modeling of complex hydrochemical systems.

Tarasankar Deb Roy's interests lie in the modeling and analysis of metallurgical processes. In his research, he is trying to achieve improved composition control during laser welding of several

George Simkovich has a conversation with Julius Szekely, professor of materials engineering and associate director of the Center for Materials Processing at the Massachusetts Institute of Technology.

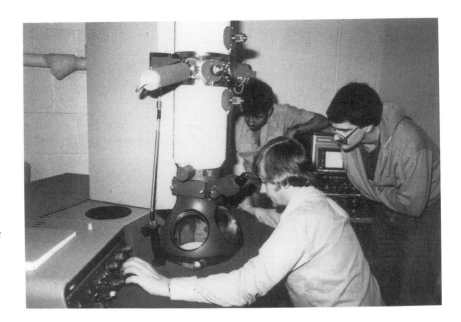

Paul Howell works with the Philips EM 420T analytical electron microscope while two students look on.

modern alloys through a better understanding of heat flow, mass transfer, and the circulation of molten metal in the weld pool. Another program is aimed at removing sulfur from coal by selective oxidation at high temperatures. W. Murray Small heads the associate degree program in materials engineering technology offered at the University's Shenango Valley Campus. His research interests are in pyrometallurgy and powder metallurgy. Of special concern is the measurement of the dissolved gas contents of liquid and solid alloys and various materials used in metal processing.

In the 1980s three faculty members were added to the staff. The research work of Lee J. Cuddy examines the efforts of prior deformation of austenite and of its cooling rate on the morphology and size-distribution orientation relationships of transformation products in steels. Paul R. Howell's research interests center on phase transformation, superplasticity, and structure property relationships. Current research is related to the application of electron optical techniques. Donald A. Koss has been program chairman of metals science and engineering since 1985. His research interests are deformation, fracture, materials processing, and composite materials. His activities range broadly from fundamental investigation of the mechanisms of both ductile and brittle fractions to studies of the deformation behavior of high-performance alloys such as intermetallics.

Merrilea Mayo, who came to Penn State in 1990, works in both the metals and ceramics fields. Her interests are in superplasticity and nanocrystalline materials. In these two realms the properties of metals and ceramics merge. For example, a superplastic ceramic is a fine-grained ceramic that is quite ductile at moderate temperatures—that is, it behaves more like a metal than a traditional ceramic; on the other hand, the room-temperature properties of an ultrafine-grained metal are such that it is extremely hard, just like a ceramic. Understanding the interplay between the mechanical properties and the ultrafine microstructures—*why* the ceramics behave like metals, and vice versa—forms the basis of Dr. Mayo's work. In the process of resolving these issues, Dr. Mayo's research examines everything from the atomistic processes of slip and diffusion, to the manufacture of bulk specimens, to the characterization and identification of unique microstructures and their desirable mechanical properties.

John W. Hanley
Distinguished Alumnus

John W. Hanley (Distinguished Alumnus 1973; Alumni Fellow 1983; B.S. Metallurgy 1942) combined metallurgical and business degrees (M.B.A., Harvard, 1947) to become president and chief executive officer and member of the board of directors of Monsanto Company. He describes himself as intensely interested in details and an admirer of thorough, thoughtful, analytical, documented "homework." John Hanley went to Monsanto after a twenty-five-year career with Proctor & Gamble Company, where he rose from sales positions to executive vice president. He has five honorary degrees from five colleges and universities. From 1977 to 1979 he served as chairman of the board of governors of the United Way of America. His citation read:

> To John W. Hanley, executive extraordinaire and highly sought-after corporate manager, for his pace-setting achievements in the corporate world; for his leadership ability, recognized throughout the business community; for his thorough, thoughtful, and analytical approach to professional goals; for his involvement in cultural and civic activities and his willingness to assume responsibility in both areas.

COOPERATIVE PROGRAM IN METALLURGY

When Amos J. Shaler became head of metallurgy in 1953, he worked actively to revitalize the Steel Fund. Because company memberships in the program had become more diversified, including base metal, specialty steel, and other related firms, the program was renamed Cooperative Program in Metallurgy to reflect the broader base. The metal companies once again responded and the new program evolved.

Although the funds were modest, many undergraduate and graduate students received aid in pursuing their education. The United States Steel Foundation graduate fellowship, established in 1955, illustrates the type of fellowships granted. It had the following conditions: "(1) The fellowship shall be known as the United States Steel Foundation Graduate Fellowship in Metallurgy. (2) The fellowship shall have as its purpose to provide an opportunity for a two-year graduate study program in the field of metallurgy to a qualified graduate student. (3) The recipient of the fellowship shall be selected by the Committee on Fellowships in the College of Mineral Industries on the usual basis for such selections. The recipient is required to hold an undergraduate degree and be enrolled for a two-year graduate program in the College of Mineral Industries."

This cooperative program still continues and provides a strong working relationship between Penn State and a range of industries. An annual meeting brings together company representatives, faculty, and students to discuss trends in the industry and future development. Because of diverse needs, the program does not sponsor specific research on projects, but it is used to fund the needs of graduate students.

George S. Rose
Distinguished Alumnus

George S. Rose (Distinguished Alumnus 1966; B.S. Metallurgical Engineering 1923) has devoted his career to the steel industry. After graduation he worked for a number of steel companies, and in 1940 he went to the American Iron and Steel Institute and rose to the position of vice president. He was instrumental in this organization's growth from a small technical and statistical organization into one of the foremost industrial associations. During World War II he was appointed to the Steel Industry Defense Advisory Committee. In 1943 he was a member of an Anglo-American team concerned with armor and armor-piercing projectiles. As a service to his alma mater, he served on the executive board of the Alumni Council. His citation read:

> To George S. Rose, for a career that has secured for him both national and international stature; for service to his country in advisory roles in World War II; and for his continuing interest in alumni affairs.

UNDERGRADUATE CURRICULUM DEVELOPMENT

Since the beginning of the metallurgy program an outstanding feature has been the continual revision to keep it up-to-date (Koss, 1987). One aspect of the revision was the change in program title required by the engineering accreditation commission, the Accreditation Board for Engineering and Technology. After long discussion the traditional name, "Metallurgy," was changed to "Metals Science and Engineering," reflecting the dual nature of the major. A more fundamental problem was determining whether the courses were appropriate for the educational needs of the 1980s.

An intensive review resulted in a significant revision of the undergraduate program. Donald Koss states: "Some courses were changed dramatically, others were changed in more subtle ways. The driving force for change had its roots in the concept that the fundamentals of metallurgy had to be stressed because our students were dealing with more and more diverse career opportunities. As a result, they would be better equipped if they were grounded in the fundamentals as opposed to knowing a great deal about specific problems. To accomplish this, increased emphasis was placed during the junior year on such fundamental-type courses as thermodynamics, kinetics, phase transformation, crystallography, and structure. It was also felt that the laboratory courses were inadequate. Many of the laboratories were devised from lecture courses, and separate laboratory courses were created that could stand on their own. There was also a response to the need for more computer use by introducing computers into both lecture and laboratory courses. This was accomplished by having department-wide computer facilities." Communication skills were emphasized: "One characteristic of Penn State metallurgy graduates has been their ability to communicate. We are continuing to encourage students to develop their ability to stand in front of small groups and present their ideas in clear, precise English."

In addition, Dr. Koss notes, "We've increased emphasis on independent study by increasing not only the number of credits but also the intensity and content of those credits. The independent study course has become the capstone design course for the metallurgy curriculum." But, he continues, "Although the theoretical work has grown in importance, the applied courses in properties and processing have been maintained. The faculty have tried to make these courses more generic rather than focused on a specific process or a specific metal or alloy, but still sufficiently applied so the students understand the applications of the fundamental concepts to practical problems. All in all, we have made extensive evolutionary changes in the attempt to modernize a program and put it in the context of today."

MODERN EQUIPMENT NEEDS

Metals science and engineering, like other materials programs, relies heavily on the characterization of metals as a means for understanding how metals and alloys behave in service. Traditionally, typical methods for characterizing metals used some type of optical microscopy combined with x-ray diffraction. In the past twenty years, there has been a virtual explosion of techniques, many of them relying on the behavior of electrons and, in many cases, on the use of high vacuum technology.

Max W. Lightner
Distinguished Alumnus

Max W. Lightner (Distinguished Alumnus 1964; B.S. Metallurgy 1929) spent his entire career intimately associated with research and development activities related to steel-making. After three years of teaching at the Carnegie Institute of Technology, he went to the Homestead District Works of U.S. Steel. In 1956, having spent most of his career at U.S. Steel, he became vice president of Applied Research. He was a recipient of the David F. McFarland Award. He was known for his important developments in steel forging and the improvement of quality. Nearly sixty years after graduating from Penn State, Max Lightner reflects: "Perhaps my fondest recollection is the inspiration I received from Dr. David McFarland to pursue a career in metallurgy. I definitely know that the basic training I received in mathematics, chemistry, and physics was most helpful to me. The encouragement I received from my various instructors filled me with the desire to work hard at my chosen profession." His citation read:

> To Max W. Lightner, for outstanding success as a scientist in the metallurgical field and as a director in planning and organizing major metallurgical operations; for his general contributions to the improvement of the steel industry; and for the many services he has performed for the professional societies to which his work is related.

Senior metallurgy students of the class of 1948, on a visit to a plant in 1948, were accompanied by two faculty members, H. Mauzee Davis, top row left, and Harold J. Read, bottom row right.

The electron microscope, in both the transmission and the scanning modes, has had a major impact on understanding the structure of metals. For example, the transmission electron microscope is now routinely used to characterize the phases present and the microstructure of materials. The scanning electron microscope is used to examine surfaces and can be adapted for chemical analysis techniques as well.

In addition, the department's recent acquisition of a scanning tunneling microscope provides the opportunity to examine the surfaces on an atom-to-atom scale of operation. To illustrate, this microscope permits examination of corrosion on a surface of a metal with a resolution that was not imaginable ten years ago. There can be no questions that the advanced electron microscope has had a large impact on the study of metals and will continue to do so in the near future.

J. L. Mauthe
Distinguished Alumnus

J. L. Mauthe (Distinguished Alumnus 1964; B.S. Metallurgy 1913, Metallurgical Engineering 1945) came to Penn State from Turkey City in Clarion County via DuBois, both in Pennsylvania. He was the University's first great football star, his feats were legendary, and his name is now enshrined in the Football Hall of Fame. During his summer vacations at Penn State he worked for steel companies. By 1937 he was general superintendent of the Youngstown District of the Youngstown Sheet & Tube Company. In 1950 he became president of the company, and in 1956 he was made chairman of the board. In 1938 he became an alumni member of the Board of Trustees and served for many years. He was a recipient of the McFarland Award in 1951. He established the J. L. Mauthe Scholarship, "in remembrance of the Class of 1913," to be given to a member of one of the varsity athletic squads with a major in the field of Metallurgy, Ceramics, or Engineering. His citation read:

> To James Lester (Pete) Mauthe, for more than a half-century of service to his alma mater as student and athlete and as trustee; for his exceptional achievements in the industrial world as executive and metallurgist; and for his concern for and interest in the advancement of education at Penn State and elsewhere.

Fletcher L. Byrom
Distinguished Alumnus

Fletcher L. Byrom (Distinguished Alumnus 1963; Alumni Fellow 1974; B.S. Metallurgy 1940) began his career in metallurgy in 1940 with the American Steel & Wire Company as sales engineer. After serving in the Naval Ordnance Laboratory in World War II, he joined the Koppers Company as assistant to the general manager of the Tar Products Division. He became president and a member of the Board of Directors of Koppers in 1960. Over the years he continued service with the University, serving as a member of the Advisory Board of the McKeesport Campus and as president of the Penn State Alumni Association. In 1967 the Penn State chapter of the American Society for Metals honored Fletcher Byrom with the David Ford McFarland Award for Achievement in Metallurgy. His Distinguished Alumni citation read:

> To Fletcher L. Byrom, for achieving a high station in the industrial world in an extraordinarily short time; for energetic and unselfish guidance of civic organizations; and for continued interest and service to his alma mater.

Van E. Leichliter
Distinguished Alumnus

Van E. Leichliter (Distinguished Alumnus 1959; B.S. Metallurgy 1930) was president of the American Steel and Wire Division of the U.S. Steel Corporation when he was honored as a Distinguished Alumnus. Immediately out of college he began work with U.S. Steel, rising to president of the division in 1956. He served as a trustee of Fern College at John Carroll University. In 1958 he was honored with the Silver Beaver Award by the Greater Cleveland Council of the Boy Scouts of America. In 1956 he received the David F. McFarland Award for Outstanding Achievement in Metallurgy. His citation read:

> To Van E. Leichliter, for the uncanny foresight that led him to forgo early gains in favor of demonstrated opportunity; for his practical insight into the problems of steel, and the part he played in resolving these problems; for his exemplary service to education in his home community; and for the human qualities that have enabled him to rise to the top in one of the nation's foremost industries.

CHANGING EMPLOYMENT OPPORTUNITIES

For many years after the beginning of the metallurgy program, the typical graduate was employed by the vigorous steel companies of Pennsylvania and adjacent areas. As the relative importance of the steel industry declined, job opportunities in other fields increased. While the steel industry still employs many of the metallurgy graduates, many companies are completely removed from the steel industry. In 1988–89 the steel companies sending representatives to interview metallurgy graduates included Inland, U.S. Steel, Allegheny Ludlum, and Florida Steel, but the list of nonsteel companies included Mobil, General Electric, McDonnell Douglas, Caterpillar, Sprague Electric, Rockwell, and others. The latter companies are not metal-producers, but metal-users. This represents the changing character of the field and the need for a curriculum that reflects these changes. Because of this shift in employment opportunities, a major demand comes from companies and industries that use metals, and their needs for metallurgists are much different from the needs of the companies who are basic metal-producers.

METALLURGY ALUMNI

A strong feature of the metals science and engineering program has been the close relationships with alumni, who have maintained a strong sense of allegiance to the faculty and the program. Tangible evidence of this has been the generous financial assistance provided for the undergraduates through alumni contributions to the Penn State Metallurgy Alumni Scholarship Fund. Initiated by Robert Lindsay in 1969, this fund has since provided thousands of dollars of aid to students.

An annual event is the special recognition given an alumnus at the David Ford McFarland Award Banquet. This has been presented since 1949 by the Penn State chapter of the American Society for Metals. The first recipient was George V. Luerssen (B.S. '15), then chief metallurgist for the Carpenter Steel Company of Reading, Pennsylvania. Alumni attend this dinner to renew friendships and become reacquainted with the faculty. It is one of the pleasant traditions of the metallurgical group.

The metallurgy program has produced an unusually large percentage of highly successful graduates who have made their mark on both the engineering and the scientific aspects of the field. To illustrate, six of the twelve Penn State alumni who are presidents or board chairmen of companies listed in the 1980 *Fortune* magazine "Directory of the 500 Largest U.S. Industrial Corporations" were metallurgy graduates: Howard O. Beaver, Jr., B.S. '48, chairman, Carpenter Technology Corporation; Fletcher L. Byrom, B.S. '40, chairman, Kopper Company; Dennis J. Carney, B.S. '42, chairman, Wheeling-Pittsburgh Steel Corporation; Joseph R. Carter, B.S. '40, chairman, Wyman-Gordon Company; John W. Hanley, B.S. '42, chairman, Monsanto Company; and Frederick C. Langenberg, Ph.D. '55, president, Interlake Inc.

Table 7.   Recipients of the David F. McFarland Award

1949	George V. Luerssen*	'15
1950	Max W. Lightner	'29
1951	J. L. Mauthe*	'13
1952	William W. Sieg*	'23, '25
1953	R. Burns George*	'22
1954	Mowry E. Goetz*	'17
1955	John A. Succop	'17, '20
1956	Van E. Leichliter*	'30
1957	Elwood D. Mairs*	'26
1958	Carl F. Hoffman*	'21
1959	Robert D. Stout	'35
1960	Manley E. Brooks	'28
1961	George H. Todd	'28
1962	James H. Keeler	'42, '51
1963	Archibald Miller, Jr.*	'31
1964	F. Gordon Benford	'33
1965	Norman B. Lane*	'27
1966	Dennis J. Carney	'42
1967	Fletcher L. Byrom	'40
1968	C. Thompson Stott	'34
1969	Jack H. Wernick	'54
1970	Joseph R. Carter	'40
1971	Adolph J. Lena	'48
1972	Howard O. Beaver, Jr.	'48
1973	Frederick C. Langenberg	'55
1974	Howard B. Bomberger	'42
1975	Robert L. Sproat	'42, '48
1976	Guy F. McCracken	'49

1977	Sam J. MacMullan	'37
1978	Frank Marold	'45
1979	Theodore B. Winkler	'39
1980	Franklin H. Beck	'43
1981	Thomas M. Krebs	'49
1982	John W. Murray, Jr.*	'40
1983	Hal L. Harman	'56
1984	Edward J. Ripling	'42
1985	John O. Brittain	'43, '51
1986	Ronald M. Latanision	'64
1987	John E. Werner	'54, '60
1988	Howard R. Peiffer	'56
1989	Rolf Weil	'51
1990	Norris B. McFarlane	'34
1991	George Simkovich	'59

*Deceased.

THE ASSOCIATE DEGREE PROGRAM

A two-year associate degree program in materials engineering technology is offered at the Shenango Valley Campus. The director of the program is Murray Small. The original program, begun in the 1970s, concentrated on the needs of the steel industry, but as the steel industry declined in the Shenango Valley, area enrollment in the program also declined. To reflect changes in the industry, the program has evolved into one now focusing on materials technology. This new program thus introduces the student not only to metals but also to polymers and ceramics. The employment base has thereby been considerably broadened and reflects trends that are also occurring at the bachelor's degree level.

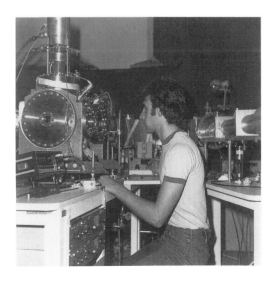

A graduate student uses the atom probe, field-ion microscope in metallurgy in 1982.

William A. Haven
Distinguished Alumnus

William A. Haven (Distinguished Alumnus 1956; B.S. Metallurgy 1909) described himself as a "metallurgical missionary." After graduation he gained experience in a number of iron and steel companies. In 1929 he joined the Iron and Steel Division of Arthur G. McKee & Company. He was a recognized authority on blast furnace operations. During his career he was granted a number of patents. One of his major contributions was his development of the A.S.T.M. standard tumbler test for metallurgical coke. His citation read:

> William A. Haven has had a long and pre-eminent career in metallurgy. Starting as an ore sampler in 1909, he became superintendent of a blast furnace three years later. His big opportunity came in 1929 after he joined Arthur G. McKee and Co., one of the world's great builders and designers of blast furnaces, steel plants, and petroleum refineries. For that firm, he fashioned the famous Magnitogorski Plant in Russia, helped build Brazil's Redona Steel Works, and afforded similar help and consultation to the governments of China, England, Colombia, Mexico, Canada, and Italy and others. He has served his own country in many ways, notably by aiding in the expansion of the steel-making industry during World War II and the Korean War. His many patents have played an important role in the world's economy.

HONORS AND AWARDS

The metallurgical faculty have received a number of awards and honors. Within the College, Earle R. Ryba, John H. Hoke, George Simkovich, and Paul R. Howell received the Wilson Outstanding Teaching Award in 1974, 1979, 1984, and 1985, respectively. In 1973 Harold J. Read received the Melvin Romanoff Award of the National Association of Corrosion Engineers for his and George Di Bari's article, "Electrochemical Behavior of High-Purity Aluminum in Chloride-Containing Solutions," and Robert W. Lindsay was awarded the Albert Easton White Distinguished Teacher Award by the American Society for Metals in 1977. Howard W. Pickering has been honored by a number of organizations. In 1985, he received the Willis Rodney Whitney Award of the National Association of Corrosion Engineers, and in 1988 he was presented with the H. H. Uhlig Award of the Corrosion Division of the Electrochemical Society for his contribution to corrosion science. In 1978 Frank F. Aplan received the American Institute of Mining, Metallurgical, and Petroleum Engineers Robert H. Richards Award.

Many of the faculty have served on committees of national organizations and received contracts for research work. In 1971 Maurice C. Inman was appointed a metallurgical investigator to NASA. George W. Healy, in 1973, served as co-chairman of a session on metallurgical chemistry at the 102nd annual meeting of the American Institute of Mining, Metallurgical, and Petroleum Engineers. William R. Bitler received a Fulbright grant from the program of educational exchange between the United States and Norway for the year 1985–86. In 1985 Howard Pickering was conference chairman of the National Association of Corrosion Engineers, and in 1989 the University of Cincinnati honored Dr. Pickering by making him a Distinguished Alumnus.

William W. Sieg
Distinguished Alumnus

William W. Sieg (Distinguished Alumnus 1955; B.S. 1923 and M.S. 1925, Metallurgy) perceived mineral industries as the basis of grassroots industry, indicating that the living standards, security, and happiness of the nation depended on the healthy condition of mineral companies. He received the McFarland Award in 1952. His citation read:

> William Wetzel Sieg, president of Titan Metal Company, is a distinguished industrial leader whose interests extend beyond his University and his local community to the state, national, and international communities. In his home town of Bellefonte, he works quietly and diligently in the cause of civic welfare. He has served as borough council president, was co-founder and first secretary of the Bellefonte Chamber of Commerce, and is a staunch friend of education. As a former president of the Pennsylvania Chamber of Commerce, he is now chairman of the board of directors of the Penn State Foundation. His thorough knowledge of the brass and copper industry has won him an outstanding reputation in the business world and made him a valuable consultant to the United States government. Penn State has previously honored him with the David Ford McFarland Award for attainment in the metallurgical industry. A humble, conscientious builder, he is, in the truest sense, an effective citizen.

Adolph J. Lena
Alumni Fellow

Adolph J. Lena (Alumni Fellow 1982; B.S. Metallurgy 1948), a metallurgist credited with the development of several special alloys, was chairman of the board and chief executive officer of Al Tech Specialty Steel. He is an honorary fellow of the American Society of Metals and has been recognized for his research accomplishments, earning, among other awards, Penn State's McFarland Award for distinguished contribution to the College.

Frederick C. Langenberg (Ph.D. '55), center, president of Interlake Inc.; Dr. Lindsay, left; and Dr. Geoffrey E. Brock (M.S. '52) look over the commemorative booklet prepared for the 75th anniversary of the metallurgy program in 1983.

POLYMER SCIENCE

The importance of polymers is rarely recognized by the average citizen. Yet such natural polymers as wood, fur, leather, wool, cotton, and a host of others have served humanity since the beginning of civilization. The word "polymer" has a Greek origin and means many (*poly*) parts (*meros*). In other words, a polymer is a macromolecule, a giant molecule.

In the nineteenth century it was discovered that synthetic and modified naturally occurring polymer materials could be produced. Work on these materials was carried out in a number of widely dispersed locations, and a variety of polymer products were produced. One interesting example is provided by the chemist C. F. Schoenbein, who was working on a nitrate solution when the flask broke and spread nitric and sulfuric acid on the floor. After wiping the floor clean, he hung his damp cloth in front of the fireplace, and in drying his cloth he realized that he had discovered a new explosive, which he called guncotton. Guncotton was considered a major advance in explosives because it produced much less smoke than gunpowder (Painter, 1980).

An early contribution was also made by Alexander Parkes, a chemist from Birmingham, England, who found that by putting castor oil and camphor together with nitrated cellulose a new material was created, which he called Parkesine. In the United States, John Hyatt produced a hard synthetic material from which he made billiard balls, and when the billiard balls were coated with nitrocellulose they exploded. This experience with nitrocellulose led Hyatt to investigate its properties in more detail. By experimentation, he eliminated castor oil from his formulations, using only camphor, and produced a hard material that could be softened by heating to about 90° C. This product, called celluloid, was a tremendous success because it was possible to produce a variety of useful products from it, from knife handles to false teeth. The stiff celluloid collar was a common trademark.

Celluloid was a chemically modified polymer, not a true synthetic. The modern processes for manufacturing fibers were further refined by the introduction of regenerated cellulose in 1892. With regard to the development of the cellulose process, it is interesting to note that William H.

Administration
Polymer Science

Department of Materials Science
Polymer Science Section

Philip L. Walker, Jr.   1972–1978

Department of Materials Science and
Engineering, Polymer Science Program

Michael M. Coleman   1978–1985
Ian R. Harrison   1985–1988
James P. Runt   1988–

Walker, a Penn State graduate of the class of 1890, together with Arthur W. Little, developed manufacturing processes for production of both yarn and film. Fibers from regenerated cellulose were called rayon, while films were known as cellophane.

Early in the twentieth century a true synthetic plastic was produced by Leo H. Baekeland. Using phenol and formaldehyde, he eventually produced a thermosetting plastic that was named "Bakelite." This material could be molded into any shape and had excellent electrical and thermal properties. It was unfortunately brittle and easily broken, but it was inexpensive and easily replaced. This material marked the birth of the polymer industry, and also the reputation that while plastic was a substitute for natural materials, such as wood or putty, it was also nondurable and fragile.

In the 1920s and 1930s, great advances were made in polymer materials. Numerous new plastics were introduced, principally from the laboratories of I. G. Farben in Germany and E. I. du Pont de Nemours in the United States. The synthesis of new materials was now based on chemical principles instead of on empirical trial and error. World War II witnessed further advances, particularly in the production of synthetic rubber.

The advancement and application of the macromolecular concept has deeply influenced scientific and technological trends. On the one hand, it has led to an understanding of those polymers responsible for life and hereditary processes, encompassed in the field of molecular biology; on the other hand, the knowledge of specific structural requirements necessary for desirable macroscopic material properties has enabled chemists to design and synthesize hitherto unknown materials or to improve on naturally occurring polymers. As a result of recent technological advances, there has been truly astounding growth in production of chemicals in the last three decades.

Within one generation in time, synthetic polymer materials established themselves as a major component of the materials spectrum. While low quality once characterized the plastics industry, the field of polymers has come to be recognized as a producer of quality products. Metals and ceramics once dominated the field of materials, but it is now recognized that plastics have a range of properties that places them in a complementary position alongside the traditional materials.

Ian Harrison, left, and James P. Runt are shown with a small-angle x-ray scattering system used in polymer characterization.

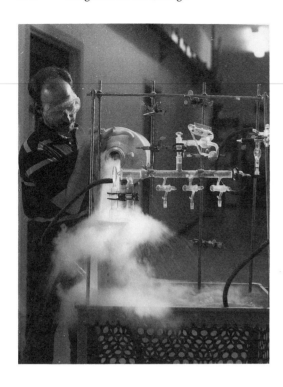

Robert Kempf, graduate student, studies
polymer synthesis.

ESTABLISHMENT OF A POLYMER SCIENCE MAJOR

Polymer science programs were established in Germany, the United Kingdom, and Japan long
before they were introduced in American universities. Even today, only a few undergraduate
degree programs exist in the United States. In most universities, one or two courses in polymers
are typically offered in chemistry or chemical engineering departments.

A number of interrelated factors may explain the long delay in introducing the study of
polymers in the United States. In the nineteenth and early twentieth centuries the metallic and
nonmetallic industries were highly developed in the United States. The availability of such products as iron and glass made it seem that there was no need for another material. Further, the early
plastics were of poor quality and many people rejected their use because of their poor reputation.

The production of polymer materials is far more complex than production of most metals and
nonmetallics. Polymer science is a multidisciplinary subject involving elements of all the traditional science and engineering fields, such as chemistry, physics, mathematics, mechanical and
industrial engineering, and the biological sciences. At first, there was no core of faculty in a single
department that could be called polymer scientists. Faculty with research interests in polymers
were dispersed in different areas. This situation still remains in many universities. The delayed
growth in polymers may also be related to the fact that American industry has been in the habit of
hiring chemists and engineers and then training them in the basics of polymer science.

The fundamental structure of the College of Earth and Mineral Sciences at Penn State provides
the ideal foundation for a polymer science program. Within the philosophy that all the materials
of the earth will be studied, polymers becomes the third corner of the materials science triangle

joining metallurgy and ceramics. After Philip Walker, then chair of the Department of Materials Science, proposed the program in 1970, lengthy discussions were required with the College of Science. Dr. Walker and Dean Miller had many meetings with representatives from the College of Science over a period of nearly two years before the program was approved by the University Senate and Board of Trustees in 1972.

The undergraduate major provides a fundamental background in basic chemistry, physics, and mathematics together with an introductory materials course and required communication skills and social science subjects. Because Ian R. Harrison and Michael M. Coleman, two of the initial members of the polymer science faculty at Penn State, graduated from the polymer program of Case Western Reserve University, the initial Penn State program drew heavily on the established major of that university (Coleman, 1978; Harrison, 1981). Over time and with the addition of new faculty, the Penn State program has developed new approaches and concepts. It now reflects the individuality of the faculty.

Polymer science courses are scheduled in the final two years; students learn the theoretical basics of polymer science in six 3-credit courses. In each course the use of computers has increased and is now strengthened by a course in computational methods in the polymer sciences. There has also been a major advancement in acquiring state-of-the-art equipment for student experimentation in the courses.

In the final year, an independent studies course permits the students to pursue an aspect of polymer science of special interest to him or her under the direction of a faculty member. James P. Runt states: "The independent study course is one of the aspects that we're quite proud of. Students come back to us and tell us that they truly enjoyed that experience. They were able to discover their own capabilities in an independent environment." The program has also been strengthened by permitting 15 credits of supporting courses, enabling the student to pursue particular areas of interest.

Randy W. Snyder, polymer science graduate student, operates the FTIR spectrometer used to probe the molecular structure of polymers.

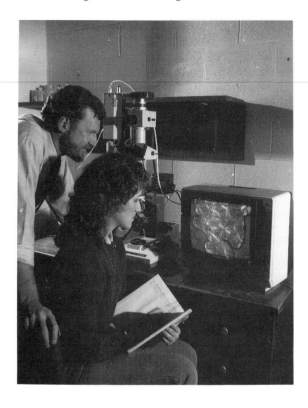

Susan Weaver, undergraduate student, studies the optical microscopy of polymers under the direction of Dr. Harrison.

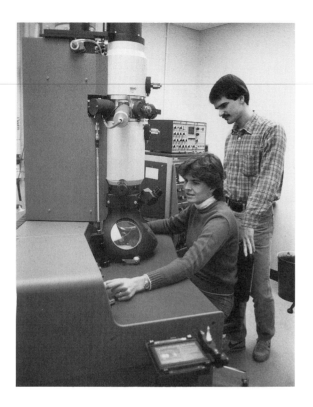

Rebecca Thompson, graduate student, operates the Philips EM 420T analytical electron microscope while her husband, Steven W. Thompson, metallurgy graduate student, looks on.

FACULTY RESEARCH INTERESTS

The research program has evolved with time, but the growing maturity of the field has brought about fundamental changes. Traditionally, the field was closely related to materials and physical chemistry. The base of study has now been broadened to include polymer synthesis, surface science, theory, and other areas.

Ian Harrison's initial research emphasized the study of polymer single crystals and fundamental understanding of crystallization. This work has continued, but has gradually broadened to the study of structure-property relationships. In recent years one of Dr. Harrison's major efforts has focused on the properties of thin films of polyethylene, a project supported by the National Air and Space Administration. There is a great need to lift materials to high altitudes. One way to do this is to have a huge balloon made up of several square miles of thin polyethylene film. Because there were problems in the early attempts to achieve this, NASA sponsored research to study the properties of such films. This research resulted in production of a film that will carry heavy loads into high altitudes. Another area of interest to Dr. Harrison is diffusion—an important area in polymers because, for example, in packaging there may be the need to exclude oxygen from certain materials. To accomplish this it is necessary to know the basic properties of the material. This involves an understanding of the relationships between the

Dr. Harrison and Michael Farr use computers to conduct a thermal gravimetric analysis.

Paul Painter and students use the Fourier Transform infrared spectroscope.

microstructure of the materials, and of how to control the diffusion of the gases in or out of a particular situation.

Michael M. Coleman and Paul C. Painter have collaborated on a number of research projects since 1977. These two researchers complement each other: Dr. Coleman has strengths as an experimentalist; Dr. Painter has become the theoretical arm of the team. One result of their collaboration has been a book on theory of vibrational spectroscopy that has been widely accepted on the international market and even translated into Russian. A dominant thrust of their work has been in the development and understanding of polymer alloys. This is a complex task; it is very difficult to mix polymers because there is usually an insignificant entropy of mixing when high molecular weight materials are mixed. Dr. Coleman and Dr. Painter believed that miscibility can be accomplished if there is a strong interaction between polymers. Experiments have been in progress for more than five years. Dr. Coleman states, "Dr. Painter has developed the theory and I've developed the practice, and we are predicting extremely well what's going on right now. We're working harder than we ever have."

James P. Runt has worked in a number of different areas related to the microstructure and properties of polymers, trying to develop some understandings of the basic structure-property relationships, particularly in multicomponent polymer systems (e.g., polymer blends and block co-polymers). Dr. Runt is interested in the areas of crystallization, phase behavior, and mechanical and electrical properties of polymers and composites. Together with Robert E. Newnham and Wayne Huebner of the Materials Research Laboratory and Ceramic Science, Dr. Runt is investigating composites of polymers and electroceramics with novel electrical properties. One area of current interest is so-called "PTC materials"—materials in which large changes in resistivity can occur as a result of changes in temperature and pressure. One focus of this work is the development of an understanding of what controls the PTC transition.

Bernard Gordon III's area of research lies in synthetic polymer chemistry. He is active in the synthesis of high-performance polymers, specifically conducting polymers. This has tremendous potential if a synthetic material with typical polymer properties which has the ability to conduct electricity, potentially like copper, can be produced. The major problem is that these polymers are not stable in air and deteriorate quickly when exposed to the elements. The thrust now is to stabilize the structure while maintaining the electrical conductivity. This remains a major challenge. Dr. Gordon is also working on synthesizing novel segmented block co-polymers with high-temperature properties and the use of delocalized carbon ions as polymerization initiators.

David L. Allara came to the polymer science faculty in 1987 from Bell Laboratories. He has begun his research with some unique perceptions of polymer surfaces and their interactions with other materials such as ceramics, metals, or another organic phase. This is an important area of

Andrew Lichkus works with Dr. Runt in the differential scanning calorimetry of polymers.

Dr. Runt and Martine Jacq in the process of determining the mechanical properties of polymers.

investigation, for example, in composites. One critical aspect of this work is the interface between two materials. The primary focus of Dr. Allara's research is the development of a molecular-level understanding of the chemistry and physics of these interfaces.

Sanat K. Kumar joined the faculty in 1988. Although his degree is in chemical engineering, he might be labeled a polymer physicist. Dr. Kumar's most recent studies have stressed theoretical and experimental aspects of the behavior of polymer systems in the vicinity of surfaces. In addition, he is interested in interfaces in semi-crystalline polymers and blends as well as thermodynamics of polymer solutions.

T. C. (Mike) Chung is the newest member of the polymer science faculty, joining the College in 1989. His area of expertise is in synthetic polymer chemistry and his interests lie in creating new polymer molecules. Specifically, his interests include synthesis of functional polyolefins via Ziegler-Natta and ionic processes and synthesis of well-defined functional and telechelic polymers via living metathesis polymerization. In this manner, new materials, many of which have potential practical applications, are created.

EMPLOYMENT OPPORTUNITIES IN POLYMER SCIENCE

Since the inception of a polymer science major at Penn State in 1972, the number of undergraduate and graduate students has grown impressively. Because the average high school student and the high school counselors may not be aware of the program of polymer science at Penn State, the freshman class is small. The program acquires a large percentage of its students by transfers from

Dr. Harrison and Beth Jordan, graduate student, use transmission electron microscopy in the study of polymers.

other majors. At the graduate level most students have a B.S. degree in chemistry, chemical engineering, or materials science. There is a general impression in the United States that perhaps 60 to 70 percent of all chemists and chemical engineers work in some way with polymers or in the polymer industry. As a result, students recognize polymer science as a viable option and are encouraged to enter the program.

The polymer science program at Penn State has engaged in an active recruitment program, particularly to attract more American students to graduate study. Because of the excellent job offers undergraduate degree recipients receive, particularly in the traditional engineering programs, there has been a reluctance to proceed on to a graduate degree program. In spite of this problem, much effort is being devoted to attracting more well-qualified U.S. citizens into the graduate program.

RELATIONS WITH INDUSTRY

Although Penn State is not located near the leading centers of the chemical industries, the faculty have excellent ties with industry. The major chemical companies, such as Dow and E. I. du Pont de Nemours, have provided undergraduate scholarships, and a number of companies such as Dow, Hoechst Celanese, and Shell actively support graduate research.

Each year the polymer science faculty sponsor a symposium on a key advanced topic. These symposiums have been well attended by people in industry. The speakers are drawn from academia and industry and are nationally or internationally known. The symposium devotes some time to research being conducted by graduate students and faculty at Penn State.

The first symposium was devoted to the general theme of polymers; the second was focused on polymer alloys; the third on polymer chemistry; and the fourth on polymer characterization. The 1989 symposium was in the area of polymer surfaces and interfaces. Dr. Runt states: "The symposia have brought many people to University Park to hear outstanding speakers and student poster presentations. We've had an excellent response." Industrial sponsorship has grown, so that by 1989 about fifteen companies have provided financial support for this event.

Polymer science B.S. graduates are actively recruited both by industrial organizations and by graduate schools. Because the demand far exceeds the supply, employment opportunities are excellent. Considering the substantial annual growth rate projected for the industry, it is unlikely that this will change in the immediate future. Since polymer materials are here to stay, there will be an increasing demand for these scientists to continue to make improved polymer products.

THE POLYMER SCIENCE CLUB

The Polymer Science Club for undergraduate students functions as a social and professional group. During the year a number of social functions, such as parties and sports events (in which normally graduates play against the undergraduates), are held. A major purpose of the club is to bring outside speakers to the program to discuss many topics, including career information. Most important, the club brings the students together so that camaraderie develops. These friendships that develop through club activities last long into the professional careers of the students.

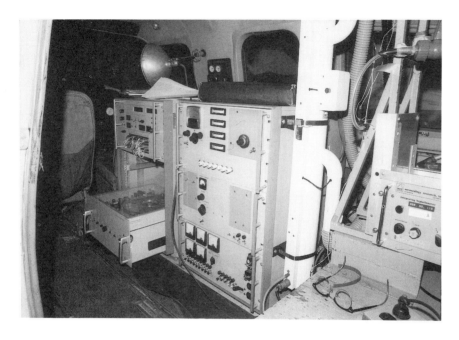

The meteorological instruments inside the weather plane *Aero Commander* 680E, which belonged to the Department of Meteorology from 1968 to 1981.

Thomas Ackerman, left, discussing computer climate simulations with graduate students.

Chapter 8 | The Department of Meteorology

The Department of Meteorology has expanded from early efforts aimed at applications in agriculture to one of the nation's largest and most successful academic departments in atmospheric science. The first catalog of the Farmers' High School, issued in 1859, listed a course in geography and meteorology that concentrated on the implications of temperature, precipitation, and other meteorological factors on crop production. The present department grew from a single faculty member located in mining engineering in the 1930s to complete undergraduate and graduate programs spanning the entire field of modern meteorology. Just as the impacts on agriculture were important in the nineteenth century, today the department is concerned with understanding the interactions of atmospheric phenomena and their impacts on the global changes that are altering the planetary environment.

METEOROLOGY AND THE SCHOOL OF MINERAL INDUSTRIES

In structuring the School of Mineral Industries, Dean Edward Steidle felt that meteorology was a fundamental earth science and played an equal role with geological sciences and geography in investigating problems covering the utilization of the earth's resources. In his volume on *Mineral Industries Education* (1950) he wrote: "While the possibility of human control of weather

Administration
Meteorology

Department of Mining Engineering

Helmut Landsberg   1934–1937

Department of Geology, Mineralogy, and Geography

Helmut Landsberg   1937–1941
Hans Neuberger   1941–1944

*Department of Earth Sciences
Division of Meteorology*

Hans Neuberger   1944–1945
Hans Neuberger   1945–1954

Department of Meteorology

Hans Neuberger   1954–1961
Charles L. Hosler   1961–1965
Hans Neuberger   1965–1967
Alfred K. Blackadar   1967–1981
John A. Dutton   1981–1985
William M. Frank   1985–

elements has been demonstrated recently by successful rain-making experiments, for a long time to come, agriculture, industry, and various other activities must rely on weather forecasting for economic planning and preparation against the adverse effects of the weather. There are many specialized problems, such as mine air conditioning, safety and smoke abatement. Thus, the principal work of meteorologists deals with the interpretation of atmospheric phenomena. Research which has been developed to the greatest extent in physical meteorology must be expanded in synoptic and applied meteorology and climatology. The proposed influence of the weather on various aspects of our daily life must be more thoroughly investigated. The increase of our knowledge of climate and weather is not only necessary for the present, but it builds a research foundation upon which future generations can rely to make increasing use of solar and wind energy. Meteorology is given equal status with other subject matter fields at Penn State."

Helmut Landsberg, former director of the Taunus Observatory of Geophysics and Meteorology at the University of Frankfurt, Germany, was the first meteorologist appointed in the School. He arrived in the fall of 1934 and was located in the Department of Mining Engineering. His duties were extremely broad and were outlined in the November 1934 issue of *Mineral Industries:* "He will teach the regular courses in geophysical methods of prospecting, climatology, and physics of mining. His research in the beginning will have to do with the general application of geophysical principles to ground movement, subsidence, roof support and the development of instruments for measuring accumulated stresses which cause strain and ruptures in rocks during mining operations. Along with the research, which is of prime importance to the mining industry in Pennsylvania, will be the development of a meteorological and seismological laboratory, including a seismograph for recording earthquakes. The entire program will be carried on in cooperation with the mining and primary mineral industries in Pennsylvania."

The instructional program in meteorology began in 1934–35, when twenty-three students took a 1-credit course in weather forecasting. Daily weather maps were drawn and forecasts issued based on methods of air mass analysis, which at that time had not yet been officially introduced into the public weather service of the United States. In the fall of 1935 two new 3-credit courses on general meteorology and physical climatology were made available. These courses were listed in the College catalog under "Geography."

In 1937 Hans Neuberger, a recent Ph.D. from the University of Hamburg, was the second faculty member appointed with training in meteorology. His talents and experiences in the field of atmospheric turbidity and his skill in designing and handling instruments made him a very valuable addition to the staff. The demand for meteorologists was also growing. The expanding air traffic and the foreshadowing of the rise in military aviation activities began to be felt in the rising demand for professional meteorologists.

In the late 1930s the Penn State meteorology program benefited from the fifteen-month visit of a European refugee and foremost Austrian climatologist, Victor Conrad, of the University of Vienna, who not only provided intellectual stimulation but also carried out research on worldwide rainfall variabilities and made a study of periodicities in Penn State's climate, using an uninterrupted series of temperature and rainfall data recorded in the Agricultural Experiment Station since 1880.

In 1938, with the construction of the new wing of the Mineral Industries Building, a larger laboratory on the top floor with a meteorological observatory platform on the roof was completed. At this time, Dr. Neuberger began an interesting series of observations on atmospheric

David R. Cook (M.S. 1977) performing soil temperature measurement experiment in meteorological instruments course, May 1975.

Hans A. Panofsky in the classroom.

Hans A. Panofsky
Evan Pugh Professor of Atmospheric Sciences

My principal interest as a university professor has always been teaching, at all levels. It is a great pleasure to share one's limited knowledge and understanding with students, and occasionally see them develop an enthusiasm for the subject. Also, teaching is good for the ego. Finally, the students' questions and reactions frequently suggest new problems that require research.

Research, to me, is mostly an adjunct to teaching graduate students. It is a special joy to find the occasional student who is creative and significantly contributes to the research. Even students who do not show great creativity may help increase the knowledge in our field, if only by a small amount.

Before and after being appointed an Evan Pugh Professor, I taught two courses almost every term. Before and after, I spent a great deal of my time with graduate students on their research. I have greatly enjoyed serving on some national scientific committees, observing how one's ideas influence public policy if only marginally.

It was fortunate that I began my career in meteorological research at a time when the subject was just starting to mature from a descriptive field into a rigorous, physical discipline. Therefore it was possible to do relatively fundamental research in subjects such as atmospheric turbulence, satellite meteorology, and atmospheres of other planets. As a result, my co-workers and I published more than 150 papers in technical journals, as well as five books.

The culmination of my career was my receipt of the Rossby Memorial Medal, the most respected prize given by the American Meteorological Society.

polarization with a polarimeter of his own design. In 1939, as the nation awakened to the needs of national defense, the School was asked to prepare courses in meteorology for a civilian pilot training program. A geophysics laboratory was converted to instruction in meteorology. This initiated a program that persisted for many years.

In 1940 a closer cooperation with the U.S. Weather Bureau began. In July of that year the Federal State Flood Forecasting Service installed a shortwave radio station on the meteorological platform of the Mineral Industries Building (Steidle Building), and by daily broadcast the College furnished weather information to the Harrisburg office of the Flood Forecasting Service. Prior to this development, Penn State had had a long history of cooperating with the weather service. As early as 1880 a climatological station had been installed in conjunction with the Agricultural Experiment Station. In an agreement between the deans of Agriculture and Mineral Industries in 1934, the Geophysics Laboratory would not duplicate records taken at the Agricultural Experiment Station. In August 1940, due in part to loss of an agricultural observer, the climate work was transferred to the geophysics laboratory. New equipment was installed and the observatory was raised to the position of a first-order station. All meteorological elements were recorded on a twenty-four-hour basis by automatically operating instruments. At that time the observatory was the only one in Pennsylvania that recorded the intensity of solar and sky radiation.

The requests for weather information from students, faculty, townspeople, government agencies, and others began as soon as Dr. Landsberg arrived at Penn State. Requests ranged from simple information, such as daily weather forecasts, to difficult problems occasionally requiring weeks of special research. On several occasions, foreign governments requested details of studies made in the geophysical laboratory.

CURRICULUM EVOLUTION

In 1940 the geology curriculum was broadened into an earth science curriculum with four major options, one of which gave students the opportunity to specialize in meteorology. This was a pioneer adventure in undergraduate meteorology instruction. The courses in meteorology were expanded, and in 1942 the first bachelor's degrees in meteorology were granted under the earth science option. Meteorology was first approved as a separate curriculum in Penn State's 1946–48 undergraduate catalog. The first two B.S. degrees and the first two M.S. degrees in the meteorology curriculum were granted in 1947, and the first Ph.D. degree was awarded in 1949 (Blackadar, 1981).

Since the first major was granted, the science and application of meteorology has undergone spectacular changes. In order to keep pace with the development, the curriculum has been revised many times and the methodology courses have undergone similar changes. All graduates are required to be proficient in the dynamics and thermodynamics of the atmosphere. Within a basic framework of courses, each student may develop a specialty option. While the forecasting option has been very popular, many other options are available to students, including specialization in hydrology, atmospheric dynamics, and air pollution meteorology. The department emphasizes breadth and flexibility in its curriculum, which has enabled its graduates to respond to a wealth of opportunities during their careers.

William Mach (Ph.D. 1978) checking micrometeorological instruments in the Roskilde Fjord at Riso National Laboratory, Denmark, July 1978.

The Department of Meteorology draws about one-third of its undergraduate enrollment from outside the state, far higher than the University percentage as a whole. Students come to the department from Florida, from all over New England, New Jersey, New York, Maryland, and many from the Midwest, particularly from Ohio. This reflects the fine reputation of the department. While there are other meteorological programs in colleges and universities in the East, none has the reputation Penn State enjoys.

RECOLLECTIONS OF
THE EARLY DEPARTMENT OF METEOROLOGY

Charles Hosler began his career at Penn State as a student in 1942. After spending three semesters in the College as a meteorology student, he spent the next three years during World War II in the Navy, going to school at another institution and also spending some time in the Pacific Theatre of operations. He returned to Penn State in 1946 and in 1948 became an instructor in meteorology.

Dr. Hosler recalls that it was a close-knit College with a strong desire on the part of the faculty to excel. At the time he joined the meteorology faculty, he was the third man, the other two being Dr. Neuberger and F. Briscoe Stephens. Dr. Hosler recollects: "We had to double in brass; we built the tables; we built the instruments. I got up in the morning at 6:00 A.M. and took the observations and put the paper in the teletype and plotted the weather maps for the classes to use and taught almost eight hours a day in many classes, as did other people who were working here. It was not until the 1950s that meteorology began to expand. Probably the most significant new faculty member was Hans Panofsky, who had been a professor at New York University. He wanted to leave New York and took a significant pay cut to come to Penn State. Shortly afterward, Alfred Blackadar came. Both were talented individuals and represented valuable additions. From that point on we really grew into an eventually world-class department."

THE AIR FORCE PROGRAM

During World War II, Penn State's Department of Meteorology was recognized for its excellent training program, and the United States Air Force recognized the need for officers with meteorological training during the Korean War. In 1951 the Air Force began sending about twenty-five students each year to a professional program leading to a second B.S. degree for them. This program initially was very important for the department. By the addition of these students, the undergraduate enrollment reached a critical mass for the first time. Dr. Blackadar reflects: "If it hadn't been for the Air Force program, we would not have been able to support the faculty and course instruction level we were giving at the time."

As the undergraduate curriculum enrollment increased, the Air Force became less significant to the growth of the program. The number of Air Force students has varied greatly and in the 1980s ranged from five to eight. These students are, however, considered important to the meteorological program; not only are they more mature, but they are carefully selected for the program so that they set a high standard for the total student body. The faculty in the department consider it important to continue the program because of the impact these students have on the regular B.S. students.

GENERAL EDUCATION

In the 1940s there was a growing general interest in meteorology, particularly in the practical aspect of weather forecasting. As a result, there was demand for a course to provide basic meteorological information to the nonmajor students. In 1948 Hans Neuberger introduced the course "Weather and Man" as an elective suitable for nontechnical students in other colleges. This course was an instant success. It continues today as "Weather and Society."

Graduate students Carl W. Benkley (M.S. 1977) and Kenneth Underwood (M.S. 1978, Ph.D. 1981) calculating antenna angles for solar measurements of cooling tower plumes at Keystone Power Plant near Indiana, Pennsylvania, September 1976.

Students in meteorological instruments course performing first outdoor tests of their self-made sensors on the roof of Deike Building, May 1973.

This course has been taught by the most highly qualified faculty in the department. About quality education in meteorology Dr. Blackadar states: "This was a great concern of mine in the years before I was department head and particularly when I was department head. I was always impressed with the way Princeton put their top-notch people in the lowest levels of undergraduate instruction. I remember taking a course in astrophysics, in which I was the only student in the course, and it was taught by a world-renowned astrophysicist. This makes sense if one is concerned about undergraduate instruction. I've tried to encourage our best people to teach our beginning-level course. This has paid off by influencing many students to become interested in meteorology as a career, and it also brought this course a high reputation for quality among the nontechnical students."

This course is taught to more than 2,500 students each year. Dr. Blackadar continues: "We always look at such courses as a kind of public relations, and meteorology is in a unique position because most people are interested in weather. In teaching meteorology, one is also teaching science. It's much more appealing to most people to be able to study scientific principles using examples they are familiar with, such as weather events and other atmospheric phenomena, rather than things that go on in a laboratory. In essence, this becomes a unique responsibility because the meteorology professor becomes an ambassador for science to the nonscientific community."

The tradition of a science course for nontechnical students continues. William M. Frank, head of the Department of Meteorology, states: "I think the popularity is due to the fact that it gives students an opportunity to relate the scientific learning process to something they can observe firsthand. A large emphasis in this course has been to explain phenomena that can be observed, not only the daily weather but also optical phenomena and atmospheric and climatic variations you can see. So the students have a more natural relation to this course. There have been many innovations over time. 'Weather and Man' was taught by television tapes on several campuses during the 1970s, with direct telephone hookups for classroom discussion and interaction. Beginning in 1988 this course was offered by satellite transmission to a number of Commonwealth Campuses. This provided not only an elective on Commonwealth Campuses but also a way to introduce meteorology to a large number of students earlier in their college careers."

Craig F. Bohren
Distinguished Professor of Meteorology

I find it strange that I am even a university graduate, let alone a beribboned university professor. Often I wake up in the morning expecting to find that the events of the past thirty years of my life have been a dream. None of them was planned, all of them accidents.

As a young man, I was not keen on going to college. Nor, given my mediocre high-school grades, were colleges keen to have me. So I first attended a two-year college that admitted all who knocked on its door, though without feeling obligated to keep them all. I had to drop out before the end of my first semester, my ship having foundered on the rocks of calculus and English composition.

At this juncture I aspired to be a machinist. I probably would be one now if I had not scored so high on an examination for apprentice machinists that the examiners advised me to return to college. Having failed to find a job, I had no choice but to do so. I spent two years studying mechanical technology, learning how to draft, weld, and operate the tools in a machine shop. Despite the pleasure I received at making things out of metal, at the end of these two years, I was dissatisfied. So I began anew, this time in mechanical engineering. At the end of my second two-year attempt at higher education, still undistinguished, I transferred to San Jose State College to complete my mechanical engineering degree. It was there that I came under the influence of Robert Clothier and also discovered my calling in life.

To help pay for my education, I took various jobs, among them grading homework papers for several professors. One of the professors was called away unexpectedly, so he asked me to teach his class. At the end of my fledging lecture, I knew from the enthusiasm of the students and my own euphoria that I was intended to be a teacher, that teaching was a field in which I could excel.

It was then I learned that to teach in a college or university one needs a doctoral degree. This was what inspired me to go to graduate school. I was not burning with ambition to do research. This was only a means to an end.

My career as a graduate student was even more checkered than my career as an undergraduate student. I began as a nuclear engineering student at the University of Arizona, then tried to switch to mathematics. But I really wanted to study physics, which I had known from my senior year. Without a degree in physics, however, I could not get an assistantship, so I reluctantly finished an M.S. degree in nuclear engineering. Then I worked in an industrial laboratory for long enough to save the money that would enable me to return to graduate school, this time in physics.

At about the time I finished all the courses and examinations for Ph.D. students in physics at the University of Arizona, the bottom fell out of the field. No one could get a job. So I began taking courses in hydrology and soil physics in the hope of combining my great love for the out-of-doors with physics in a way that would make me more employable. For three years I worked as a research associate in the School of Renewable Natural Resources, still without a doctorate and all but having abandoned hope of getting one. But in a chance encounter with two of my physics professors, John Kessler and Donald Huffman, they insisted that I do enough research for a dissertation. They were adamant that I should finish.

So I began working in Huffman's laboratory doing light scattering experiments. My interests, however, soon turned to theory. For years, I couldn't get going on my research, but once I found a problem to my liking, I solved it in three weeks, solely by my own efforts.

The problem was light scattering by a particle with mirror asymmetry. This resulted in a paper still cited today and included in two collections of landmark papers. Publishing this paper was a heady experience, a major turning point in my life. It showed me that I was naturally endowed with insights into optical phenomena. I was then thirty-five years old, hardly a prodigy.

For the next three years I was an expatriate in Wales. When I returned to the United States I was unemployed and nearly destitute. In my wanderings in search of work, I returned to the University of Arizona, where by chance I ran into Louis Battan, late director of the Institute of Atmospheric Physics. When I told him the reason for my visit, he offered me a temporary one-year job teaching elementary meteorology, a subject about which I knew very little. During this year, Battan tried to find me a more permanent position. He wrote to various institutions on my behalf without my having asked him.

Because of Battan's stature in meteorology, I was invited to Penn State to interview for a position in meteorology. My honesty (some call it stupidity), however, was my undoing. I made the heretical assertion that I wasn't keen to chase after research grants. Hence, I was not offered the job. But, again, chance smiled on me. The man to whom the job was offered took it, but continued to look for something more to his liking. When he found it, he left Penn State high and dry just before the term was about to begin. This was a perfidious act and a stupid one, given that meteorology is a small field. Yet I was its beneficiary. I was offered the job, although under terms that are still painful to recall: nontenure track assistant professor at an insultingly low salary. But I couldn't refuse: I was almost forty, and hadn't had a real job in twelve years.

Thus it was that I ended up at Penn State teaching meteorology, a field in which I have no formal education. Ten years later, I was named the first distinguished professor of meteorology. I am pleased about this, of course, but I am saved from smugness by knowing that whatever I may have achieved is the result mostly of chance and the help of teachers who had more faith in me than I myself did.

EXTENSION AND CORRESPONDENCE COURSES

The development of extension and correspondence work in meteorology began at an early date. One of the first efforts occurred in 1941, when the Engineering Defense Training Program requested a course on engineering applications of meteorology. The course was offered through the Extension Division of the School in Harrisburg and Pittsburgh. During this program more than two hundred students were trained in meteorology for the Civilian Pilot Training Program.

In the 1930s the new requirement of the Civil Service Commission for professional meteorologists spurred requests for correspondence instruction. Early in 1939 a 3-credit course on aeronautical meteorology was prepared and was an immediate success. It was followed two years later by a second 3-credit course on climatology, for which a three-hundred-page textbook had to be written. Beginning in the late 1940s the demand for correspondence work grew greatly. Hundreds of students enrolled in these courses. In 1946 F. Briscoe Stephens became the coordinator of meteorology correspondence. In this position he undertook the writing and servicing of the correspondence courses in meteorology. The department has continued to offer a variety of correspondence courses.

ASSOCIATION WITH OTHER INSTITUTIONS

The Department of Meteorology has had a long tradition of association with other institutions. As early as 1940 a seminar of the American Meteorological Society (AMS) met regularly on the campus, and in 1955 the seminar was reorganized as an AMS student chapter that conducts a variety of activities.

In the mid-1950s, national scientific awareness focused on the opportunities for better weather prediction that were becoming available through the use of satellites and computers and on the need to marshal the human and physical resources commensurate with the magnitude of the undertaking. Recognizing this need, several meteorological department heads from around the nation met at Penn State in 1958 and drew up articles to incorporate what is now the University Corporation for Atmospheric Research (UCAR). With leadership and management by the universities and funding by the National Science Foundation, the National Center for Atmospheric Research (NCAR) was established by the Corporation in Boulder, Colorado. Penn State meteorologists have been active in the management and scientific direction of the UCAR since its founding.

Since 1966, a strong informal association has developed between the Department of Meteorology and the Danish National Research Laboratory in Risø when Niels Busch spent several years at Penn State. Subsequently four other meteorologists spent extended leaves here, and four Penn State meteorologists visited Risø in a similar capacity.

John Norman and Zellman Warhaft (Aerospace Engineering) discussing turbulence measurements in a cornfield at Rock Springs Agricultural Research Center, August 1976.

PUBLIC SERVICE

The faculty of the Department of Meteorology has always been strongly committed to public service. By the late 1940s the public demanded more-sophisticated weather information. In 1948, when the School's meteorological observatory was receiving more than 2,500 phone calls a year for weather information, a desperate graduate student began a system of hoisting color-coded flags atop the Mineral Industries Building to indicate upcoming conditions, a procedure that continued for ten years.

The increase in the number of households with television brought new opportunities for public-service weather forecasts, and in 1957 Charles Hosler began a daily broadcast at noon on WFBG-TV, Altoona, on the program "Farm, Home, and Garden," popularly known as "Make Hay with Hosler." The importance and appeal of such forecasts was emphasized unmistakably in the 1960s when the program was suspended due to the lack of adequate equipment to receive facsimile maps and forecasts directly from the National Meteorological Center in Washington. A group of Pennsylvania farmers spontaneously collected about $2,500 and presented it to the University, requesting continuation of the television forecasts. This effective demonstration by citizens had a great impact on the University administration. Support for public-service forecasting has grown, and the weather program in its various formats has continued to increase in popularity to become the most widely viewed program originated by the University. The program, now "Weather World" under the guidance of Frederick J. Gadomski and Paul G. Knight, is produced by the Penn State Weather Communications Group, a joint venture of the departments of Meteorology, Speech, and Learning and Telecommunications (which operates WPSX-TV for Penn State). This fifteen-minute nightly show provides not only a comprehensive weather forecast but also a wide variety of weather information. It is available to half a million homes via Pennsylvania Public Television Network and Pennarama, an educational cable service. The Weather Communications Group also sponsors a special interdisciplinary course.

Micrometeorological instrumentation from Penn State, Argonne National Laboratory, and Oak Ridge Turbulence and Diffusion Laboratory installed at Rock Springs field site for comparative air pollution-related measurements, June 1985.

John Norman discussing temperature measurements with student Steven G. Perry (M.S. 1977, Ph.D. 1985) during meteorological instruments course field experiments, May 1975.

The expanding public-service function brought celebrity status to the university forecasters, who received more and more requests to give lectures on aspects of the weather to groups across the state. But this visibility was to have its disadvantage, as Dr. Hosler learned when his extensive research program on clouds, precipitation formation, and cloud-seeding was popularly misinterpreted as contributing directly to a severe drought in the 1960s. The culmination of this unfortunate misconception was the enactment of state legislation that effectively disabled all useful research on weather modification at the University and brought to an abrupt end a valuable program of potential benefit to Pennsylvania agriculture.

INITIAL RESEARCH EFFORTS

The productivity and diversity of the meteorological research in the 1930s and 1940s was quite remarkable. True scientists of their day, Dr. Landsberg and Dr. Neuberger applied the mathematics, physics, and geophysics in which they had been trained to a daunting array of atmospheric problems. Dr. Neuberger's resourcefulness and skill in designing and working with instruments were particularly valuable to a faculty with a total equipment and supply budget of $200 and a laboratory that had only one instrument of each type for student use. Considerable ingenuity was required to provide adequate equipment for laboratory instruction and the ambitious research program of the two faculty members.

The articles published by Dr. Landsberg were on a wide range of topics, including earthquake prediction, the design of an instrument for measuring mine subsidence, the study of rock falls in mines, the use of special glass developed by Dr. Landsberg and Dr. Woldemar Weyl (later Evan Pugh Professor of Ceramics) to measure ultraviolent dosimetry, the influence of pressure patterns on deep-focus earthquakes, the statistical evaluation of cyclone movement and precipitation cycles, rock-core testing by radioactive methods, a major study of atmospheric suspensions with applications to both fog and dust in underground mines, a new method for measuring gravity, the use of solar energy for melting ice, optical measurement of sky light using a polariscope designed and constructed by Dr. Neuberger, the documentation of local tornadoes, and pioneering aerial photography of an unusual "Northern Light" display in central Pennsylvania in September 1938. In the period from 1934 to 1941, Dr. Landsberg presented no fewer than fourteen papers before technical societies.

Hans Neuberger, in his poem "Compensation," asked, "How will the sky feel / when the flight of birds / is only shadowed trace / across the fog?" This question suggests Dr. Neuberger's intense drive throughout his professional career to understand the mechanics of the sky. For decades he personally and meticulously observed conditions affecting atmospheric purity. In his student days he spent a year camping in a tent on the North Sea island of Sylt measuring fog conditions, and later he took fog readings at the Mid-State Airport with a fog tube he had developed to predict fog formation.

Dr. Neuberger was a pioneer in the use of scientific measurements in the field of meteorology. During World War II he was concerned with the effect of atmospheric conditions on aviation. In 1943 he wrote an article on meteorology specifically for pilots. In 1948 he developed an inexpensive method of obtaining temperature, humidity, and pressure readings above 5,000 feet by use of a large balloon. Dr. Neuberger stated many times that the public had to have an understanding of atmospheric conditions if they were to appreciate weather forecasting and maintaining an unpolluted atmosphere. His text, *Weather and Man* (1948), with F. Briscoe Stephens, explained just what weather was, what we needed to know about weather, and how it affected our daily lives. One of his early texts, *Introduction to Physical Meteorology* (1951), helped students solve theoretical and mathematical problems in the field.

One of his unique ventures that drew wide public interest was his study of the meteorological aspects of paintings. He studied the "weather conditions" of more than 12,000 paintings of outdoor scenes from the last few centuries, hypothesizing and illustrating how the climatic environment of the artists influenced the hues and general meteorological features of the paintings. In addition, he wrote and published more than two dozen poems and several articles on such topics as meteorological imagery in language, music, and art. Dr. Neuberger is not only a scientist but a man of artistic taste and finesse.

Carl W. Benkley (M.S. 1977) monitoring data records during meteorological instruments course field experiments, May 1975.

Beginning in 1952, with the appointment of Hans Panofsky, continuing with the arrival of Alfred K. Blackadar in 1955, and with the cooperation of John L. Lumley and Hendrik Tennekes in Penn State's Department of Aerospace Engineering, the Penn State faculty in atmospheric turbulence achieved a prominence and reputation that became world renowned. Another research theme was the development of dynamic and synoptic meteorology by such faculty members as Edwin F. Danielsen, Robert T. Duquet, and Hans Neuberger.

In the mid-1960s, with the arrival of John A. Dutton, research in general circulation meteorology with a more rigorous and formal use of mathematics applied to meteorology began. Dennis W. Thomson has been responsible for the development of research in instrumentation. As a result Penn State's department is the national leader in the development of observational equipment.

Another research theme, developed by such faculty members as Thomas T. Warner and Richard A. Anthes, has been the introduction of numerical weather prediction models that have been applied operationally to the prediction of atmospheric circulation systems that produce severe weather. Penn State has been at the cutting edge of modeling the atmosphere. One family of modeling studies has emphasized nonlinearity in prototypes with fewer degrees of freedom. Some models have stimulated and contributed to the models of very complex processes. They are thus at the very forefront of dynamical systems research and are helping to reveal common aspects of almost all the systems encountered on the face of the Earth.

INSTRUMENTATION AND RESEARCH DEVELOPMENTS

In the early days of the Department of Meteorology much of the simple equipment was built by the faculty. The first major acquisitions came when weather-forecasting equipment was needed. In the 1950s the instrumental capability was guided primarily by Charles Hosler and his interest in cloud physics and weather modification. In 1958 Dr. Hosler managed to acquire an army surplus M-33 radar, which was useful both for his research and for giving a picture of the weather in the local vicinity that could be obtained no other way. For fifteen years this radar was used to teach precipitation patterns in central Pennsylvania and to chart wave flows across the Alleghenies.

As Dr. Hosler's research grew, he needed and obtained in 1963 a Piper Twin Comanche aircraft through a grant from the National Science Foundation. The plane was used by Hosler and his graduate students to make cloud measurements for studying cloud physics and performing cloud-seeding precipitation experiments. In 1966 the first plane was replaced by a twin-engine Aerocommander capable of lifting heavier equipment.

The research emphasis shifted from cloud physics to air quality in the 1960s. The Environmental Protection Agency announced plans to identify a "select research group" in air pollution meteorology and to fund a five-year program. Penn State competed with twelve other universities in the nation and won the award. This grant provided $2 million and was a major source for equipment in the department for many years. One of the chief activities was conversion of the airplane to make air quality measurements.

In the early 1970s John J. Cahir became interested in trying to find a way to analyze weather data automatically, using computers. The acquisition of a digital minicomputer was the beginning of the computer laboratory. Before this time, observations had to be decoded and plotted on

Student launching a radiosonde balloon with radar reflector.

weather maps by hand and then analyzed by personal observation. As a result of Dr. Cahir's work, a very large computer facility evolved capable of automatically analyzing weather data that is received at a rate of thousands of bits per second. This type of operation has set a pattern for many other universities and for the National Weather Service.

In the 1980s Penn State became the international leader in the development and application of ground-based wind-profiling systems. Dennis W. Thomson has designed, constructed, and tested a variety of profiling systems. Penn State is the first university in the world to have profiling radars for continuously measuring atmospheric winds and turbulence. It is also the first to have a comprehensive set of microwave and millimeter-wave radiometers for continuously monitoring tropospheric temperatures and humidity profiles. In 1988 a special mm-wave Doppler radar was constructed to provide measurements of the velocities of timing cloud water drops. Only one other radar of this type exists in the world. Other equipment includes the unique microwave radiometer that is operated jointly with the Department of Electrical Engineering to provide stratospheric and mesospheric measurements.

For more than a decade now, a technological revolution in meteorological measurements has been in progress. Department Head William Frank states: "We are now dealing with state-of-the-art high-technology equipment requiring knowledge both of remote-sensing of the atmosphere and of how to detect signals. It's moving away from the days of relatively simple barometers and thermometers and into a world of electromagnetic signals."

SPONSORED RESEARCH

The sponsored research of the department has increased dramatically. As recently as the 1970–71 academic year, the total federal and industrial research funding was $300,000. By 1975–76 this had risen to $516,000, and the $1,348,000 mark was reached in 1983–84. By 1990–91 the sponsored research totaled about $4,800,000. The most dramatic single increase was an award

Students studying weather maps in Walker Building.

from the Office of Naval Research, which will total nearly $7,000,000, to establish a research center devoted to marine atmospheric studies. Government agencies sponsoring meteorological research include the National Science Foundation, the National Aeronautics and Space Administration, the U.S. Department of Commerce, the U.S. Department of Agriculture, and the Air Force. The growth in research funds has made it possible to increase the faculty from seventeen members in 1980 to twenty-four in 1990.

MODERN FACULTY RESEARCH THEMES

The meteorology faculty are investigating some of the nation's most complex meteorological problems. A critical mass of faculty has been assembled as funds became available to expand the research program. Although each faculty member is a specialist, the total contributions extend across the entire field. Most important, the specialties reveal the wide array of problems that are now being investigated.

Thomas P. Ackerman's interests cover a broad range of climate-related topics. A primary focus involves field programs that acquire and analyze radiometer data at both solar and infrared wavelengths in order to determine the effects of clouds and changes in cloud properties on cloud microphysics and radiation. A long-term research program centers on the climatic impact of aerosols, including those produced by volcanic eruptions, anthropogenic activity, and catastrophic events. In addition, Dr. Ackerman participates in the development of new computational techniques and applications in transfer theory and remote-sensing.

Bruce A. Albrecht's research interests include atmospheric convection, turbulence, microphysical measurements in the boundary layer, and cloud-climate interactions. A major focus of his research has been the development of methods for representing cloud processes in climate models, and understanding how clouds regulate climate. He was a scientific observer during the Global Atmospheric Research Program Atlantic Tropical Experiment (GATE) in 1974 and was

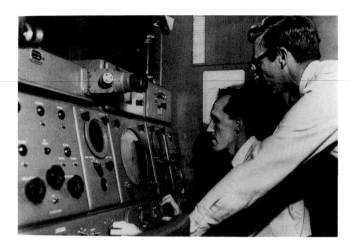

Charles Hosler, right, using radar scope to search for storm.

the lead scientist for the first International Satellite Cloud Climatology Project Regional Experiment, Intensive Operations, in 1987.

Peter R. Bannon is a theoretical dynamic meteorologist who attempts to create simple models of atmospheric flows. Through modeling he isolates specific processes and effects. These include a demonstration of a mechanism showing that middle-latitude atmospheric motions affect weather in the tropics during the summer Indian monsoon. In his work on frontogenesis he prepared the first model of moist slantwise convection.

Alfred K. Blackadar's major research interests lie in micrometeorology and planetary boundary layer modeling. He has developed a computer model of the boundary layer. The model treats most of the important processes that occur in the boundary layer: turbulent transfer, convection, surface interfacial transfer of scalar quantities, soil heat and moisture transports, moisture storage in and transport through vegetation, and transfer of short- and long-wave radiation in the atmosphere. The model is being used for real-time prediction.

Craig F. Bohren concentrates on studies of noctilucent clouds, radar backscattering by hydrometers, infrared backscattering by atmospheric aerosols, optical phenomena in the atmosphere and the sea, and radiative transfer in snow and ice. He writes a regular column, "Simple Demonstration Experiments in Atmospheric Physics," for *Weatherwise*.

William H. Brune's research interests are in atmospheric photochemistry and trace chemical species, photochemistry, kinetics of atoms and molecules in the gas-phase and in surfaces and spectroscopic detection techniques. He has developed state-of-the-art instruments based on spectroscopic and photochemical principles to detect trace constituents in the atmosphere and to study photochemistry and kinetics in the laboratory. A recent discovery of Dr. Brune's is the detection of halogen radicals in the antarctic ozone hole and in the northern high-latitude atmosphere during spring.

John J. Cahir investigates intermittent or local physical processes in the atmosphere that can have an impact on short-range weather forecasts. He is experimenting with techniques for using remotely sensed wind observations to study disturbances that can alter weather conditions. Dr. Cahir also studies climatological anomalies and their relationship to medium-range forecasting.

Toby N. Carlson devotes his research to the remote-sensing of surface moisture, the modeling of plant canopies, and severe local storms. He is interested in the modeling of such features as the effects of differential soil moisture on the evolution of mesoscale features within the large-scale

Department of Meteorology weather aircraft.

environment, the formation of elevated mixed layers and their effect on convection and precipitation, and the relationship between relative-wind quasi-isentropic motion of air, the structure of baroclinic waves, and the associated cloud patterns.

In his early years at Penn State, John H. Clark was interested in the dynamics of the upper atmosphere. In recent years he has focused on the dynamics of mesoscale systems in the lower atmosphere, such as fronts and associated convective phenomena. This has led to such completed research as mesoscale implications of airflow over mountains on cyclogenesis. In 1984–85, during a sabbatical leave, he worked with a mesoscale research group of government and community meteorologists interested in studying severe weather in the central United States.

Judith A. Curry's research is currently focused on understanding the interactions between clouds, radiation, and air chemistry in the high-latitude regions, and understanding the processes that maintain the polar ice caps. The long-term goal of this research is to improve the parameterization of high-latitude physical processes global climate models to assess past and future climatic change in this region.

Rosa G. de Pena investigates both the chemistry of precipitation as related to the natural and anthropogenic emissions of pollutants into the atmosphere, and the in-cloud and below-cloud removal processes of these pollutants. She is also active in the development of methods for measuring dry deposition of particles and gases and in establishing source-receptor relationships via circulation of air parcel trajectories.

John A. Dutton's interests span a number of topics of nonlinear atmospheric dynamics. Recent research efforts focus on the properties of attractors of hydrodynamical systems, on problems of predictability, and on global properties of atmospheric flow.

Gregory S. Forbes strives to be a versatile meteorologist and educator blending teaching and research, and he bridges the gap which tends to separate university researchers from practicing forecasters. This blend of research, teaching, and operational skills has placed him in demand when American agencies and foreign countries need advice on upgrading their weather services. Because of his forecasting experience, Dr. Forbes has served as chief of the forecasting office for such research programs as the Genesis of Atlantic Lows Experiment in 1986 and the Experiment on Rapidly Intensifying Cyclones Over the Atlantic in 1988–89. He has provided forecasts for University commencements and is a weather forecaster for Penn State Football Radio. In his research Dr. Forbes is particularly interested in violent storms. Using a movie of a tornado containing multiple funnels, he was the first to compute the winds within the individual vortices. On a larger scale, he has studied small systems that sometimes occur over lakes and oceans, and he is particularly interested in the use of new observing tools, such as the Doppler radar wind profilers, to improve weather forecasting.

William M. Frank's research has two basic themes. His tropical cyclone research, which began during graduate student days, has relied on new archival data sets and computational resources to analyze large-scale circulations of these storms. These studies have led to an understanding that tropical cyclones are large weather systems that interact with the surrounding flow over thousands of kilometers and are not merely intense, local storms.

The second research theme presents a more elusive target. It has become evident that computer models of atmospheric phenomena are handicapped by their ability to simulate the effects of small but intense cumulus clouds. The difficulty results from the relatively coarse grid sizes of the models and the limited resolution of the initialization data. Dr. Frank has attacked the problem, known as parameterization, for more than a decade using both diagnostic analyses and computer models.

Alistair B. Fraser concentrates on atmospheric scattering by both regular and irregular particles, on atmospheric refraction, and on using artificial intelligence to make weather forecasts.

J. Michael Fritsch has been particularly interested in the study of severe storms. As a result of his studies, it is now recognized that complexes of thunderstorms can interact with each other and

The department heads of the Department of Meteorology at the 50th anniversary of the program. From left are John A. Dutton, Alfred Blackadar, Hans Neuberger, Helmut Landsberg, Charles Hosler, and Hans Panofsky.

their environment in such a way as to produce completely new and independent weather systems. These systems play a key role in daily weather events and in the global earth-atmosphere-ocean-hydrologic system. By use of a computer the first successful explicit three-dimensional simulation of the development of such weather systems was achieved. By this procedure the predictability limits were extended beyond those previously considered theoretically possible.

Frederick J. Gadomski and Paul G. Knight are primarily interested in weather forecasting. They coordinate the educational and public service activities of the Penn State observatory and are directors of the Penn State Weather Communications Group. They produce the weeknight weather magazine program, "Weather World," on the Pennsylvania Public Television Network. Frederick Gadomski believes that the television program provides a vehicle to explore effective ways to present weather information to the mass media.

Carl R. Chelius has a primary responsibility in teaching the general education courses in the Department of Meteorology. These courses are significant in providing the nontechnical student with a basic understanding of weather and climate. Students are much more aware of the physical world in which they live after a course from Dr. Chelius. In his research interests he has engaged in experiments using the aircraft the department owns. He was the pilot on flights to the island of St. Croix, where sampling of both seeded and unseeded trade wind cumuli occurred to determine the effects of seeding on rainfall. He also engaged in sampling lake-effect snowstorms over Lake Erie.

James F. Kasting does theoretical modeling of past atmospheric composition and climate. He is interested in the formation of the Earth and its atmosphere and in the difference between the Earth and the other terrestrial planets. He is also concerned with the origin of life and with the effect of life on the atmosphere, and vice versa, especially with regard to long-term variations in atmospheric CO_2 and O_2.

Dennis Lamb has research interests in the interactions of atmospheric pollutants with clouds that lead to their mutual modification and to the acidification of rain and snow, as well as to the photochemical origins of secondary aerosol particles comprising smog. In addition, he studies various microphysical processes involving the ice phase to understand ice crystal growth habits, cloud glaciation, precipitation formation, and latent heat release mechanisms.

John J. Olivero is interested in remote measurements of the composition (trace gases, aerosols, and ions) and structure in the middle atmosphere that provide information on photochemical processes and circulation. His specialty is ground-based microwave radiometry. He is also working on intercomparisons of rocket and radiosonde observations with operational satellite retrievals. Another long-term project includes the study of noctilucent (polar mesospheric) clouds.

Nelson L. Seaman has developed several different numerical models to investigate the dynamics of mountain-influenced flows, sea breezes, extratropical storm development, pollution transfer, and the influence of urban development on the atmospheric boundary layer. In recent studies Dr. Seaman and his graduate students have observed the first successful combination of winds by radar-profilers into three-dimensional numerical forecasts using four-dimensional data assimilation.

Hampton N. Shirer's convection studies concentrate on the development and evolution of cloud streets, stratocumulus decks, and three-dimensional convective cells as functions of larger-scale atmospheric forcing. He collaborates with Robert Wells, a mathematics professor, in studying the structures and types of solutions to the equations of motion, developing general objective methods for designing low-order models of atmospheric flows, investigating the proposed routes to chaos in hydrodynamic systems, and determining limits on the predictability of fluid flows. The models developed are called low-order models, for they are highly truncated systems of ordinary differential equations. Studies of these models have established Penn State as an atmospheric center of excellence in this area.

Warren M. Washington
Distinguished Alumnus

Warren M. Washington (Distinguished Alumnus 1991; Alumni Fellow 1989; Ph.D. Meteorology, 1964) has spent his career at the National Center for Atmospheric Research in Boulder, Colorado, where he directs its Climate and Global Dynamics Division. He specializes in computer modeling of the Earth's climates. He is co-author of *An Introduction to Three-Dimensional Climate Modeling* (1986), which is considered the standard reference on the subject, and he has more than eighty papers in professional journals. In 1990 Washington was named by Energy Secretary James Watkins to his advisory board. He chaired the National Research Council advisory panel for *Climate Puzzle,* a film produced for the 1986 PBS television series "Planet Earth." He was on the President's National Advisory Committee on Oceans and Atmospheres from 1978 to 1984 and chaired its panel that issued the 1982 report on the future of the National Weather Service. He is a fellow of the American Geophysical Union, the American Meteorological Society, and the American Association for the Advancement of Science. In 1988 Washington was one of sixteen black scientists and engineers whose work was featured in a traveling exhibit, *Black Achievers in Science*. His citation read:

> To Warren M. Washington for his intensive study of the Earth's atmosphere and climate, and for using his knowledge to educate both the public and the government about human effects on the planet.

A unique course in nonlinear hydrodynamics has been developed by Dr. Shirer. In fall 1983 the course began to evolve in the preparation of notes and an outline. By fall 1984, graduate students gave a series of lectures on selected topics and began to write chapters for a book. After a number of revisions, the book became a reality in early 1987, with the original students listed as authors of various chapters. This approach has been enthusiastically adopted by the meteorology faculty, and in fall 1987 a set of fourteen seminar courses was approved by the Graduate School.

Dennis W. Thomson's interests are in the remote sensing of atmospheric structure and processes using electromagnetic and acoustic techniques. The department's diverse set of Doppler acoustic and microwave systems for measurement of various structure and state parameters, winds, and turbulence from the surface to more than 18 km height have all been developed under his guidance. Other research that he directs includes development of environmental monitoring systems for analysis and prediction of toxic corridors and studies of sound propagation in the Earth's surface and planetary boundary layers.

The research of Thomas T. Warner has focused on numerical modeling of regional scale (state to continental scale) meteorological processes, with an emphasis on precipitation-producing storm systems. This research has resulted in the development of a three-dimensional numerical model of small-scale atmospheric processes, an effort that began in 1972 under Richard A. Anthes and has continued with the collaboration of Nelson Seaman. This weather-prediction model is currently one of only a few general-purpose models that is used to develop improved numerical weather prediction techniques and an improvised understanding of atmospheric processes. Dr. Warner's model applications have ranged from the study of heavy-rainfall-producing weather systems to local climate changes from urban-induced temperature anomalies and circulations, to tropical storm systems such as hurricanes. The objective is to apply the model to the operational forecast models of the National Weather Service.

Peter J. Webster investigates extratropical weather, particularly the anomalous equatorial forcing related to El Niño. Other studies include the general problem of wave transports between the northern and southern hemispheres, the low frequency variability of monsoonal rain events, and such orographic features as cold air damming to the east of the Appalachians.

George S. Young's studies are concentrated in the area of boundary layer turbulence and mesoscale weather systems. The interactions of these two scales of atmospheric motion are of particular interest. His studies include the investigation of mesoscale convective systems, marine stratocumulus capped boundary layers, and the development of analog forecasting techniques.

Turbulence is a particularly difficult problem in physics—there is yet no satisfactory theoretical model of it—but steady progress has been made through experiment and, more recently, numerical simulation on the supercomputer. John C. Wyngaard uses these techniques to study turbulence in the lower atmosphere. Atmospheric turbulence differs from that in engineering devices in two important ways: it is dominated by buoyancy effects, either stabilizing or destabilizing, and it has a vastly larger range of spatial scales. The latter makes atmospheric turbulence particularly challenging, since a complete description must cover scales of motion from 1 mm to about 1 km. Measuring turbulence over this range of scales requires sensors ranging from Doppler radars to acoustic and hot-wire anemometers, all of which he and colleagues plan to use in experiments at nearby field sites. One goal of his research is improved representations of turbulent transfer processes in numerical models of weather and climate.

The weather station in Deike Building. Alfred Blackadar, second from left, and John Cahir, second from right, are preparing a weather forecast with students.

Richard E. Hallgren
Alumni Fellow

Richard E. Hallgren (Alumni Fellow 1987; B.S. 1953 and Ph.D. 1960, Meteorology) began his career as operations research analyst for IBM Corporation from 1960 to 1963. Other positions he has held include science adviser to the assistant secretary of commerce (1964–66); director of world weather systems at the Environmental Science Service Administration (1966–69); associate administrator of Environmental Monitoring and Prediction at the National Oceanic and Atmospheric Administration (1971–73); and assistant administrator of the Weather Bureau at the National Weather Service (1983–88). He is presently executive director of the American Meteorology Society and the U.S. representative to the World Meteorological Organization. He has received the Arthur S. Flemming Award, the U.S. Department of Commerce Gold Medal, and the Charles F. Brash Award of the American Meteorology Society. His research centers on cloud physics, atmospheric electricity, and meteorological systems.

AWARDS AND HONORS

The members of the meteorology faculty have received many awards and honors. The following is a representative listing.

The American Meteorological Society has honored a number of faculty members for major research contributions. Hans Panofsky gained international recognition by receiving the Meisinger Award and the Carl-Gustaf Rossby Research Medal. William Frank received the Banner I. Miller Award for outstanding work on the science of hurricanes and tropical meteorological forecasting. Alfred Blackadar and Charles Hosler were honored with the Charles Franklin Banner Award. Richard Anthes and J. Michael Fritsch have received the Charles Leroy Meisinger Award. Peter Webster received the Jules Charnoy Award for his research on monsoons and global-scale dynamics.

Faculty members have served as officers and committee members of many organizations. Charles Hosler and Alfred Blackadar have been president of the American Meteorological Society. John Dutton and Charles Hosler have been officers and served on many committees of the University Corporation for Atmospheric Research. John Cahir has been president of the National Weather Association. A number of faculty have served as editors of professional journals. Peter Webster and J. Michael Fritsch have been chief editors of the *Journal of Atmospheric Services*. Alistair Fraser has been on the editorial board of *Weatherwise*. John Cahir, John B. Hovermale, William Frank, and Bruce Albrecht have been editors of the AMS's research journal, *Monthly Weather Review,* and Alfred Blackadar was chairman of the AMS Publications Commission for six years.

Faculty members have also served on national committees. Charles Hosler was elected to the National Academy of Engineering and has been a member of the Commission on Physical Sciences, Mathematics, and Resources of the National Research Council. He was appointed by

President Richard Nixon to a three-year term on the National Advisory Committee on Oceans and Atmosphere and serves as a member of the National Academy of Science's National Academy of Engineering Committee advising to the National Oceanic and Atmospheric Administration. Hans Panofsky was chairman of a national working group established to assess the knowledge of atmospheric turbulence.

A number of other honors have been received by faculty members. Rosa de Pena was awarded a fellowship by the Argentine Council for Scientific and Technologic Research to carry out research in the Observatori Puy do Dome at Clermont Ferrand in France. Dennis Thomson and John Cahir have held the G. J. Haltiner Research Chair Professorship at the Naval Postgraduate School in Monterey, California. Hans Panofsky was elected an honorary member of the Royal Meteorological Society. Faculty receiving the Penn State Wilson Teaching Award include Craig Bohren, John Cahir, Alistair Fraser, and Hampton Shirer. Peter Webster received the Wilson Research Award and also the American Meteorological Society's Charney Award. Hans Panofsky was honored by being appointed an Evan Pugh Professor of Atmospheric Science, the most distinguished professorship in the University. Alfred Blackadar received the Alexander von Humboldt Service Award.

An integrated 9-Ch microwave radiometer.

GOALS FOR THE FUTURE

The Department of Meteorology has a sound foundation on which to build. The undergraduate and graduate programs are recognized for their excellence worldwide. Although the research program has already achieved acclaim for its excellence, a major goal is to expand research activities. An immediate goal is to continue to strengthen the doctoral program. In 1989 about 30 percent of the graduate students were enrolled in the Ph.D. program. Plans are to increase this ratio to about 50 percent through more aggressive recruiting and through increased levels of long-term sponsored research. In order to accomplish this the graduate program is under continuous review. Recent changes include the replacement of the M.S. comprehensive examination with a new core of graduate courses, and adoption of a policy that encourages the most promising students to proceed directly from the B.S. to the Ph.D. degree program.

Chapter 9 | The Department of Mineral Economics

The earliest known use of the term "mineral economics" was by the U.S. Bureau of Mines in the 1920s to classify a few new positions. Gradually a number of mineral scientists, largely mining engineers and economic geologists, began to recognize the need for economic evaluation of mineral deposits and their exploitation. The first major research projects in mineral economics were begun by the Brookings Institution in the late 1920s and early 1930s. They included a series of seminars resulting in a number of published studies.

The Washington group of government specialists who were members of the American Institute of Mining, Metallurgical, and Petroleum Engineers (AIME) began to interact with the mineral economists of the Brookings Institution. This led to a series of public lectures jointly sponsored by Brookings and the Washington section of the AIME in 1931. Out of these lectures came the first book, entitled *Mineral Economics*, published by the AIME in 1932. The chapters of this book outlined the field, world mineral distribution, cycles of production, special aspects of selected mineral commodities, strategic minerals of the period, certain policy issues, mineral price behavior, and property evaluation.

The School of Mineral Industries was the pioneer academic institution in North America establishing courses in mineral economics. In structuring the academic programs of the School, Dean Edward Steidle wrote: "The mineral industries are concerned primarily with the production, transportation, processing, and marketing of raw materials. These activities involve economic problems which constantly tend to grow more complex. The professional economist has

---

Administration
Mineral Economics

Department of Materials Technology
Division of Mineral Economics

William M. Myers	1946–1951
John J. Schanz	1951
John D. Ridge	1952–1954

Department of Mineral Economics

John D. Ridge	1954–1975
William A. Vogely	1975–1988
Adam Z. Rose	1988–

---

contributed much to their solutions. Nothing has done more to change our economic structure than the impact of technical progress. And this progress is based on a constantly expanding use of our mineral resources. This has introduced problems whose solution requires a knowledge of the interrelated fields of geology, technology, and economics. Mineral economics deals with this combination. Technical graduates are trained in methods of production and processing. Little or no attention is commonly paid to the characteristic trends of the industries in which they will participate. As they advance to executive positions they are confronted with problems of competition, marketing, taxation, labor relations and conservation of the essential minerals upon which the existence of their industry depends. Instruction in mineral economics must supply the fundamentals necessary for the appreciation and intelligent handling of these conditions" (Steidle, 1952).

ESTABLISHMENT OF THE DEPARTMENT

At Penn State, mineral economics was transformed from an informal activity to an established academic discipline. To develop the field of mineral economics, William M. Myers was appointed assistant professor of mineral economics in the Department of Mineral Technology in 1937. When he arrived on campus, there were no courses titled "Mineral Economics," and he began his academic career by teaching Geology 482, Metallic Mineral Deposits.

When it was demonstrated that this course filled a need in the programs of students, a new course was created, Geology 487, titled Mineral Economics in 1941. The course description was: "A survey of the fundamental problems related to the production, processing, and marketing of minerals." In the structuring of the academic program of the College in 1945, it was recognized that mineral economics should become a degree-granting program. On May 10, 1946, the Board of Trustees approved the organization of a new curriculum in mineral economics—the first curriculum of its type in the world—and Dr. Myers became the first head of the program. From its inception the program granted both undergraduate and graduate degrees. The first B.S. degree was awarded by Penn State in June 1947, the first M.S. in January 1948, and the first Ph.D. in June 1954—all to John J. Schanz.

A major task of the new department was to establish clearly defined areas of study. In 1956 John D. Ridge wrote: "The boundaries are becoming more specific, but no field of work can ever become completely isolated from related areas. The mineral economist, like the agricultural economist, is more concerned with commodities than the economist, and is mainly interested in functions. He is definitely more interested in management and economics than the mineral engineers. Though he shares an interest in management, operations, and economics with the industrial engineer and the business administration graduate, he confines himself to dealing with the peculiar economic problems associated with ore bodies and their exploitation and extraction and primary utilization of their products."

In discussing the philosophical evolution of mineral economics William A. Vogely indicates: "Mineral economics continues to concentrate on applying the science of economics to the mineral sector. In addition to their training in the economic aspects of minerals, all students are required to get a grounding in one of the technological/science fields, such as geology, materials science, or mining engineering. This type of training provides a tie between economics on one side and science/technology on the other. This relationship is necessary for defining and analyzing public and industrial policy problems in the field of mineral economics. There is then a concentration of efforts on policy areas and decisions using the tools of mineral economics to better advise society about its fundamental needs for minerals." This professional evolution that has evolved over the years appears to be sound.

Richard Gordon, professor of mineral economics, in his office in Walker Building.

CURRICULUM DEVELOPMENT

The first curriculum was structured by Dr. Myers in 1946 with the establishment of the major. The mineral economics courses included principles of mineral economics, mineral conservation, plus courses on metals, nonmetallics, and fuels. Courses were available at the undergraduate and graduate levels. In 1951 and 1952, courses on mineral valuation and the analysis of mineral data were added (Ridge, 1953). Because of a growing interest in the mineral economy of the Soviet Union a course on that subject was begun in 1954 and offered for a few years.

While the structure of the courses has nominally remained quite stable, there has been a remarkable change in teaching philosophy and methodology (Schanz, 1960). The courses in the 1940s and 1950s were largely descriptive. In the 1960s the modern tools of economic analysis were introduced into the program. Particular emphasis is still placed on the wide variety of applications of mathematics to the treatment of theoretical problems and the practical evaluation of economic data. Virtually all courses in the department require a knowledge of advanced mathematics and make use of the University's computer facilities to solve a wide variety of the problems in mineral economics. The electronic computation equipment belonging to the department is heavily used.

The Department of Mineral Economics introduced these tools when their use was much more limited than is presently the case (Vogely, 1980). By extensive efforts of faculty to keep up with new trends, and the infusion of new faculty members, departmental skills have advanced with the expansion of economic analysis and its applications. As economics generally has become less accessible to nonspecialists, the department has devoted considerable effort to utilizing advanced methods in ways that better convey the results to nonspecialists.

In the early 1970s the undergraduate major was redesigned to provide greater coherence in coursework outside the department. Previously, considerable freedom had been given to take a smattering of courses from many fields, such as business, economics, science, and engineering. Subsequently students have been required to be more selective and to take several courses in one area. This could be in any related field. The dominant choices include various areas of business administration, but others have concentrated on branches of mineral engineering or economics.

The department has long offered a course for seniors in which the principles learned in previous semesters are applied to a concrete problem. The approach has evolved with developments in the curriculum, student backgrounds, and faculty interests. When the course started, computational proficiency meant access to mainframe computers. Use of a computer business game adapted to mineral industry problems was thought to provide critical integrating skills. Teams of students were set up to compete with each other in running imaginary companies in hypothetical industries. As more work is being done on microcomputers, and the use of elaborate models is a more standard part of the curriculum, emphasis has shifted to teaching broader techniques for problem-solving and undertaking fresh studies of problems in actual markets.

Although mineral economics courses are not required in any other program at Penn State, students select these courses as electives. "Introductory Mineral Economics" normally has about one hundred students from a wide variety of programs each semester. Because minerals are of such great importance in our industrial civilization, many students desire a basic understanding of their place in our economy. The introductory course provides this general education background. William Vogely has taught this course since his arrival at Penn State, for he believes that senior professionals should teach basic undergraduate courses. From the experiences in this course, many students develop an interest in the major and transfer to the mineral economics major.

Many students from the Colleges of Earth and Mineral Sciences and Engineering also elect upper-level courses in mineral economics. These courses provide supplementary training to many science and engineering fields. The analytical and technical courses are particularly valuable elective courses for a wide variety of majors.

ENROLLMENT TRENDS

After a major in mineral economics was established, an important task was to attract students to a program that was unknown in American universities. Student response to the major was quite encouraging, and in the fall of 1946 eleven students enrolled. This figure rose to twenty-one in the fall of 1947 and held fairly constant until 1950. In the ten years between 1946 and 1956 the department conferred fifty bachelor's degrees, thirteen master's degrees, and one doctorate. These students found a great variety of positions available to them, including government service, management and administration, engineering, marketing, teaching, research, banking and investment, and graduate study (Schanz, 1960).

Similar to enrollment in most of the College's other curricula, enrollment in the mineral economics major has fluctuated over time. This is a reflection of the fortunes of the mineral industries in general, and of the frequently shifting preferences of students concerning fields of study. During the 1950s, periods of less favorable business conditions in the mineral industries resulted in unwelcome publicity about an oversupply of personnel in the mineral fields. These declines were particularly serious for any field with which the typical high school graduate was not familiar. This situation was compounded further for mineral economics, which was heavily dependent on transfers from the technical and engineering curricula of the University.

At one point during the decade these retrenchments in enrollments caused the department's student population to shrink to less than a dozen undergraduates and a few graduate students. This sharp decline endangered the program's future and reduced the number of professionally trained mineral economists flowing to both industrial and government positions, which in turn further harmed the program's ability to attract attention to its merits.

Fortunately enrollments did tend to rally briefly, but the department remained small compared to most departments in the College. At this critical juncture, the University at the beginning of the 1960s engaged in an intensive evaluation of all of its departments. The mineral economics program, its faculty, and its future potential were included in this examination. All reviews were conducted by outside experts who came to the University and provided detailed examinations of programs. The mineral economics review panel evaluated the department favorably and recommended that the program be continued and strengthened with additional faculty who had professional economics training. The reviewers emphasized that the mineral economics program must maintain its relationship not only with professional economists but also with the earth sciences and related mineral sciences.

Beginning in the early 1960s, with a growing awareness of the nation's needs for minerals, interest in hiring professionally trained mineral economists grew. Rapid price increases for oil and metals in the late 1970s led to heightened concern about mineral supplies. Some studies, such as that sponsored by the Club of Rome, emerged suggesting that inadequacy of mineral resources and rapidly rising population and pollution would lead to world economic collapse. Interest in mineral problems greatly expanded, as did research support. Also, undergraduate enrollment grew to approximately 140 in the late 1970s. The graduate enrollment was maintained in the 1970s in the range of thirty to forty students by a deliberate decision to hold the numbers to those who could be professionally prepared by the available faculty.

In the 1980s, with the waning concern about energy shortages and a softening of mineral prices, the demand for mineral economists declined. Consequently enrollment at the undergraduate level dropped to about sixty students. There has also been a decline in funds from government, industry, and research sponsored by private foundations. As a result, financial aid for graduate students has declined. In recent years the graduate program has had between ten and twelve students in residence, but major effort at student recruitment in 1989 resulted in a rise in graduate student enrollment, indicating that the goal of a total enrollment of thirty students could be met in the near future. Although even at this level the program is relatively small, the department continues to produce a large percentage of the nation's mineral economists and, most important, these graduates are in some of the most prestigious mineral positions of government, industry, and universities.

EARLY RESEARCH TRENDS

Since the early days of the Department of Mineral Economics, research has played a major role in its activities. Because the scope of the field was not clearly defined at first, faculty publications have been important in delineating the boundaries of the discipline. For many years, each issue of *Mineral Industries* contained an article on some aspect of mineral economics written by Dr. Ridge, John J. Schanz, and other faculty members. The articles dealt with the entire spectrum of the field of mineral economics. Many articles considered aspects of a single mineral problem, often at a specific site. Others had a broader theme, including stockpiling of minerals, world trade, regional problems, trend studies, exploration and development, and statistical techniques.

Beginning in the 1960s the mineral economics studies became more analytical and quantitative. Examples of these types of study were Richard L. Gordon's "Optimization of Input Supply Patterns in the Case of Fuels for Electric Power Generation," the first published survey of fuel-buying practices and an effort to develop some principles of contracting. This type of analysis became a major concern among economic theorists in the 1970s. DeVerle P. Harris's 1973 paper, "A Subjective Probability Appraisal of Metal Endowment of Northern Sonora," was an effort to develop more sophisticated techniques to infer economic factors from geologic survey data, and George H. K. Schenck's 1973 paper, "Cost Estimation in Evaluation of Mineral Ventures," attempted to present the more sophisticated methods of investment appraisal that have come to be widely used by industry. Dr. Ridge and Dr. Schanz began to develop economic policies to solve problems confronted by the mineral industries. A number of studies, such as John E. Tilton's 1974 "On U.S. Energy R&D Policy: The Role of Economics" considered the factors necessary for development of a U.S. mineral policy.

In developing the research program, support was received from a wide variety of sources beginning in the 1950s: the Ford Foundation, Resources for the Future, and the U.S. government, particularly the Bureau of Mines and the National Science Foundation. Further recognition has come through requests to prepare special studies for various conferences, for professional meetings, and for anthologies.

Mineral economics students using the computer to analyze mineral data.

FACULTY PROFILES

The following selected faculty profiles present a cross section of the teaching and research of the Department of Mineral Economics.

William M. Myers was initially trained as a geologist, and after working with mining companies in Peru, Arizona, and Oregon he went to the U.S. Bureau of Mines; he became concerned with economic problems in nonmetallic mineral technology. After studying the economics of nonmetallics, he wanted to get more training in this area. Nearly twenty years after receiving his bachelor's degree from Syracuse, he earned his Ph.D. from the University of Michigan in economic geology with an emphasis on mineral economics and technology.

Dr. Myers then resumed his career as a professor, for he believed this setting provided the best opportunity to inform the public of the importance of minerals in the American economy. Writing widely about the problems of mineral industries in Pennsylvania, he felt that research and teaching must be interrelated and that teaching by residence instruction, correspondence, and continuing education was necessary in order to reach the total population. Furthermore, he recommended combining formal instruction with field experiences whenever possible. Dr. Myers was particularly concerned with mineral conservation in the United States, especially in Pennsylvania. In April 1944, in the *Mineral Industries* bulletin, he wrote: "The depletion of high-grade material will force diversion to lower grade ores than had been previously considered commercially useful. The necessity for the development of new technologies and men trained in these operations will constantly increase. A more exact knowledge of the reserves of material left for future use and the rate at which it is being consumed will be necessary, and the work of the geologist in exploration and of the mineral economist in tracing the influence of technology on reserves will become complex and essential."

A recognized authority on the nonmetallic industries, Dr. Myers was co-author of a classic book in this field that was published in 1951, just prior to his death at age sixty-one. Gemstones were a favorite topic, and he had a valuable collection of books on gemstones of the world.

During talks with students, he liked to casually call attention to an unusual ring he wore. Most would not recognize the light-gray speckled stone as silicious oolite, the only semi-precious gemstone found near State College.

John D. Ridge came to Penn State as an economic geologist, but in 1951 he became the head of the Department of Mineral Economics, a position he held until his retirement in 1975. Dr. Ridge maintained teaching and research careers in both mineral economics and economic geology, and for much of his term as department head he was also an assistant dean of the College. At least in the last decade of his career he maintained the traditional approach to mineral economics through his graduate seminar class that discussed classic books about mineral problems. His writings on mineral economics provided the foundation for development of the field in other American universities. He conducted extensive research on the geology of the major ore deposits of the world. His administrative efforts brought the department faculty to its present size. He assembled a group of scholars who established Penn State as the first major center for the study of mineral economics in the nation and directed the introduction of people trained in economics into the faculty. In turn, Penn State's Department of Mineral Economics has provided the faculty for many of the newly developing academic centers of mineral economics.

John J. Schanz began his career at Penn State in 1948 as an instructor in mineral economics immediately after receiving his bachelor's degree. He remained at Penn State, rising to the rank of professor, until 1967. His interests were largely in the economics of fuels with particular emphasis on Pennsylvania. Dr. Schanz was one of the pioneers of the field who also had a major influence in molding the disciplinary structure of mineral economics. On leaving Penn State he became professor of natural resources at Denver University and organized the research program in energy economics at that university's research institute. He later held positions at Resources for the Future and the Library of Congress. He is currently adjunct professor of mineral economics at the Colorado School of Mines.

Richard T. Newcomb became a member of the faculty in 1965 as assistant professor. Trained as an economist, he was primarily interested in mineral resources and economic development. In 1972 he left Penn State to go to West Virginia University to develop a new program in mineral economics. Dr. Newcomb was particularly interested in modeling mineral markets and did valuable work on fuel and, more recently, on nonferrous metals. He is currently a professor at the University of Arizona.

DeVerle Harris joined the Department of Mineral Economics in 1966 after receiving his Ph.D. from the department and spending some time in private industry. While at Penn State he pioneered the subject of geostatistical resource appraisal. Dr. Harris left the University in 1974 to found the mineral economics program at the University of Arizona, where he continues to be a prolific scholar and a valued consultant to industry and government.

John E. Tilton became a member of the mineral economics faculty in 1972. He was particularly concerned about policy decisions in mineral economics as they affected market demand at both the national and the international level. At a time when there were dire predictions of the exhaustion of minerals, Dr. Tilton presented the viewpoint that minerals would not be in short supply in the foreseeable future. Market demand and price adjustments would maintain an adequate supply of minerals for the world's economy. He resigned in 1984 to take a position at the Colorado School of Mines, where he became head of the economics department in 1988.

Mark N. Lowry was a member of the faculty between 1983 and 1988. His major contribution to mineral economics focused on advancing understanding of the short-run behavior of mineral markets. He made a number of pioneer applied advances in economics to mineral markets. These include the development of a new statistical method for incorporating expectations into short-run market models and the extension of the theory of competitive storage to crude and refined oil products. Dr. Lowry also did innovative statistical work on the relationships between mineral stocks and prices for mineral futures.

George H. K. Schenck, who taught in the department from 1965 until his retirement in 1989, was particularly concerned with mineral market analysis, mineral taxation, and laws and regulations affecting the mineral industries. His state-sponsored study on valuation of coal land taken for highways in Pennsylvania was instrumental in recovering a large amount of revenue for the state. A leader in using modern teaching techniques, Dr. Schenck was the first instructor in a large mineral economics course to require the use of personal computers by undergraduates for problem-solving. Earlier he was the first in the College to use television recordings so that students would evaluate and improve their oral class discussion. Dr. Schenck had a strong commitment to the College, to the University, and to community-service activities. He was the founder and leader of the Penn State Independent Faculty, a group opposed to faculty unionization. He was also a founder and leader of the community-wide organization involved in a major zoning issue in State College.

Richard L. Gordon came to the mineral economics department in 1964. His primary goal has been to provide, through his teaching, research, and public service, useful analyses of mineral problems. Dr. Gordon states: "Mineral Economics was created to encourage interaction among economics, geosciences, and mineral science and technology. I have tried hard to foster this interaction in various ways. I have had people from different disciplines serve on thesis committees and cooperate on research ventures. I often make presentations before audiences of noneconomists and serve on many committees concerned with developing interdisciplinary research and teaching programs. Throughout my career, the College of Earth and Mineral Sciences has been an outstanding place in which to conduct my work. Its devotion to excellence, independence, and integrity greatly facilitates my efforts. The College has fostered the transformation of mineral economics from the casual efforts of a few largely self-taught participants into a systematic and effective discipline. We have seen ourselves imitated by at least three U.S. universities and several abroad."

Dr. Gordon has been a prolific scholar, with six books, eight monographs, and more than a hundred other publications to his credit. He has published in a wide variety of journals, ranging from *Science* to the *Journal of Political Economy*. Although he is a specialist in coal economics, he has dealt with many other mineral issues. His research has been supported by Resources for the Future, the National Science Foundation, the U.S. Bureau of Mines, and the Electric Power Research Institute. But his classroom responsibilities are not neglected. In discussing his teaching he states: "My objective is to challenge the students and myself to master tools essential to their long-run performance in mineral market analysis. I quickly learned that my work in research and policy advice contributed substantially to improving the content of my courses." He has taught a variety of courses ranging from the introductory undergraduate course to a graduate course in quantitative methods. In recent years he has concentrated on the introductory course for graduate students and a graduate course in energy economics.

Prior to coming to Penn State, William A. Vogely spent twenty-three years with the federal government. He served as chief economist and assistant director of the U.S. Bureau of Mines and natural resources adviser to the secretary of the interior and chief of the Office of Economic Analysis; he ended his government career as deputy assistant secretary of energy and minerals. While at the Interior Department, Dr. Vogely had a major role in advancing the field of mineral economics. He was instrumental in ensuring that more of the bureau's market studies employed sound analytic techniques. Even more important, he led the way toward introducing economic

A desk computer used by mineral economics students.

principles into policy-making, persuading many Interior Department officials that such analyses were valuable. He also established himself as a major force in the mineral economics profession through his active involvement in the leading organization in the field.

Dr. Vogely began at Penn State as professor of mineral economics in 1974 and succeeded John Ridge as chair in 1975, a post he held until 1988. He obtained major grants for research from the National Science Foundation and Resources for the Future for studies in mineral supply fluctuations and mineral material modeling, respectively. He developed a graduate course in mineral policy analysis, first co-listed with economics, and now an integral part of the curriculum of the graduate program in policy analysis. He edited the third and fourth editions of *Economics of the Mineral Industries,* the standard reference textbooks on mineral economics, published by the AIME. He also co-edited two other books and is the author of numerous articles.

A professional goal of Dr. Vogely is to apply the tools of the economics profession toward a better understanding of the energy, minerals, and materials sectors of the national and world economies and implications for public policy. He states: "These objectives involve not only conducting analyses and giving advice to decision-makers, but also teaching economic principles to colleagues with engineering and scientific training as well as developing my own understanding of the constraints placed by the technologies and scientific principles on energy, minerals and materials production and use." Dr. Vogely has concentrated his research on minerals market structure and policy analysis.

Timothy J. Considine came to the department in 1986 from the Congressional Budget Office and Bank of America. While in the Economics and Policy Research Department at Bank of America, he conducted special studies on tax reform and federal budget policies and developed the economic forecast. At the U.S. Congressional Budget Office he published two studies on natural gas decontrol policies and advised Congress on energy policy. His major areas of research are production economics and applied econometrics. His recent work has focused on materials economics, applied demand analysis, recycling, and energy inventory models. He is also examining the impact of technological innovations and environmental and trade policies on the competitive structure of the steel industry. Other research interests include energy-economy interactions, the natural gas industry, minerals in developing countries, and world mineral trade.

Adam Z. Rose joined the Department of Mineral Economics as its head in 1988. He came to Penn State following seven years at West Virginia University. From 1975 to 1981 he was on the faculty of the Department of Economics at the University of California, Riverside. Prior to that he served for a year as senior council economist for the New York State Council of Economic Advisors. Dr. Rose's main emphasis in recent years has been analyzing the socioeconomic and environmental impacts of the mineral industries. He has analyzed these effects in terms of impacts across income brackets, economic sectors, occupational categories, minority groups, and geographic regions. Since coming to Penn State, Dr. Rose has taken an active role in graduate recruitment and in the restructuring of the graduate program. This includes his initiation of graduate courses in energy and the environment and in natural resources and economic development, both paralleling his research interests. He has initiated a major research project, funded by the National Science Foundation, on the role of external financing of regional investment and its implications for regional economic growth. He has also begun research on the economics of global warming.

Katherine T. McClain joined the department in 1990 after receiving her B.S. in mineral economics from Penn State and a Ph.D. in economics at the University of California, San Diego. She is the first female faculty member of the department and only the second to hold a tenure-track position in mineral economics in the United States. Dr. McClain focuses her attention on quantitative methods, nonfuel minerals, and environmental policy. Dr. McClain is interested in how the world around us is changing today and what implications those changes have for future resource management and availability. She is currently considering what impact municipal recycling programs will have on resource markets and on what impact the siting of locally unwanted land uses will have on local communities. She is also exploring how modern econometric techniques can be

A mineral economics class taught by Adam Rose, head of the Department of Mineral Economics.

useful in studying minerals, materials, and energy resources. She particularly enjoys teaching and interacting with students: "While I must admit to being a fairly demanding and rigorous teacher, I work very hard to make sure that every student is fully understanding and enjoying the material. In my classes the emphasis is on teaching students how to think, not merely on transferring an accumulation of facts from my head to theirs." Dr. McClain teaches undergraduate courses on quantitative analysis of mineral markets and economics of the mineral industries, and at the graduate level teaches forecasting and time series analysis.

AWARDS AND HONORS

The mineral economics faculty has been recognized for a number of activities. The American Institute of Mining, Metallurgical, and Petroleum Engineers has presented its Economics Award to William A. Vogely, John E. Tilton, Richard L. Gordon, John J. Schanz, and Richard T. Newcomb. In 1989 Penn State recognized the excellent research of Richard Gordon by granting him the Faculty Scholars Medal in Social and Behavior Sciences. Also in 1989 Dr. Gordon's contribution to training people who have prominent positions in the Venezuelan government and its nationalized oil industry was recognized by presenting him with the Andres Bello Award (first class) by the Venezuelan Ministry of Education. John D. Ridge served as an officer of many societies, including vice president and president of the International Association on the Genesis of Ore Deposits. He is also a fellow of the Geological Society of America and the Mineralogical Society of America.

Many of the mineral economics faculty have served as editors or on the editorial boards of the major journals in their field. For example, Dr. Vogely has been co-editor and editor of the journal *Materials and Society* since 1976. In this capacity he has helped to develop an outlet for significant articles dealing with the economics of the policy issues concerning energy, minerals, and materials. Adam Z. Rose serves on the editorial boards of the *Journal of Regional Science* and *Resources Policy*. Dr. Gordon is the book review editor of the *Energy Journal* and serves on the editorial board of the *Energy Journal* and *Resources and Energy*.

Many faculty members have served on important government and professional committees. For example, Dr. Gordon served on the Commission for Fair Market Value Policy for Federal Coal Leasing, Dr. Ridge served on the National Academy of Science's Committee on Technical Aspects of Critical and Strategic Materials, and DeVerle Harris served on the National Commission on Materials Policy. Dr. Gordon served as program chairperson for the Council of Economics at the ninety-ninth meeting of the American Institute of Mining Engineers. Dr. Gordon, Dr. Vogely, and Dr. Schenck have served as chair of the AIME Council of Economics. Dr. Rose serves as the American Economic Association representative to the American Association for the Advancement of Science. More recently, Dr. Vogely has taken the lead in organizing a new professional group—the Mineral Economics and Management Society.

Dr. Vogely has served two terms on the National Materials Advisory Board, has chaired a study by the U.S. Office of Technology Assessment on natural gas availability, and has served as a consultant to numerous government agencies and private firms. The Bank of America honored Timothy Considine by awarding him their Sibert Economics Forecasting Award in 1986 for his work in macroeconomic forecasting, and Dr. Considine also received the Young Scholars Award from the U.S. Department of the Interior for his work on materials economics. He has been a consultant to the Office of Technological Assessment, the National Governors Association, the California Energy Commission, the U.S. Department of Energy, and the Pennsylvania Attorney General's Office. Dr. Rose has served as a consultant to such clients as the U.S. Bureau of Mines, the National Coal Association, the California Air Resources Board, the Appalachian Regional Commission, the Los Angeles Mayor's Office, the West Virginia Independent Oil and Gas Association, and Public Interest Economics. He also received a Woodrow Wilson Fellowship and the American Planning Association's Outstanding Program Planning Honor Award.

PROSPECTIVE

At Penn State, mineral economics has been transformed from an informal activity to an established academic disicpline. From its origin nearly a half-century ago the department has taken the broadest possible view of minerals. Energy, metals, and the nonmetallics are all considered in their various stages from exploration to their final use. This breadth is the strength of the department and provides the foundation for the future.

Because mineral economics is an issue-driven discipline it is likely to go through many changes in emphasis in the years ahead. The breadth of the department has become increasingly more evident. Creation of its affiliated Center for Energy and Mineral Policy Research in 1987 clearly identified the faculty's expertise in the energy field and regulatory policy. More recently, there has been an emphasis on materials, ranging from established products, such as steel, to the economics of synthetics and composites. As a reflection of its broader base, the department is giving serious consideration to changing its name to the Department of Mineral, Material, and Energy Economics. But even this designation falls short of capturing the breadth of the faculty's experience and research interests. Recent initiatives that represent the basis for future activities include strengthening the cooperative effort with the Department of Mineral Engineering in the Mineral Engineering Management Program and construction of a Pennsylvania Economic Forecasting and Policy Simulation Model in collaboration with members of the College of Business Administration and the Department of Geography. Moreover, members of the department have begun to participate in research and policy debates on such long-term environmental issues as global warming and sustainable economic development.

The department has been fortunate in having been staffed by leaders in the field. Dr. Myers led in establishing the legitimacy of the field. Dr. Ridge consolidated that position and presided over the introduction of more formal economic analyses into the program. Dr. Vogely's appointment represented the change in leadership as it evolved from a geologist self-taught in economics to a person trained in economics. The evolution of the increased role of formal economics in the program has continued with Dr. Rose's appointment. Dr. Rose is also committed to broadening the department's focus.

The faculty of the Department of Mineral Economics continues to be at the cutting edge of the discipline. They are widely recognized for their contributions to the literature of the field, they hold leadership positions in major organizations, and they are widely consulted by government agencies and industry. While the program was originally envisioned primarily to train personnel for industry and governments, graduates have become the leaders in establishing mineral economics not only in a number of American universities but also abroad in such countries as South Africa and Venezuela. The high standard set by the faculty provides the foundation for even greater accomplishments in the future.

Chapter 10 | The Department of Mineral Engineering

The Department of Mineral Engineering has been created to promote efficiency by providing a close interrelationship among disciplines dealing with the engineering aspects of the mineral extraction industries. The department consists of two majors: (1) mining engineering with options in mining and mineral processing, and (2) petroleum and natural gas engineering. There is also the interdisciplinary graduate program in mineral engineering management and the interdisciplinary research program in the Generic Mineral Technology Center on Respirable Dust.

THE MINERAL ENGINEERING MANAGEMENT PROGRAM

In the early 1960s it became evident, due to the growing complexity and capital-intensiveness of mineral operations, that education in management principles and practices should be an inherent part of the mineral engineering graduate's education. It was also felt that management training had to be preceded by a broad and thorough understanding of the technical elements of the student's chosen discipline within the mineral field.

The level of involvement of mineral engineers in management activities has tended to follow a pattern. Initially, some responsibility is given for the supervision of semi-skilled personnel and

---

Administration

Mineral Engineering

Department of Mineral Engineering

David R. Mitchell	1945–1954

Division of Mineral Engineering

David R. Mitchell	1954–1967

Department of Mineral Engineering

Thomas V. Falkie	1969–1974
Robert L. Frantz	1974–1984
Raja V. Ramani	1984–

Mineral Engineering Management

Boris J. Kochanowsky	1968–1970
Thomas V. Falkie	1970–1974
Raja V. Ramani	1974–

---

limited staff functions. Then, in just a few years, management duties expand as the individual progresses to become a team leader, project supervisor, and department head. Any further advancement in the organization usually requires that the engineer devote a still greater proportion of time to management decision-making rather than to engineering problems. Consequently, many mineral engineers become part of general management.

With management skills, the mineral engineer is able to make a unique contribution to the company. Such an individual is able to understand not only the problems of the engineer but also the problems of the manager. The decision-making process is thereby improved because the individual is able to understand the complex interactions of the many technical and economic aspects of a problem.

In order to provide the engineer with a bachelor's degree with management skills, Boris J. Kochanowsky, now professor emeritus of mineral engineering management, developed the Mineral Engineering Management Program in 1968, leading to the master of engineering degree. Unique in the United States, this graduate program was designed to prepare engineers for advancement into top managerial positions in mineral and mineral-related fields. The program has strong affiliations with the College of Engineering and the College of Business Administration.

Initially the goals of the program were described as educating engineers for advancement into production management positions. In general, the students were graduates of the engineering branches of the mineral industries—mining, petroleum, mineral processing, metallurgy, and ceramics and such closely allied fields as civil, geological, chemical, and industrial engineering. Industrial experience was preferred, but not required, for admission into the program.

Since the program was initiated, many changes have occurred in the management field. Broad philosophical issues concerning technology and industrialization, quality of life, and environmental conservation confront mineral industries management today. These issues have complicated management's problems and call for greater decision-making and problem-solving skills on the part of managers than ever before. In addition, major legislation pertaining to the environment at federal, state, and local levels has been enacted. This affects almost every aspect of the mineral industries and provides still more problems for those in management.

Planning and engineering functions in the mineral fields are now being filled by engineers and scientists from many different disciplines, such as biology, ecology, and environmental engineering, and this has added still further to the need for management education. Managers from this pool of engineering and scientific talent need a broad knowledge of the various technical disciplines. Further, there is a fundamental need for development of the organizational structure in which these specialists and their managers can function most effectively.

In view of these changing needs, the Mineral Engineering Management program has evolved so that not only those with engineering backgrounds but also those with experience or education in allied fields, such as ecology and mineral economics, can enter the program. The academic programs for the nonengineering students are individually developed to include basic courses in engineering and specific mineral fields.

The strength of the program lies in the development of a course of study tailored to each student's individual background and experience, and adapted, insofar as possible, to meet his or her specific goals. The course content reflects the need for today's manager to be familiar with statistics, computer programming, and operations research. Courses that emphasize the application of management sciences in the specific mineral field of interest to the student are recommended. Required for all students is a course that provides an overview of mineral engineering management problems and their solutions through the use of case studies. In addition to the coursework, a scholarly written report on a suitable topic is required, in order to ensure that a student is able to develop valid alternatives in reaching a valid management decision.

Management methods and controls that are routinely used in the traditional manufacturing industries are not easily transferred to the extraction industries. Traditional methods must often undergo considerable modification before they can be successfully applied to a mineral industry.

More than eighty students have graduated with degrees in mineral engineering management. These graduates have made a major contribution to the management field both in the United States and abroad. There remains, however, a great need for additional innovative research and development in management techniques for the mineral industries. Advancements in engineering will be diminished unless skilled mineral managers can implement sound development policies in the industry.

GENERIC MINERAL TECHNOLOGY CENTER ON RESPIRABLE DUST

Mining is among the oldest occupations, and the illnesses associated with mining have long been known. Nevertheless, preventive measures have not been widely practiced. For example, "black lung disease" was a common illness in coal miners. It is now recognized that this problem can be

Elliott Spearin, an M.S. graduate student in mineral processing in 1979, studies the nature of solids and the energy at interfaces as a necessary prelude to an understanding of the floculation and dispersion of particles, and crushing and grinding in the ore flotation process.

alleviated through legal, medical, engineering, and social controls. The Federal Health and Safety Act of 1969 provides the basic legislation to control the dust of mines. In order to enhance the medical and engineering controls, the Generic Mineral Technology Center on Respirable Dust was established at Penn State to further the understanding of the scientific engineering and biomedical aspects of fine particles in mines and mills.

The center is performing research in five major areas of dust generation and control. It is concerned with the amount of dust created with the breakage of coal, the transportation and deposits of dust, particle characterization, dust-lung interactions, and the relationship of the coal miners to the coal seam—that is, mining system–worker location interactions that will keep the dust away from workers or the workers away from the dust.

These studies were begun in 1983, and by 1988 funding totaled more than $11 million. Not only the faculty at Penn State are involved; cooperation has developed with the Hershey Medical School, the Universities of West Virginia and Minnesota, and the Massachusetts Institute of Technology. The scope of the research has been continually expanded. In the mid-1980s Michigan Technology became affiliated with the group with a specialty on diesel particulates. The interaction of the hot diesel fumes with coal dust, and the effect these tars have when they are breathed into people's lungs, are being investigated.

It is being increasingly recognized that health and safety in the mines is of fundamental importance to the future of the mining industry. The investigation of the health problems in coal mining is at the forefront of modern research. A fundamental objective of this program at Penn State is to disseminate new knowledge to the mining industry. Three conferences have been held (in 1984, 1986, and 1990) to inform the mining industry of the research advances being made in the Center.

MINERAL PROCESS ENGINEERING

Since the beginning of the industrial revolution in the eighteenth century, the world has experienced an insatiable demand for energy and mineral materials. The high-quality resources were exploited first. As production increased, the minerals extracted from the earth were not suitable for direct utilization. For example, until recently iron ore bodies of the United States were composed of sufficiently high-grade material (greater than 50 percent iron) and were low enough in other impurities that they could be shipped directly to the blast furnace. The low-grade ore (about 25 percent iron) must now be beneficiated to secure a product of about 65 percent iron. This preparation of the ore is the fundamental work of mineral processing engineers. It is a job that has become more and more important in time, because the mining industry must extract from the earth materials of lower and lower grades, while the mineral utilization industry is demanding ever higher-grade products as a source of raw materials.

THE ORIGIN OF MINERAL PROCESSING

Peter T. Luckie, professor of mineral processing, indicates that mineral processing has been practiced for centuries in an attempt to improve the quality of the earth's raw materials: "Mineral processing traces its origins back to medieval and early Renaissance practices" (Luckie, 1980). Antoine Marc Gaudin pointed out in his *Principles of Mineral Dressing* (1967): "Information concerning the operations of the past is not so full as might be wished . . . largely because educated Athenians and Romans would not lower themselves to such 'common' duties as are implied in technological description or discussion." Consequently, most of the description of very early practices in mining and mineral processing appear in *De Re Metallica* by Georgius Agricola, published in 1556. This book details the state of the art in Europe at the time of the Renaissance. In his introduction to chapter 8 Agricola states: "First of all, I will explain the methods of preparing the ores; for since nature usually creates metals in an impure state, mixed with earth, stones and solidified juices, it is necessary to separate most of these impurities from the ores as far as can be, before they are melted, and therefore I will now describe the methods by which the ores are sorted, broken with hammers, burnt, crushed with stamps, ground into powder, sifted, washed, roasted and calcined." The book is profusely illustrated with drawings showing in great detail the various steps in mining and mineral processing as it was done more than four centuries ago.

From medieval and early Renaissance times to the present, the importance of being able to process fine particles has become increasingly evident. Particle properties—for instance, those caused by magnetism and surface chemistry—have been studied in order to bring about separation.

Dr. Luckie continues his explanation of the evolution of mineral processing by examining the production of gold in the United States:

> The first producers of gold had a rather easy job of it in that gold nuggets could be found in stream beds and simply picked up. In this case, nature had already extracted the mineral from its ore and done the processing of it. All that remained was the hand-sorting of the desired material from the sands of the stream bed. However, it was not long before these types of nuggets were depleted, and the gold producers had to find other sources. Close examination of the stream-bed sands revealed small pieces of gold mixed in with the larger quantity of stream-bed material. In this case, nature had extracted the mineral, but had not processed it.
>
> By carefully panning the bed material, that is, washing it with a swirling action that removed the bed sand, leaving behind the heavier gold particles, the old prospector could obtain gold dust. When the quantity of gold particles in the stream-bed material was too small to make panning worthwhile, this process was replaced by another known as sluicing. A wooden trough—the sluice—was constructed and a flowing stream of water was directed into it. The materials in the water stratified into layers due to the different specific

Administration
Mineral Processing

Department of Mineral Engineering
Division of Mineral Preparation

Shiou-Chuan Sun	1945–1947
Albert M. Keenan	1947–1948
Raymond E. Zimmerman	1948–1950
Shiou-Chuan Sun	1950
H. Beecher Charmbury	1950–1954

Department of Mineral Preparation

H. Beecher Charmbury	1954–1962
Harold L. Lovell	1962–1968
Frank F. Aplan	1968–1971

Department of Materials Science
Mineral Processing Section

Frank F. Aplan	1971–1978

Mineral Engineering Department
Mineral Processing Section

Leonard G. Austin	1978–1979
Peter T. Luckie	1979–1986
Richard Hogg	1986–

gravities, so that the heavier particles were trapped behind the riffles in the bottom of the sluice. In this wooden trough, the prospector had basically reproduced the action of nature that had concentrated the gold particles in the stream in the first place. The sluice was operated for a time and then the gold particles were removed. Although such concentrating of an ore is only one phase of mineral processing, it is the heart of the operation.

Eventually, the sources of gold that could be recovered by sluicing declined, and then the prospector went underground to extract veins of gold-bearing rock. Some of these veins produced gold nuggets that were obtained simply through crushing the rock and then picking them out. This process—the liberation of a mineral from the gangue (worthless) material associated with it by fracturing the ore—is another of the mineral processing unit operations.

Other prospectors found gold-bearing rock containing small particles of gold. In this case, they crushed the rock to liberate the gold particles and then sluiced the crushed ore the same way they had sluiced stream-bed materials to concentrate and separate the gold particles.

Eventually, the ore declined in gold content to such an extent that all that was left existed as only flakes in a quartz matrix. Then it was necessary to go to still higher technology to obtain the valuable metal, and amalgamation was one of the methods used. The gold ore pulp, that is, a mixture of fine particles and water, was passed over surfaces coated with mercury, and the gold particles dissolved in the mercury. This process could be stopped periodically and the amalgam of gold and mercury recovered. The mercury was then distilled from the gold and reused.

Another popular method of gold recovery was—and still is—cyanidation. In this process, the gold is dissolved with cyanide and the liquid separated from the solid impurities. Then the gold is precipitated from the cyanide solution by the addition of zinc dust. The zinc is recovered from the gold and reused while the gold is sold to mints for final purification. Today, substantial quantities of gold and silver are obtained as by-products of the smelting of nonferrous metals such as copper and lead. (Luckie, 1980)

BASIC MINERAL PROCESSING

Four fundamental procedures are employed in mineral processing: characterization, liberation, sorting, and disposal (Luckie, 1980).

Characterization is the examination of the ore to determine its composition, specifically for its valuable mineral content and its gangue, or waste, material. Many of the ores contain several valuable minerals, which makes the concentrating more challenging. The same is true with coal in that there may be several impurities with complex chemical relationships.

Liberation involves the creation of particles that contain a high percentage of valuable minerals and other particles with a high percentage of gangue. In this process, particles with various concentrations of the desired mineral are created. Liberation is achieved by size reduction—crushing and grinding of run-of-mine ore, sometimes reducing it down to particles of 50 microns or less in size.

Sorting entails separating the liberated ore into concentrate (material containing particles with a high concentration of the desirable mineral) and tailings (material containing particles with a very low concentration of desirable minerals). During the process, material called middlings, which contains intermediate concentrates of desirable mineral, can be produced. The sorting is done

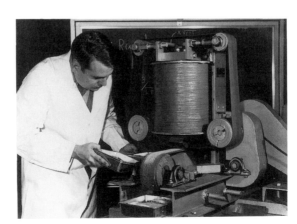

Dean Peter Luckie (Ph.D. 1972) using differences in natural magnetism in a high-intensity magnetic separator in order to separate minerals from one another.

physically by utilizing differences in such particle characteristics as size, shape, specific gravity, and magnetic susceptibility. When physical differences do not successfully separate the particles, chemicals are used to alter the surface properties of the particles, either by creating size differences by attracting some particles into agglomerates while dispersing others, or by selectively creating particles that are hydrophobic (water-hating) or hydrophilic (water-loving). Such particles can be separated by selective attachment to air bubbles—the froth flotation process. Alternative processes involve dissolution of the mineral, which makes it possible to perform separations in the liquid phase. One such approach is the use of liquid/liquid extraction where the metal ion from a mineral species preferentially enters liquid B, leaving the impurities in Liquid A. Sometimes the dissolved minerals are removed by ion-exchange methods similar to those used in the household water softener in which the metal ion displaces another ion in and ion exchange, resin material.

Disposal is the process of cleaning up the various solid and liquid materials that are created when producing the mineral concentrates. Solids are separated from the liquids that are recycled, all in an environmentally acceptable manner. This involves solid/liquid separation, water treatment, agglomeration, and other operations.

THE DEVELOPMENT OF MINERAL PROCESSING AT PENN STATE

Courses in mineral preparation were developed in the early 1890s in the new mining curriculum. In the *Report of the Pennsylvania State College for 1894,* a course on the mechanical treatment of ores is described in the listings under mining engineering. Students learned the principles of mineral preparation by working on models of coal washers, ore-dressing mills, and a coal breaker.

The real value of mineral preparation had to wait, however, until the richest ores were mined. As a consequence, mineral processing at Penn State became recognized as a separate discipline in 1944, becoming one of the six divisions in the Department of Mineral Engineering. Because mineral processing lies between the mining of the mineral and its utilization, the program has frequently been administratively located in other areas. In 1954 the division became the Department of Mineral Preparation and remained an independent unit until 1971, when the department became the Mineral Processing Section within the Department of Materials Science. At this time the undergraduate major was discontinued and replaced by an Extractive Metallurgy Option within the Metallurgy B.S. program. In 1978 the section became a part of the Department of Mineral Engineering, where it had begun over three decades earlier. The undergraduate program was now offered as an option in the mining engineering program.

While the undergraduate enrollment in mineral processing has been small, the graduate program has flourished. More than 130 M.S. and over 45 Ph.D. degrees have been awarded. The graduate students have come from both science and engineering backgrounds. The graduate courses are oriented toward specialized knowledge in the fundamental principles of comminution, classification, physical and nonphysical concentrations, particle technology, applied surface chemistry, hydrometallurgy, flocculation, solid/liquid separation, agglomeration, process analysis and control, and the mathematical modeling of processes.

A major aspect of the graduate program is research oriented toward analysis and modeling of grinding circuits, flotation, flocculation, and mixing/transport; colloidal behavior of particles in liquid media; solid-liquid interfaces, influence of atomic defects in the structure of material on its separation behavior; the rheology of particulate systems; sulfur and ash removal from coal; and

A mineral processing laboratory about 1940.

the treatment of process water. The program seeks to achieve a balance between research on general process principles and applied research on coal, metallic ores, and industrial minerals.

FRANK APLAN AND MINERAL PROCESSING

Frank F. Aplan came to the college on January 1, 1968, as professor of mineral preparation and head of the Department of Mineral Preparation. He reflects on his arrival and the development of the mineral processing program:

> I felt fortunate to be able to come to Mineral Preparation as its chairperson because there had been a long history of accomplishments going back to the 1920s when David Mitchell began work in the field. David Mitchell initiated the classic coal preparation volumes published by the American Institute of Mining Engineers. He was one of the outstanding pioneer coal preparation engineers in the nation. Herbert H. Kellogg, now at Columbia University, was a member of the faculty specializing in flotation from 1943 to 1946, and in 1946 S. C. Sun, recently graduated from M.I.T., formed the faculty.
>
> Over the years a very good faculty had been developed, particularly H. Beecher Charmbury, Harold Lovell, Theodore Spicer, and S. C. Sun, each of whom has done some very good work. When I arrived, we decided it would be desirable to build on the traditional strengths and to extend into new areas. Since I had a professional background in ores and industrial minerals, we began to place some emphasis in these directions. There was not only an academic but also a practical reason for doing this. Sometimes the job situation is good in coal and poor in ores, and sometimes good in industrial materials, so that by developing a

balanced program in the study of materials, but also having some courses that are not oriented to any one commodity, students widen their job opportunities.

Shortly after I arrived, Leonard Austin and Richard Hogg joined our faculty. In order to keep at the forefront of the field it was decided to stress particulate matter systems which include the creation, characterization, separation and agglomeration of particles. In order to accomplish this, a number of courses were developed to stress both particle technology and applied surface chemistry, the flotation, flocculation, dispersion, and separation of various particles then based on surface chemistry. Penn State has been a pioneer in these endeavors and has one of the strongest programs in the nation.

Another area that received special attention was in chemical processes and solutions. These processes were commonly known as chemical metallurgy or hydrometallurgy. Strength in this area was provided by Daniel McLean and myself. A little later, Dr. Osseo-Asare joined the faculty to develop this area further, and his efforts have gained an international reputation.

Another major innovation in the program was the development of courses in the mathematical modeling of plant processes. If the operations of a plant are to be monitored so that maximum throughput can be achieved and problems can be detected instantly, there must be closed-loop computer control of the process.

To be effective, mathematical models must be developed to describe these situations. Leonard Austin and Richard Hogg provided the foundation for modeling studies, for each had practical industrial experiences in modeling. We have now been able to apply modeling not only to courses but also to research programs. It has reached a stage where we have gone into a number of industrial plants to apply these procedures to real applications in the plant.

RESEARCH PROJECTS IN MINERAL PROCESSING

The following research projects illustrate some of the endeavors of the mineral processing faculty in investigating the critical problems of maintaining the flow of minerals required by our modern industrial society. In applying the techniques of mineral processing, it is not sufficient to produce a mineral product of higher quality; in the process the environment must be preserved.

Richard Perry collects froth containing the desired minerals from a laboratory froth flotation mixer, 1970s. In this flotation testing, he is examining various reagents and types of minerals in order to improve the recovery and grade of processed materials.

Frank F. Aplan
Distinguished Professor of Metallurgy and Mineral Processing

Life as a professor in the College of Earth and Mineral Sciences has been a challenge, a thrill, and a joy. For the engineering-based programs in our College (ceramics, fuel, metallurgy, mining, mineral processing, and petroleum and natural gas), the professional disciplines are small, the industries we represent are often large, and the problems to be solved are great. No need to be bored or lack yet another problem to be solved. *One person can make a positive contribution and a difference!!!*

As with most E&MS faculty, my duties have been reasonably well balanced between teaching and research and between undergraduate and graduate students. Teaching undergraduates keeps you young—always be prepared for that unexpected "Why?" An inadequate answer will bring out that "Don't put me on" expression on the student's face. Teaching is my first love. The course "Elements of Mineral Processing" has furnished its own reward—the satisfaction I take in former students who have succeeded. I'm not necessarily talking about one who has become a captain of industry, but about anyone who has earned the respect of peers in little or big things. A fringe benefit of being a professor is the thrill of having a former student tell you, years later, how much your course was appreciated. On a few occasions, parents of former students have expressed appreciation for their son's or daughter's development. You walk about two feet off the ground after one of those encounters.

A faculty member has a great deal of latitude in research direction. I chose to focus on the integration of theory and practice to solve what I considered important industrial problems. This choice probably reflects my fifteen years of industrial experience prior to coming to Penn State. When I arrived at Penn State, as a department head, I proceeded to enlarge our offerings in mineral processing to put our students in the best possible competitive position upon graduation. Today our graduates are well versed in coal, ore, and industrial mineral processing and have additional strengths in particle technology, applied surface chemistry, hydrometallurgy, and the mathematical modeling of processes. They can, and do, handle a broad variety of jobs.

Historically, the mining industry has encompassed geology, mining, mineral processing, and metallurgy. This industry has a great deal of breadth and a long and illustrious history leading up to its present highly technological state. Its history has allowed me to use my profession as both a vocation and an avocation. Avocationally, one of my hobbies is to visit old mine, mill, and smelter sites of the West and from the ruins try to decipher the process used—sort of an archaeometallurgy hobby. I have hundreds of slides on the subject and will give a slide-lecture at the drop of a hat. The excellent collection of journals in the EMS library, dating back to the late century, has been very helpful. This allows me to check on the validity of my observations at long-abandoned mining operations. Why, I asked myself, should a small (at that time) eastern school have such an extensive collection? Two answers came through with crystal clarity: (1) E&MS, since its inception as the School of Mines in 1890, has had a series of superb librarians and (2) in the early days, when library space was woefully short, the faculty members kept whole collections of journals in their offices and these were subsequently turned over to the library as space became available.

This spirit of camaraderie continues today. In our College, I have long noted that some of our best teachers are our best researchers. In these days where large universities seem to have trouble reconciling research and devotion to teaching, E&MS has long practiced a philosophy that considers both. Such a philosophy is instilled from the top, and E&MS has had a series of excellent deans dating back into the nineteenth century. When I first arrived at Penn State, two of the people whom I met really impressed me: Dean Hosler was enthusiastic about both his research and his introductory course in meteorology. A dean teaching? Yes, and mighty happy about it too. The other person who impressed me was Bob Stefanko, head of the Department of Mining Engineering. For years Bob had been confined to a wheelchair as the result of an unfortunate accident. Never mind his physical problems— he bubbled over with enthusiasm about his research on controlling methane buildup in mines and waxed eloquent when he described what he was doing in his mine electrical systems course. I decided then and there they would be proper role models.

It has been my good fortune to be part of a unique College, where good teaching and good research are combined to produce an important product: capable graduates.

Beneficiation of Ores

Beneficiation of ores was one early endeavor of the mineral processing faculty. In 1943 David R. Mitchell proposed a survey of the iron ore of Pennsylvania. This occurred at a time when it was evident that iron ores of the Lake Superior region were being depleted and it was believed that the exhaustion of these ores would be a severe blow to the iron and steel industry of western Pennsylvania. Dr. Mitchell recognized that the ores of Pennsylvania were of low grade and could be utilized only after beneficiation. Although the survey of the iron-ore resources of the state was not undertaken, the foundation was laid for a program in mineral beneficiation in the college.

Reprocessing Abandoned Culm Banks

In the early 1960s, H. Beecher Charmbury, Harold L. Lovell, and Theodore S. Spicer initiated a project to recover coal from abandoned culm banks. The project was funded by the U.S. Department of Health, Education, and Welfare. A coal preparation plant with a capacity of about 50 tons an hour was designed and constructed at a coal mine owned by the Barnes & Tucker Coal Company, near Barnesboro. Coal from local sources was trucked to the site. The processes of cleaning the coal were studied and evaluated, and the studies provided the basic information needed for removing coal from culm banks in the state. Thus a valuable resource has been recovered. The reworking of the culm banks became economically advantageous for the anthracite industry. In the 1980s about two-thirds of all anthracite produced was reprocessed. While reprocessing surface "waste" has proven economical in recovering coal, the remaining material has frequently had a high concentration of pyrites. These pyrites may provide the basis for the production of acid water draining from the region. Thus, while one problem may be solved, another remains.

The Hollywood Acid Mine Treatment Plant

The water problem in Pennsylvania mining began with the production of coal. For decades, however, the main concern was the interference of water with coal production in deep mines and the associated safety implications. The concern for the environmental aspects of water-quality degradation was long in developing. The first actual action related to this concern, in which Pennsylvania was a pioneer, was the passage of the Pennsylvania Clean Stream Act in 1937. This

Grinding laboratory studies are geared toward reducing the energy consumed during grinding and producing desired size distributions in ores. Here, Zvi Rogovin (Ph.D. 1983) works with a continuous ball mill.

act has been amended many times. In the 1967 amendments the Pennsylvania legislation introduced an entirely new concept in water-quality control. This act established effluent guidelines on the quality of the water that could be discharged from a mining operation, coupled with the requirements for a permitting system.

Because the techniques of controlling water quality were in the initial stages, the mining industry sought help from the state and the University. The mining industry asked whether a system could be developed that is large enough to be meaningful and yet still be used for research to develop an economically feasible system that meets the state's effluent guidelines.

As a response, the state acquired an abandoned deep-mine and surface-mine site at Hollywood, a small village on the border of Clearfield and Elk counties. At this site a mine drainage facility was designed and funded by the Pennsylvania Department of Mines and Mineral Industries and the former Federal Water Pollution Control Administration, later to become a part of the U.S. Environmental Protection Agency. Harold Lovell was appointed director of the project.

The treatment plant, with a hydraulic capacity of 300 gallons a minute, was unique in that it was a large engineering unit consisting of a series of basic operations. These could be combined in an almost infinite number of ways to allow the study of different systems and the use of many types of chemical reagents, from the simplest limestone to very elaborate materials, such as alkalies, and even gaseous sources such as ammonia.

Besides its versatility, the plant was unique in several other ways. It was an elaborate facility providing for automatic control of numerous variables, including the continuous chemical analysis of all pertinent water characteristics. In addition, there was the capability of measuring power consumption, a major cost factor in this type of engineering.

Within the unit operations a number of special features existed, among them the use of bacteria to complete the oxidation of iron as a major operation within the water treatment. The settling lagoon design provided for utilization of high-molecular-weight flocculants. The large volume of sludge was a problem, however, first in drying the material and second in disposing of it. This remained a major problem throughout the plant's operation.

The plant was in operation about four years. During this period a great amount of information was collected on the maintenance of quality water during and after the mining operation. Although the problems of water quality were not solved completely, the industry had a greater awareness of the problem, and the first scientific and engineering steps had been taken to solve it.

Comminution

Another traditional area of study in mineral preparation is in comminution—the process of crushing and grinding ores, rock, coal, and cement into finer sizes. The first major laboratory in the College used to study all phases of beneficiating minerals from the highly theoretical small-scale laboratory batch-type experiments to large-scale pilot plant operation was completed in 1954. This facility made possible research and development work on the preparation of all types of metallic and nonmetallic ores and coal. The laboratory included offices, chemical control facilities, and equipment for crushing, grinding, screening, classification, and concentration of materials. In 1954 Dr. Charmbury stated: "When the new laboratory is completed, it will be comparable to any one of the country's most outstanding school or commercial laboratories."

In 1957 Leonard G. Austin began research on size reduction. He applied the concepts of population balance (keeping track of the rate at which particulates are created and destroyed) and reactor theory (defining movement of the solids through the size-reduction device, which had been recently developed) to creating a mathematical model for batch grinding. Dr. Austin extended the treatments to grinding circuits and developed methods for measuring rates of breakage in ball mills. This method of analysis and the design of grinding machines and circuits has been extended to several other types of grinding devices at Penn State. Because the cost of energy used in size reduction is increasing rapidly, and ore grades are becoming lower and thus require more size reduction, the sophisticated computer design procedure developed at Penn State is being adopted by designers and users of size-reduction equipment.

Changing a four-foot decanter tumbling mill that can be used with or without grinding media.

Processing Coal to Remove Sulfur

Most of the coal of Appalachia has a high sulfur content. This impurity became a critical factor in coal production with the passage of the Clean Air Act of 1970, which recognized that sulfur was undesirable because it contributes to air pollution. During combustion, sulfur is converted to sulfur dioxide. Also, sulfur can be associated with other elements, forming compounds that have been identified as major contributors to the slagging and fouling problems associated with the combustion of coal in a boiler.

Because the sulfur content must be reduced in Appalachian coals in order to meet Clean Air Act standards, this has become a major research endeavor in the Department of Mineral Processing. The cleaning of coal is a tremendously complex problem. The difficulty with sulfur removal is understanding what is achievable through physical beneficiation and what is not. As Frank Aplan and Peter Luckie state: "The various constituents in coal have different properties. Therefore, it should be possible to separate them, one from another, using the differences in their properties if that difference is sufficient and if the individual constituents can be conveniently liberated, one from another. Unfortunately, this condition is strictly hypothetical. It is impossible to achieve complete liberation of the organic constituents from the inorganic constituents. And even if all the inorganic constituents could be separated from the organic constituents, the sulfur would still contaminate both groups. This is because the sulfur can be found both in the chemical structure of the organic constituents, hence there is both organic and inorganic sulfur."

A basic goal in coal processing is the removal of as much sulfur as possible from the coal. The traditional method is to take raw coal from one to six inches in diameter and crush it to a size small enough for the pyrite to be separated from the coal. In this process, the coal is ground for subsequent treatment to coarse, intermediate, and fine sizes. Coarse cleaning involves gravity-separation procedures such as jigging and heavy media cycloning. These devices are low-cost, high-capacity, and effective means of cleaning coal.

The Penn State mineral processing engineers have found that coarse cleaning, though effective, has two disadvantages: first, the nature of the pyrite and ash may be such that they are not well liberated at the coarse size and that finer crushing is needed and second, the cleaning device, when set at a certain specific gravity to produce the desired product, will reject all particles heavier than this specific gravity, including not only refuse but also particles that contain both coal and refuse constituents.

Because there is a critical need to remove sulfur if coal is to continue to command a substantial share of the fuel market, the research emphasis today is on the intermediate and fine cleaning. To solve the fine-cleaning problem, the froth flotation process was applied.

Shiou-Chuan Sun began studies of coal flotation in the 1950s. In the flotation process, coal particles, usually $\frac{1}{32}$ inch or smaller, are placed in aqueous suspension in a large mixing tank called a flotation cell. After mixing, the coal particles attach themselves to air bubbles that rise to the surface, where they are skimmed off. The flotation process has the greatest potential of all fine-cleaning processes, but it has been underused and is in many ways still in a stage of research, development, and plant testing. The flotation process is being advanced by Frank Aplan, a recognized leader in the field at the present time. Further research is now proceeding on the most efficient method of rejecting pyrite and other materials from the coal. Subhash Chander is using applied surface and colloid chemistry in developing the froth flotation process. These mineral processing techniques include fine particle treatment, aqueous electrochemistry, and hydrometallurgy.

Although sulfur is only one constituent of coal, it has gained the attention of many people from highly diverse backgrounds. Consequently, its removal from coal places great demands on the talents of the coal processing engineers. Even if only part of the sulfur in coal can be removed by coal processing, it is still cheaper to remove as much as possible before combustion than it is to attempt to remove all the sulfur in the gas-stream after substitution. Another advantage of coal processing prior to combustion is that the quality of the coal is improved by providing a more uniform product. Any coal-utilization scheme operates more efficiently when it receives a uniform feed. Coal cleaning research will remain at the forefront of mineral processing research for the foreseeable future.

Particle Systems

The extraction of minerals from ores invariably involves the production, handling, processing, and separation of particle systems. In many ways, particulate materials can be regarded as a distinct form of matter, analogous to but different from gases, liquids, or solids. They possess their own characteristics and behavioral relationships. A mineral process engineer is required to understand and deal with the characteristics and properties that are unique to the particulate state. But the importance of particulates extends far beyond the mineral processing field. Many foods, pharmaceuticals, cosmetics, detergents, inks, paints, fertilizers, and pesticides have problems of production identical to those in the processing of minerals. As a consequence, the mineral processing program at Penn State has broadened its scope to encompass specific applications to mineral processing. Richard Hogg states: "We believe that, in doing so, not only can we contribute to other areas, but we provide greater breadth of background. We have placed recent Ph.D. graduates in the chemicals, paint, and aerospace industries as well as in the more traditional areas of minerals and coal. The mineral processing section is also playing a leading role in the development of the recently established, university-wide Center for Particle Science and Engineering."

CHANGES IN RESEARCH PHILOSOPHY

Before 1970 most of the research at Penn State in mineral processing was directed toward specific empirical problems—for example, how to clean a certain type of coal or beneficiate a certain type of ore. Beginning in the 1970s, the research began to concentrate on processes, that is, what makes a particular process work, what the effects of numerous variables on the process are, how

Dr. Chander uses a high-speed videocamera for recording the rapid movement of particles.

processes can be optimized, and how processes can be modeled mathematically so that simulations of processes can be performed in order to study entire plants in the laboratory.

As Dr. Hogg says: "The most significant change in the last twenty years in research has been the extensive use of modeling techniques in the Department of Mineral Processing. Their use occurs at several different levels. Models are widely used for such individual operations as grinding, crushing, processing, flotation, separation, and others. By the use of models, individual operations can be evaluated. But an even more important research trend is the ability to develop whole plant simulations. By the use of the computer the total operation can be evaluated. For example, individual laboratory tests may seem to indicate very important results, but once they are applied in a plant other factors may be more important, and what appeared workable becomes a failure. By the use of models, sensitive factors that control the operation of the plant can be isolated. As a result, the trend in the department is toward the integrated systems approach to gain an understanding as to how the individual operations function together as a complete unit."

EMPLOYMENT OPPORTUNITIES

Mineral processing engineers traditionally work for companies that produce mineral products, such as coal, iron, phosphates, copper, uranium, aluminum, titanium, cement, crushed stone, and glass sand. Within such companies, the mineral engineer engages in engineering, planning, operations, and research. The following are typical positions held by mineral processing engineers who are graduates of Penn State. Dale A. Augenstein (B.S. '69, M.S. '71, Ph.D. '74) is president of K & J Coal Company; S. David Irons (B.S. '62, M.S. '66) supervises research for Bethlehem Steel; Elliott Y. Spearin (B.S. '69, M.S. '71, Ph.D. '79) conducts research for Inland Steel; Kevin C. Thompson (B.S. '72, M.S. '78) is a senior metallurgical engineer with BHP–Utah Minerals Inc.; William E. Porter (B.S. '70) is vice president of Consolidation Coal Company; and Sidney M. Cohen (B.S. '55) is director of research and development of the Fuller Company.

Mineral processing engineers also work for firms that design, engineer, construct, and research the systems used to produce minerals, and for companies that manufacture the equipment or produce the supplies, such as chemicals, that are used to prepare and concentrate the ore. For example, Richard F. Wesner (B.S. '47, M.S. '48), the first Penn State graduate in mineral processing, is past president of Kennedy Van Saun Corporation; Thomas R. Wood (M.S. '80) is with Bechtel Corporation; Thomas H. Wentzler (B.S. '69, M.S. '71) is president of Tetra Technologies; and Terry E. Stauffer (B.S. '64, M.S. '68) is manager of technical application of Leeds and Northrup Company.

HONORS, AWARDS, AND PROFESSIONAL ACTIVITIES

The high caliber and achievements of the mineral processing faculty have been recognized nationally and internationally through several prestigious honors and awards. Frank F. Aplan, Distinguished Professor of Metallurgy and Mineral Processing, has been elected to the National Academy of Engineering and has received the Robert H. Richards and Arthur F. Taggart awards of the AIME. He was awarded an honorary degree (Minl. Engr.) by the Montana College of Mineral

Richard F. Wesner
Alumni Fellow

Richard F. Wesner's (Alumni Fellow 1990; B.S. 1947 and M.S. 1948, Mineral Preparation) education was interrupted by World War II, and he enlisted as an Air Corps cadet and served eighteen months in the China-Burma-India theatre. Following his discharge as a first lieutenant, he returned to Penn State to complete his B.S. degree and earn an M.S. in mineral preparation engineering.

He joined the McNally Pittsburg Manufacturing Corporation of Pittsburg, Kansas, as a field service and coal process engineer in 1948. In 1954 he moved to Boone County Coal Corporation, where he served as vice president and general manager of mining operations for five years. Following a brief return to McNally Pittsburg in Wellston, Ohio, Wesner became executive vice president of one of the McNally groups of companies, the Kennedy Van Saun Corporation (Danville, Pennsylvania) in 1963. Three years later he was named president and CEO, retiring in 1988.

Under his leadership, Kennedy Van Saun was a dynamic industrial corporation that played a significant role in the Danville economy. Richard Wesner succeeded as a business leader and established a company reputation for sound technology based on continuous research and development. He is currently the president of a firm of mining consultants in Pittsburgh, Pennsylvania.

Science and Technology and received the Centennial 100 Award from the South Dakota School of Mines and Technology. In 1989 he was the first recipient of the Engineering Foundation Award, henceforth known as the Frank F. Aplan Award "for contributions to further understanding of coal and mineral processing," and in 1991, he was elected a honorary member of the American Institute of Mining, Metallurgical, and Petroleum Engineers "for his innovative, prolific and productive career of outstanding contributions to the integration of theory and practice of processing coal, ore and industrial minerals."

Leonard G. Austin, emeritus professor of fuels and mineral engineering, has received the Antoine M. Gaudin Award of the AIME, and the Percy W. Nicholls joint engineering award of the AIME-ASME. He has also received the Babcock Power Award of the Institute of Energy (London). Most recently, Dr. Austin was selected to receive the Arthur F. Taggart Award of the AIME (1991).

H. Beecher Charmbury, emeritus professor of mineral preparation, was the first recipient of the Joan Hodges Queneau Environmental Award of the Audubon Society and received the Environmental Conservation Distinguished Service Award of the AIME.

David R. Maneval, former assistant professor of mineral preparation, was also a recipient of the AIME's Environmental Conservation Distinguished Service Award.

Richard C. Klimpel, adjunct professor of mineral processing, is also senior scientist for the Dow Chemical Company, one of only four engineers (and the only nonchemical engineer) who have been honored with this title in the history of the company. Dr. Klimpel has received the Robert H.

Richards Award of the AIME and has been named Inventor of the Year for both Dow Chemical Company and the state of Michigan. In addition to his duties at Dow, Dr. Klimpel is an active participant in the mineral processing program at Penn State.

Frank Aplan, Richard Hogg, and Peter Luckie have received the Matthew and Anne C. Wilson Outstanding Teaching Award at Penn State.

The diverse expertise of the faculty is reflected in their active membership in numerous professional societies, including the American Chemical Society, the American Institute of Chemical Engineers, the American Filtration Society, the Electrochemical Society, and the Fine Particle Society, in addition to the American Institute of Mining, Metallurgical, and Petroleum Engineers (AIME). Frank Aplan, Leonard G. Austin, and Richard Klimpel have all been honored as Distinguished Members of the Society of Mining Engineers of AIME. These three have also served on the board of directors of the Society of Mining Engineers and as chair of the Mineral Processing Division.

The faculty have been especially active in the prestigious Engineering Foundation Conferences program. Dr. Aplan was chair of the Engineering Foundation Board from 1985 to 1987. Frank Aplan, Leonard Austin, Subhash Chander, Richard Hogg, Richard Klimpel, and Peter Luckie have all organized and chaired conferences on mineral, coal, and fine-particle processing under the auspices of the Engineering Foundation.

THE FUTURE

The faculty, facilities, and research funding provide the foundation for the mineral processing program at Penn State. The basic goal will continue to be to educate young engineers so that they will be equipped to solve the myriad of particle processing problems facing the mineral industries. As our mineral resources are depleted, efficient and economical mineral processing becomes of ever greater importance to the future well-being and security of the United States.

MINING ENGINEERING

Mining is a unique basic industry devoted to taking materials out of the earth. It thus removes from the earth a nonrenewable, or "wasting," asset. Mines are developed not where the miner chooses but where the natural deposits are found. A mineral is as likely to be found under a city as in the farthest reaches of the most distant continent. In addition, the mining industry, depending as it does on irreplaceable resources, must assume responsibility for achieving maximum utilization of its resources. Gone are the bonanza days when the rich ores could be skimmed off and the leaner ores left behind. The modern challenge of a mining engineering department is to provide scientific and engineering training so as to make worthwhile the natural hidden material resources for man's use, and at the same time achieve their conversion into a useful material as efficiently as possible with a minimum of disruption to the other resources of land, water, and air.

George Deike presents "watch award" to mining engineering student Allen D. Gray, Jr., at the cornerstone-laying dinner for the Mineral Sciences Building in 1949.

ESTABLISHMENT OF A MINING ENGINEERING CURRICULUM

On October 4, 1890, the Executive Committee of The Pennsylvania State College adopted a resolution establishing a curriculum in mining engineering. In 1891 the state legislature enacted laws that made it possible to erect and equip a building for the mechanic arts, including mining engineering, and in 1893 an appropriation for the maintenance of a Department of Mining Engineering was passed. The catalog for the same year contained the first curriculum offered in mining engineering. The Department of Mining Engineering was the foundation on which the present College of Earth and Mineral Sciences has been built.

TRAINING MINING ENGINEERS AT PENN STATE

In the late 1930s David Mitchell described the training of the mining engineer. He quoted Agricola's *De Re Metallica*, published in 1556, which stated "what a miner should know," the term "miner" being used in the same sense as mining engineer is used today. According to Agricola, the miner should have mastered the following areas of knowledge: geology ("that he may know what mountains, what valley, can be prospected most profitably"), chemistry and mineralogy ("that he must be familiar with the many varied species of earth—metals—compounds"), mining ("He must have a complete knowledge of all underground work"), metallurgy ("There are the various systems of assaying and of preparing substances for smelting"), and the general sciences, of which Agricola states: "There are many arts and sciences of which the miner should not be ignorant: first, philosophy, that he may discern the origin, course, and nature

---

Administration
Mining Engineering

Department of Mining Engineering

Magnus C. Ihlseng	1893–1900
Marshman E. Wadsworth	1901–1906
Walter R. Crane	1907–1919
William R. Chedsey	1919–1938
David R. Mitchell	1938–1946

Department of Mineral Engineering
Division of Mining Engineering

Richard D. Snouffer	1946–1948
Arnold W. Asman	1948–1953

Division of Mineral Engineering
Department of Mining Engineering

Arnold W. Asman	1954–1957
Howard L. Hartman	1957–1963
David R. Mitchell	1963–1964
Robert Stefanko	1964–1967

Department of Mineral Engineering, Mining Section

Robert Stefanko	1967–1969
Thomas V. Falkie	1969–1974
Lee W. Saperstein	1974–1987
Stanley C. Suboleski	1988–

---

of subterranean things; second, medicine, that he may be able to look after the health of his diggers; third, astronomy, that he may judge the direction of the veins; fourth, surveying, that he may estimate how deep a shaft would be sunk; fifth, arithmetical science, that he may calculate the cost in the working of the mine; sixth, architecture, that he may construct the machines and structures; next he must have a knowledge of drawing; lastly, there is the law—."

Professor Mitchell recognized that this was "truly a formidable array of subjects, and yet the busy mining executive or consultant of today must be versed in as many subjects." He continued: "It has been said frequently that the broad training of the mining engineer especially fits him for administrative positions, and further, being well grounded in the sciences, he may specialize in a number of different directions." At Penn State the course structure has evolved with advancing technology and changing economic conditions (Snouffer, 1947). Besides the traditional courses in mining engineering, such as mine design, materials handling, and power systems, a variety of new courses reflecting modern trends in the industry have been added. Because Pennsylvania is a major producer of surface coal, a number of surface mining courses (surface mining systems and design, surface mining sedimentation control, and surface mining cut planning) are offered. In the mining industry, economic conditions are extremely important, so that a course in mineral property evaluation is now offered. Work has also been expanded in geostatistics and rock mechanics, and more emphasis is being placed on fluid flow through porous media. These new courses, which require a new emphasis in teaching at both the undergraduate and graduate levels, reflect the development of a highly sophisticated mining technology.

ENROLLMENT TRENDS

The first mining students at The Pennsylvania State College enrolled in the 1890s in the newly created Department of Mining Engineering. There were between ten and twenty students in the mining program. In 1899, when the graduating class of The Pennsylvania State College numbered forty-three, six of the students were mining engineers. Because coal production was rising and great technological advances were occurring, there was a growing demand for the mining engineer. By 1906 mining engineering was a popular program on the campus, with a total enrollment approaching one hundred. This interest in mining engineering remained high with an average annual enrollment of about seventy-five students until 1925.

After 1925, coal production experienced a precipitous decline, and enrollment in mining engineering declined drastically to under thirty-five in the 1930s. While the students who graduated in mining engineering had little difficulty securing good jobs in the industry, the general perception was that mining was a dying industry, due largely to competitive fuels, and that it held little prospect for a sound future.

The Charles B. Manula Microcomputer Laboratory.

Between 1950 and 1970, within the United States, many mining programs in universities were abolished, but the program at Penn State was continued because it was recognized that a service was still being provided to the industry and that a long-range viewpoint was required. There would be a need for mining engineers in the future. During these bleak years the program was maintained by a few American undergraduate students, a graduate student program consisting largely of foreign students who were supported by industry and government contracts, and a small continuing education program.

In the late 1950s, when enrollment had reached a low ebb in mining, the department introduced a student-trainee cooperative program to bolster enrollment. This program allowed a student to alternate work and study and to secure a B.S. degree in five years, and at the conclusion of this program the student had completed two years of industrial experience. Howard L. Hartman contacted mining companies to convince them that this was a good idea. The companies responded by sponsoring a number of students in the degree program.

The freshman class enrolled in 1960 had more than twenty students, in contrast to the two to six students who had previously entered the program. The students recognized the considerable value of this program:

1. Two years of experience can bring a higher starting salary and a more responsible job.
2. Up to three years of mining experience are required for a B.S. mining degree, and five years for a nondegree worker before he or she may take the examination for first-class foreman's papers in Pennsylvania. Much of this experience is gained prior to graduation in the student-trainee program.
3. Salaries, or wages, paid to the student during the work period offset some expenses.
4. Cooperative training, which involves no postgraduation obligation on the part of either the student or the employer, gives each the opportunity to evaluate the other.
5. The training period allows the student time to formulate his or her plans in terms of the kind of mining career (operations, research, sales, exploration, etc.) desired after graduation.

The department has now developed a list of mining company sponsors. The student, in cooperation with an adviser, selects a suitable sponsor. Concerns such as the distance from home, the city size, the mineral commodity, and the type of work involved are resolved with the trainee, who is then asked to apply to the companies that seem suitable. By making contact with the potential sponsor, the trainee demonstrates willingness to accept sponsorship. When accepted by a sponsor, the student intersperses college study with work for the company.

In the 1970s, as a response to the world's energy crisis, coal once again became an important source of energy to the nation. Because few mining engineers had been trained during the previous two decades, the demand for mining engineers was at an all-time high. As a response, salaries were at the top level. Undergraduate enrollment increased from about twenty students in 1970 to a peak of almost 450 in 1979. There were also thirty graduate students at University Park and ninety associate degree students located on the three Commonwealth Campuses of Altoona, Fayette, and New Kensington. In order to staff the increased enrollment during the 1970s, the faculty doubled to a total of twenty-six.

The enrollment peaked in the late 1970s at the time of maximum coal production in Pennsylvania. Since then, coal production has declined about 25 percent in the state, due largely to such factors as declining oil prices and clean air legislation. The undergraduate enrollment has experienced a significant decline to about forty students in the fall semester of 1991. Government and industry contracts have maintained graduate enrollment.

High-pressure apparatus for determining rates of diffusion of methane in coal.

COAL CONFERENCES

During the 1930s a number of coal conferences were held at the School. The first occurred on November 10 and 11, 1933. The stated purpose of the conference was to "offer the possibility of concerted attack on certain general and more or less fundamental problems." The 1933 conference was "attempting to aid the solution of the important question of more profitably utilizing the fine sizes of coal." The conference papers included discussion on the mining of coal with relation to the cleaning and the production of fine sizes, the preparation of the fine sizes of bituminous coal and anthracite, and the nonfuel use of the fine sizes of anthracite. To promote the maximum opportunity for making acquaintances among the conference participants, an informal dinner was held at the Nittany Lion Inn followed by an open house in the Mineral Industries Building.

In 1934 the American Institute of Mining and Metallurgical Engineers, Coal Division, held their fall meeting at Penn State. This meeting was largely "in recognition of Penn State's long established Mining Engineering course, the large number of her prominent alumni in the coal industry, the relatively new course in Fuel Technology, and the accompanying research work on coal." The papers of this meeting, such as "Sealing Abandoned Bituminous Mines," "Trends in Underground Lighting," "Rate of Face Advance," and "Machine Mining on the Pitch," were largely devoted to practical coal-mining problems.

The coal conferences of the 1930s gave visibility and recognition to the mining program at Penn State. Many of the leading mining engineers in the United States and foreign countries participated. Few endeavors have been more successful.

ASSOCIATE DEGREE PROGRAMS

In the late 1960s it was recognized that the mining industry needed a level of training that fell between that expected of an hourly employee and that expected of the engineer. Responding to the requests of the mining industry for more technological training, Robert Stefanko, then department head, organized Penn State's first associate degree program in mining technology. As one of the first such programs in the nation, it began on the Penn State Fayette Campus in the fall of 1969. This program was successful, and the associate degree was next extended to the Altoona and New Kensington campuses.

Because of specialization of operations in the mining of coal, three options were developed. The production option provided the broadest training and was offered at each of the three campuses. Because of the importance of strip mining, a surface mining option was developed at the Altoona Campus. The third option was in mine maintenance and was offered only at the Fayette Campus. The Fayette Campus had four faculty members; Altoona had three; and New Kensington had one. Because of the decline of coal production in Pennsylvania in the 1980s, the mining technology programs have now been suspended.

RESEARCH TRENDS

For many years the mining faculty devoted its efforts to training mining engineering students. Progress in the development of mining machinery began in the 1930s but since then has been nothing less than phenomenal. As the easily mined coals and metal ores were exploited, advances

---

William Bellano
Distinguished Alumnus

William Bellano's (Distinguished Alumnus 1974; Alumni Fellow 1973; B.S. Mining Engineering 1936) long career in mineral extracting and processing industries ranged worldwide. In 1972 he chose early retirement as president of Occidental Petroleum Corporation to concentrate on education, public service, and corporate directorships. Penn State capitalized on his talents and commitment to education by honoring him as a member of the inaugural Alumni Fellow group.

Mr. Bellano wrote of his student days: "It was easy to know and recognize fellow students and the faculty. There was also an environment of accessibility that was conducive to a good education. There was no place to hide, no excuse for failure to learn. I wrote my senior thesis under Dr. Helmut Landsberg. At that time Dr. Landsberg conducted undergraduate studies on the effects of atmosphere and physical conditions on roof support and subsidence. Dr. Landsberg submitted a copy of my thesis to the AIME contest for the best paper on mining by a mineral industries college graduating senior. I was awarded first prize. Upon graduation, Dr. Landsberg gave me a copy of *Don Quixote*. Included was a postscript that I 'should dream of things to do, but unlike Don Quixote I should avoid jousting with windmills.' "

His Distinguished Alumnus citation read:

> To William Bellano, internationally recognized industrialist and energy resource expert, for his unceasing crusade urging a sound national energy policy; for his dynamic corporate and civic leadership; and for sharing it all with the current Penn State generation as a visiting Alumni Fellow.

Jesse F. Core III
Distinguished Alumnus

Jesse F. Core III (Distinguished Alumnus 1966; B.S. Mining Engineering 1937), in his professional life, witnessed a steady expansion of responsibility in the coal industry. After working for a number of coal companies, he began work with the U.S. Steel Corporation in 1951 and rose to vice president in charge of coal operations. He was active in many professional and local organizations. His devotion to Scouting is attested by the coveted Silver Beaver Award he holds. His citation read:

> To Jesse F. Core, for outstanding development as a leader in the coal and steel industry; for his many contributions to professional organizations; and for noteworthy service to Scouting and the honor bestowed on him for that service.

in efficiency were necessary for the industry to supply the growing demands for energy and raw material. In terms of equipment, machine loading of the blasted mineral is one of the most important elements of the mining process. The time it takes to load material is a primary measure of efficiency. The Penn State faculty worked closely with mining machinery companies to develop modern machinery in the 1930s and 1940s.

With the application of mechanization in mining, efficiency increased. Probably more than any other single element, the application of production control to mining was instrumental in establishing the pattern of modern mining technology. Penn State was a national leader in these developments. The basic foundation for production control was the simple time study. Having such a useful and well-developed tool permitted mining engineers to evaluate critically how personnel and machinery performed. From these data, cost predictions could be made.

A modern program of research was begun at Penn State in the mid-1950s when Howard L. Hartman, then department head, recognized that the mining industry continued to lag in scientific and technological advancements. In order to reduce accidents in mines, a great deal more had to be known about rock mechanics. Although its importance was long recognized, the study of the mechanics of rocks developed very slowly; perhaps the general attitude of neglect was prompted by the complexity of the problems. By the 1950s, with more sophisticated, mathematical techniques, rapid means of analysis and computation, and precise, rugged measuring devices available to the engineer, the time had come to develop the field. Robert Stefanko became an early national leader in the study of rock mechanics.

In order to develop the research program, the Rock Mechanics Laboratory was established at Penn State in 1957. To coordinate the work in rock mechanics, an Annual Symposium on Rock Mechanics was jointly sponsored with the Colorado School of Mines, the University of Minnesota, and the University of Missouri.

In the 1950s mechanization was rapidly replacing manual labor in all phases of the mining activities. This technological revolution in turn created many new problems in planning and production technology. As a consequence, a highly complex operational system evolved. The problems arising from this new system had to be solved by a more rational and rigorous approach. Economic and cost relations had become so complex that management could not issue a

Edward Steidle
Distinguished Alumnus

Edward Steidle (Distinguished Alumnus 1967; B.S. Mining Engineering 1911) came to the School of Mining and Metallurgy in 1928 when it was housed in a wooden shack. Its faculty of twelve taught 144 undergraduate majors on an annual instruction budget of less than $60,000. An allocation of $50 for postage made up the school's total research fund, and $32 took care of extension needs. On his retirement in 1953 the School of Mineral Industries had a physical plant valued at $5 million, more than 200 people on its staff, 590 undergraduate majors, and 170 graduate students. More than $1 million in research funds were granted by the federal government alone, and extension service reached every part of Pennsylvania. His citation read:

> To Edward Steidle, for wisdom and energy in developing one of the nation's outstanding schools in the mineral industries and service; for distinguished service not only to the United States but to other governments; for writings and teaching which have gained him many honors; and for inspirational leadership to those who have had the privilege of working closely with him.

George H. Deike, Jr.
Distinguished Alumnus

George H. Deike, Jr. (Distinguished Alumnus 1967; B.S. Mining Engineering 1931) began his career with the Mine Safety Appliances Company, rising to the position of secretary and vice chair of the board. He and his father served for nearly half a century on Penn State's Board of Trustees. He was active in his home community of Wilkinsburg and was elected to the borough council, a founder of the Blackridge Civic Association, and a director of Columbia Hospital. His citation read:

> To George H. Deike, Jr., for continued service to the University; for a highly successful career as engineer and administrator; for exceptional community service through public office, charitable, and youth organizations, and for professional activities related to safety in the mining industry.

command in one department of an operation without affecting controls in other departments. Management could no longer afford the luxury of quick decision-making that characterized the days of the simple operation.

During the 1950s a relatively new scientific approach began to aid mining in the complex area of planning and decision-making. Charles B. Manula was at the forefront of the development of the new discipline of operations research. In the next decade Penn State became a recognized

Ventilation Laboratory for studying atmospheric conditions in mines.

leader in the development of operational models. By means of these models the efficiency of mining was improved by controlling the organization of the mining system through the shaping and testing of new ideas and by optimizing practices in the field of production technology.

Operation research is particularly important for the application of mathematical models to the mining industry. Model construction involves the preparation of iconic or analogic flowcharts of the system under study. Computer modeling of surface mining systems began about 1966, and by 1971 models had been developed that were widely accepted in the industry. These state-of-the-art models analyzed such aspects as equipment selection, mining methods layout, and plant design. In the mid-1970s a complete design of a mine was developed by a number of graduate students under the direction of Dr. Manula.

Ventilation of mines has been a recognized problem since mining began. It was the earliest major research program conducted by the department. In 1930, when Steidle Building was constructed, a ventilation laboratory was built into the basement. This facility made it possible to recreate actual mining ventilation conditions. Over the years the ventilation tunnel has been upgraded. Airflow measurements within the model tunnel have been automated and extended by remote sensors. Projects in ventilation network theory, diesel emissions underground, and dust control have demonstrated the high caliber and diversity of the research accomplishments of the faculty. In response to the ventilation research, Howard Hartman prepared the volume *Mine Ventilation and Air Conditioning* in 1961. This volume has long been recognized as the principal effort in this area. In 1981 it was revised, and Hartman wrote: "This second edition is a team effort. It is essentially a Pennsylvania State University effort: all the authors are students, fellow faculty, or colleagues of mine, and most share my Penn State origins. . . . I have been assisted in this task by two co-editors, Jan M. Mutmansky and Y. J. Wang, both also Penn State graduates."

Because many coal seams in Pennsylvania have a high methane gas content, Robert L. Frantz and Robert Stefanko have investigated the possibility of utilizing the methane output of mines. They have studied methane movement in mines in the attempt to recover the gas before the coal is mined, thus reducing the possibility of an explosion.

Eileen Ashworth, visiting professor of mining engineering, in Ventilation Laboratory.

In recognition of the increasing importance of surface mining, a number of the faculty, including Lee Saperstein (now at the University of Kentucky), Raja V. Ramani, and L. Barry Phelps, have organized projects in planning reclamation of surface mines. Of particular interest has been the integration of mining with land use and environmental planning. A major study was conducted by Charles Manula on the feasibility of large-scale open-pit mining of anthracite coal for use by power plants.

A major research interest of a number of faculty members has been the development of advanced machine and mine systems. Robert Frantz and Robert H. King have evaluated mine systems that use increased mechanization, remote control, and automation systems. The research of the mining faculty has increasingly used computer programs and simulation studies to advance the field of mining engineering. With variations for underground and surface mining, these simulators have evolved into some of the most complete and powerful design tools in the world.

RESEARCH UNITS

Three research units for investigating specific problems are located in the mining engineering program. These are the Geomechanics Section, the SOHIO Center for Longwall Mining, and the Mine Electrical Laboratory.

The Geomechanics Section

The Geomechanics Section was established in 1976 as an outgrowth of the original Rock Mechanics Laboratory. This new unit was needed because of the rapidly increasing industrial and governmental activities in the geomechanics area and the expanding interest from graduate students with a variety of engineering and science backgrounds in the fundamental and applied mechanics of geological materials. From the early research on the behavior of "hard rocks," the field has developed rapidly to include studies in such areas as mine design and safety, natural gas storage, the properties of building stones, rapid excavation, and blasting and surface subsidence, as well as more fundamental research into the physical behavior of geologic materials. Both research and teaching have been extended into the "soft rock" area, as well as such fields as tunneling, slope stability, and underground storage.

H. Reginald Hardy, Jr., professor of mining engineering, has been chair of the Geomechanics Section since it began in 1976. In 1978 Z. T. Bieniawski, former head of the Rock Mechanics Division of the Council for Scientific and Industrial Research in South Africa, joined the section as professor of mineral engineering.

Although the section offers no degrees, thirteen students completed M.S. and Ph.D. degrees on acoustic emission/microseismic related topics by 1991. Most students were from mining engineering, but civil engineering, geology, and geophysics students have also completed their research in the Rock Mechanics Laboratory. Faculty from mineral engineering provide courses and assist graduate students in specialized aspects of their program. In addition, a special series of geomechanics seminars is held each semester to further ensure personal contact among program participants.

Jerome W. Woomer
Distinguished Alumnus

Jerome W. Woomer (Distinguished Alumnus 1964; B.S. Mining Engineering 1925; E.M. 1931) headed one of the nation's major consulting mining engineering firms. Many of the leading companies of the world retained his service. After World War II he helped the governments of England and France to revitalize their mining economies. His specialties included mineral valuation and appraisal and mine design. His citation read:

> To Jerome W. Woomer, for an exemplary career as a consulting engineer whose services are sought by governments and industries throughout the world; and for his activities on behalf of professional organizations in the mining field.

John T. Ryan, Jr.
Distinguished Alumnus

John T. Ryan, Jr. (Distinguished Alumnus 1961; B.S. Mining Engineering 1934) was president both of the Mine Safety Appliances Company and its research corporation and chair of Callery Chemical Company. He began work with Mine Safety Appliances in 1936 and was elected president in 1953. He was a trustee of the Thomas Alva Edison Foundation, chairman of the Pittsburgh Board of the Federal Reserve Bank of Cleveland, and a director of many companies. He has served on the advisory board of Duquesne University and a member of the Citizens Assembly. His citation read:

> To John T. Ryan, Jr., for his earnest and dedicated participation in the civic life of his community; for his espousal and solicitation of broad citizen support for worthy community endeavors, especially in the field of educational television; and for the tireless devotion that has rendered invaluable his services to his alma mater.

James C. Gray
Distinguished Alumnus

James C. Gray (Distinguished Alumnus 1960; B.S. Mining Engineering 1925) began his career with the Hudson Coal Company of Scranton. After twelve years he went to the U.S. Steel Corporation, advancing through various positions before becoming vice president of operation in 1954. Mr. Gray was active in professional and civic organizations and served on the executive committee of the American Institute of Mining and Metallurgical Engineers. His citation read:

> To James C. Gray, for his steady advance in the industry he serves with such great distinction; for his deep commitment to and participation in professional and civic affairs; for his exemplary citizenship; and for his personal dedication to his alma mater.

Luther C. Campbell
Distinguished Alumnus

Luther C. Campbell (Distinguished Alumnus 1958; B.S. Mining Engineering 1915) began his career in Nevada as superintendent of a gold and silver mining company, a job he held until he was commissioned as a first lieutenant in the Air Corps in 1917. From 1919 to 1927 he held many positions in the coal industry. In 1927 he joined Eastern Gas and Fuel Association, rising to be vice president in 1943. He was president of the National Coal Association from 1942 to 1956. His citation read:

> To Luther C. Campbell, for his major role in converting coal mining from a back-breaking job to a modern, mechanized industry; for his pioneer efforts in obtaining benefits for miners and their families; for an unprecedented record in promoting industrial safety; and for constant encouragement of promising young men.

Although no formal graduate program exists, formal graduate courses span the major areas of the field. One undergraduate course, Rock Mechanics, and a series of ten graduate courses are available. No other university provides such a number and range of formal scheduled courses in this discipline.

Facilities for instruction and research in geomechanics are among the best and most modern of any American university. The Rock Mechanics Laboratory includes a testing facility housing a fully programmable 200,000-pound-capacity electrohydraulic testing machine and apparatus for conducting and monitoring a wide range of rock mechanic tests, a creep laboratory, and an electronic and instrumentation shop. Facilities are also available for a wide range of studies on microseismics and acoustic emission phenomena, roof bolt design, failure criteria, and mechanical properties.

Edward G. Fox
Distinguished Alumnus

Edward G. Fox (Distinguished Alumnus 1956; B.S. Mining Engineering 1925) was associated with the anthracite industry of Pennsylvania when he secured his first job in 1921 as a miner for a company he was later to serve as president. During his career he held many positions in anthracite mining companies. When the Philadelphia and Reading Coal and Iron Company organized a subsidiary unit, the Shen-Penn Products Company, to carry out stripping operations in Shenandoah in 1946, Mr. Fox became president of the subsidiary. In 1947 he became manager of the parent company, and in 1951 he became president. His citation read:

> Edward George Fox has devoted most of his life to coal, and, as president of the Reading Anthracite Company, is one of the distinguished leaders of this industry. Born in the hard-coal region, he took his first job in a colliery, succeeded to the general managership, and eventually to higher offices elsewhere. A man of keen judgment, he knows labor and management alike and serves both as chairman to the Anthracite Operation Wage Agreement Committee and on the Anthracite Board of Conciliation. The industry's national respect has made him a director of the American Mining Congress. At home, where he has benefited many institutions, including the Good Samaritan Hospital and the Children's Home, he is recognized as a valued citizen.

There is also equipment for field measurement of in situ stresses and laboratory facilities for evaluation of such equipment. A Photoelastic Laboratory with facilities for carrying out three-dimensional model studies using the "frozen stress technique" has been developed. There are also extensive microseismic field research facilities.

Research in geomechanics reflects the interdisciplinary nature of the field. Among the projects was a major long-term research endeavor aimed at developing acoustic emission/microseismic (AE/MS) techniques. Since 1966 well over $1 million in research funds have been expended. To date, research includes studies on underground gas storage reservoirs, longwall coal-mining, the effects of underground blasting on surface stability, mine and tunnel roof stability, earthquake prediction, and a variety of other instrumentation and fundamental topics. More than fifty scientific papers, proceedings, monographs, and technical reports have been published on these activities.

The study of geomechanics began at Penn State with research associated with mining problems some forty years ago. This type of research remains at the core of the field. In the past twenty years the boundaries of geomechanics has expanded, due in part to a resurgence of interest in the methods developed in the geotechnical field. Further, it has become increasingly clear that a common area of interest exists between fields. Disciplinary studies differ mainly with respect to the scale of the specific problems under investigation, and the frequency range of the associated acoustic emission/microseismic activity. In general, AE/MS studies in the geotechnical fields overlap at low frequencies with seismology and at high frequencies with material-science-related AE/MS studies. This overlap presents a number of advantages, since specialized instrumentation and experimental techniques have been under development for a number of years in both areas.

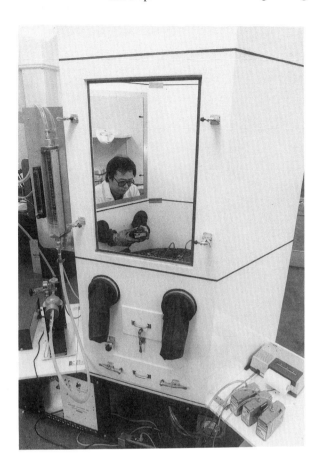

Dust Laboratory in mining
engineering.

Students in the Elders Ridge mine
training program.

A brief review of a number of recent acoustic emission/microseismic field-oriented research activities in the geotechnical area shows that research has been conducted in longwall coal studies, rock bolt monitoring, and the effects of blasting and slope stability. One of the most interesting studies was on the stability of natural gas storage reservoirs.

During the period 1966–82, the Rock Mechanics Laboratory was involved in research associated with the mechanical ability of underground gas storage reservoirs. These studies assumed greater importance after the energy crisis of the early 1970s. Because it is economically desirable to store gas at the maximum possible pressure, studies sponsored by the Pipeline Research Committee of the American Gas Association were conducted to estimate the optimum operating pressures for underground gas storage reservoirs and to evaluate their stability under such operating conditions.

Although research in slope stability has been relatively limited in the past, the Rock Mechanics Laboratory is carrying out a study for the Pennsylvania Department of Transportation to evaluate the feasibility of using AE/MS techniques to evaluate the stability of highway rock slopes. At a site on Interstate 80 near Lamar an array of ten geophones has been permanently installed in holes drilled at the top of the slope. The technique also includes an evaluation of the characteristics of AE/MS activity generated from rock-block sliding, small-scale surface fractures, surface impact, and falling rocks. Source location studies using simulation have also been undertaken, and an automated system for monitoring rock fall has been developed.

The SOHIO Center of Longwall Mining

In 1983 Standard Oil of Ohio decided to provide funds for research in activities that could be of significant benefit to the company and to the energy industry in general. To initiate the program, SOHIO invited universities across the nation to submit projects in about fifteen broad scientific and engineering areas. Out of an initial one thousand responses, thirty-six groups were invited to submit detailed proposals. From this number a prestigious committee selected five universities to which grants of $2 million each were given.

The Massachusetts Institute of Technology received a grant to establish a center for the study of offshore petroleum drilling technology, primarily in the Arctic region. The second area selected went to Stanford University for studies in petroleum reservoir technology. The third area was in crop generation and located at the University of Illinois. The fourth area was in membrane technology, located at the University of Cincinnati. The fifth area was in mining technology for the development of longwall mining, for which the Department of Mineral Engineering at Penn State was selected, with Robert Frantz and Raja Ramani as coordinators.

The Longwall Mining Center at Penn State has investigated a number of problems. These include an innovative mining system and a systems analysis approach for longwall planning, utilizing computers. Another study centers on strata control. Here the research projects have to do with pillar and floor design for longwall mining stability, and also microseismic examinations of the mine roof for early warning of roof fall predictions. Other studies have concentrated on mining ventilation and electrical systems.

This Center has advanced the knowledge of longwall mining and has provided a depth of knowledge on some of the most complex problems. This information has been transferred to the industry through a number of specialized short courses. Because longwall mining is highly efficient, it is a major technical advance in making the coal industry competitive in the total energy market.

Mine Electrical Laboratory

Starting with Robert Stefanko's early work and the later efforts of Lloyd A. Morley, Robert H. King, Christopher J. Bise, and Jeffrey L. Kohler, the mine electrical power research at Penn State developed into one of the top two programs in the United States. The program began with developing some fundamental concepts of mine electrical safety. Christopher Bise evaluated high-voltage, cable-complex performance in mine power systems in his doctoral dissertation. These efforts evolved into the establishment of the Mine Electrical Laboratory, a facility that addresses electrical engineering applications in the mineral industries.

The basic research in the Mine Electrical Laboratory involved protective relaying, cable construction and repair, ground faults, transients, and enclosures for use in hazardous atmospheres. This has contributed greatly to electrical safety in mines and to more efficient utilization of electrical power. A major recent contribution of this laboratory is its sensitive monitoring of electrical ground faults. Its uniqueness lies in its sensitivity. If a person cut through an electrical cable that ordinarily would electrocute him or her, this monitor is so fast that the power is cut before a shock occurs. Although the principle was long known, the difficulty in developing a practical system was that there were so many trippings of the power system that it was not practical. A safe system was devised in the Penn State labs, and the system is now in commercial production. This device will save the lives of scores of miners and is one of the great inventions to come out of this University.

The laboratory, under the direction of Jeffrey Kohler, is unequaled in the world in terms of capabilities and experience of its personnel in mine electrical work. It consists of a number of units. The power lab has high-voltage and high-current supplies for component testing and evaluation. There are also cable-testing mechanisms for determining the life-cycle of cables and cable splices, cold-blend apparatus for testing cables and a master test facility for evaluating such cable properties as abrasion resistance and flammability, and equipment for testing partial discharge and water testing in high-voltage cables, couplers, and components. There is a mine power center and mine rectifier for powering mine equipment and conducting laboratory tests. A complete model of a substation, switchhouse, load center, and rectifier exists. The laboratory's motor and generator facilities include all major motor and generator types, ranging in size from 5 to 100 horsepower.

Mining engineering students using testing equipment in the Rock Mechanics Laboratory.

The monitoring and control unit has available a monitoring system and sensors, and evaluation facilities. Specific equipment includes logic controllers, microprocessors, and minicomputers for developing, implementing, and evaluating control functions. In the artificial intelligence unit the installed equipment includes computers and software for developing expert systems. A special feature is the use of robotics for investigating expert systems controls. The robotics unit has a CMT3 robot and supporting equipment for investigating sensory and control issues. With regard to instrumentation, the laboratory has a full complement of electronic equipment to support instrument development and testing, a wide range of materials for in-mine data collection and processing, signal processing equipment for data analysis, and explosion-proof instrumentation carts. It also has a gravel test track available for testing machine-mounted instrumentation.

CONTINUING EDUCATION

Continuing education is a traditional branch of education in mining engineering. As coal production increased in the anthracite and bituminous fields in Pennsylvania in the nineteenth century, it was recognized that working conditions in the mines were extremely dangerous and that the accident rate was high. Consequently, the state legislature passed a number of laws and regulations requiring certification of all underground supervisors.

Extension Services

In response to these industrial needs, the Mineral Industries Extension Service was begun in 1893 under special maintenance appropriations by the state legislature for the Department of Mining Engineering. This organization provided the first extension training in the United States in the mining industry.

From 1894 to 1899, twenty-seven extension bulletins were printed by Penn State and distributed free to the mining industry. To develop the program further, mining instructors presented a series of free lectures "to the mining employees at their customary places of assembly upon matters of interest to them in their occupation."

Mobile microseismic field facility of the Rock Mechanics Laboratory.

In 1899, legislative action reduced the college appropriations, and the mining extension work had to be abandoned. Extension services were resumed in 1908 with the assistance of friends from the YMCA and the Central Pennsylvania Coal Producers Association. The program again experienced a hiatus after 1915 but was revitalized in 1919 through a small college appropriation, a grant-in-aid from the Central Pennsylvania Coal Producers Association, and the utilization of federal Smith-Hughes funds, in cooperation with the State Departments of Public Instruction and Mines. Up to that time, all the extension instruction had been given by the resident staff in mining, but a full-time extension director was also hired to develop the needed courses.

In 1923 the State Departments of Mines and Public Instruction entered into a formal agreement with the School of Mining and Metallurgy to assist the School in its extension work. Classes were organized for miners to take the examination for certification of competency as an underground supervisor. Mimeographed lesson material was used at first, but beginning in 1927 mining and mining teacher-training lessons were printed in pamphlet form.

EXPANSION OF EXTENSION PROGRAMS

With the establishment of the Extension Division in the School by Dean Steidle, the first program to be increased was in mining engineering. In 1931 a three-year program of 144 hours of training in night classes began. The state funds were given directly to the local school boards and the instruction was recommended to the Penn State extension supervisor by the local school boards. The instructors then had to be certified to teach by the State Department of Public Instruction. If the instructors passed the test, they were given a Vocational Extension Certificate good for one year and renewable if the services were satisfactory. Because the instructors were employed locally, they could appreciate not only the educational needs of the industrial workers but also the local social and economic conditions that had a direct bearing on all local educational programs. Each instructor had to have an educational background that met not only the standards of the School of Mineral Industries but also at least six years of industrial experience, or its equivalent, in the industry from which the vocational students came.

SPECIAL TRAINING PROGRAMS

A number of programs were developed in the 1940s and 1950s to prepare workers for specific jobs.

The National Emergency Defense Training Program

By the 1940s equipment maintenance was becoming a special problem because of increasing mechanization in the mines. During World War II, when older equipment could not be replaced, a special program was created. As a result the U.S. Office of Education established the Defense and War Training Program to prepare workers to understand the problems associated with machinery maintenance. Special test material was prepared, but, equally important, courses were developed in cooperation with manufacturers who were quite willing to lend equipment for use by classes in various locations. The equipment was shifted from course site to course site as the demand for certain machines became known.

Particularly significant was the training of workers in the preparation of coal. Many companies had preparation plants with workers so poorly trained that little coal was actually cleaned. By training these workers, coal preparation became a fundamental part of the coal industry.

The Mining Electro-Mechanical Association

As the coal-mining industry became increasingly mechanized there was a need for a continuing program in training workers to repair machinery. Donald C. Jones recognized the need and in the late 1940s attempted to get the Coal Mining Institute of America to undertake this project. The institute rejected the idea, however, but felt it should ultimately be pursued. Jones then enlisted the aid of mining equipment manufacturers, specialists from the U.S. Bureau of Mines, and of course Penn State faculty. In 1948 this group formed the Mining Electro-Mechanical Association. A central committee that developed small groups throughout the state was formed. These small groups asked manufacturers to send representatives to address the miners on the use and care of certain types of machinery. The meetings took place from October to May with a final state banquet. This organization continues to play a major role in educating the mining people about the development and maintenance of various modern mining machines.

The Coal Sales Staff

In the 1950s, a program to provide information about coal to sales staff was provided by the Extension Division. The sales staff recognized that they needed to understand the different types of coal if they were to sell in the national market. As a result, they requested short courses to provide information about coal quality, seam differences, market perspectives, and other pertinent information. This program was extended to other fields in the College, including petroleum and natural gas. Industry representatives came not only from the United States but from many other countries too. The program was so successful that it was copied by a number of other institutions, particularly the University of Texas.

OFF-CAMPUS TRAINING PROGRAMS

Mining Extension has operated specialized training programs in off-campus locations. These special courses have served a particular need in the mining industry. In the bituminous mining area, a separate faculty in the field was often employed to meet the specific needs of these programs.

Elders Ridge Program

The Elders Ridge Program was established in 1965 and existed until 1984. The program was initiated under the Manpower Development and Training Administration and continued under the Comprehensive Employment and Training Act (CETA). The basic purpose of the program was to take unemployed and underemployed persons and train them to become mine mechanics and electricians. During the nineteen years the program existed, more than 1,400 people graduated.

The program initially began as a one-year course of study but in a relatively short time was reduced to six months. The classes consisted of sixty students with a variety of backgrounds.

Jesse B. Warriner
Distinguished Alumnus

Jesse B. Warriner (Distinguished Alumnus 1954; B.S. Mining Engineering 1905) spent his entire career in the anthracite industry. His first professional job was with the Lehigh Valley Coal Company. In 1913 he joined the Lehigh Coal and Navigation Company as chief engineer, following in the footsteps of his brother. He became president in 1930, a position he held until 1947, when he became chairman of the board of directors. In addition, he served for twenty-six years on the Anthracite Board of Conciliation. During his participation in wage-contract negotiations he won praise from management and labor alike as a fair-minded capable negotiator.

Lewis E. Young
Distinguished Alumnus

Lewis E. Young (Distinguished Alumnus 1952; B.S. Mining Engineering 1900) taught mining at Iowa State College and at the Colorado School of Mines and then served as director of the Missouri School of Mines, before entering the University of Illinois to earn his doctorate in industrial economics. After leaving Illinois in 1918 he joined the staff of the Union Electric Company at St. Louis and was responsible for the first complete mechanization of a coal mine in Illinois. As a specialist in the mechanization of underground mines, he was a consultant on a worldwide basis. He contributed many papers in the field of mine mechanization, mine management, mine taxation, and mine subsidence. He held honorary degrees from the University of Missouri and the Colorado School of Mines.

George H. Deike, Sr.
Distinguished Alumnus

George H. Deike, Sr. (Distinguished Alumnus 1952; B.S. Mining Engineering 1903) began his career as a mining engineer in the coal industry. In 1912 he joined the Bureau of Mines. In 1914, with John T. Ryan, he organized the Mine Safety Appliances Company. His interests were extensive. He was a director of the Potter Bank and Trust Company and of the Carbon Monoxide Eliminator Corporation, president of Catalyst Research Corporation, and director and president of the Pittsburgh Athletic Association. He was a master of the George W. Guthrie Masonic Lodge, Pennsylvania Consistory, and grand master of the Grand Lodge of Masons of Pennsylvania.

John J. Forbes
Distinguished Alumnus

John J. Forbes (Distinguished Alumnus 1952; B.S. Mining Engineering 1911) interrupted his grade school education in 1896 at the age of eleven to begin his mining career as a "breaker boy" in Shamokin, Pennsylvania. His entire career after 1915 was spent at the U.S. Bureau of Mines, where he rose from first-aid miner to director. During his years at the Bureau he gained recognition as one of the foremost figures in mine safety. He supervised the Mineral Production Security Division created by Congress during World War II. He supervised such health and safety activities as accident-prevention education, investigation of disasters, federal coal-mine inspection, contact of mine fires, and mine-flood prevention.

Toward the end of the program, a number of women were accepted and graduated from the program. This reflected a major change in the hiring of women in the mining industry. There were even a few brothers, a father-daughter team, and a husband-wife team in the program. The course included not only practical training but also the mathematics, physics, and chemistry students would need to understand the basic principles of the maintenance of mine electrical and mechanical equipment and apply them upon completion of the program. In the program's later years the operation and maintenance of diesel equipment was also introduced.

Many of the students in this program had been unemployed or underemployed for years, and many of them were receiving welfare. During the training program the students were given a stipend sufficient for them and their families to live on. A large percentage of the students immediately found jobs in the mines after their graduation. Most of the others secured jobs in which they could apply their training. Most important, however, was that these people had become productive workers. In a few instances the lives of the students were enhanced even if a job was never secured.

The Power Plant Maintenance Course

In 1982 the Pennsylvania Electric Company and the Elders Ridge faculty developed a program through which Penn State would provide basic maintenance training to power plant employees. This consisted of training in basic maintenance functions of small motors and pumps that make up a large percentage of the workload in utility plants. This program trained fifty-four employees at seven generating stations in classes of 130 hours extending over a four-week period. This initial maintenance training program developed into a regular in-house training program for the power company.

The Florence Simulated Mine Program

The Florence (Pennsylvania) Simulated Mine Program began in 1972 and continued until 1978. Coal companies in western Pennsylvania sent miners who had at least six months of mining experience to this program. At graduation from the program, the miners became operators of the various types of machinery in modern underground mines. Training took place in an above-ground simulated mine that was equipped with such modern equipment as a continuous miner, a

Dedication of the Mine Electrical Laboratory.

roof bolter, a shuttle car, and a scoop. Students received instruction and gained experience not only in the safe operation of all types of equipment but also in the fundamentals of mining. They also learned the basic checking processes to ensure that the machinery was ready to operate and, in addition, learned to service mining machinery. A simulated continuous miner was utilized to gain proficiency in machine controls. More than one thousand machine operators were trained for the coal industry in this program.

After graduation the miners returned to the companies that sponsored them. This program greatly improved the safety and efficiency of the mining trainers, thus increasing productivity and making coal more competitive with other fuels.

The United Mine Workers

In 1973 the Department of Mineral Engineering received a grant from the U.S. Bureau of Mines to hold seminars on mine health and safety issues for representatives of the United Mine Workers. Thirty-one seminars were conducted in thirteen states. The basic purpose of this program was to provide union health and safety representatives with up-to-date technical and other types of information that could then be taken directly to the mines to better safety conditions and workers' health. In 1974 the United Mine Workers ratified a contract with the coal companies that mandated the first nationwide training program for coal miners. Under this program, Penn State received a grant to develop a model mine training program and a training manual.

Courses for Mining Instructors

Between 1977 and 1980 the mining faculty developed a special program of short courses to train mining instructors. This program consisted of twelve different short courses attended by about 150 people. These people then trained other miners in new health and safety developments.

The Miner Training Program

Penn State's miner training program has evolved considerably since the early 1970s. In addition to health and safety, today's training emphasis includes the areas of efficiency and the worker's ability to prevent loss—not only human losses due to injury and illness but also losses due to inadequacies in the various components of the mining operations, whether it be safety, production, or maintenance. Companies desiring in-field training services from the four full-time instructors are required to submit detailed information including number of employees, location of proposed field training site, location of the job(s) site, accident information and reports, ground control plans, emergency response system, fire-fighting procedures, and blasting information. The next step for the Penn State trainer is to conduct an on-site safety audit tour of the mine site and to review with company officials compliance with federal, state, and company regulations. In this process the trainer discusses past accidents and potential deficiencies in the compliance system and begins to develop site-specific personalized training material utilizing 35 mm slides or videotapes of personal workplace observations. Utilizing this resource material, and a Pennsylvania Mine Injury Report (PMIR) that is an adaptation of MSHA's Safety and Health Technology Center (SHTC) injury data, the trainer is able to tailor the training classes in terms of company-specific problem areas developed from the scientific data bases or personalized workplace observations. The four trainers are distributed across the state in both coal and metal/nonmetal locations and serve both industries.

A major goal of the program is the continued development of high-quality, site-specific training programs that address the effectiveness and efficiency issues facing today's mine operator and the transfer of this knowledge to industry. Since the beginning of funding under the State Grants Program, several hundred companies have been served and more than 40,000 miners have received training or retraining.

Training Resources Applied to Mining (TRAM)

Since 1972, Penn State and West Virginia universities have jointly sponsored TRAM as a three-day national training conference for the mining industry. In this annual conference three concurrent tracks are conducted in such programs as Supervisory/Management Training, Maintenance Training, and Mandatory/Instructor Development Training. This premier training conference, consisting of workshops and papers and the associated proceedings volume, continues to be the primary means of providing technology transfer in the coal, metal, and nonmetal industry.

Penn State Provost William Richardson, left, and Congressman John Murtha, right, at the dedication of the Mine Electrical Laboratory.

TECHNICAL MINING EDUCATION

As mining became increasingly complex, and with rapid advances in technology, it became evident that mining personnel needed to be updated by intensive specialized short courses. The mining faculty consequently expanded their offerings in highly technical short courses. These courses range from the traditional elements of underground and surface mining to advanced courses in such diverse topics as exploration, mine development, coal preparation, mine electricity, strata control, ventilation, drainage, environmental concerns, mine safety, management, and preparation for the mining engineer professional engineering examination. Because engineers are now trained in computer application, most of the short courses are computer-oriented. Twenty to thirty short courses are offered annually, bringing hundreds of industry and government personnel to the campus for this technical instruction.

King Wu
Alumni Fellow

King Wu (Alumni Fellow 1988; M.S. Mining Engineering 1945) was the first international alumnus honored as an EMS Alumni Fellow. This award recognized his outstanding achievements of fifty years of service in the Chinese mining industry. King Wu served as a member of the National Committee of the Chinese Peoples' Political Consultive Conference in 1982 and 1988 and was recently named a Standing Member of the National Committee of that conference. He is vice chair of the Energy Research Association and a member of the State Committee of the World Energy Conference. He serves as director of the China Association for the Advancement of International Friendship.

He came to the United States first in 1942 and spent two years as an engineer with the Pittsburgh Coal Company. While in Pittsburgh he met many Penn State mining engineers and decided to enter the graduate program. In 1945 he was the only Chinese student in the School of Mineral Industries. He has retained close relations with the University and in 1986 established the Penn State Club of Beijing.

H. Douglas Dahl
Alumni Fellow

H. Douglas Dahl (Alumni Fellow 1987; B.S. 1965, M.S. 1967, and Ph.D. 1969, Mining Engineering) is an outstanding alumnus of the Penn State mining engineering program. During his undergraduate days at Penn State he worked as a student trainee with the National Steel Corporation and attended graduate school as a National Service Foundation trainee. His subsequent professional career has been a model of development and continuous achievement, first with Continental Oil Company and later with Consolidation Coal Company. In 1982 he was promoted to executive vice president of Engineering, Exploration, Environmental Affairs, and Non-Mining and was concurrently elected a member of CONSUL's board of directors. Dr. Dahl's contributions to rock mechanics research and their application to strata control problems, including mathematical modeling and numerical solutions to mine subsidence phenomena, have been both original and substantial. In recognition of this significance, he was awarded the National Society of Mining Engineers' prestigious Rock Mechanics Award in 1985.

Between May 1985 and September 1987 the mining faculty studied the means of providing more in-depth service to the small mine operators of Pennsylvania in order to provide mine technical, safety, and health information. Many small operations do not have the staff to utilize technology readily to resolve their problems. It would be desirable to develop a program that has many similarities to Penn Tap or Agricultural Extension in helping small mine operators utilize the latest technology to attack their problems. This would be in the spirit of the land-grant colleges.

NATIONAL AND INTERNATIONAL SYMPOSIUMS

The mining engineering section is a member of several national and international consortiums and co-sponsors and hosts these prestigious symposiums. It is a founding member of the International Symposia on the Application of Computers in the Mineral Industry and hosted the sixth, fourteenth, and nineteenth symposiums in 1966, 1976, and 1986. The department has also hosted the fourteenth U.S. National Rock Mechanics Symposium (1972), the third Mine Productivity Symposium (1976), the second International Symposium on Innovative Mining Systems (1986), and the third U.S. Mine Ventilation Symposium (1987).

MINING AND ENVIRONMENTAL CONCERNS

Traditionally the mining industry has been looked upon by the general public as a destroyer of the land. The Penn State Department of Mining has been in the forefront in the attempt to change this perception. As Dr. Ramani states, "Pennsylvania has long had a very positive policy in terms of environmental protection. In the mid-1960s when the state developed the program 'Operation Scarlift,' much of the research for the state was done by the mining faculty. Throughout the years, faculty projects have focused on waste disposal, controlling acid mine drainage, and reclamation of strip-mined lands. The College has worked with the College of Agriculture, particularly the School of Forest Resources, for the revegetation of the spoil banks. Further, the faculty has worked with the Environmental Protection Agency and the Office of Surface Mine Management and Enforcement to ensure both that present practices do not destroy the land and that past practices of poor reclamation can be rectified. It is now recognized that the miner has a responsibility not only to the mining industry but also to society as a whole."

AWARDS AND HONORS

The mining faculty have received many of the highest awards given by the mining industry. In 1988 Derek Elsworth received the prestigious Manuel Rocha Medal of the International Society for Rock Mechanics. The Rocha Medal is presented annually to an outstanding young researcher in rock mechanics on the basis of an international competition. In the same area, H. Reginald Hardy, Jr., has received the Gold Medal Award of the Acoustic Emission Working Group

The Mine Electrical
Laboratory.

(AEWG), an international organization of more than two hundred professionals. Dr. Hardy was honored as an AEWG Fellow in 1983 and received the AEWG Achievement Award in 1985.

Raja V. Ramani was honored as the first recipient of the Award for Educational Excellence from the Pittsburgh Coal Mining Institute of America in 1986. The award was granted for "his contributions to the theory and practice of mine ventilation and to education through teaching, research and consultation." In 1990 Ramani also received the Environmental Conservation Award of the American Institute of Mining, Metallurgy, and Petroleum Engineers (AIME), and the Howard Erveson Award of the Society for Mining, Metallurgy, and Exploration (SME).

In 1984 Z. T. Bieniawski received the AIME Rock Mechanics Award for "outstanding contributions in scientific and practical application of strata control to coal mining and rock tunneling."

Robert Stefanko also received many awards, including the Donald S. Kingery Memorial Award, the National University Extension Association 1978 Faculty Service Award, and the AIME's Industry Education Award.

The mining faculty have served on many national committees and held offices in professional organizations. Robert Stefanko was an active member of the American Institute of Mining, Metallurgy, and Petroleum Engineers, holding the office of president of the Society of Mining Engineers. Raja Ramani was the 1977 chair of the Minerals Engineering Division of the American Society for Engineering Education. He also chaired the National Research Council's Committee on Post-Disaster Survival and Rescue in 1979 and has served as chair of the International Council for the Application of Computers in Mineral Industry for the years 1983–87. Lee W. Saperstein was vice chair of the Engineering Accreditation Board for Engineering and Technology from 1985 to 1987. He was responsible for coordinating the accreditation inspection of 387 engineering programs at ninety-two academic institutions. He also served on the National Research Committee for Mineral and Energy Resources. Z. T. Bieniawski has served as Chairman of the U.S. national Committee on Tunnelling Technology and Vice-President of the International Society for Rock Mechanics. Among the present faculty, Robert L. Frantz, Jan M. Mutmansky, Raja V. Ramani, and Stanley C. Suboleski are Distinguished Members of the Society for Mining, Metallurgy, and Exploration, an honor restricted to 1 percent of the membership. The Matthew J. Wilson teaching award has also been given to H. Reginald Hardy, Jr., Lloyd A. Morley, Christopher J. Bise, and Raja Ramani.

Lloyd Morley and students in the Mine Electrical Laboratory.

MINING AND THE FUTURE

In the late 1980s the situation in the academic training of mining engineers is somewhat similar to that of the 1960s. Undergraduate enrollment in mining and mineral processing is low. Dr. Ramani believes, however, that there is a fundamental need for a mining engineering program at both the undergraduate level and the graduate level. He states:

> There is an ever-rising demand for the fuels, metals, and nonmetals of the earth. . . . To satisfy this demand, there is a need to maintain a supply of mining engineers. So there is no question whether the mining engineering program will survive. The major question is, In what form? The future belongs to those who can achieve increased efficiencies by an innovative application of emerging technology and new solutions to long-standing problems. The academic programs must remain dynamic with a continuing restructuring.
>
> In order to do this, we are looking at new programs in such areas as geotechnical engineering and geological engineering. There is also a need for mineral engineering management programs at the undergraduate level. There may be a need to expand the program from four to five years. If this is done, the basic mining program will be achieved in four years and the fifth year will be devoted to a specialty.
>
> At the graduate program and research level, there are many areas for new initiatives. These include monitoring of motor control and automation systems, robotics, and innovative extractive systems. Electrical power is still the most convenient way to operate machines, but advancements can be made in the utilization of power. There is the continuing problem of utilizing the space left underground when a mine is abandoned. Underground open space for disposal of waste must also receive more attention. The utilization of mine water is also a fundamental issue. Land-use planning after mining will be of even greater importance in the future than in the past. The health and safety problem will remain a

critical issue, for in mining there will be dust, and if this dust is toxic there are fundamental problems to solve. There will be new types of mining, such as oil-shale mining. This calls for an entirely new type of technology. Literally this will involve the creation of a chemical factory inside the earth. The disposal of nuclear waste in underground cavities is essentially a mining problem. There are even some spectacular possibilities in mining. These include new research in mining the extraterrestrial resources on the moon. George Deike has provided the College with an endowment of nearly a million dollars, and some of these funds are now being used to begin initial study of this type of mining.

These are only a few examples of programs and research that the future holds. The challenge will be to integrate all aspects of the mining engineering program. Our thrust is, thus, in both teaching and research, so that we can provide the best trained engineers for industry, government, and research organizations.

Jeffrey Kohler and student with the mining program robot.

PETROLEUM AND NATURAL GAS ENGINEERING

The modern petroleum industry of the world began at Titusville, Pennsylvania, in 1859. The peak primary production of oil occurred in Pennsylvania late in the nineteenth century, and peak secondary production occurred in the late 1930s. In order to maintain the petroleum industry of Pennsylvania, the petroleum and natural gas program of Penn State has played a unique role. Even as oil production declined in Pennsylvania, Penn State was and has been recognized for its research on advanced recovery schemes. It is now recognized throughout the world as one of the leading centers for developments in reservoir engineering enhanced oil recovery.

DEVELOPMENT OF THE PROGRAM

The initial course in petroleum and natural gas engineering was listed in the College catalog of 1907–8, labeled "Mining 3" and entitled "Prospecting and Well Drilling." The course description read: "Methods employed in shallow and deep boring and in materials of varying degrees of hardness. Use of the rod and rope type of drills, also the rotary forms, as the diamond and steel toothed forms. Cementation as applied to drilling operations. Surveys of bore holes and apparatus employed." While there is evidence that this course was designed to serve the petroleum industry of Pennsylvania, it disappeared shortly from the catalog.

The development of the petroleum and natural gas curriculum did not proceed from the well-developed mining program. Its origin lay in the growth of the geological sciences. In the 1920s there was a concerted effort in the United States to discover and develop new oil reserves. Exploration endeavors created a demand for petroleum geologists. To meet this demand, courses in petroleum geology and allied areas were added to the geology curriculum.

The major impetus to develop a research and teaching program in petroleum and natural gas engineering at Penn State came in 1929, when the state legislature appropriated $50,000 for the purpose of developing a research program in petroleum on the campus. Because the grant was designed to develop the petroleum refining and oil production aspects of petroleum, the fund was divided between the Schools of Mineral Industries and Chemistry and Physics. In the School of Mineral Industries the money was assigned to the Department of Geology.

To implement the grant, Clark F. Barb, assistant professor of oil and gas production research, and Paul G. Shelley, instructor in oil and gas production, were hired, along with two assistants in petroleum research. In the early years of the program, there was a rapid turnover of the faculty. In 1932 only Kenneth B. Barnes remained in the program from the previous year. George H. Fancher, an assistant professor, was hired in 1932 and remained until 1934. In 1935 Gerald L. Hassler joined the faculty and Kenneth B. Barnes was replaced by Ralph H. King. In 1936 Sylvain J. Pirson and Francis C. Todd joined the faculty as assistant professors of petroleum and natural gas engineering. Samuel T. Yuster was advanced in rank from a research assistant to assistant professor. During this building period, there were two to four research assistants in the program each year. Most of them were highly qualified scientists and engineers. For example, in 1935 the research assistants were Earl S. Hill, who had a Ph.D. from the California Institute of Technology, and Samuel Yuster and Donald R. Blumer, who had Ph.D.'s from the University of Minnesota. The scientific maturity of these men made it possible for the research output in petroleum and natural gas to begin immediately and to be soon recognized as at the forefront in the nation.

In 1931 the B.S., M.S., and Ph.D. programs were initiated. A full range of courses was offered, including ten at the undergraduate and six at the graduate level. During 1933/34 the program of instruction was revised, with options in production and refining added. The next year, 1934/35, the courses of study were stabilized as a broad, general curriculum in petroleum and natural gas engineering. As the graduate program developed at Penn State it became the practice to hire the recent baccalaureate graduates to carry out research on an apprenticeship basis. Although this is a common practice today, it was relatively new in the 1930s.

This course of study was developed with the advice of two advisory bodies: the petroleum and the natural gas advisory boards, consisting of petroleum and natural gas engineers. As a consequence the curriculum was both pragmatic and scientific, not only preparing students to deal with the practical problems of drilling and production but also with a scientific emphasis on secondary recovery. When Penn State granted its first Ph.D. in petroleum engineering in 1942, only two

Administration
Petroleum and Natural Gas
Engineering

Department of Geology

Chesleigh A. Bonine	1931–1935
William R. Chedsey	1935–1936

Department of Petroleum and Natural Gas Engineering

Sylvain Pirson	1936–1946

Department of Mineral Engineering, Division of Petroleum and Natural Gas Engineering

Samuel T. Yuster	1946–1950
John C. Calhoun	1950–1955
Robert L. Slobod	1955–1957

Department of Petroleum and Natural Gas Engineering

Robert L. Slobod	1957–1960
C. Drew Stahl	1960–1969

Department of Mineral Engineering, Petroleum and Natural Gas Engineering Section

C. Drew Stahl	1969–1984
Turgay Ertekin	1984–

other such degrees had been granted in the United States. Penn State led the nation in the development of the petroleum engineering graduate education.

In the formative years the program was located in the Department of Geology with Chesleigh A. Bonine in charge from 1931 to 1935 and William R. Chedsey in charge from 1935 to 1936. The expanding enrollment in petroleum and natural gas engineering convinced many that direction of the program should be placed in the hands of a petroleum engineer, and in 1936 the Department of Petroleum and Natural Gas Engineering was established with Sylvain Pirson becoming the first head and serving for ten years before transferring to become head of geophysics. The initial staff included Gerald L. Hassler, Samuel T. Yuster, Donald R. Blumer, Harry Krutter and Bennett Ellefson and Luther T. Bissey. In the late 1930s Kurt H. Andresen, Thomas G. Cooke, H. Beecher Charmbury, and John C. Calhoun were added to the research staff. Dr. Yuster specialized in petroleum technology in the testing of petroleum products and also was in charge of the water-flooding projects.

Dr. Pirson devoted his time to reorganizing the newly created department to meet the increased student load (Pirson, 1940). Enrollment had grown to eighty-one students by the fall of 1936, consisting of thirty-two freshmen, twenty sophomores, seventeen juniors, ten seniors, and two graduate students. The undergraduate enrollment was second only to that of metallurgy. Prior to this time the freshman class had been limited to twenty-five students, but the expanded research facilities made it possible to enlarge the freshman class. Many of the students transferred into the program from other science and engineering majors.

Besides performing his instructional activities, Dr. Pirson carried on an extensive research program. A major contribution was his interpretation of three-layer resistivity curves. He presented methods of interpretation that offered a means of solving a three-layer resistivity curve while obtaining the thicknesses and resistivity of the individual layers. In addition to editing and revising the *Petroleum Encyclopedia* in 1942, Dr. Pirson wrote *Oil Reservoir Engineering,* which helped usher the field of oil reservoir engineering to the status of a science. The work of Dr. Pirson expanded the research of the department from water flooding per se to the broader issue of the performance of the underground reservoir. As a result he played a key role in consolidating the

Student laboratory of Petroleum and Natural Gas.

Norman J. Rubash
Distinguished Alumnus

Norman J. Rubash (Distinguished Alumnus 1986; B.S. Petroleum and Natural Gas Engineering 1954) has been a petroleum industry leader for nearly three decades, serving Amoco in the United States and abroad before becoming Amoco's corporate executive vice president in 1985 responsible for worldwide production, exploration research, gas marketing, planning, and economic activities. In the period from 1970 to 1985, when he was chief petroleum engineer for Amoco's international operations, his family lived in fifteen homes in six states and three foreign countries, each time "as though we would stay forever."

Of his college experience he reflects: "Dean Steidle was firmly at the helm of the School of Mineral Industries, and every freshman was required to take his introductory course, Mineral Industry. Surely to this day everyone who took that course must appreciate the importance of 'irreplaceable resources' and must have a full understanding of the meaning of 'conservation' in the broadest sense." He continues: "Penn State was far more than curriculum and classes. It was also the first opportunity for most students to begin striking out on their own, apart from family. We met and learned how to get along with people from different backgrounds."

His citation read:

> To Norman J. Rubash for attaining worldwide prominence as a leader in the petroleum industry; for marshaling his considerable energy and intellect to conquer new challenges; and for caring enough to translate regard into activity on behalf of his fellow man.

principles of reservoir engineering as an advanced discipline, which he carried from Penn State to the Stanolind Oil and Gas Company and later to the University of Texas.

With the establishment of a department the equipment in petroleum and natural gas engineering was strengthened. A new oil production laboratory for undergraduate instruction was equipped. Additional intensive instruction in secondary methods of recovery had long been needed, and completion of this new laboratory with its physical testing equipment facilitated this work. The facilities of the new laboratory included a means to determine porosity (with the Washburn-Bunting porosimeter and the Russell Volumeter); to measure air permeability of core samples; to measure oil saturation of oil sands by the retort and extraction methods; to determine water in oil sands; to measure hydrogen ion concentrations in oil field waters; and to study oil field emulsions and their treatment. A combination petrographic and chemical microscope was available for studying oil sand by use of thin sections. The laboratory was equipped with an experimental gas-lifting device that provided students with an opportunity to calculate the efficiency of different systems of oil-well blowing. A five-spot flooding pattern for illustrating the secondary recovery method of oil production by water drive was set up.

In the existing petroleum refining and natural gas laboratory, several new pieces of equipment were installed. These included a Pensky-Martens and a closed A.S.T.M. flash point tester, and a unitized gas analyzer. Special facilities were available for experiments on natural gas, such as

Victor G. Beghini
Distinguished Alumnus

Victor G. Beghini (Distinguished Alumnus 1985; B.S. Petroleum and Natural Gas Engineering 1956) began his career with Marathon Oil Company in 1956, and after serving the company in many capacities he became president of the Marathon Petroleum Company, a subsidiary that brought Marathon's worldwide supply, transportation, refining, and marketing operations under a single corporate umbrella. Of his undergraduate days at Penn State he says: "I remember the four years I spent at Penn State primarily for two things. Professors, such as Drew Stahl, Emil Burcik, and Luther Bissey, took an interest in the quality of your work and in your future. Drew Stahl had a particular impact because he had a burning desire to make sure each of us got the best petroleum engineering foundation there was in the country. Second, the courses relating to reservoir engineering were a Penn State forte, and upon going to work it was proved early on that a PSU graduate had a leg up as a result of the emphasis on reservoir theory. I believe the discipline of using engineering logic to reach answers to decisions is the most important thing I got from my education."

He has maintained close ties to Penn State, where he has chaired the C. Drew Stahl Fund campaign to equip and support an Enhanced Petroleum Recovery Laboratory. His citation read:

> To Victor G. Beghini, energy specialist and corporate executive, for his superior performance in management, for his professional attainments in the fields of energy, supply, transport, refining, and marketing, and for his personal commitment to the educational excellence of the University.

calibration of pressure gauges with the dead-weight gauge tester, determination of the specific gravity by use of the Edwards gas density balance, calibration of orifice and Venturi meters, orifice discharge coefficients determination, liquid flow measurements, and flow control tests and similar instrumentation.

EARLY RESEARCH ACTIVITIES

Early research activities in petroleum and natural gas engineering at Penn State received support from three groups: the Pennsylvania Oil Producers Association of the Bradford District, the Pennsylvania Grade Crude Oil Association, and the Pennsylvania Natural Gas Men's Association. With this support an active research program investigating a wide range of topics was initiated by the faculty in the 1930s.

One of the earliest of these investigations was a study by Kenneth B. Barnes and his graduate students. This early work stands as a monumental endeavor in the systematic determination of the properties of porous media. Other pioneer studies followed. In 1934 the relationship between permeability and Poiseuille's Law for flow in capillaries was reported in a School bulletin. The concept of relative permeability and its relation to fluid saturation was presented in 1936–37, but without

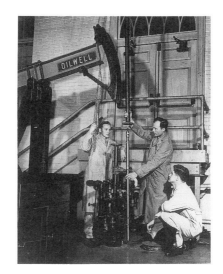

Drilling rig in the Petroleum and Natural Gas Lab in 1946.

the word "relative" being used. The effect of pressure on gas permeability was studied in the laboratory in the late 1930s and later was developed by John C. Calhoun in his doctoral dissertation.

The concepts of interfacial tension forces in porous media and threshold pressure were noted in reports as early as 1936, with contact angles and adhesion tension in two-phase flow being mentioned in 1935. Phase distribution in porous media and the relation of pore structure and interfacial tension to displacement were discussed at the Petroleum and Natural Gas Conference of 1936.

Methods of calculating water-flood histories, allowing for permeability profiles, were developed about 1944 and tested against field behavior. These methods are still being used. In pioneer work "Tarner's method" for predicting primary field behavior was developed in the PNG laboratories in 1944. This calculation was the first approach to predicting oil field behavior.

Penn State was also a pioneer in research on the addition of various materials to injection water to increase oil recovery. As early as May 1932, *Mineral Industries* described injection experiments using soap, sodium carbonate, and other materials. Later, numerous surfactants were tried and the possibility of a chromatographic wave was suggested.

THE PETROLEUM AND NATURAL GAS CONFERENCES

Beginning in 1930 Petroleum and Natural Gas Conferences were held annually in the School of Mineral Industries. These conferences were an opportunity to showcase the activities of the newly created petroleum and natural gas curriculum. The May 1932 issue of *Mineral Industries* stated: "Before the meeting of the first Conference in October 1930 no organized effort had been made to study the problem of these important industries as (bringing together those interested) in their improvements. In addition to focusing attention on some of the outstanding problems, the First Conference proved of great educational value, both to the students at the College specializing in Petroleum and Natural Gas Engineering and to others in attendance." Conferences were spon-

George E. Trimble
Distinguished Alumnus

George E. Trimble (Distinguished Alumnus 1984; B.S. Petroleum and Natural Gas Engineering 1942), who began his career as a roustabout in a small independent company, had achieved a distinguished international career with Exxon before retiring in 1973. In 1976 he came out of retirement to build Aminoil, the energy subsidy of R. J. Reynolds Industries Inc., into the second largest independent petroleum exploration and production company in the nation. In 1978 he was named president and chief executive officer, and in 1981 chairman of the board. Besides his professional career he dedicated time to the community as a volunteer in Junior Achievement, Little League baseball, Rotary, the volunteer fire department, and his church. Of his student days at Penn State, Mr. Trimble remembers, "The faculty had a sincere, dedicated interest in you as a person. The faculty taught you not only engineering but also an appreciation of going forth to serve. You were a part of a family." His citation read:

> To George E. Trimble, international petroleum expert, for his lifelong commitment to providing consistent energy sources for the nation, for his expertise in foreign commerce, and for his dedicated concern for his community.

sored by the Bradford District of the Pennsylvania Oil Producers Association, the Pennsylvania Grade Crude Oil Association, and the Pennsylvania Natural Gas Association. These early conferences were attended by some of the leading scientists and engineers of the period.

These meetings not only brought the leaders of the petroleum field to Penn State but also gave the Penn State faculty an opportunity to demonstrate research undertaken in the department. A 1931 paper by Kenneth B. Barnes, "Preliminary Experiments in Oil Recovery," indicates the early emphasis on secondary recovery research. "The oil recovery experiments have been conducted in the petroleum research laboratory of the School of Mineral Industries. The data obtained so far appear to substantiate the various field tests which have been made. There are some indications that subsequent experiments may show the way to an increased percentage of recovery per acre." During the third conference, in 1933, George H. Fancher and James A. Levin presented research on "Some Physical Characteristics of Oil Sands." This study, conducted in the petroleum laboratories, investigated "the permeability of actual oil sands by means of test pieces cut out of core samples. Accurate knowledge of the permeability of oil sands is vital to the intelligent operation of secondary recovery methods."

In 1934 the annual conference of the American Petroleum Institute, Division of Production, Eastern District, was held at the School. Dean Steidle addressed the conference, and Harry B. Northrup gave a talk entitled "Employee Education." At the 1935 conference Earl S. Hill continued presentations on secondary recovery with his paper "Methods of Determining the Saturation of Oil Sand Samples." In 1936, when the conference stressed the importance of the injection of gas, Gerald Hassler presented his work on "The Production of Oil by Gas Drive."

At the tenth conference in 1941, Harry Krutter presented a paper, "The Mechanics of Oil Expulsion by Air in Porous Media," reviewing the history of gas and air drive development since its inception in 1911 and giving the results of experiments designed to obtain information on the effect

G. Montgomery Mitchell
Distinguished Alumnus

G. Montgomery Mitchell (Distinguished Alumnus 1975; B.S. Petroleum and Natural Gas Engineering 1949) was the former president and chief executive officer of the Transcontinental Gas Pipe Line Corporation for petroleum management before leaving to go to Stone and Webster Management Consultants Inc. as an expert troubleshooter for petroleum management. He has served on many boards, including the Federal Power Commission's National Gas Survey execution advisory committee and the Independent Natural Gas Association of America. His citation read:

> To G. Montgomery Mitchell, industrial executive and expert troubleshooter, for solving management problems with astuteness and finesse; for achieving distinction in a field vital to the stability of the nation's energy resources; for demonstrating exceptional executive skill in the oil and gas industries.

of air drive as a secondary recovery medium. A second paper at the 1941 conference was given by Paul D. Krynine and treated the relationships of porosity and permeability of cementation by calcium carbonate and secondary silica. The paper also discussed the possible relative influence of primary sedimentary and postdepositional diagnostic tectonic factors on cementation.

EVOLUTION OF THE RESEARCH PROGRAM

One of the fundamental goals of Dean Edward Steidle was the development of the petroleum and natural gas secondary recovery program in order to aid the state's declining oil industry. In 1950 Alfred W. Gauger and J. P. ("Dick") Jones of Bradford went to the University of Oklahoma to invite John C. Calhoun, Jr., to become head of the program. Dr. Calhoun writes: "They were very interested in upgrading the research program for petroleum and natural gas, and I know that a strong research and doctoral program was one of my desires. However, I did not place the excellency of the research program higher than that of the program of instruction or in outreach activities to industry. My interest in the oil industry in the Appalachian area was, however, a key factor in my decision to return to Penn State. The University was not able to pay what I considered to be a competitive salary, and four oil companies in the Bradford area agreed, under the leadership of Dick Jones, to supplement my salary through private arrangements. The willingness of Penn State administrators to work with industry in order to obtain a supplement for me was evidence of the importance of this program to the institution."

The research program established in the 1930s by Samuel Yuster and others was expanded under the direction of John Calhoun. A wide variety of projects were undertaken, beginning in the 1950s with a concentration on reservoir engineering. The early leaders in this endeavor were Ralph F. Nielsen, Emil J. Burcik, Luther T. Bissey, Robert L. Slobod, C. Drew Stahl, and S. M. Farouq-Ali, among others (Nielsen, 1951). One major project dealt with the solubility of natural gas in oil. This was a fundamental study, for the amount of gas in oil determines the movement of the fluid into the well and thus is a controlling factor in production. In a laboratory experiment, natural gas was compressed in a steel U-tube. The compressed gas entered the equilibrium cell containing oil, at a constant temperature, and by constant agitation of this cell all the gas dissolved in the oil. The increase in oil volume due to the dissolved oil could be measured and the potential oil production determined.

Another experiment involved prior gas injection; gas was injected into wells before water flooding. Experiments were undertaken using cores of unconsolidated sand and porous media to measure the amount of gas moving through the sand. Some of the experiments involved simulation models of oil field conditions. The basic purpose of this type of study was to determine if this type of gas injection increased production.

A third area of study explored the role of viscosity in water flooding. When gas is dissolved in oil, the viscosity is lowered. The viscosity of oil determines not only the rate of flow but also how much oil is left in the oil sand after the oil field has been abandoned. The role of viscosity in water injection, with or without prior gas injection, was investigated by Carl W. Sherman, a graduate student in the 1950s. After being employed in the oil industry for many years, he returned to Penn State in the 1970s as a faculty member.

There has been much controversy over the possible gains in production that result from applying a vacuum to a producing well. In the PNG laboratories these types of studies were conducted. The first experiment involved the use of a vacuum to release additional gas from the well. This release of gas amounted to an extension of the so-called dissolved gas drive beyond the point where gas release would stop without a vacuum. A second mechanism involved a decrease in pressure toward the producing well so oil would move from a higher to a lower pressure, and the third mechanism was the addition of water flooding to create a vacuum. These studies were helpful in determining efficient field operations.

In the 1950s, research was also carried out on a number of displacement studies. The original studies of displacement were usually on a macroscopic scale, which provided only crude estimations of porosity. In the PNG laboratories a chemical microscope was used to reveal the motion of gas and liquid at the capillary level. The displacement of oil and water was observed in terms of how it influenced the production of oil. When oil is removed from a porous rock it must be replaced either by gas or by another liquid.

Penn State petroleum and natural gas graduate students Steven Enedy, left, and Richard Fulcher, right, are investigating the use of solvents to increase oil recovery from oil reservoirs. The study begins with the injection of oil into sandstone cores. Then various solvents are forced through the rock to determine to what degree of efficiency they will remove the oil.

Flow rates are checked in the Gas
Measurements Laboratory.
Checking recording orifice meters
are Emil J. Burcik, Luther T. Bissey,
and C. Drew Stahl, about 1960.

The study of capillary pressure was another project. In the displacement of oil by water or gas, certain retentive forces must be overcome. One measure of the degree of retention is provided by the capillary pressure. By use of capillary pressure measurements, it was possible to determine the wettability of sands by oil and water. In this procedure it was demonstrated that Bradford oil sand is preferentially wet by oil and the Venango sand is preferentially wet by water. Such information was important in determining the procedure for other physical measurements on the sand. It was also important in the search for methods of releasing the retentive forces and thereby increasing the amount of oil recovery.

In the 1940s the laboratories conducted a series of relative permeability studies under the direction of James H. Henderson and Samuel T. Yuster. These studies of the relative permeability of a sand to oil and water, or to gas and oil, were important in predicting the production behavior of a reservoir. This was a major research endeavor, and the resulting method for measuring relative permeability came to be known in the industry as the "Penn State Method." The measurements had become so exact that they were considered the nearest possible approach to what these values are in the reservoir during production.

The systematic study at Penn State of miscible displacement began in 1952 with the proposal of the "equilibrium cell" theory for calculating transition (mixing or dispersion) zone compositions. Experimental work on the alcohol slug process, a forerunner of numerous miscible slug processes, was reported in 1959. Modified and combination slugs, slug sizes, flow velocities, sand types, fluid properties, and other variables were all investigated by the Penn State researchers.

Experimental work on micellar-polymer displacement of testing oil began in the laboratories in 1966. The early micellar research program, applied to the Bradford field, dealt largely with the determination of optimum slug sizes for various micellar compositions. Later work covered a range of variables: rate effects, polymer type and concentration, and polymer slug size. The study of polymer flooding was supervised by Emil J. Burcik, whose area of expertise was in rock and fluid properties and phase behavior. His text on fluid properties is considered a classic and has been used throughout the world.

John C. Calhoun
Alumni Fellow

John C. Calhoun (Alumni Fellow 1976; B.S. Petroleum and Natural Gas Engineering 1937; M.S. 1941; Ph.D. 1946) began his career as an oil field roustabout in McKean County, Pennsylvania, and became a world-renowned energy expert. Once head of Penn State's Department of Petroleum and Natural Gas Engineering, he ended his academic career as vice president for academic affairs at Texas A & M University.

It was recognized that if research work in petroleum production was to have any value, the quantitative information obtained from laboratory studies would have to be applied to the behavior of an oil field. Such application had to involve mathematical calculations. To demonstrate this, in the 1960s C. Drew Stahl completed a series of calculations showing how laboratory data could be applied to production behavior during a gas or air drive. A system in which the permeability varies from top to bottom in a preassigned manner was treated mathematically, using as a measure of the degree of heterogeneity a distribution coefficient known as the "Lorenz factor."

The research work in petroleum production constituted an integrated program. Each project was benefited by and partially dependent on the results of other projects. Since petroleum engineering is an applied science, it was recognized that there had to be cooperation with the research laboratories of the major oil companies. The kind of close relationship between university and industrial research that exists between the petroleum and natural gas program at Penn State and the nation's leading oil companies over the decades is rare.

Because the future of oil production is tied to enhanced recovery, the faculty plans to advance the traditionally strong position that has been achieved in reservoir engineering. Turgay Ertekin states: "We want to continue our important role in the area of reservoir engineering. Most of the water-flooding techniques and relative permeability measurement procedures now employed in the oil fields have been developed in Penn State laboratories." A major thrust in advancing reservoir engineering came with the application of computers. Dr. Ertekin notes: "We have been able to develop a series of models beginning with simple techniques but advancing now into the most complex processes of fluid movements. By use of these models we are able to describe the processes that affect the recovery of oil. Some of our models are now used by the petroleum industry throughout the world."

THE CENTER FOR ENHANCED OIL RECOVERY

The petroleum and natural gas program at Penn State has major laboratories for the study of reservoir, drilling, and production problems. These are all outfitted with the most modern equipment. The drilling laboratory has a drilling simulator, which makes it possible to simulate the actual drilling process of the field. The students therefore get a hands-on approach to drilling problems. The department now has a completely equipped computation laboratory. Each student has a per-

S. M. Faroque-Ali in the Petroleum and Natural Gas Laboratory with core samples used in tertiary oil recovery studies.

sonal computer to do the work required in different courses. Students not only do work for specific courses but also get the opportunity to become more familiar with advanced computer techniques.

In April 1987 the program celebrated a major achievement when the C. Drew Stahl Center for Enhanced Oil Recovery was established. The opening of the Center culminated a year-long fundraising effort that brought widespread alumni support and major contributions from corporations and companies associated with the oil industry. The success of the effort was a tribute to the blue-ribbon Stahl Fund Committee, composed of alumni from the PNG program and chaired by Victor G. Beghini, a 1956 B.S. recipient and president for worldwide production of the Marathon Oil Company.

The Enhanced Oil Recovery Center is named to honor Dr. Stahl, who served as chair of the petroleum and natural gas program from 1960 to 1985. The ability to raise more than $1 million for the laboratory reflects the esteem that Dr. Stahl's former students have for him. It also affirms that Penn State's PNG program is one of the strongest in the United States.

In the new center Penn State faculty will have the opportunity to use the latest computer-assisted instrumentation to investigate some of the most complex oil recovery problems. They will work closely with the oil industry in analyzing existing technology and developing and testing new processes. The center will also be used to acquaint students with the latest developments in petroleum engineering.

THE UNDERGRADUATE PROGRAM

The undergraduate curriculum has been modified over time to reflect the changing technology of the discipline. In the early period it was a pragmatic program providing the essentials for an engineering career in the petroleum industry. As new techniques evolved, new courses were developed to provide students with up-to-date knowledge of the day so they could be at the forefront of the field. In the late 1970s the program was accredited by the Accreditation Board for Engineering and Technology.

Sintran simulator in the Petroleum and Natural Gas Laboratory.

A number of new courses have been introduced since then. The widespread interest in tertiary recovery methods, together with the research effort in this area, has resulted in development of a tertiary recovery course offered at the senior level. Another new required course deals with mathematical modeling of petroleum reservoirs and is offered by Dr. Ertekin, who also has developed a well test analysis course that enrolls students from a number of engineering disciplines. A well-log analysis course has also been designed for practicing field petroleum engineers. Robert W. Watson has developed a course on the application of the fundamental sciences to engineering design, and Jamal H. Abou-Kassem has devised a course on numerical reservoir modeling. Michael A. Adewumi, who conducts research in the area of multiphase flow in pipes, teaches courses in production engineering. Abraham S. Grader teaches courses in applied reservoir engineering and analysis and performs research in fluid dynamics. He also has been instrumental in establishing advanced computer facilities for students and faculty.

Dr. Farouq-Ali introduced the use of computers in the Department of Petroleum and Natural Gas Engineering in the reservoir modeling course, one of the first courses in the United States to take advantage of simulation using the computer. At the time he introduced the course, the department did not have its own computers, so the students had to use the University mainframe computer, which presented a number of problems because many times the students could not use the University computers until late at night. However, funds were not immediately available to purchase departmental computers.

This problem was solved in a unique way. A graduate of PNG, George Trimble ('42), past senior vice president of Exxon, visited Drew Stahl in his office at Penn State. During the conversation, Dr. Stahl demonstrated the use of computers in reservoir modeling. As Mr. Trimble was leaving he asked how much he needed to purchase computers in the department. Dr. Stahl replied, off the top of his head, "Sixteen thousand dollars." Mr. Trimble said, "Write me a letter asking for $16,000 and my company will have a check on your desk." The money came immediately, and within a year a computer lab was established.

After the computers were installed, Mr. Trimble made a return visit to the campus to see them function. He was fascinated by the complex problems, such as the designing of an oil and gas separator, that undergraduate students were solving with the aid of computers. He commented, "I've been thinking, Am I glad I went here when I did! These kids are so smart now, I never would have graduated." Use of the computer has been extended, under the direction of Dr. Ertekin, to essentially all the courses in the petroleum and natural gas program. The computer is now a fundamental teaching aid, with more than forty personal computers and three multiuser computers available within this program alone.

THE STUDENT BODY

With the establishment of the petroleum and natural gas program in the 1930s, the undergraduate student body grew to more than 100, but with the decline of the Pennsylvania oil industry after 1940, the student body was small until the energy crisis of the 1970s. Student enrollment experienced a dramatic increase, including a much higher proportion of women students. Undergraduate enrollment peaked in the early 1980s at about 450, including about forty women. Because of the great shortage of petroleum engineers in the United States, the starting salary for a newly graduated bachelor's degree student was the highest in the engineering field in the United States. Since then, enrollment has declined greatly at the undergraduate level, but graduate enrollment has been more steady.

The composition of the student body has varied greatly between undergraduate and graduate students. Most of the undergraduates were traditionally from the United States, predominantly Pennsylvania. However, in the 1980s a greater percentage of undergraduates were coming from foreign countries. In contrast, the graduate students have traditionally come from many areas of the world, particularly Venezuela and the Middle East but also many other countries. At times more than 50 percent have been international students. As a result of the wide geographical background of students, Penn State's graduates, with both undergraduate and graduate degrees, are found in the industry throughout the world.

A major feature of the student program is the large number of scholarships and fellowships at both the undergraduate level and the graduate level. Almost every major oil company in the

Scott Heckman uses the Core Flood Station.

United States now provides three to four scholarships for undergraduate training. The Pennsylvania Oil and Gas Association and the Pennsylvania Grade Crude Oil Association have traditionally provided a number of scholarships. The fellowships made available by oil companies provide funds for students to carry on research programs.

STUDENT ORGANIZATION

The student chapter of the Society of Petroleum Engineers has long been active on campus. With the aid of the faculty, they sponsor field trips to the oil fields of the state, and many attend the monthly meeting of the Pittsburgh Section of the Society of Petroleum Engineers. But most important, the Penn State student chapter is recognized by the National Society of Petroleum Engineers as one of the best in the nation. This provides recognition for student accomplishments that could not be obtained in any other manner.

CONTINUING EDUCATION

Dissemination of the knowledge developed in the Penn State laboratories to the industry has long been a major endeavor of the faculty. In the early 1950s Dr. Calhoun initiated a series of special continuing education courses for training those working the industry. He states: "I had a course in reservoir engineering for practicing engineers in Bradford. The course was presented in the evenings, and I commuted to Bradford to give it. It was, however, the Standard Oil Company of

Scott Heckman and Majdolin Hanna use the CAT-scanner to study formations.

James Brannigan talks with Deans Charles Hosler and John Cahir at the dedication of the C. Drew Stahl Center for Enhanced Oil Recovery.

California that allowed me to place continuing education activity on a basis parallel to that of the research program. Standard of California initially requested that this course be given in either Houston or San Francisco. My response was that I would do the course if it would be given at Penn State. They accepted this condition. The continuing education course was given several times for engineers from Standard of California who came to the campus. It was followed by courses given for Sun Oil Company and finally to petroleum engineers from oil companies. This use of continuing education in petroleum engineering was a first among American programs." This kind of academic relationship with industry has continued. Dr. Stahl began giving short courses to Continental Oil Company but expanded the offerings to many other companies. These short courses have enhanced the reputation of the petroleum and natural gas engineering program at Penn State, and industry has responded by providing funds for scholarships and facilities for laboratories.

A continuing education program in petroleum and natural gas was developed to train oil field workers in the new techniques of oil recovery. As in the mining industry, these courses were offered in the oil fields of Pennsylvania and were a fundamental part of the PNG program. Among the directors of the program were Oscar F. Spencer and Richard Harding. In the 1950s, to serve the needs of the students, Spencer wrote five books for these courses, including *Petroleum and Natural Gas Engineering* and *Secondary Recovery*. The program was discontinued in 1969 as oil production declined in the state.

HONORS AND AWARDS

Petroleum and natural gas faculty members have received a number of awards. C. Drew Stahl was the recipient of the 1987 Distinguished Achievement Award for petroleum engineering faculty given by the Society of Petroleum Engineers. In 1986 Mark A. Klins received the Outstanding

Young Member Service Award of the Society of Petroleum Engineers for "his noteworthy civic contributions, especially his work with disadvantaged children, and for his contributions to the Society's publication program as author and technical editor in the area of reserve estimation, reservoir engineering and enhanced oil recovery."

The faculty have always maintained a high degree of personal contact with students, even at times of very high enrollment. This effort has been recognized by the College for four of the PNG faculty: Turgay Ertekin, C. Drew Stahl, Syed M. Farouq-Ali, and Abraham S. Grader have received the Wilson Outstanding Teaching Award.

A number of the faculty have been active in professional societies. George Slater served as vice chair of the Society of Petroleum Engineers, and Carl W. Sherman and Mark A. Klins were directors of the Pittsburgh Chapter of the Society of Petroleum Engineers.

Selected Bibliography

Alexander, Shelton S. 1981. "The Geophysics Graduate Program." *Earth and Mineral Sciences* 50 (May–June), 54–57.

Allen, John Eliot. 1949. "The Penn State Polylith." *Mineral Industries* 18 (March), 1+.

Aplan, Frank F., and Peter T. Luckie. 1982. "Methods of Processing Coal to Remove Sulfur." *Earth and Mineral Sciences* 51 (January–February), 26–29.

Asman, Arnold W. 1949. "Opportunities in Mining Engineering." *Mineral Industries* 18 (May), 1+.

Barron, Eric J. 1988. "The Earth System Science Center." *Earth and Mineral Sciences* 57, no. 3, pp. 44–48.

Bates, Thomas F. 1947. "New High Magnification Laboratory of the Mineral Industries School." *Mineral Industries* 16 (January), 1–2.

———. 1952. "The New Mineral Constitution Research Laboratories." *Mineral Industries* 21 (February), 1–6.

Bell, Maurice E. 1961. "Materials Science: A Plan for Research and Graduate Study." *Mineral Industries* 31 (October), 1, 3–7.

Bell, Maurice E., Joseph B. Bodkin, Maurice C. Inman, and Norman H. Suhr. 1969. "A Facility for Analytical Research and Science Analysis: The Mineral Constitution Laboratories." *Earth and Mineral Sciences* 38 (May), 61–65.

Blackadar, Alfred K. 1981. "Meteorology at Penn State: 47 Years of Quality Education and Public Service." *Earth and Mineral Sciences* 50 (March–April), 37–40.

Bonine, C. A. 1939. "Geology Department Grows." *Mineral Industries* 9 (November), 1+.

———. 1941. "Field Training at M.I. Camp." *Mineral Industries* 10 (February), 1+.

Cathles, Lawrence M. 1982. "Mineral Deposits Research Review for Industry, 1982." *Earth and Mineral Sciences* 52 (Fall), 5–8.

Charmbury, H. B., and D. R. Mitchell. 1954. "Mineral Preparation Facilities at Penn State." *Mineral Industries* 24 (October), 1–3.

Coleman, Michael M. 1978. "Polymer Science: A Discipline Whose Time Has Come." *Earth and Mineral Sciences* 48 (December), 17, 20–23.

Comer, Joseph J. 1961. "The Mineral Constitution Laboratories." *Mineral Industries* 31 (December), 1, 3–7.

"Co-operative Educational Programs for Mineral Industries Workers." 1949. *Mineral Industries* 19 (December), 1+.

"Co-operative Research in Metallurgy." 1935. *Mineral Industries* 5 (December), 1–2.

Coxey, James R. 1947. "The Pennsylvania Ceramics Association." *Mineral Industries* 17 (October), 1–3.

Davis, H. M. 1955. "A Philosophy of Education in the Mineral Sciences." *Mineral Industries* 24 (April), 1–7.

"Dean Steidle Honored at School Banquet." 1953. *Mineral Industries* 22 (May), 1–8.

Deasy, George F. 1948. "Geography on a University Level." *Mineral Industries* 17 (May), 1–2.

"Deike Building Dedication." 1967. *Earth and Mineral Sciences* 36 (June), 5–9.

"Employer Hires an M.I. Graduate." 1955. *Mineral Industries* 25 (December), 1–16.

Farouq-Ali, S. M., and H. H. M. Totonji. 1979. "Petroleum Reservoir Modelling: What It Can and Cannot Do." *Earth and Mineral Sciences* 48 (April), 49–52.

Frantz, Robert L., and Raja V. Ramani. 1982. "Mineral Management: Its Unique Aspects." *Earth and Mineral Sciences* 52 (Fall), 1–4.

"The Future of Resident Instruction in the College of Mineral Industries, 1955–1975." 1955. *Mineral Industries* 25 (November), 1–6.

Gauger, A. W. 1939. "Fuel Technology at Penn State." *Mineral Industries* 8 (May), 1+.

———. 1942. *Fuel Technology: Curriculum and Career*, Curriculum 14. State College, Pa.: Mineral Industries Experiment Station.

———. 1943. "Mineral Industries Research: An Endowment Policy for Pennsylvania." *Mineral Industries* 12 (May), 1–4.

Gaus, John E. 1950. "Growth of a Museum." *Mineral Industries* 19 (April), 1–2.

Gensamer, M. 1946. "Mineral Technology: An Organic Limit." *Mineral Industries* 15 (January), 1–4.

"Geology Department Improves Facilities for Scientific Study." 1937. *Mineral Industries* 6 (January), 1.

Gold, David P. 1976. "Summer Field Program in Geosciences." *Earth and Mineral Sciences* 45 (June), 65+.

———. 1981. "The Geology Graduate Program." *Earth and Mineral Sciences* 50 (May–June), 52–54.

Graham, E. K. 1987. "High P/T Facilities and Research Directions." *Earth and Mineral Sciences* 56 (Spring), 40–46.

Graham, E. K., and C. P. Thornton. 1981. "Geosciences at Penn State: Development, Current Status, and Future Prospects." *Earth and Mineral Sciences* 50 (May–June), 49–52.

Griffiths, J. C. 1966. "Future Trends in Geomathematics." *Earth and Mineral Sciences* 35 (February), 1–4.

Guber, Albert. 1973. "Penn State's Spring Term Marine Science Program: A Unique Educational Venture." *Earth and Mineral Sciences* 43 (November), 9–13.

Harrison, Ian R. 1981. "Penn State's Polymer Science Program." *Earth and Mineral Sciences* 50 (July–August), 67–68.

Hewes, R. B. 1951. "A Supervisory Training Program for the Mineral Industries." *Mineral Industries* 23 (October), 1–4.

Hipple, John A. 1954a. "Research for the Mineral Industries." *Mineral Industries* 23 (February), 1–5+.

———. 1954b. "Future Growth of Mineral Industries Research." *Mineral Industries* 23 (May), 1–5.

Howell, B. F., Jr. 1988. "Some Thoughts on the Development of Geosciences at Penn State." *Earth and Mineral Sciences* 57, no. 3, pp. 38–43.

Howell, Paul R. 1982. "Analytical Electron Microscopy." *Earth and Mineral Sciences* 51 (July–August), 68–70.

Hummel, Floyd. 1969. *Nelson W. Taylor: In Commemoration*. State College, Pa.: Penn State.

Inman, Maurice C. 1969. "Electron Microscope:

Prime Tool for Materials Science." *Earth and Mineral Sciences* 39 (October), 1–5.

Insley, Herbert. 1945. "The Earth Sciences: An Organic Unit." *Mineral Industries* 14 (February), 1–4.

Jackson, Lucille. 1941. "The Mineral Sciences Library, 1931–1941." *Mineral Industries* 11 (December), 1–2.

Jones, D. C. 1955. "A Brief History of the College of Mineral Industries." *Mineral Industries* 24 (January), 1–6.

Keith, M. L. 1963. "Mineral Conservation Section." *Mineral Industries* 32 (June), 1, 6–9.

Kellogg, Herbert H. 1946. "Mineral Preparation: An Old Cut, a New Technology." *Mineral Industries* 15 (May), 1–3.

Kerrick, Derrill M. 1980. "Geology Summer Field School: The Culmination of Classroom Training." *Earth and Mineral Sciences* 49 (January–February), 25, 30–32.

———. 1981. "The Geochemistry and Mineralogy Graduate Program." *Earth and Mineral Sciences* 50 (May–June), 49, 57–59.

———. 1987. "An Historical Perspective on High P/T Research in Geosciences." *Earth and Mineral Sciences* 56 (Spring), 34–39.

Koss, Donald A. 1987. "Metals Science and Engineering." *Earth and Mineral Sciences* 56 (Summer), 67.

Landsberg, Helmut. 1941. "Geophysics at Penn State, 1934–1941." *Mineral Industries* 11 (November), 1–3.

Lindsay, Robert W. 1981. "Metallurgy at Penn State Approaches Its 75th Year." *Earth and Mineral Sciences* 50 (July–August), 61–64.

Luckie, Peter T. 1980. "Mineral Processing: Attacking the Problem of Declining Ore Quality." *Earth and Mineral Sciences* 49 (May–June), 49–54.

McFarland, D. F. 1939. "Metallurgy at Penn State." *Mineral Industries* 9 (October), 1+.

Miller, E. Willard. 1946. "The Field of Modern Geography." *Mineral Industries* 15 (April), 1–4.

———. 1952. "Geography: A Dynamic Earth Science." *Mineral Industries* 22 (November), 1–4.

———. 1980. "Dr. Edward Steidle: A Man of Vi-

sion." *Earth and Mineral Sciences* 50 (September–October), 1+.

———. 1982. "Geography at Penn State: A Discipline of Spatial Analysis." *Earth and Mineral Sciences* 51 (March–April), 37, 43–46.

"M.I. Alumni Play Prominent Roles in Modern Industry." 1955. *Mineral Industries* 24 (February), 1–6.

"Mineral Industries at The Pennsylvania State College." 1932. *Mineral Industries* 1 (February), 1–3.

"Mineral Industries Bldg. Named to Honor Former Dean, Edward Steidle." 1978. *Earth and Mineral Sciences* 47 (May), 57+.

"Mineral Industries Extension Courses Organized Under Smith-Hughes Plan." 1931. *Mineral Industries* 1 (December 22), 1–2.

"Mineral Industries Graduates." 1954. *Mineral Industries* 24 (December), 1–16.

"The Mineral Industries Undergraduates Speak." 1954. *Mineral Industries* 23 (January), 1–12.

"Mineral Sciences Cornerstone." 1949. *Mineral Industries* 18 (April), 1+.

Mitchell, D. R. 1945. "Mineral Engineering: An Organic Unit." *Mineral Industries* 14 (April), 1–4.

"A Modern Organization and a Modern Plant for a Modern Job." 1955. *Mineral Industries* 24 (March), 1–3.

Murphy, Raymond E. 1932. "Geography and Mineral Economics at Penn State." *Mineral Industries* 1 (March), 1.

———. 1933. "Geographic Survey Being Planned for Pennsylvania." *Mineral Industries* 3 (December), 1–2.

———. 1934. "The Geography of Johnstown, Pennsylvania: An Industrial Center." Mineral Industries Experiment Station, Pennsylvania State College, Bulletin 13.

———. 1935. "Johnstown and York: A Comparative Study of Two Industrial Cities," *Annals of the Association of American Geographers* 25 (1935), 179–96.

———. 1940. "Geography Looks Ahead." *Mineral Industries* 9 (March), 1+.

Myers, W. M. 1943. "Enrollment Trends in the M.I. School." *Mineral Industries* 12 (January), 1–2.

Neilly, Mary S. 1980. "A Brief History of the College of Earth and Mineral Sciences." *Earth and Mineral Sciences* 50 (September–October), 1–8.

Nelson, Harlan W. 1937. "Fuel Technology: A Curriculum of Increasing Importance." *Mineral Industries* 6 (May), 1.

Nielsen, R. F. 1951. "Graduate Research in Petroleum Production." *Mineral Industries* 20 (April), 1+.

"1970 Graduation at Elders Ridge." 1970. *Earth and Mineral Sciences* 39 (February), 37+.

Northrup, H. B. 1941. "M.I. Extension Work Reviewed." *Mineral Industries* 10 (May), 1–2.

———. 1944. "A Half Century of Extension Service." *Mineral Industries* 14 (October), 1–4.

Osborn, E. F. 1956a. "The Future Availability of Graduates in Fuel Technology." *Mineral Industries* 25 (January), 3+.

———. 1956b. "Significant Changes During the Past 50 Years in Education in the Mineral Industries Fields." *Mineral Industries* 25 (February), 1–3+.

Painter, Paul C. 1980. "From Guncotton to Bakelite: The Early History of Polymer Science." *Earth and Mineral Sciences* 49 (July–August), 61–64.

Palmer, Howard B. 1981. "Fuel Science at Penn State." *Earth and Mineral Sciences* 50 (July–August), 65–66.

Panofsky, H. A., Rosa De Pena, and Dennis W. Thomson. 1981. "Research at Penn State on Turbulence and Air Quality." *Earth and Mineral Sciences* 50 (March–April), 40–42.

"Pennsylvania's School of Mineral Industries." 1940. *Mineral Industries* 10 (November), 1–6.

"Pennsylvania's School of Mineral Industries." 1953. *Mineral Industries* 22 (April), 3–8.

"A Pictorial Review of the College of Earth and Mineral Sciences." 1968. *Earth and Mineral Sciences* 37 (June), 73–77.

Pirson, S. J. 1940. "Petroleum and Natural Gas Engineering at Penn State." *Mineral Industries* 9 (January), 1–2.

———. 1946. "Laboratory of Applied Geophysics and Geochemistry." *Mineral Industries* 16 (December), 1–2.

Ramani, R. V. 1981. "Mineral Engineering Management: Challenges and Opportunities." *Earth and Mineral Sciences* 50 (January–February), 30–31.

Ridge, John D. 1953. "Mineral Economics and the Mineral Industries." *Mineral Industries* 22 (April), 1–5.

Rindone, Guy E. 1981. "Ceramic Science and Engineering at Penn State: Past, Present, and Future." *Earth and Mineral Sciences* 50 (July–August), 61, 68–71.

Robinson, Clair W. 1945. "The Mineral Industries Museum." *Mineral Industries* 14 (January), 1–3.

Roy, Rustum. 1963. "The Materials Research Laboratory." *Mineral Industries* 32 (May), 1, 6–8.

Saperstein, Lee W. 1981. "Mining Engineering Achieves New Heights at Penn State." *Earth and Mineral Sciences* 50 (January–February), 25–28.

Schanz, John J., Jr. 1960. "Evolution of the Mineral Economics Curriculum." *Mineral Industries* 29 (June), 7–8.

Slingerland, Rudy L. 1982. "Coastal Studies at Wallops Island, Va." *Earth and Mineral Sciences* 51 (May–June), 57–79.

Snouffer, Richard D. 1947. "Revised Mining Engineering Curriculum." *Mineral Industries* 16 (February), 1–2.

"Some War Efforts of the School of Mineral Industries." 1942. *Mineral Industries* 11 (January), 1–4.

Spackman, William, Jr. 1963. "Another Cornerstone to the World's Finest College of Mineral Industries." *Mineral Industries* 32 (March), 1+.

Spicer, T. S. 1981. "Fuel Technology: Opportunities Unlimited." *Mineral Industries* 21 (November), 1–3.

Stahl, C. Drew. 1972. "The Future Supply of Petroleum Engineers: An Impending Crisis." *Earth and Mineral Sciences* 42 (November), 14–15.

———. 1981. "Petroleum and Natural Gas Engineering at Penn State: Then and Now." *Earth and Mineral Sciences* 50 (January–February), 25, 31–34.

Steidle, Edward. 1939. "M.I. Studies Inaugurated in 1859." *Mineral Industries* 8 (April), 1+.

———. 1942. "Mineral Industries Education Cannot Remain Static." *Mineral Industries* 12 (February), 1–7.

———. 1947. "New Mineral Laboratory Building." *Mineral Industries* 16 (April), 1–3.

———. 1948. "Roots of Human Progress." *Mineral Industries*, vols. 17, 18, editorial series.

———. 1950a. "Philosophy for Conservation." *Mineral Industries* 18 (1949); 19, editorial series.

———. 1950b. *Mineral Industries Education.* State College, Pa.: The Pennsylvania State College, 1950.

———. 1951. "Wanted: Mineral Industries Colleges." *Mineral Industries*, vols. 20, 21, editorial series.

———. 1952. *Mineral Forecast, 2000 A.D.* State College, Pa.: The Pennsylvania State College.

Steidle, Edward, and W. M. Myers. 1942. "The Last Chapter in Mineral Industries Education: A Preliminary Report." *Mineral Industries* 11 (May), 1–12.

Taylor, Nelson W. 1950. "Penn State Ceramics Program." *Mineral Industries* 9 (February), 1+.

———. 1940. "A Report on the Development of the Department of Ceramics from 1923/24 to 1939/40." In *Nelson W. Taylor: In Commemoration.* State College, Pa.: Penn State.

Thomson, Dennis W. 1987–88. "New Perspectives on Atmospheric Structure and Dynamics." *Earth and Mineral Sciences* 57, no. 1, pp. 1–6.

Thornton, Charles P. 1981. "The New Undergraduate Program in Geosciences." *Earth and Mineral Sciences* 50, no. 3, pp. 31–32.

"Unique Art at Penn State." 1935. *Mineral Industries* 5 (November), 1–2.

Venuto, Louis J. 1965. *The Creation of a College.* University Park, Pa.: The Pennsylvania State University.

Vogely, William A. 1980. "Mineral Economics: A Mature Profession." *Earth and Mineral Sciences* 49 (July–August), 61+.

Weyl, Woldemar. 1944. "Glass Science Research Foundation." *Mineral Industries* 13 (May), 1–4.

Williams, Anthony V. 1971. "Computers and Geography at Penn State." *Earth and Mineral Sciences* 40 (June), 65–68.

Wright, C. C. 1941. "Research in Coal Described." *Mineral Industries* 10 (January), 1–2.

Zimmerman, Raymond E. 1950. "Opportunities in Mineral Preparation Engineering." *Mineral Industries* 19 (January), 1+.

Index